Computer Communications and Networks

T0191529

For other titles published in this series, go to
www.springer.com/series/4198

The Computer Communications and Networks series is a range of textbooks, monographs and handbooks. It sets out to provide students, researchers and non-specialists alike with a sure grounding in current knowledge, together with comprehensible access to the latest developments in computer communications and networking.

Emphasis is placed on clear and explanatory styles that support a tutorial approach, so that even the most complex of topics is presented in a lucid and intelligible manner.

Nick Antonopoulos • Lee Gillam

Editors

Cloud Computing

Principles, Systems and Applications

 Springer

Editors
Nick Antonopoulos
University of Derby
School of Computing and Mathematics
Kedleston Road, DE22 1GB
Derby
UK
N.Antonopoulos@derby.ac.uk

Lee Gillam
University of Surrey
Department of Computing
Guildford, Surrey, GU2 7XH
UK
L.Gillam@surrey.ac.uk

Series Editor
Professor A.J. Sammes, BSc, MPhil, PhD, FBCS, CEng
Centre for Forensic Computing
Cranfield University
DCMT, Shrivenham
Swindon SN6 8LA
UK

ISBN 978-1-4471-2580-8   ISBN 978-1-84996-241-4 (eBook)
DOI 10.1007/978-1-84996-241-4
Springer London Dordrecht New York Heidelberg

Cover design: SPi, Puducherry, India

Printed on acid-free paper

Springer is part of Springer Science+Business Media (www.springer.com)

Foreword

Cloud computing is increasingly being used for what was known as 'on-demand' and 'utility computing'. The services provided, the APIs and the applications that can be hosted by these Cloud providers have superseded the use of the Grid, and are increasingly becoming popular with users. There are obviously two sides to the services that are provided by Cloud providers: those that are supplied by commercial entities, such as Amazon and Google, and those that are open-source systems, such as Open Cirrus[1] and Eucalyptus.[2]

There are currently three cloud-based delivery models. Software as a Service (SaaS), where the consumer uses an application, but does not control the operating system, hardware or network infrastructure. In this situation, the user steers applications over the network. Next is Platform as a Service (PaaS), where the users host an environment for their applications. The users control the applications, but do not control the operating system, hardware or network infrastructure, which they are using. Finally, there is Infrastructure as a Service (IaaS), where the user accesses 'fundamental computing resources' such as CPU, memory, middleware and storage. The consumer controls the resources, but not the cloud infrastructure beneath them.

Service providers try to provide simplified software installation, maintenance and a centralised control over the software used. The end-users can access the cloud-based services 'anytime' and from 'anywhere'. Naturally, this type of access is based on the bandwidth that a user has over the Internet and therefore poor interconnections mean that the use of cloud-based resources is not viable. Unfortunately, most current cloud-based systems use different APIs and protocols, which means that collaboration and sharing of data is difficult at this point in time. It is interesting that the Open Grid Forum is looking at Cloud-based API and protocols, so that systems can share and work together in the future.

Many users and organisations are uncomfortable with the idea of storing their data and applications on system infrastructure and services they do not control. In addition, migrating workloads to a shared infrastructure increases the potential for unauthorised access and exposure of sensitive data. Cloud-based systems need to

---

[1] Open Cirrus, http://opencirrus.org/

[2] Eucalyptus, http://open.eucalyptus.com/

be consistent around authentication, identity management, compliance and access-related technologies, which are becoming increasingly important. Within the cloud-security model, the user needs to trust the vendor's security model, consider a customer's inability to respond to audit findings, potentially obtain support for investigations, deem indirect administrator accountability, ensure that proprietary implementations cannot be examined, and cope with the loss of physical control on the remote clouds being used. In addition, it may be a case that a user wants to use sensitive data on a cloud-based system, in which case it would be useful to be able to encrypt the data so that it is safe and cannot be stolen by other users.

There is also a need on cloud-based systems for Quality of Service (QoS) and Service-Level Agreements (SLAs). The contract between customers and service providers needs to be negotiated and agreed. Various performance metrics (e.g., uptime, throughput, and response time) need to be guaranteed to the users. Also, certain management details need to be exposed to the users of the system. This aspect of the service will require logging and efficient monitoring of the resources used by the users, so that they can see that they are potentially accessing the resources that were originally negotiated. There also needs to be well-documented security capabilities provided to the users, and the providers must recompense users where there are penalties for non-performance.

Cloud computing relies on separating user applications from the underlying infrastructure using virtualisation. The host operating system provides an abstraction layer for executing a virtual guest operating system. A key aspect of virtualisation is the 'hypervisor' and potentially the 'virtual machine monitor'. Cloud-based systems use para-virtualisation, which includes a binary bus between the various virtual machines that are being executed. Para-virtualisation provides a much faster and more efficient virtualisation system than other virtual systems. Virtualisation enables the guest operating systems to execute in isolation of the other operating systems, and it also enables a range of legacy applications to be run. In addition, on a Cloud-based system, it is possible to run multiple types of operating systems across the system, which potentially also helps to increase the utilisation of physical servers. Virtualisation also allows the portability of virtual servers between physical servers and it can increase the overall security of the physical host server. It is well known for example that many HPC applications are only 15–20% efficient, and it is possible when executing these applications on Cloud-based services that overall there is better program efficiency. In addition, for HPC applications, the system will also need to be able to schedule the virtual machines (VMs) efficiently, as it will be important that the constituting parts of the application are placed closely together to reduce communication latencies and give high inter-VM bandwidth as well. Another aspect is that the Cloud-based systems have the possibility to optimise the use of resources, reduce the amount of electrical power used as well as the capability to provide efficient Green IT computing.

An unfortunate aspect of current Cloud-based systems is the hyperbolae and publicity broadcast about them, without detailed information about the services, protocols and applications that can be executed on these systems. Just like previous distributed systems (e.g. CORBA, Jini and the Grid), it is very important for the potential end-user to know about the architecture, services, protocols, inter-opera-bility, security, scalability and performance, reliability, user interfaces and poten-tially payment for services in the context of Cloud computing.

This book provides a thorough and timely examination and exploration of the services, interfaces and the types of applications that can be executed on Cloud-based systems. In addition, the book discusses the interfaces used to access the underlying services, the pros/cons of using virtualisation, the range and scope of applications that can be executed, the security used by these services, the user inter-faces and aspects such as service-level agreements and the quality of service pro-vided. The applications that execute on a Cloud-based system need a computational model, storage capabilities and potentially inter-process/thread communication. In addition, it is important to understand the scalability and performance capability of the systems being used. This book covers a wide range of topics related to Clouds and it includes chapters about tools and technologies for building Clouds, taxono-mies of cloud-based systems and analysis of security and data confidentiality issues. There are discussions about the interoperability challenges related to the numerous protocols and APIs, methods for mixing Grids and Clouds together, resource management tools, potential Peer-to-Peer cloud-based provisioning, the policies, economics and costs-based benefits of Clouds, as well as Service-Level Agreements in Grids and Cloud-based systems. Therefore, it will be a useful tool for researchers and professionals aiming to understand and use Cloud systems for scientific and commercial purposes.

University of Reading, UK   M. Baker
Winter 2010

Preface

Introduction

Cloud computing appears to have emerged very recently as a subject of substantial industrial and academic interest, though its meaning, scope and fit with respect to other paradigms is hotly debated. For some researchers, Clouds are a natural evolution towards full commercialisation of Grid systems, while for others they may be dismissed as a mere rebranding of the existing pay-per-use or pay-as-you-go technologies. From either perspective, it appears that 'Cloud' has become the label of choice for accountable pay-per-use access to a wide variety of third-party applications and computational resources on a massive scale. Clouds are now supporting patterns of less-predictable resource use for applications and services across the IT spectrum, from online office applications to high-throughput transactional services and high-performance computations involving substantial quantities of processing cycles and storage. The current notion of Clouds seems to blur the distinctions between Grid Services, Web Services, and data centres, amongst others, and brings considerations of lowering the cost for relatively bursty applications to the fore.

Currently, there appears to be an increasing demand for Cloud computing in general. Major IT and e-commerce vendors such as Amazon, Google, IBM, Microsoft, and Sun have joined a variety of technology and service providers in offering Clouds. In turn, this generates significant demand for reference materials that provide coverage for this topic, ranging from standard developer guides to advanced expositions of research into Cloud design, optimisation and management. Interest in Cloud computing, as a concept or system design abstraction, is compounded and further strengthened by an inherent relationship to service-oriented computing. Clouds may be considered by some as a reincarnation and an extension of service-oriented computing that covers computational hardware-based resources as well as software, with concomitant business benefits in cost reduction where such services scale efficiently.

For the scientific community, Cloud computing offers interesting characteristics and challenges. Some of these exist at the intersection between computing and economics, where the key question is how to develop a Cloud infrastructure that provides the required quality of service; from a network economics perspective, this relates to the design and deployment of an adaptive pricing mechanism that provides both for a competitive edge and a profitable venture. At the same time, end-users (both potential consumers and providers) need to be able to understand the similarities, differences, benefits and disadvantages of Clouds over numerous existing paradigms including Grids, High-Performance Computing, Peer-to-Peer (P2P) systems and so on. P2P, Grid, High-Performance Computing and Web Services are very pertinent fields that have received significant and sustained research interest in the design and deployment of large-scale and high-performance computational resource-sharing systems. Collectively, these form the de facto basis for methods and techniques that will be re-appraised, re-used or re-designed to construct performance-driven Cloud platforms capable of satisfying the four cornerstones of quality of service:

1. Efficiency: The execution and coordination of the services is optimised in terms of data traffic and latency. Data traffic is typically one of the main cost factors in any distributed computing framework and thus its reduction is a standard long-term goal of such systems. Latency is arguably one of the most important factors affecting customer satisfaction and therefore it should also be within specified acceptable limits.
2. Scalability: These platforms should scale well to massive customer bases. They must also withstand demand of multiple bursty applications during peak times and endure the 'flash crowds' phenomenon familiar in overly successful marketing strategies and provisioning for popular websites at key times.
3. Robustness: The services need continuously high availability by design, with effective use of redundancy and graceful failover. Where users are charged for the expected successful use of computational facilities, it is imperative to understand the risk of failure, either to remove the probability of failure, or to use this information to offer appropriate compensation schemes.
4. Security: Appropriate security provisions must exist for both data and applications to protect both the providers and consumers from malicious or fraudulent activities. Without adequate security provisioning, it is highly unlikely that any commoditised platform would become a serious consideration for business computing.

To ensure commercial success, effective Clouds will be expected to provide guaranteed quality of service to customers by satisfying these four cornerstones.

This book is targeted at providing a thorough and advanced treatment of the state-of-the-art in Cloud computing that addresses the above topics and highlights and clarifies the conceptual and systemic links with other distributed computing approaches.

The book has four key objectives:

(i) To explore the relationship of Cloud computing to other distributed computing paradigms, namely Peer-to-Peer, Grids, High-Performance Computing and Web Services
(ii) To present the principles, techniques, protocols and algorithms that can be adapted from other distributed computing paradigms to the development of successful Clouds

(iii) to present current Cloud applications and highlight early deployment experiences

(iv) to elaborate the economic schemes needed for Clouds to become viable business models.

The first two objectives are firmly rooted in extant discourse of distributed computing and a desire to understand the potential of all these technologies in constructing purpose-specific hybrid solutions. The remaining objectives are closely linked to commercial demand for understanding how such technologies can shape successful and profitable businesses.

Expected Audience

This book should be of particular interest for the following audiences:

- **Researchers and doctoral students** working specifically in Cloud computing research, implementation and deployment, primarily as a reference publication. Similarly, this book should be useful to researchers in related, or more general fields, such as distributed computing, software engineering, Web Services, modelling of business processes, and so on.
- **Academics and students** engaging in research-informed teaching in the above fields. This book can serve as a good collection of articles to facilitate a broad understanding of this subject and as such may be useful as a key reference text in such teaching.
- **Professional system architects and developers** who could decide to adapt and apply in practice a number of the techniques and processes presented in the book.
- **Technical managers and IT consultants** as a book that demonstrates the potential applicability of certain methods for delivering efficient and secure commercial electronic services to customers globally.

These audiences will find this publication appealing as it combines three distinct scholarly contributions: first, it identifies and highlights state-of-the-art techniques and methods for designing Cloud systems; second, it presents mechanisms and schemes for linking Clouds to economic activities; third, it achieves balanced coverage of all related technologies that collectively contribute towards the realisation of Cloud computing.

Book Overview

The book contains 21 chapters that were carefully selected based on peer review by at least two expert and independent reviewers. The chapters are split into four Parts:

Part 1: Cloud Base

This section aims to cover the essential definitions, characteristics and concepts behind Cloud computing. The chapters included in this section collectively introduce the reader to Cloud computing and its essential architectural principles. As a result, chapters in this section are either tutorial in nature or provide critical literature surveys in the field.

Chapter 1 presents a number of mainstream technologies for building and managing Cloud architectures. The authors provide a detailed description of virtual machine frameworks and present the MapReduce programming model, which is suitable for large-scale data processing.

Chapter 2 describes a detailed taxonomy of Cloud computing architectures that may promote clarity and reusability of key concepts in Cloud design. The authors use this taxonomy to identify key similarities and differences between various approaches to Cloud computing and underline areas for further development.

Chapter 3 analyses the applicability of Cloud computing in e-Science. It focuses on classifying different Cloud architectures in terms of their ability to provide the services required for large-scale scientific experiments and calculations.

Chapter 4 examines the differences between Cloud and Grid computing. The authors explain how the user- and task-centric design philosophy of Clouds makes this technology more appealing to typical end-users.

Chapter 5 provides a high-level overview of various standards for, and related to, Cloud computing. It explores the key features of each standard in terms of interoperability, security and portability and assesses the potential for market adoption of the standards presented.

Part 2: Cloud Seeding

This section builds on the introductory material of Part 1 and provides in-depth coverage of how Clouds can be designed and how emerging technologies such as P2P fit with Cloud computing in general. It includes chapters that propose novel techniques and systems for making Clouds scalable, efficient and fault-tolerant computing platforms.

Chapter 6 presents an innovative computational paradigm called Cloud@Home that merges Peer-to-Peer computing with Clouds. The Cloud@Home aggregates the computational resources of many low-power systems, and the authors demonstrate how this pool of resources can subsequently be managed and used by different communities of users.

Chapter 7 exploits a novel peer-to-peer model for replicating and managing job states in an efficient and decentralised way. The authors use this model to enhance the fault tolerance of the MapReduce programming paradigm in highly dynamic environments that exhibit significant failure rates.

Chapter 8 introduces a novel network-centric Cloud architecture that provides enhanced end-to-end connectivity services. The framework facilitates vertical and horizontal communication integration of Cloud applications and the authors demonstrate its usefulness in decoupling connectivity from the underlying network implementations.

Chapter 9 presents a new workflow-based framework called YPL-PC that supports the development of (private) scientific Clouds. The authors base their work on the YML workflow programming paradigm and show how their framework can effectively integrate dedicated and volunteer computing resources to support large-scale scientific applications.

Chapter 10 discusses the benefits of mixing Clouds with more traditional computing platforms. It focuses on the design of a new high-level framework that supports the smooth transition of an application from a cluster or Grid to a Cloud.

Chapter 11 describes a novel mechanism for extending a Grid computing environment to use on-demand Cloud resources in order to achieve better performance. The authors achieve this by modifying the Grid resource management architecture, and through experimentation demonstrate the performance gains of their framework in workflows with large data sets.

Chapter 12 presents a new peer-to-peer Cloud architecture called Cloud Peer. The system creates and manages an overlay network of virtual machines and the authors demonstrate how it supports load balancing and scalable resource discovery.

Chapter 13 discusses the applicability of Cloud computing for high-throughput scientific applications. It shows that the Nimrod/G toolkit can handle both volunteer resources and commercial services. Through a case study, the authors conclude that an appropriate mixture of Grid and Cloud computing provides an ideal platform for high-performance scientific computations.

Part 3: Cloud Breaks

This section covers a range of challenging issues associated to Cloud computing that, if not addressed properly, may limit adoption. It includes chapters that discuss legal issues, security and limitations. Specifically, the questions here relate to how data is protected in such environments to account for privacy, confidentiality, and so on, and what legislative and regulatory challenges are faced.

Chapter 14 provides an overview of a wide spectrum of legislation and regulations applicable to Cloud computing. The authors present a detailed analysis of the considerations that potential Cloud users should make in order to protect their processes and data.

Chapter 15 discusses interoperability issues and open development frameworks for Cloud computing. It presents current standardisation efforts and identifies future key challenges in data confidentiality in particular.

Chapter 16 discusses security and risk issues related to Cloud computing, including privacy, trust and data control. The authors use this analysis to propose a new information asset classification model to assist Cloud users when choosing amongst Cloud delivery and deployment models.

Chapter 17 focuses on the security controls that need to be deployed in order to increase the adoption of Cloud computing. This discussion leads to a set of recommendations on how various security layers can be incorporated in typical private or public Cloud provisions.

Part 4: Cloud Feedback

This section aims to argue a business case for Cloud computing by debating the impact of Clouds. Can Clouds be the basis for deploying successful digital economies? Are there any lessons learned from specific case studies involving the use of Clouds for business applications?

Chapter 18 assesses frameworks for the distribution and enforcement of policies in Cloud architectures. The authors explore the use of the Service-Oriented Architecture (SOA) Policy Enforcement Point (PEP) as a policy portal and show that this can be an effective security model for Cloud-based services.

Chapter 19 describes in detail the PeRvasive Infrastructure of Services for Media (PRISM) project that provides a Cloud-based media infrastructure to support network access to BBC content. The deployment of this system is discussed, and it is shown that the system is capable of handling petabytes of data for on-demand viewing.

Chapter 20 discusses the economic forces and business drivers affecting the adoption of Cloud computing. It provides a detailed analysis of the costs and benefits of using Clouds as well as the overall quality of experience of Cloud end-users and its link to Service-Level Agreements (SLAs).

Chapter 21 discusses the challenges that would be entailed in constructing a price comparison service for Cloud resources. Service-Level Agreements (SLAs) would be a key component in such a service and experiments are presented for costing applications on a local Grid and a public (Amazon EC2) and private (Eucalyptus) Cloud.

Acknowledgements The editors are grateful to the peer-review panel for supporting this book including, in no particular order, Anand Govindarajan, Bhaskar Prasad Rimal, Bin Li, Blair Bethwaite, Brian Amedro, Cyril Onwubiko, David Abramson, Hai Jin, James P. Durbano, Fabrice Huet, Francesco Palmieri, Ian Lumb, Jinlei Jiang, Kevin Mcdonald, Lakshmanan G, Rajiv Ranjan, Scott Morrison, and Terence Harmer. The editors are deeply apologetic to anyone whom they have forgotten.

The editors also wish to thank the Springer's editorial team for their strong and continuous support throughout the development of this book.

University of Derby, UK Professor Nick Antonopoulos
University of Surrey, UK Dr Lee Gillam
Winter 2010

Contents

Part IV   Cloud Feedback

Part I
Cloud Base

Chapter 1
Tools and Technologies for Building Clouds

Hai Jin, Shadi Ibrahim, Tim Bell, Li Qi, Haijun Cao, Song Wu, and Xuanhua Shi

Abstract With cloud computing growing in popularity, tools and technologies are emerging to build, access, manage, and maintain the clouds. These tools need to manage the huge number of operations within a cloud transparently and without service interruptions. Cloud computing promises lower costs, faster implementation, and more flexibility using mixtures of technologies, and the associated tools are critical for achieving this.

In this chapter, we survey several state-of-the-art techniques for building clouds, starting with virtualization technology. We briefly introduce virtual machines (VMs) and their main features. Then, we introduce the main tools to manage VMs (hypervisors and virtual infrastructure managers) as well as the major technologies used to manage VMs in a public cloud. We then present *MapReduce*, a powerful model that makes it easier to write programs that take advantage of the power of cloud computing. We conclude by examining four web services tools and technologies that are built for cloud computing.

1.1 Introduction

Computing is being transformed by a new model, *cloud computing*. In this model, data and computation are operated somewhere in a "cloud," which is some collection of data centers owned and maintained by a third party.

Cloud computing refers to the hardware, systems software, and applications delivered as services over the Internet. When a cloud is made available in a pay-as-you-go manner to the general public, we call it a *Public Cloud*. The term *Private Cloud* is used when the cloud infrastructure is operated solely for a business or an organization. A composition of the two types (private and public) is called a *Hybrid*

H. Jin (✉)
Services Computing Technology and System Lab, Cluster and Grid Computing Lab,
Huazhong University of Science and Technology, 430074, Wuhan, China
e-mail: hjin@hust.edu.cn

N. Antonopoulos and L. Gillam (eds.), *Cloud Computing: Principles,*
Systems and Applications, Computer Communications and Networks,
DOI 10.1007/978-1-84996-241-4_1, © Springer-Verlag London Limited 2010

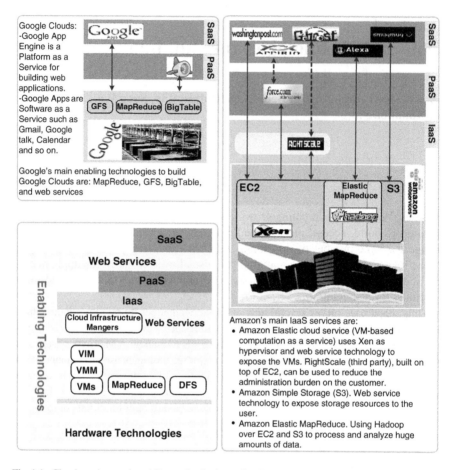

Fig. 1.1 Cloud services and enabling technologies, using Amazon and Google systems as examples

Cloud, where a private cloud is able to maintain high service availability by scaling up their system with externally provisioned resources from a public cloud when there are rapid workload fluctuations or hardware failures.

In general, cloud providers fall into three categories (shown in Fig. 1.1):

- Infrastructure as a Service (IaaS): offering web-based access to storage and computing power. The consumer does not need to manage or control the underlying cloud infrastructure but has control over the operating systems, storage, and deployed applications.
- Platform as a Service (PaaS): giving developers the tools to build and host web applications (e.g., APPRIO [1], a software as a service provider, is built using the Force.com [2] platform while the infrastructure is provided by the Amazon Web Service [3]).

- Software as a Service (SaaS): applications that are accessible from various client devices through a thin client interface such as a web browser.

The shift toward cloud computing is driven by many factors including ubiquity of access (all you need is a browser), ease of management (no need for user experience improvements as no configuration or backup is needed), and less investment (affordable enterprise solution deployed on a pay-per-use basis for the hardware, with systems software provided by the cloud providers) [4]. Furthermore, cloud computing offers many advantages to vendors, such as easily managed infrastructure because the data center has homogeneous hardware and system software. Moreover, they are under the control of a single, knowledgeable entity.

1.1.1 Cloud Services and Enabling Technologies

For the purposes of this chapter, we define cloud computing as data centers plus a layer of system software services designed to support the creation and scalable deployment of application services. Our goal here is to examine the tools and technologies used to build these clouds.

The data center hardware consists of thousands of individual computing nodes with their corresponding networking and storage subsystems, power distribution and conditioning equipment, and extensive cooling systems. Such data centers currently power the services offered by companies such as Google, Amazon, Yahoo, and Microsoft's online services division.

Cloud services (remote data and computation) are exposed as simple and user-friendly **web services**. For example, Microsoft's ADO.NET (originally called *Astoria*) [5] provides the tools to expose any data object from a collection, stored in a database or other form, as a URI to an encoded form using a standard such as JSON or ATOM representation, and Google's AppEngine [6] provides a way to deploy a remote Python script that becomes a web service that can access data in their *BigTable* database system.

To deliver highly available and flexible services (i.e., computation as a service), and owing to the maturity of *virtualization technology*, *Virtual Machines* (VMs) are used as a standard for object deployment in the cloud. VMs decouple the computing infrastructure from the physical infrastructure. In addition, VMs allow the customization of the platform to suit the needs of the end-user. For example, in the Amazon Elastic Compute Cloud (EC2) [7], the customer selects his/her preferred VM image (virtual appliance) from a list of various versions of Linux and Windows servers configured with different web servers and databases. Alternatively, they can customize a system to best meet their needs and deploy the new application in the VM. Amazon provides a basic set of web services that can be used to deploy the VM, create an instance, and secure it. Multiple instances can be created to support demand as needed, although this requires more system administration and management. Thus, some organizations have developed *virtual infrastructure* tools to manage and monitor VMs in a pool of distributed resources (e.g., Enomaly

[8] and OpenNebula [9]). In addition, third-party application hosting framework service companies, like RightScale [10] and Elastra [11], have emerged to provide higher-level application deployment tools on top of EC2, thereby reducing the administration burden on the customer.

Because of the huge amount of data stored by a cloud, efficient processing and analysis of data has become a challenging issue. The Google *MapReduce* [12] model has proven to be an efficient approach for data-intensive cloud computing (e.g., Google uses its MapReduce framework to process 20 petabytes of data per day). MapReduce has been advocated as a good basis for data center computers in general [13].

1.2 Virtualization Technology

Virtualization is the idea of partitioning or dividing the resources of a single server into multiple segregated VMs. Virtualization technology has been proposed and developed over a relatively long period. The earliest use of VMs was by IBM in 1960, intended to leverage investments in expensive mainframe computers [14]. The idea was to enable multitasking – running multiple applications and processes for different users simultaneously. Robert P. Goldberg described the need for virtual machines in 1974: "Virtual machine systems were originally developed to correct some of the shortcomings of the typical third generation architectures and multiprogramming operating systems – e.g., OS/360" [15]. During the 1980s and 1990s, the prevailing approach to computing was distributed systems, client-server applications, and the inexpensive x86 server [14]. Recently, owing to the rapid growth in IT infrastructure, we have seen the emergence of multicore processors and a wide variety of hardware, operating systems, and software. In this environment, virtualization has had a resurgence of popularity. Virtualization can provide dramatic benefits for a computing system, including increased utilization, energy saving, rapid deployment, improved maintenance capability, isolation, and encapsulation. Moreover, virtualization enables applications to migrate from one server to another while they are still running, without downtime, providing flexible workload management, and high availability during planned maintenance or unplanned events [16–22].

There are numerous reasons that virtualization is effective in practical scenarios, for example [23,24]:

- Server and application consolidation: under virtualization, we can run multiple applications at the same time on the same server, resulting in more efficient utilization of resources.
- Configurability: virtualization allows dynamic configuration and bundling of resources for a wider variety of applications than could be achieved at the hardware level – different applications require different resources (some requiring more storage, others requiring more computing).

- Increased application availability: VM checkpointing and migration allow quick failure recovery from unplanned outages with no interruption in service.
- Improved responsiveness: resource provisioning, monitoring, and maintenance can be automated, and common resources can be cached and reused.

1.2.1   Virtual Machines

A VM is a software implementation of a machine (i.e., a computer) that executes programs like a physical machine [25]. This differs from a *process* VM, which is designed to run a single program, such as the Java Runtime Environment (JRE). A *system* VM provides a complete system platform that supports the execution of a complete operating system (OS).

The VM lifecycle has six phases: create, suspend, resume, save, migrate, and destroy. Multiple VMs can run simultaneously in the same physical node. Each VM can have a different OS, and a *Virtual Machine Monitor* (VMM) is used to control and manage the VMs on a single physical node. A VMM is often referred to as a *hypervisor*. Above this level, *Virtual Infrastructure Managers* (VIMs) are used to manage, deploy, and monitor VMs on a distributed pool of resources (cluster or data center). In addition, *Cloud Infrastructure Managers* (CIMs) are web-based management solutions on the top of IaaS providers (see Fig. 1.2).

1.2.2   Virtualization Platforms

Virtualization technology has been developed to best utilize computing capacity. Server virtualization has been described as follows: "In most cases, server virtualization

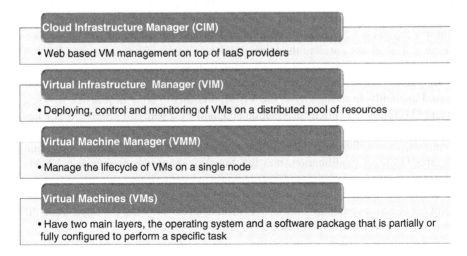

Fig. 1.2 Different layers of VM management tools and technologies

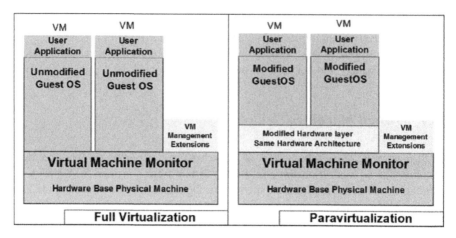

Fig. 1.3 A comparison between full virtualization and paravirtualization VM hypervisors [33]

is accomplished by the use of a hypervisor (VMM) to logically assign and separate physical resources. The hypervisor allows a guest operating system, running on the virtual machine, to function as if it were solely in control of the hardware, unaware that other guests are sharing it. Each guest operating system is protected from the others and is thus unaffected by any instability or configuration issues of the others" [26].

Virtualization methods can be classified into two categories according to whether or not the guest OS kernel needs to be modified, as shown in Fig. 1.3: (1) *full virtualization* (supported by VMware [27], Xen [28], KVM [29], and Microsoft Hyper-V [30], etc.), and (2) *paravirtualization* (currently supported only by Xen). Full virtualization emulates the entire hardware environment by utilizing hardware virtualization support, binary code translation, or binary code rewriting, and thus the guest OS does not need to modify its kernel. Having full virtualization is important for running non-open-source operating system such as Windows, because it is too difficult to modify the Windows kernel without source code. Paravirtualization requires the guest OS kernel to be modified to become aware of the hypervisor. Because it need not emulate the entire hardware environment, paravirtualization can attain better performance than full virtualization.

In paravirtualized architecture, OS-level information about the VM can be passed explicitly from the OS to the VMM, and this is done in practice to some extent [31,32]. Any explicit information supplied by a paravirtualized OS is guaranteed to match what is available inside the OS. However, in some important environments, the explicit approach is less valuable, and because paravirtualization requires OS-level modification, that functionality cannot be deployed in VMMs running beneath legacy or closed-source operating systems anyway.

Table 1.1 compares some of the most relevant commercial and open-source software (OSS) technologies for server virtualization, showing the main trade-off between the product's performances.

Table 1.1 Comparison of some of the most relevant commercial and open-source software (OSS) tools for server virtualization [34]

VMM	Type	Highlights	Guest performance	License
KVM [29]	Full virtualization	Assigns every VM as a regular Linux process	Close to native	Open source
Xen [28]	Paravirtualization	Supports VM migration on fly	Native	Open source
VMware [27]	Full virtualization	Provides a mature product family to manage virtual infrastructure	Close to native	Commercial
Microsoft hyper-V [30]	Full virtualization	Able to trap guest calls	Close to native	Commercial

1.2.3 Virtual Infrastructure Management

A *Virtual Infrastructure Manager* (VIM) is responsible for the efficient management of a virtual infrastructure as a whole, by providing basic functionality for deploying, controlling, and monitoring VMs on a distributed pool of resources. This is done by communicating with their VMMs. The major issues being addressed by the cloud community are:

- Improving the distributed and efficient management of the virtual infrastructure as a whole (i.e., deployment, control, and monitoring)
- Providing self-provisioning of the virtual infrastructure
- Improving the integrity and interoperability of the different virtualization technologies (different hypervisors such as Xen, VMware) as well as the different cloud providers
- Providing administrators with a uniform user-friendly environment that enables access to a wider range of physically distributed facilities improving productivity

Accordingly, many organizations have introduced virtual infrastructure management tools as shown in Table 1.2.

In addition to specific systems such as those listed in the table, open standard organizations such as OGF and DMTF contribute many standards for remote management of cloud computing infrastructures. The scope of the specifications covers all high-level functionality required for the life-cycle management of VMs. Some of these standards have been widely adopted to construct grid and cloud systems, such as the Open Grid Forum *Open Cloud Computing Interface* (OCCI) [40], The *Open Virtualization Format* (OVF) [41], and the virtualization API (*libvirt*) [42].

Table 1.2 Comparison of some of the most relevant commercial and open-source software (OSS) tools for virtual infrastructure management

System name	Brief description	VM hypervisor	Cloud type
Enomaly [8]	A programmable virtual cloud infrastructure for small, medium, and large businesses. Their Elastic Computing Platform (ECP) helps users to design, deploy, and manage virtual applications in the cloud, and also significantly reduces administrative and systems workload. A browser-based dashboard enables IT personnel to simply and efficiently plan deployments, automate VM scaling and load-balancing, and analyze, configure, and optimize cloud capacity.	Xen, KVM	Private and public
Eucalyptus [35]	"Elastic Utility Computing Architecture Linking Your Programs To Useful Systems" – is an open-source software infrastructure for implementing cloud computing on clusters. The current interface to Eucalyptus is compatible with Amazon's EC2, S3, and EBS interfaces, but the infrastructure is designed to support multiple client-side interfaces.	Xen, KVM, VMware	Private and public
Nimbus [36]	Nimbus has been developed in part within the Globus Toolkit 4 framework and provides interfaces to VM management functions based on the WSRF set of protocols. There is also an alternative implementation implementing Amazon EC2 WSDL.	Xen	Private and public
Open Nebula [9]	Orchestrates storage, network, and virtualization technologies to enable the dynamic placement of multitier services (groups of interconnected VMs) on distributed infrastructures, combining both data center resources and remote cloud resources, according to allocation policies.	Xen, KVM, VMWare	Private, hybrid, and public cloud (EC2, Elastic Hosts[37])
Usher [38]	The design philosophy of Usher is to provide an interface whereby users and administrators can request VM operations (e.g., start, stop, migrate, etc.) while delegating administrative tasks for these operations out to smart plug-ins. Usher's implementation allows for arbitrary action to be taken for nearly any event in the system.	Xen	Virtual cluster
VNIX [39]	With VNIX, administrators can deploy various VMs rapidly and easily on computing nodes, and manage them with related configuration from a single easy-to-use management console. In addition, VNIX implements several specialized features, involving easy monitoring, fast deploying, and autoconfiguring.	Xen	Cluster

1.2.4   *Cloud Infrastructure Manager*

A *Cloud Infrastructure Manager* (CIM) is a web-based solution focused on deploying and managing services (deploying, monitoring, and maintaining the VMs) on top of *Infrastructure as a Service* (IaaS) clouds. Third-party application-hosting framework service companies provide higher-level application deployment tools on top of IaaS. Some of these solutions are listed in Table 1.3.

Table 1.3 Cloud infrastructure management solutions

System name	Brief description	Pricing	Cloud provider	Users
Rightscale [11]	Rightscale is a cloud management environment, cloud-ready server template and best-practice deployment library, adaptable automation engine, and multi-cloud engine.	Starting at US$500, monthly fee	Amazon web services, GoGrid, FlexiScale	G.ho.st, Animoto, and MeDeploy [43]
Elastra [12]	Elastra's main features are: application infrastructure modeling, federated hybrid cloud management, lifecycle orchestration, and deployment management.	Pricing not published	AWS	
Kaavo [44]	IMOD is for Application-Centric Management of virtual resources in the clouds. It provides easy-to-use web interface for deploying, running, and managing complex multiserver n-tier applications in the cloud.	Pricing not published	EC2	The 451 Group and Infoworld [45]
CohesiveFT [46]	PN-Cubed is a commercial solution that enables customer control in a cloud, across multiple clouds, and between private infrastructure and the clouds.	Starting with US$5,000 per year	EC2, Elastic hosts	

1.3   The MapReduce System

Google's MapReduce [12] is a programming model that demonstrates a simpler way to develop data-intensive applications for large distributed systems. It can be leveraged to utilize the resources available through a cloud.

The MapReduce [12] system runs on top of the *Google File System* (GFS) [47], within which data is loaded, partitioned into chunks, and each chunk replicated. Data processing is co-located with data storage: when a file needs to be processed, the job scheduler consults a storage metadata service to get the host node for each chunk, and then schedules a *map* process on that node, so that data locality is exploited efficiently. At the time of writing, because of its remarkable features including simplicity, fault tolerance, and scalability, MapReduce is by far the most powerful realization of data-intensive cloud computing programming. It is often advocated as an easier-to-use, efficient, and reliable replacement for the traditional programming model of moving the data to the computation.

The MapReduce abstraction is inspired by the Map and Reduce functions, which are commonly used in the functional languages such as Lisp [12]. Users express the computation using two functions, map and reduce, which can be carried out on subsets of the data in a highly parallel manner. The runtime system is responsible for parallelizing and fault handling. The steps of the process are as follows. They are illustrated by the widely used "wordcount" example in Fig. 1.4:

- The input is read (typically from a distributed file system) and broken up into key/value pairs. The key identifies the subset of data, and the value will have computation performed on it. (In the example, the keys are each input word read from files A, B, and C, and the values are all a count of one.) The map function maps this data into sets of key/value pairs that can be distributed to different processors.

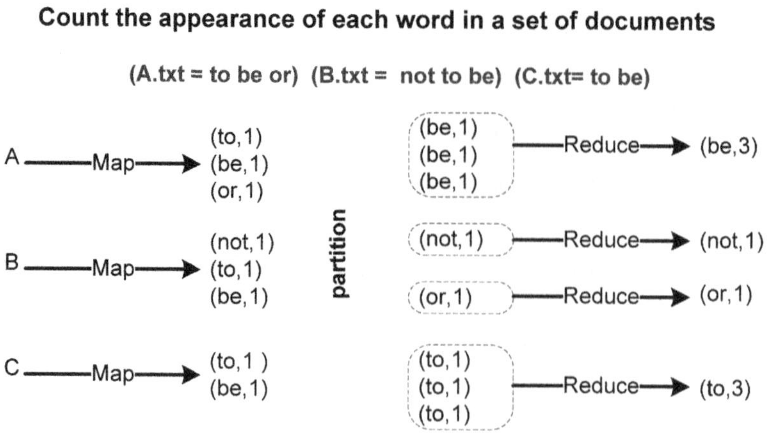

Count the appearance of each word in a set of documents

(A.txt = to be or) (B.txt = not to be) (C.txt= to be)

Fig. 1.4 Illustrate the *Map* and *Reduce* functions using the Wordcount Example

- The pairs are partitioned into groups for processing, and are sorted according to their key as they arrive for reduction. (In the example, the pairs are now grouped according to the key.)
- The key/value pairs are reduced, once for each unique key in the sorted list, to produce a combined result. (In this example, this will be the count of each word).

MapReduce has been applied widely in various fields including data- and compute-intensive applications, machine learning, and multicore programming. Moreover, many implementations have been developed in different programming languages for various purposes.

The popular open source implementation of MapReduce, Hadoop [48], was developed primarily by Yahoo, where it processes hundreds of terabytes of data on at least 10,000 cores [49], and is now used by other companies, including Facebook, Amazon, Last.fm, and the *New York Times* [50]. Research groups from enterprises and academia are starting to study the MapReduce model as a better fit for cloud computing, and explore the possibilities of adapting it for more applications.

1.3.1 Hadoop MapReduce Overview

The Hadoop common [48], formerly called the Hadoop core, includes filesystem, RPC (remote procedure call), and serialization libraries, and provides the basic services for building a cloud computing environment with commodity hardware. The two main subprojects are the MapReduce framework and the Hadoop Distributed File System (HDFS).

The HDFS is a distributed file system designed to run on commodity hardware. HDFS is highly fault-tolerant and so can be deployed on low-cost hardware. HDFS provides high throughput access to application data and is suitable for applications that have large data sets. The Hadoop MapReduce framework is highly reliant on its shared file system, and it comes with plug-ins for HDFS, CloudStore [51], and the Amazon Simple Storage Service (S3).

The MapReduce framework consists of a single master JobTracker and one slave TaskTracker per cluster-node. The master is responsible for scheduling the jobs' component tasks on the slaves (i.e., it queries the HDFS master Namenode about data block locations and assigns each task to the TaskTracker that is closest to where the data to be processed is physically stored), monitoring them, and re-executing any failed tasks. The slaves execute the tasks as directed by the master.

1.4 Web Services

To support cloud computing infrastructure efficiently, and to express business models easily, designers and developers need a group of web services technologies to construct a real, user-friendly, and content-rich set of applications on the top of their clouds. This section introduces four fundamental tools and technologies, which can be employed to construct cloud applications viewed at the infrastructure, architecture, and presentational level. These technologies are: Remote Procedure Call (RPC), Service-Oriented Architecture (SOA), Representational State Transfer (REST), and Mashup.

1.4.1 RPC (Remote Procedure Call)

Reliable and stable communications among cloud resources are fundamental to the infrastructure, and thus are an important consideration. Remote Procedure Call (RPC) has proven to be an efficient mechanism for implementing the client-server model in a distributed computing environment. It was proposed initially by Sun Microsystems as a great advancement in comparison with sockets (e.g., the programmer is not concerned with the underlying communications, since they are embedded inside the RPC). In RPC, the client must know what features the server provides, which are indicated by a service definition, written in IDL (Interface Description Language). An RPC call is a synchronous operation that suspends the calling program until the results of the call are returned. When an RPC is compiled, a stub is included in the compiled code that represents the remote service. When the program runs, it calls the stub, which knows where the operation is and how to reach the service. The stub will send the message through the network to the server. The result of the procedure is returned to the client in the same way.

Many commercial products built over the RPC mechanism have been practically proven as efficient and convenient to construct enterprise applications.

In 2002, Microsoft released the .NET Remoting [52], which was incrementally evolved from DCOM and Active X, to support. NET applications intercommunicating in a loosely coupled environment. Similar to RPC stubs, .NET Remoting initializes the "Channel" objects to proxy the remote calls. To improve the transparency and convenience, the procedure of serialization and marshalling will be completed automatically by .NET runtime. Each .NET Remoting object is identified as a unique URL and safely accessed by clients remotely.

Extending from Java Remote Method Invocation (RMI) [53], Java community presents a complete specification J2EE [54] to standardize the communications among loosely coupled Java components. The enhancements include Enterprise Java Beans (EJB), connectors, servlets, and portlets. The complete J2EE structure of specifications helps designers to easily construct business logic and assists developers in clearly implementing them. Although .Net Remoting and J2EE have been widely adopted by the industry, RPC mechanism is not feasible to construct Cloud applications. One of the problems with RPC is that RPC implementations, as shown in Table 1.4, can be incompatible with each other. To use one of the possible implementations of RPC will result in a high dependence on the particular RPC.

Table 1.4 Web service toolkits comparisons

	Age	Dep.	Transport	Key Tech.	Categories	Implementations
RPC	1974	–	TCP/IP	Stubs, IDL	Infrastructure, IaaS	Java RMI [52], XML RPC, .Net Remoting [53], RPyC, CORBA
SOA	1998	WS-RPC	HTTP,FTP, SMTP	WSDL UDDI SOAP	Architecture level, PaaS	IBM Websphere, Microsoft .Net IIS, Weblogic
REST	2000	HTTP	HTTP,FTP, SMTP	Web-oriented	Architecture level, DaaS	RIP, Rails, Restlet, Jboss RESTEasy, Apache CXF, Symfony
MASHUP	2000 later	REST SOA RSS	HTTP	Web-oriented (Web 2.0)	Application level, SaaS	Google Mashup editor, JackBe, Mozilla Ubiquity

1.4.2   SOA (Service-Oriented Architecture)

The goal of a Service-Oriented Architecture (SOA) [55,56] is to composite together fairly large chunks of functionality to form service-oriented applications, which are almost entirely built from the existing software services. SOA hired a bunch of open standards (1) to wrap the components in different localized runtime environment (e.g., in Java or .NET); (2) to enable different clients including pervasive devices free access; (3) to reuse the existing components to compose more services. This significantly reduces development costs and helps designers and developers to concentrate more on business models and their internal logic.

SOAs use several communication standards based on XML to enhance the interoperability among application systems. As the atomic access point inside an SOA, the web services are formally defined by three kernel standards: Web Service Description Language (WSDL), Simple Object Access Protocol (SOAP), and Universal Description Discovery and Integration (UDDI). Normally, the functional interfaces and parameters of specific services are described using the WSDL. Web services exchange messages are encoded in the SOAP messaging framework and transported over HTTP or other internet protocols (SMTP, FTP, and so forth). A typical web service lifecycle envisions the following scenario: A service provider publishes the WSDL description of their service in a UDDI, a registry that permits Universal Description Discovery and Integration of web services. Subsequently, service requesters can inspect the UDDI and locate/discover web services that are of interest. Using the information provided by the WSDL description, they can directly invoke the corresponding web service. Further, several web services can be composed to achieve more complex functionality. All the invocation procedures are similar to RPC except that the communications and deployments are described in open standards.

Moreover, the open standards organizations such as W3C, OASIS, and DMTF contribute many higher-level standards to help different users construct their reusable, interoperable, and discoverable services and applications. Some of these standards were widely adopted to construct grid and cloud systems, such as Web Services Resources Framework (WSRF) [57], Web Services Security (WS-Security) [58], Web Services Policy (WS-Policy) [59], and so on.

1.4.3   REST (Representative State Transfer)

REST [60] is an architectural style that Roy T. Fielding, now chief scientist at Day Software, first defined in his doctoral thesis. REST stipulates mechanisms for defining and accessing resources in specific distributed systems such as the web. In a REST implementation, resources are addressed via uniform resource identifiers (URIs). That is, a given URI is used to access the representational state of a resource, and also to modify that resource. For example, web URLs can be used to give descriptive information about resources, and consumers then need to know only the URL to read the information. Furthermore, an authorized user can also modify the information if needed.

REST defines three architectural entities as follows [60–62]:

* Data elements: resource identifiers such as URIs and URLs, and resource representations, such as HTML documents, images, and XML documents
* Components: Origin servers, gateways, proxies, and user agents
* Connectors: Clients, servers, and caches

The representational state for resources in an HTTP-based REST system should be accessed using the standard HTTP methods.

A simple breakdown of these methods is as follows: GET is used to transfer the current representational state of a resource from a server to a client; PUT is used to transfer the modified representational state of a resource from the client to the server; POST is used to transfer the new representational state of a resource from the client to the server; and DELETE is used to transfer information needed to change a resource to a deleted representational state.

1.4.4   Mashup

A mashup has been defined in Wikipedia [63] as "a web page or application that combines data or functionality from two or more external sources to create a new service. To be more precise, Mashup technology concentrates on the following tasks

[64]: (1) Deep access to existing enterprise services and data/content repositories; (2) SaaS-style web-based Mashup assembly and use; (3) Assembly models that are truly end-user friendly with very little training required; and last, but certainly not least, (4) a credible management and maintenance plan for IT departments that must support a flood of public end-user built and integrated apps."

Mashup is concerned with the API (application) level. When building Mashups, the developer is always dependent on the providers of the services. As shown in the figure, Mashup requires that the XMLHttpRequest is made to third-party domains. By compositing services and data from SOA, REST, RSS, ATOM, and other RPC-like web servers, a Mashup API can conveniently bind the data with AJAX scripts to deliver a service to end-users.

Some Mashup editors have been implemented to help developers easily construct Web 2.0 and cloud-oriented applications; currently two are available, Google Mashup Editor [65] and Mozilla Ubiquity [66].

1.4.5   Web Services in Practice

All the aforementioned web services tools and technologies have been widely implemented by industry and open-source organizations. Table 1.4 also lists their main attributes in terms of when they were proposed, dependencies, transport mechanism, key technology, categories, and implementations. Understanding these features can help developers to quickly adopt the appropriate technologies and develop their clouds effectively.

1.5   Conclusions

This chapter has presented the main tools and technologies for building and operating clouds. Virtualization technology is foundational to cloud computing because it provides a safe and flexible platform using VMs, VM Monitors, Virtual Infrastructure, and Cloud Infrastructure Managers. Virtualization technology is still developing rapidly, and some of the limitations that currently exist are likely to be addressed as virtualization technology becomes more mature. We have also presented the MapReduce programming model, which is a particularly useful approach for processing huge amounts of data because the computation is close to the data.

Finally, we have reviewed a number of different web services technologies that provide an easy interface for users to configure and access cloud resources.

Cloud computing is a powerful way to provide computing resources, and the tools for creating and maintaining cloud systems and their services are becoming increasingly flexible and easy to use, providing users with easy on-demand access to massive computing power and storage that previously would only have been available to extremely well-resourced organizations.

Acknowledgments This work is supported by National 973 Key Basic Research Program under grant No.2007CB310900, NSFC under grants No.60673174 and No.60973037, Program for New Century Excellent Talents in University under Grant NCET-07-0334, Information Technology Foundation of MoE and Intel under grant MoE-INTEL-09-03, and National High-Tech R&D Plan of China under grant No.2006AA01A115.

References

1. APPRIO Homepage (2009) http://www.appirio.com/
2. Force.com Homepage (2009) http://www.salesforce.com/platform/
3. Amazon Web Services (2009) http://aws.amazon.com/
4. Barroso LA, Urs Hölzle U (2009) The datacenter as a computer: an introduction to the design of warehouse-scale machines. Morgan & Claypool, USA
5. ADO.NET Data Service (formally Astroia) (2009) http://msdn.microsoft.com/en-us/data/bb931106.aspx
6. Google AppEngine (2009) http://code.google.com/appengine/
7. Amazon Elastic Cloud Computing (2009) http://aws.amazon.com/ec2/
8. Enomaly Elastic Computing (2009) http://www.enomaly.com/
9. Open Nubela Homepage (2009) http://www.opennebula.org/
10. Rightscale Homepage (2009) http://www.rightscale.com/
11. Elastra Manage ComplexITy Homepage (2009) http://www.elastra.com/
12. Dean J, Ghemawat S (2008) MapReduce: simplified data processing on large clusters. Commun ACM 51(1):107–113
13. Patterson DA (2008) Technical perspective: the data center is the computer. Commun ACM 51(1):105
14. Vmware (2009) http://www.vmware.com/virtualization/history.html
15. Goldberg RP (1974) Survey of virtual machine research. IEEE Comput Mag 7(6):34–45
16. Waldspurger CA (December 2002) Memory resource management in VMware ESX server. In: Proceedings of the 5th symposium on operating systems design and implementation (OSDI '02), Boston, MA
17. Fraser K, Hand S, Neugebauer R, Pratt I, Warfield A, Williamson M (2004) Safe hardware access with the Xen virtual machine monitor. In: OASIS ASPLOS 2004 workshop
18. Clark C, Fraser K, Hand S, Hansen JG, Jul E, Limpach C, Pratt L, Warfield A (2005) Live migration of virtual machines. In: Proceedings of the 2nd symposium on networked systems design and implementation (NSDI '05), Boston, MA
19. Garfinkel T, Pfaff B, Chow J, Rosenblum M, Boneh D (2003) Terra: a virtual machine-based platform for trusted computing. In: Proceedings of the 19th ACM symposium on operating systems principles (SOSP '03), Bolton Landing (Lake George), New York
20. Bressoud TC, Schneider FB (1995) Hypervisor based fault tolerance. In: Proceedings of the fifteenth ACM symposium on operating systems principles, ACM Press, pp 1–11
21. Petrini F, Kerbyson DJ, Pakin S (2003) The case of the missing supercomputer performance: achieving optimal performance on the 8,192 processors of ASCI Q. In: Proceedings of SC '03, Washington, DC, USA
22. Koch K (2002) How does ASCI actually complete multi-month 1000-processor milestone simulations? In: Proceedings of the conference on high speed computing
23. Foster I, Zhao Y, Raicu I, Lu S (2008) Cloud computing and grid computing 360-degree compared. In: the Proceedings of the grid computing environments workshop
24. Nanda S, Chiueh T (2005) A survey on virtualization technologies, RPE Report, February. www.ecsl.cs.sunysb.edu/tr/TR179.pdf
25. Virtual Machine (Wikipedia) (2009) http://en.wikipedia.org/wiki/Virtual_machine

26. IBM white paper (2009) Seeding the Clouds: Key Infrastructure Elements for Cloud Computing. ftp://ftp.software.ibm.com/common/ssi/sa/wh/n/oiw03022usen/OIW03022USEN.PDF
27. VMware – Virtual Infrastructure Software (2009) http://www.vmware.com.
28. Xen Homepage (2009) http://www.xen.org/.
29. Kernel-based Virtual Machine (2009) http://kvm.qumranet.com.
30. Microsoft Hyper-V (2009) http://www.microsoft.com/hyper-v-server/en/us/default.aspx
31. Pratt I, Warfield A, Barham P, Neugebauer R (2003) Xen and the art of virtualization. In Proceedings of the 19th ACM symposium on operating systems principles (SOSP '03), Bolton Landing (Lake George), New York
32. Whitaker A, Shaw M, Gribble SD (2002) Scale and performance in the Denali isolation kernel. In: Proceedings of the 5th symposium on operating systems design and implementation (OSDI'02), Boston, MA
33. MSDN Architecture Center, Mapping Applications to the Cloud (2009) http://msdn.microsoft.com/en-us/library/dd430340.aspx
34. Comparison of platform virtual machines (Wikipedia) (2009) http://en.wikipedia.org/wiki/Comparison_of_platform_virtual_machines
35. Eucalyptus system Homepage (2009) http://www.eucalyptus.com/
36. Nimbus Homepage (2009) http://workspace.globus.org/
37. Elastic Hosts Homepage (2009) http://www.elastichosts.com/
38. McNett M, Gupta D, Vahdat A, Voelker GM (2007) Usher: an extensible framework for managing clusters of virtual machines. 21st Large installation system administration conference
39. Shi XH, Tan H, Wu S, Jin H (2008) VNIX: managing virtual machines on clusters, pp 155–162. Japan-China joint workshop on frontier of computer science and technology
40. OGF Open Cloud Computing Interface Working Group (2009) http://www.occi-wg.org/doku.php
41. VMan Initiative (2009) http://www.dmtf.org/initiatives/vman_initiative/
42. libvirt: The virtualization API (2009) http://libvirt.org/
43. RightScale – Testimonials (2009) http://www.rightscale.com/customers/
44. Kaavo Homepage (2009) http://www.kaavo.com/home
45. Kaavo – Testimonials (2009) http://www.kaavo.com/testimonials
46. CohesiveFT Homepage (2009) http://www.cohesiveft.com/
47. Ghemawat S, Gobioff H, Leung ST (2003) The google file system. In: the proceedings of the 19th ACM symposium on operating systems principles, Lake George, New York
48. Hadoop (2009) http://lucene.apache.org/
49. Yahoo! (2009) Yahoo! Developer Network. http://developer.yahoo.com/blogs/hadoop/2008/02/yahoo-worlds-largest-production-hadoop.html. Accessed September 2009
50. Hadoop Credits Page (2009) http://hadoop.apache.org/core/credits.html. Accessed September 2009
51. CloudStore (Formely Kosmos File System) (2009) http://kosmosfs.sourceforge.net/
52. .NET Remoting, http://en.wikipedia.org/wiki/.NET_Remoting
53. Java RMI, http://en.wikipedia.org/wiki/Java_RMI
54. J2EE, http://en.wikipedia.org/wiki/J2EE
55. Service Oriented Architecture (Wikipedia) (2009) http://en.wikipedia.org/wiki/Service-oriented_architecture
56. Service-architecture – Service-oriented architecture (SOA) definition (2009) http://www.service-architecture.com/web-services/articles/service-oriented_architecture_soa_definition.html
57. WSRF (2009) http://www.oasis-open.org/committees/wsrf/
58. WS-Security (2009) http://www.oasis-open.org/committees/tc_home.php?wg_abbrev=wss
59. WS-Policy (2009) http://www.w3.org/Submission/WS-Policy/
60. Goth G (2004) Critics say web services need a REST. IEEE Distribut Syst Online 5(12): 1–1
61. Vinoski S (2008) RESTful web services development checklist. IEEE Internet Comput 12(6):94–96
62. Vinoski S ((2007) REST eye for the SOA guy. IEEE Internet Comput 11(1):82–84

63. Mashup (web application hybrid), http://en.wikipedia.org/wiki/Mashup_(web_application_hybrid)
64. Webmashup.com blog, http://www.webmashup.com/blog/category/learn/ (accessed 1 October 2009)
65. Google Mashup Editor (2009) http://en.wikipedia.org/wiki/Google_Mashup_Editor
66. Mozilla Ubiquity (2009) http://ubiquity.mozilla.com/

Chapter 2
A Taxonomy, Survey, and Issues of Cloud Computing Ecosystems

Bhaskar Prasad Rimal, Eunmi Choi, and Ian Lumb

Abstract Cloud computing has emerged as a popular computing model to support processing of volumetric data using clusters of commodity computers. Nowadays, the computational world is opting for pay-for-use models. Hype and discussion aside, there remains no concrete definition of cloud computing. This chapter describes a comprehensive taxonomy for cloud computing architecture, aiming at a better understanding of the categories of applications that could benefit from cloudification and that will address the landscape of enterprise IT, management services, data governance, and many more. Then, this taxonomy is used to survey several cloud computing services such as Google, Force.com, and Amazon. The usages of taxonomy and survey results are not only to identify similarities and differences of the architectural approaches of cloud computing, but also to identify the areas requiring further research.

2.1 Introduction

Cloud computing appears to be a highly disruptive technology, which is gaining momentum. It has inherited legacy technology as well as new ideas on large-scale distributed systems. The concept of cloud computing addresses the next evolutionary step of distributed computing. The goal of this computing model is to make a better use of distributed resources, put them together in order to achieve higher throughput, and be able to tackle large-scale computation problems. The computing power nowadays is easily available for massive computational processing. For example, image processing on Amazon Elastic Cloud Computing (EC2) [20] for New York Times is a great success story for Amazon. The input of 11 million articles (4-terabytes of TIFF data) was processed successfully using Amazon Simple Storage Service

E. Choi (✉)
School of Business IT, Kookmin University, Jeongneung-Dong,
Seongbuk-Gu, Seoul, 136-702, Korea
e-mail: emchoi@kookmin.ac.kr

N. Antonopoulos and L. Gillam (eds.), *Cloud Computing: Principles,*
Systems and Applications, Computer Communications and Networks,
DOI 10.1007/978-1-84996-241-4_2, © Springer-Verlag London Limited 2010

(Amazon S3), EC2 as hardware, and Hadoop [19] with MapReduce as software framework [29]. The output data was 1.5 terabytes of PDF format, processed within 24 h at a computation cost of just $240. Google has used MapReduce to process 20 petabytes[1] of data a day [1]. Similarly, Google used MapReduce running on 1,000 servers to sort 1 terabyte of data in just 68 s [40]. Hive/Hadoop [51] cluster at Facebook stores more than 2 Petabytes of uncompressed data and routinely loads 15 Terabytes of data daily [50]. Such scenarios prove that cloud computing is becoming cheaper, faster, and easy for massive distributed processing and scalable storage.

Cloud computing is not a completely new concept for the development and operation of web applications. It allows for the most cost-effective development of scalable web portals on highly available and fail-safe infrastructures. In the cloud computing system, we have to address different fundamentals like virtualization, scalability, interoperability, quality of service, failover mechanism, and the cloud delivery models (private, public, hybrid) within the context of the taxonomy. The taxonomy of cloud includes the different participants involved in the cloud along with the attributes and technologies that are coupled to address their needs and the different types of services like "XaaS" offerings where X is software, hardware, platform, infrastructure, data, and business.

The taxonomy is more than defining the fundamentals that provides a framework for understanding the current cloud computing offerings and suggests what is to come. It is provoking those who would seek a single, canonical definition of the term cloud computing. The main idea behind this taxonomy is to find out the technical strength, weakness, and challenges in the current cloud systems and we suggest what should be done in future to strengthen the systems. The emergence of cloud fabrics will enable new insights into challenging engineering, medical, and social problems. The cloud taxonomy should not be a gigantic construct that muddies the water of service development. It should be consistent with a set of principles that provides architectural and design guidance on the usage and crafting of services. It should provide understandable and consistent guidelines that provide clarity and reusability. For that reason, this taxonomy is intentionally small and fuzzy, i.e. the boundaries of the service layers are not rigid with regard to an emerging service.

Taxonomic information is essential for cloud service providers, enterprise firms, and border authorities to detect, manage, and control invasive alien components. Taxonomy identifies and enumerates the components of cloud computing that are providing basic knowledge underpinning management and implementation of the cloud spectrum. Taxonomy is more than defining the fundamentals that provides a framework for understanding the current cloud computing offerings and suggests what is to come. The criteria for defining the taxonomy is based on the core ideas of distributed systems for massive data processing. The criteria focus on cloud architecture, virtualization management, services, fault tolerance, and we analyze mechanisms like load balancing, interoperability, and scalable data storage.

---

[1]Disk Storage: 1,000 Megabytes = 1 Gigabytes, 1,000 Gigabytes = 1 Terabytes, 1,000 Terabytes = 1 Petabytes

This chapter tries to define taxonomy and survey of "Cloud Computing" based on recent advances from academia and industry as well as our experience. This chapter also describes the comparative study of different cloud service providers and their systems. The chapter is organized as follows. Section 2 introduces the background and related work. Section 3 defines the taxonomy of cloud computing. Section 4 describes the classification and comparative study of cloud computing ecosystems. Findings are discussed in Section 5. Some of the issues and opportunities are explained in Section 6. Finally, Section 7 concludes the chapter.

2.2 Background and Related Work

XaaS implies everything as a service [17] like SaaS (Software as a Service), PaaS (Platform as a Service), HaaS (Hardware as a Service), DaaS ([Data center, Database, Desktop] as a Service), IaaS (Infrastructure as a Service), BaaS (Business as a Service), FaaS (Framework as a Service), OaaS (Organization as a Service), etc. There are many cloud computing systems like Amazon EC2, Google App Engine (GAE), Microsoft Azure, IBM Blue Cloud, Nimbus, 3 Tera, etc. There is, however, no standard taxonomy, as everyone tries to define cloud computing and its services in their own way. There has been prior work reflecting the taxonomy of cloud computing. The taxonomy described by the Cloud Computing Use Case Discussion Group [23] is categorized into three views: service developer, service provider, and service consumers. This taxonomy does not cover the data holding governance structure. Crandell [21] defines a taxonomy based on product offerings. He divided the product offerings into three layers, namely Application in the cloud (Salesforce and other SaaS vendors), Platform in the cloud (GAE, Moso, Heroku), and Infrastructure in the cloud (Amazon Web Services, Flexiscale). This taxonomy is attractive for any company with an application that runs in a data center or with a hosted provider, that does not want to reinvent the wheel or pay a premium. Laird's [22] Cloud Vendor Taxonomy gives the classifications and vendors with that related group. This taxonomy divides the cloud vendors into Infrastructure (Public Cloud, Private Cloud), platform (Biz User Platforms, Dev Platform), services (Billing, Security, Fabric Mgmt, System Integrators), and applications. This taxonomy gives a visual map of the SaaS, PaaS, and cloud computing industries. Forrester's Cloud Taxonomy [24] is categorizing cloud services by IT-Infrastructure vs. Business value and by the level of privacy. This taxonomy focuses on the dimensions of privacy and business value. It focuses on the modes of cloud computing (Public Scale-Out Clouds, Public Server Cloud, Virtual Private Scale-Out Clouds, Virtual Private Server Clouds, Private Clouds, Virtual Private SaaS, Public SaaS, PaaS, On-Premises, ASP Concepts, etc.) To provide an even clearer and more explicit view over cloud computing applications, we propose several incremental enhancements of those taxonomies. In this paper, we will adjust, refine, and extend those taxonomies, making them even more suitable and flexible for cloud computing.

2.3   Taxonomy of Cloud Computing

Several taxonomies [21,22,24] of the cloud computing blueprint can be found, but most were created from the perspective of vendors that are part of the landscape and not from the perspective of enterprise IT, the consumers of cloud services, and software. This taxonomy is split into seven major sections as shown in Fig. 2.1.

This includes architecture, virtualization management, core services, security, data governance, and management services. The subtaxonomy core services include replication, discovery, and load balancing. A scalable, robust, and intelligent replication mechanism is crucial to the smooth operation of cloud computing. Another subtaxonomy security includes encryption/decryption, privacy, federated identification, authorization, and authentication. Ultimately, the cloud computing taxonomy describes certain patterns in *how to understand the cloud components and how to do things.* At the same time, it needs to provide some specific grounding to address the complex issues of integration of services within cloud computing that focus on providing computable semantic interoperability.

2.3.1   Cloud Architecture

Cloud architecture is the design of software applications that use Internet accessible and on-demand service. Cloud architectures are underlying an infrastructure that is

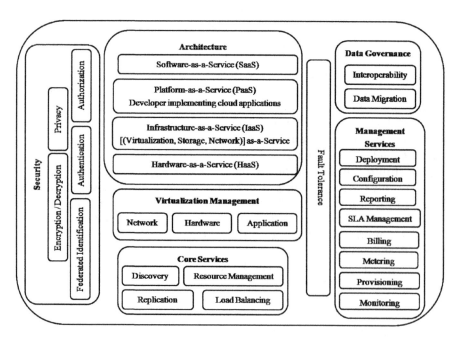

Fig. 2.1   A taxonomy of cloud computing

used only when it is needed to draw the necessary resources on-demand and perform a specific job, then relinquish unneeded resources, and dispose of them after the job is done. The services are accessible anywhere in the world, with the cloud appearing as a single point of access for all the computing needs of consumers. Cloud architectures address the key difficulties surrounding large-scale data processing.

2.3.1.1 Services and Modes of Cloud Computing

There are different categories of cloud services such as infrastructure, platform, and applications. These services are delivered and consumed in real time over the Internet. We discuss these services in the broader view.

Software-as-a-Service (SaaS)

Software as a Service is a multitenant platform. It uses common resources and a single instance of both the object code of an application as well as the underlying database to support multiple customers simultaneously. SaaS [3,4], commonly referred to as the Application Service Provider model, is heralded by many as the new wave in application software distribution. Examples of the key providers are SalesForce.com (SFDC), NetSuite, Oracle, IBM, and Microsoft, etc.

Platform-as-a-Service (PaaS)

Platform-as-a-Service provides developers with a platform, including all the systems and environments, comprising the end-to-end lifecycle of developing, testing, deploying, and hosting of sophisticated web applications as a service delivered by a cloud base. It provides an easier way to develop business applications and various services over the internet (e.g. a real state service provider). Creating and maintaining an infrastructure is the most time-consuming work in the on-premises systems. PaaS was invented to solve exactly this problem. Key examples are Google AppEngine, Microsoft's Azure, Heroku.com, etc. Compared with conventional applications development, this strategy can slash development time, offer hundreds of readily available tools and services, and quickly scale.

Hardware-as-a-Service (HaaS)

In HaaS model, the vendor allows customers to license the hardware directly. According to Nicholas Carr [18], "the idea of buying IT hardware or even an entire data center as a pay-as-you-go subscription service that scales up or down to meet your needs. But as a result of rapid advances in hardware virtualization, IT automation, and usage metering and pricing, I think the concept of hardware-as-a-service – let's call it HaaS, may at last be ready for prime time." This model is advantageous to the enterprise users, since they do not need to invest in building and managing data centers.

Infrastructure-as-a-Service (IaaS)

Infrastructure-as-a-Service is the delivery of computer infrastructure as a service. Aside from higher flexibility, a key benefit of IaaS is the usage-based payment scheme. This allows customers to pay as they grow. Another important advantage is that of always using the latest technology. Customers can achieve a much faster service delivery and time to market. Key examples are GoGrid, Flexiscale, Layered Technologies, AppNexeus, Joyent, and Mosso/Rackspace, etc. Basically, cloud mode can be defined by three types (1) Private Cloud: Data and processes are managed within the organization without the restrictions of network bandwidth, security exposures, and legal requirements that using public cloud services across open, public networks might entail. Some examples are Amazon VPC, Eucalyptus, Enomaly, VMWare, Redplaid, Platform computing, and Intalio. (2) Public Cloud: Describes cloud computing in the traditional mainstream sense, whereby resources are dynamically provisioned on a fine-grained, self-service basis over the Internet, via web applications/web services, from an off-site third-party provider who shares resources. Some examples are Zimory, Azure, SunCloud, Amazon EC2, SymetriQ, GigaSpaces, Rackspace, and Flexiscale. (3) Hybrid Cloud: The environment is consisting of multiple internal and/or external providers. Some example are RightScale, Asigra Hybrid Cloud Backup, Carpathia, Skytap, and Elastra.

2.3.2   Virtualization Management

Virtualization Management is the technology that abstracts the coupling between the hardware and operating system. It refers to the abstraction of logical resources away from their underlying physical resources in order to improve agility, flexibility, reduce costs, and thus enhance business value. Basically, virtualizations in cloud are of different types such as server virtualization, storage virtualization, and network virtualization. A common interpretation of server virtualization is the mapping of single physical resources to multiple logical representations or partitions. In a virtualized environment, computing environments can be dynamically created, expanded, shrunk, or moved as the demand varies. Virtualization [2] is therefore extremely well suited to a dynamic cloud infrastructure, because it provides important advantages in sharing, manageability, and isolation. Different solutions are available to manage virtual machines such as XEN, VMWare, KVM, VirtualBox, Microsoft Virtual Machine Manager and many more. Virtualization management deals with the different types of virtualizations in the context of cloud computing such as Desktop Virtualization (Virtual PC), Network Virtualization, Storage Virtualization,

Server Virtualization (Virtual Server), Application Virtualization (SoftGrid Application Virtualization), and Presentation Virtualization (Terminal Server). Storage capacity and performance are scalable because there is no central bottleneck. When expected demand exceeds higher server utilization, the storage can be scaled (horizontal scalability or vertically scalability) to meet them. One study from Gartner [25] shows that fewer than five million PCs were "virtualized" in 2006; by 2011, that figure will rise to between 480 million and 846 million. In another study, Gartner also estimated [26] that revenue from hosted virtual desktop will more than triple from $74.1 million to $298.6 million in 2009, while revenue from server virtualization management software will increase 42% from $913.9 million in 2008 to $1.3 billion in 2009. Revenue from server virtualization infrastructure will grow 22.5% from $917 million in 2008 to $1.1 billion in 2009. These data give a direction that is the major infrastructure for cloud computing. Therefore, it is the essential component for the cloud taxonomy. It has several benefits such as test and development optimization, resource maximization, business cost reduction, and much more.

2.3.3   Core Services

This section focuses on the core services of cloud computing. In core services, we will discuss discovery, replication, load balancing, and resource management in details.

2.3.3.1   Discovery and Replication

Service discovery promotes reusability by allowing service consumers to find the existing services. RESTful services [48] support discovery and reuse at design time. Replication can be used to create and maintain copies of an enterprise's data at these sites. When events affecting an enterprise's primary location occur, key application services can effectively be restarted and run at the remote location incurring no capital expenditure, only operational expenditure, until such time as the primary site is brought back online. Replication (Eager and Lazy) [54] keeps all replicas as a part of one atomic transaction. Replication technology is available in storage arrays, network-based appliances, and through host-based software.

2.3.3.2   Load Balancing

Load balancing prevents system bottlenecks due to unbalanced loads. It also considers implementing failover for the continuation of a service after failure of one or more of its components. This means that a load balancer provides a mechanism by which instances of applications can be provisioned and deprovisioned automatically without changing network configuration. This is an inherited feature from grid-based computing for cloud-based platforms. Energy conservation and resource consumption are not always a focal point when discussing cloud computing; however, with proper load balancing in place, resource consumption can be kept to a minimum. This not only serves to keep costs low and enterprises "greener," it also puts less stress on the hardware infrastructure of each individual component, making them potentially last longer. Load balancing also enables other important features such as scalability.

2.3.3.3 Resource Management

Cloud computing provides a way of deploying and accessing massively scalable shared resources on demand, in real time, and at affordable cost. Cloud resource management protocols deal with all kinds of homogeneous and heterogeneous resource environment. Management of virtualized resources, Workload and resource scheduling, Cloud resource provisioning with QoS, Scalable resource management solutions are the concerning points. Dynamic resource scheduling across a virtualized infrastructure for those environments is another issue for cloud.

2.3.4 Data Governance

When data begins to move out of organizations, it is vulnerable to disclosure or loss. The act of moving sensitive data outside the organizational boundary may also violate national regulations for privacy. In Germany, passing data across national boundaries can be a federal offence. Governance in the cloud "who and how" is the big challenge for enterprise clouds. Governance places a layer of processes and technology around services (location of services, service dependencies, service monitoring, service security, and so on) so that anything occurring will be quickly known [45]. There are some questions that need to be solved before mission critical data and functionality can be moved outside a controllable environment.

2.3.4.1 Interoperability

Interoperability means easy migration and integration of applications and data between different vendors' clouds. Owing to different hypervisors (KVM, Hyper-V, ESX, ESXi), VM technologies, storage, configuring operating systems, various security standards and management interfaces, many cloud systems are not interoperable. However, many enterprises want interoperability between their in-house infrastructure and the cloud. The issue of interoperability needs to be addressed to allow applications to be ported between clouds, or to use multiple cloud infrastructures, before critical business applications are delivered from the cloud. Most clouds are completely opaque to their users. Most of the time, users are fine with this until there is an access issue. In such situations, frustration increases exponentially with time, partly because of the opacity. Is a mechanism like a network weather map required? In other words, some form of monitoring solution like autonomous agents.

2.3.4.2   Data Migration

Data migration between data centers or cloud systems are important concerns of taxonomy. While migrating data, some considerations should be taken into account like no data loss, availability, scalability, cost–efficiency, and load balancing. User should be able to move their data and applications any time from one to another seamlessly, without any one vendor controlling it. Seamless transfer, as in mobile communication, is required for cloud computing to work. Many enterprises do not move their mission critical data and applications to the cloud because of vendor lock-in, security, governance, and many more complications.

2.3.5   Management Services

The management services contain deployment, monitoring, reporting, service-level agreement, and metering billing. We discuss these in detail.

2.3.5.1   Deployment and Configuration

To reduce the complexity and administrative burden across the cloud deployment, we need the automation process life cycle. RightScale Cloud Management Platform addresses three stages of the cloud application deployment lifecycle, namely design, manage, and deploy. Automated configuration and maintenance of individual or networked computers, from the policy specification, is very important in the computing arena; it improves robustness and functionality without sacrificing the basic freedoms and self-repairing concepts. That is why, to handle complex systems like cloud environment and data center, we need such configuration management. Tools such as cfengine [35], Chef from Opscode-chef [42], rPath [41], and Puppet are available as configuration management frameworks. These tools help software developers and engineers to manage server and application configuration by writing code, rather than running commands by hand.

2.3.5.2   Monitoring and Reporting

Developing, testing, debugging, and studying the performance of cloud systems is quite complex. Management cost increases significantly as the number of sites increases.

To address such problems, we need monitoring and reporting mechanisms. Monitoring basically monitors the SLA lifecycle. It also determines when an SLA completes and reports to the billing services. There are some services that monitor the cloud systems and produce health reports such as Hyperic HQ [32], which monitors SimpleDB, SimpleQueue Service, and Flexible Payment Service, all offered by Amazon. It collects the matrix and provides a rich analysis and reporting.

2.3.5.3   Service-Level Agreements (SLAs) Management

Users always want stable and reliable system service. Cloud architecture is considered to be highly available, up and running 24 h × 7 days. Many cloud service providers have made huge investments to make their system reliable. However, most cloud vendors today do not provide high availability assurances. If a service goes down, for whatever reason, what can a user do? How can users access their documents stored in the cloud? In such a case, the provider should pay a fine to the consumer as compensation to meet SLAs. An SLA specifies the measurement, evaluation, and reporting of the agreed services level standards such as [39]:

1. How raw quality measures will be used to evaluate agreed service component.
2. How the raw quality measures will be qualified as a service quality measure.
3. How the qualified quality measures will be used to estimate the service quality levels.
4. How the results of service evaluation will be reported.
5. How disputes on service-level evaluation will be resolved.

Currently, Amazon offers a "99.9% Monthly Uptime Percentage" SLA for Simple Storage Service (Amazon S3) and credit is limited to 10% [38]. Amazon credits 25% of charges if the availability drops below 99.0%, whereas 3Tera Virtual Private Data Center (VPDC) service will include a 99.999% availability SLA that is supposed to help assure customers about putting mission-critical apps and services in the cloud.

2.3.5.4   Metering and Billing

Transparent metering and billing will increase the trust level of users towards cloud services. Pay-as-you-go subscription or pay-as-you-consume model of billing and metering are popular for cloud. This service gets the status of the SLA, and invokes the credit service, which debits the user credit card or account and informs the user. There are many pricing strategies such as RAM hours, CPU Capacity, Bandwidth (Inbound/Outbound Data Transfer), Storage Space (gigabytes of data), Software License Fee), and Subscription-Based Pricing. There are some interesting new billing models such as GoGrid prepaid cloud hosting plan [33] and IDC cloud billing research [34], which are great examples of moving cloud pricing models towards telecom models.

2.3.5.5   Provisioning

Self-service application provisioning enables application developers to set up application infrastructure, such as Java application servers, databases, and messaging servers, without any help or assistance from infrastructure teams. Self-service application provisioning hides the complexity of the enterprise cloud from application developers and empowers them to set up and configure complex application infrastructure with the click of a button. By building a self-service portal for on-demand provisioning, we can reduce process overheads. Provisioning can help to manage the resource management, workload management, and autorecovery and task and process automation.

2.3.6   Security

Security is one of the main hurdles for enterprises to move their in-house data to public cloud. Most public cloud providers do not guarantee the security of the data while being transported to the public cloud. Many discussions around cloud computing are centered around this topic. In June-August 2009, several social networking sites such as Twitter, Facebook, Livejournal, and Google blogging pages were hit by DDoS attacks [43], [44]. DDoS are more robust and potentially simpler to implement in noisy environments such as EC2. Corporate information is not only a competitive asset, but it often contains information of customers, consumers, and employees that, in the wrong hands, could create a civil liability and possibly criminal charges. The key challenges of cloud security are performance, risk management, governance, design, and deployability. Building trust between various cloud stakeholders (users, corporations, network, and service providers) is a major consideration [49]. Establishing best practices of security in cloud computing for an end-user could be a good idea; for example, customers should talk with software vendors about licensing, or should know the network scheme.

2.3.6.1   Encryption/Decryption

Customers who worry about the privacy of their information should encrypt their data before moving it to the cloud. The provider should provide the utilities to simplify the process of encrypting the files and storing them in the cloud; similarly, for retrieval decryption will need. Cloud provider can use an Advanced Encryption Standard (AES) that may be AES-128, AES-192, or AES-256.

2.3.6.2   Privacy and Federated Identity

In cloud computing, a data center holds information that would more traditionally have been stored on the end-user's computer. This raises concerns regarding user privacy protection, since the users do not "own" their data. Also, the move to centralized services may affect the privacy and security of users' interactions. Federation is the act of combining data or identities across multiple systems. Federation can be done by a cloud provider or by a cloud broker. Each user can subscribe to a portal and be given an access card, which will be used to identify the subscriber at this particular portal or other portals in collaboration.

2.3.6.3 Authorization and Authentication

In public clouds, safeguards must be placed on machines to ensure proper authentication and authorization. Within the private cloud environment, one can track, pinpoint, control, and manage users who try to access machines with improper credentials. Single sign-on is the basic requirement for a customer who accesses multiple cloud services.

2.3.7 Fault Tolerance

In case of failure, there will be a hot backup instance of the application, which is ready to take over without disruption. Cloud computing outages extend into the more refined version of cloud service platforms. Some outages have been quite lengthy. For example, Microsoft Azure had an outage that lasted 22 h on March 13–14, 2008. Cloud reliance can cause significant problems if downtime and outages are removed from your control. Table 2.1 shows failover records from some cloud service provider systems. These are the significant downtime incidents. Reliance on the cloud can cause real problems when time is money.

Google has also had numerous difficulties with its Gmail and application services. These difficulties have generated significant interest in both traditional media and the blogosphere owing to deep-seated concerns regarding service reliability. The incidents mentioned here are just the tip of the iceberg. Every year, thousands of websites struggle with unexpected downtime, and hundreds of networks break

Table 2.1 Outages in different cloud services

Services and outage	Duration	Date
Microsoft Azure: malfunction in Windows Azure [5]	22 h	Mar 13–14, 2008
Gmail and Google Apps engine [6]	2.5 h	Feb 24, 2009
Google search outage: programming error [7]	40 m	Jan 31, 2009
Gmail: site unavailable due to outage in contacts system [8]	1.5 h	Aug 11, 2008
Google AppEngine partial outage: programming error [9]	5 h	Jun 17, 2008
S3 outage: authentication service overload leading to unavailability [10]	2 h	Feb 15, 2008
S3 outage: single bit error leading to gossip protocol blowup [11]	6–8 h	Jul 20, 2008
FlexiScale: core network failure [12]	18 h	Oct 31, 2008

or have other issues. So, the major problem for cloud computing is how to minimize outage/failover to provide reliable services. It is important to adopt the well-known Recovery-Oriented Computing (ROC) paradigm [46] in large data centers. Google uses Google File System (GFS) [47] or distributed disk storage; every piece of data is replicated three times. If one machine dies, a master redistributes the data to a new server.

2.4   Classification and Comparison between Cloud Computing Ecosystems

Even though there has been some comparative research on cloud computing from academia and enterprise perspectives, there remains an absence of a comprehensive technical study. We study cloud computing systems in terms of various classifications such as infrastructure technology, and solutions, PaaS provider, and open source. This section provides a technical comparison of several technologies and cloud providers. Tables 2.2–2.3 compare between different infrastructure technologies and solution providers such as Amazon Web Service (AWS), GoGrid, Flexiscale, and Moso. Tables 2.4–2.6 compares different SaaS and PaaS service providers such as Google AppEngine (GAE), GigaSpaces, Azure, RightScale, SunCloud, and Salesforce.com (SFDC). Similarly, Tables 2.7–2.8 compare open source cloud-based services like Eucalyptus, Open Nebula, Nimbus, and Enomaly.

2.5   Findings

Based on the proposed taxonomy, comprehensive technical studies, and survey, we notice some of the findings from different cloud computing systems that may help in future for new development and improvement on the existing systems.

2.5.1   Cloud Computing Infrastructure Technology and Solution Provider

In EC2 architecture, users are able to monitor and control their applications as an instance but not as a service. To achieve service manageability, the following capabilities are required: application-defined SLAs, such as workload capacity and concurrent computational tasks, dynamic provision of additional services to handle additional workload, and "Focal Server" approach. AWS is becoming popular as a de facto standard; many cloud systems are using a similar API. Eucalyptus is an open-source implementation of the AWS APIs. The biggest concern of current cloud computing system is auditing of the security controls and mechanism in terms of

Table 2.2 Cloud computing infrastructure technology and solution provider(12)

Features	AWS	GoGrid	Flexiscale	Rackspace cloud
Computing architecture	EC2 allows uploading XEN virtual machine images to the infrastructure and gives client APIs to instantiate and manages them	Dedicated computer resources on grid architecture	– Data center architecture – Automonically reconfiguring for infrastructure to cater to fluctuations in the demand	– Merge the idea of cloud computing with the traditional managed/shared server environment – Private Cloud's single-tenant architecture
Virtualization management	Xen hypervisor	Xen hypervisor	XEN-based hypervisor to provide hardware virtualization on Intel VT	VMware ESX Server
Service	IaaS, Xen images	IaaS	IaaS	IaaS
Load balancing	Balance incoming requests and traffic across multiple EC2 instances by using Round-Robin algorithm	F5 load balancing, Round-Robin algorithm	Uses migration of virtual servers between physical nodes. It supports both horizontal and vertical scaling	By request balancing algorithm -Simple software Load Balancer using a Cloud-Server-Scale CloudServer horizontally or vertically
Fault tolerance	System should automatically alert, failover, and re-sync back to the "last known state" as if nothing had failed	Instantly scalable and reliable file-level backup service	It provides full self-service for start/stop/delete, and changes memory/CPU/ storage/IPs of virtual dedicated servers	Share an IP between two servers. Heartbeat application runs on both Master and Slave

Table 2.3 Cloud computing infrastructure technology and solution provider (2\2)

Features	AWS	GoGrid	Flexiscale	Rackspace cloud
Interoperability	Support horizontal Interoperability, e.g. interoperability among EC2, Eucalyptus, etc.	Interoperable with other clouds such as GigaSpaces	Applications can be deployed once and managed transclouds to run on Amazon, GoGrid, and Mosso	– Open Cloud manifesto – Provides open specs for Cloud Servers APIs and Cloud Files APIs
Storage	– Amazon Simple Storage Service (S3) – Amazon SimpleDB	– Connecting each server to Private Network – Transfer protocols (RSYNC, FTP, SAMBA, SCP) to transfer data to and from Cloud Storage	Fully virtualized high-end SAN/ NAS back-end and uses a NetApp FAS3050 (hybrid SAN/NAS device, maximum storage capacity of 168TB spread over 336 drives)	– Storage is based on Rackspace Cloud Files – Uses limelight network
Security	AWS Secret Access Key, Type II (SAS70 Type II) certification – firewall, X.509 certificate, SSL-protected API	– Secure VLAN management – PrimeCloud service for hosted private cloud with no resources shared with other customers	Provides Virtual Private Servers, which gives privacy of a dedicated server	Encrypted communication channel, API Access Key, session authentication token
Programming framework	Amazon Elastic MapReduce framework. Supports Java, Ruby, PHP, etc.	Supports languages: Java, Python , Ruby, PHP	Flexiscale API support C, C #, C++, Java, PHP, Perl, and Ruby	Supports .NET, Java, Python, Ruby, PHP

Table 2.4 Cloud computing PaaS and SaaS provider(13)

Features	GAE	GigaSpaces	Azure	RightScale	SunCloud	Salesforce.com
Computing architecture	Google geo-distributed architecture	Space base architecture	An internet scale cloud services platform hosted in Microsoft data centers, which provides an OS and a set of developer services	– Multiserver clusters – Gives virtual private Servers monitoring system – Cloud management platform – Provides Elastic IPs	– Solaris OS, and Zetta-byte File System (ZFS) – Q-layer enabled for Data Warehouse and enterprise resource planning – Open dynamic infrastructure management strategy	Multitenant architecture with metadata-driven model
Virtualization management	Multitenancy	GigaSpace Service Virtualization Framework	Hypervisor (based on Hyper-V)	Xen hypervisor	– Hypervisor (Sun xVM Server) – OS (Solaris Containers) – Network (crossbow) – Storage (COMSTAR, ZFS) and applications (Glassfish and Java CAPS	Multitenancy architecture. It improves separation between shared and private data and logic.
Service	PaaS	PaaS	PaaS	PaaS	PaaS	SaaS Confined to API

Table 2.5 Cloud computing PaaS and SaaS provider(2\3)

Features	GAE	GigaSpaces	Azure	RightScale	SunCloud	Salesforce.com
Load balancing	Automatic scaling and load balancing	Performed through GigaSpaces high-performance communication protocol over EC2	Built-in hardware load balancing	High Availability Proxy load balancing in the cloud	Horizontal scalability, Vertical scalability	Load balancing among tenants
Fault tolerance	– Automatically pushed to a number of fault-tolerant servers – App Engine Cron Service	Uses OpenSpaces Service Virtualization Framework (SVF)'s failover capabilities	If a failure occurs, SQL data services will automatically begin using another replica of the container	Basic, intermediate, and advance Failover Architectures for using Elastic IPs	Resource based scheduling of service request	Self-management and self-tuning
Storage	Bigable distributed storage	In-memory data grid technique uses for front-end to the database. MySQL acts as in-sync persistence storage in the background	– SQL Server Data Services (SSDS) – Allows storing binary large objects (blobs) and can be geo-located	Open storage model, MySQL backups are Elastic Block Store (EBS) are saved to S3	Sun cloud storage WebDAV API, and Sun Cloud storage object API	Force.com database, which is tightly integrated with Apex programming language

Table 2.6 Cloud computing PaaS and SaaS provider(3l3)

Features	GAE	GigaSpaces	Azure	RightScale	SunCloud	Salesforce.com
Interoperability	Interoperability between platforms of different vendors and programming languages	Interoperability between different programming languages such as Java, .NET, and C++	Interoperable platform can be used to build new applications to run from the cloud or enhance the existing applications	Integrated management dashboard, application can be deployed once and managed across clouds	– Open source philosophy and java principles – Interoperability for large-scale computing resources across multiple clouds	Application level integration between different clouds
Security	– Google Secure Data Connector – SDC uses TLS-based server authentication – SDC uses RSA/128-bit or higher AES CBC/SHA	Support Amazon Security Groups, built-in SSH tunneling	– Security token service (STS) creates Security Assertion Markup – Language token according to rule	Private VLANs – Assign Multiple Security Groups	– User-provisioning and meta directory solution – Process and user rights management trusted extensions	– SysTrust SAS 70 Type II – Users and security, programmatic and platform security framework
Programming framework	MapReduce programming framework that support Python, Java as Java Servlet API, JDO, and JPA	Supports for Spring/Java, .NET, C++	Microsoft .NET, PHP	Ruby, PHP, Amazon's Simple Queue Service	Solaris OS, Java, C, C++, FORTRAN, RESTful, Java, Python, Ruby	Supports for .NET, C # Apache Axis (Java and C++)

Table 2.7 Open source based cloud computing services (12)

Features	Eucalyptus	OpenNebula	Nimbus	Enomaly elastic computing platform
Computing architecture	Ability to configure multiple clusters, each with private internal network addresses, into a single cloud	– Focused on the efficient, dynamic, and scalable management of VMs within data centers – Based on Haizea scheduling	– Client-side cloud computing interface to Globus-enabled TeraPort cluster – Context Broker combines several deployed virtual machines into "turnkey" virtual clusters	– A clustered virtual server hosting platform; ElasticDrive, a distributed remote storage system; and GeoStratus, a private content delivery network – Uses GlusterFS for scaling to several petabytes
Virtualization management	Xen hypervisor	Xen, KVM, and on-demand access to Amazon EC2	Xen Virtualization	KVM supports Xen OpenVZ and Sun's Virtual Box, Xen hypervisor
Service	IaaS, Xen images	IaaS	IaaS	IaaS
Load balancing	Simple load balancing cloud controller	Nginx Server configured as load balancer, used round-robin or weighted selection mechanism	Launches self-configuring virtual clusters, i.e. the context broker	– Uses user-mode load-balancing software with its own network stacks that runs over Linux and Solaris in the form of a virtual server – Supports different load-balancing methods, including round-robin, random, hash, and least resource
Programming framework	Hibernate, Axis2, and Java	Java, Ruby	Python, Java	Ruby on rails, PHP, Python

Table 2.8 Open source based cloud computing services (2\2)

Features	Eucalyptus	OpenNebula	Nimbus	Enomaly elastic computing platform
Fault tolerance	Separate cluster within the Eucalyptus cloud reduces the chance of correlated failure	– The daemon can be restarted and all the running VMs recovered – Persistent database backend to store host and VM information	Checking worker nodes periodically and recovery	Overflow, disaster, and failover services
Interoperability	Multiple cloud computing interfaces using the same "back-end" infrastructure	Interoperable between intracloud services such as access Amazon EC2 and elastic hosts cloud via plug-in	Standards: "rough consensus and working code"	Cloud portability and interoperability to cross cloud vendors
Storage	Walrus (the front end for the storage subsystem)	– Database, persistent storage for ONE data structures – SQLite3 backend is the core component of the OpenNebula internal data structures	Provides secure management of cloud disk space giving each user a repository view of VM images and works with globus GridFTP	Multiple remote cloud storage services (S3, Nirvanix, and CloudFS), uses MySQL for data sharing
Security	WS-security for authentication, Cloud controller generates the public/private key	Firewall, virtual private network tunnel	PKI credential required Works with Grid proxies VOMS, Shibboleth (via GridShib), custom PDPs	"Clustered" handling of security

user level. Amazon S3 lacks in access control that supports delegation and auditing, and makes implicit trust assumptions between S3 and clients [52]. Amazon's work [13] towards Statement on Auditing Standards No.70: Service Organizations, Type II (SAS70 type II) certification may be helpful for those concerned with widely varying levels of security competency. Generally, this is better than no certification whatsoever. Some of the important security aspects of cloud-centric computing are secure cloud resource virtualization, security for cloud programming models, binary analysis of software for remote attestation and cloud protection, cloud-centric regulatory compliance issues, and mechanisms and foundations of cloud-centric threat models that need to be considered for future cloud work.

2.5.2 Cloud Computing PaaS and SaaS Provider

Google App Engine (GAE) provides a useful basis for people and companies to make web applications from scratch without needing to worry about infrastructure. GAE provides for automatic scaling and load balancing. This alone will be worth while for a certain class of application developers. GAE has some clear advantages and lowers the barriers to entry for startups and independent developers. The potential problem is lock-in that creates risk and more cost for long term. The lock-in is caused by custom APIs such as BigTable, Python launcher, accounts and transparent scaling for both Python scripts and database. Google App Engine uses master/slave replication between data centers. They chose this approach to provide low latency writes, data center failure survival, and strong consistency guarantees.

GigaSpaces use an In-Memory Data-Grid (IMDG) technique to manage state data in a database, which bridges the bottleneck of scalability. It provides all the basic features of a high-end Data Grid as well as unique features, such as continuous query and seamless integration with external data sources, and makes it extremely easy to deploy, modify, and ensure high availability for applications running on Amazon EC2.

GigaSpaces's Space-Based Architecture (SBA) approaches are based on the Tuple Space model [53] that can meet the challenge of running low-latency transactional applications in a highly distributed environment such as Amazon EC2.

Security isolation is managed via virtualization in Azure. The Azure Fabric Controller is a service that monitors, maintains, and provisions machines to host the application that the developer creates and stores in the Microsoft cloud. Azure storage provides persistent, redundant storage in the cloud. It can store data in three different ways such as Blobs (large binary data), Queues (service communication abstraction), and Tables (service state and user data). Storage can be geo-located, which means you can choose in which region it can be hosted.

The agile nature of Sun Cloud provides multiple hardware architectures to customize systems for workload, multitenancy, and resource sharing among a large pool of users allowing centralized infrastructure with lower costs. Sun modular data center is flourishing and ten times faster to deploy than a conventional data center.

Sun's open storage provides a unique business model, which provides snapshot, replication, and compression without additional cost for data services. Hybrid cloud architecture is very important. One of the nice mechanisms of it is the open storage model that is provided by Sun Cloud, which is a new and unique business model as well.

SFDC introduces the Force.com metadata-driven, multitenant, internet application platform. In multitenant architecture, a single instance of the hosted application is capable of servicing all customers (tenants). Not all clouds are using virtualization. Clouds like GAE and SFDC use completely different technologies to create multitenancy. From the developer point of view, multitenancy is not the main event.

2.5.3   Open Source Based Cloud Computing Services

The role of open source cloud computing is to build mechanisms around digital identity management [14], and outline technological building blocks that are needed for controllable trust and identity verification. Nimbus supports the OASIS WSRF standard [32] that defines a framework and uses web services to model and access stateful resources. Enomaly cloud is focusing on the issue of interoperability, which is essential for enterprise cloud system. Most of the open source clouds are providing IaaS.

2.6   Comments on Issues and Opportunities

There are some issues related to mechanisms such as security, privacy, (erosion of) data integrity, load balancing, interoperability, and scalable storage. Cloud computing services often provide common business applications online that are accessed from a web browser, while the software and data are stored on the servers. One of the issues is an integration of data and application across clouds. This involves leveraging technology such as EAI (enterprise application integration), EII (enterprise information integration or federated database), and ESB (enterprise service bus). The market prognosis suggests raising the subscription fees as cloud vendors provide higher performance, scalability, availability, better support, and security. Transmitting huge volumes of multimedia data across clouds will continue to be a challenge, and needs further research. Discovery and composition of the services between multiple clouds is also a promising arena for enterprise cloud. Clouds have a different paradigm for resource utilization, so they need a different paradigm for managing these resources. Each previous revolution in computing also revolutionized how resources were managed. Collaborating amongst different technologies, businesses, and people in cloud computing will be an issue that will enable the enterprise to play a role as well. Quality assurance and information security are always challenging. Researchers should leverage identity and security management for business units. Furthermore, there are opportunities for the provision of a new range of privacy services. As the user requirement changes, functionality and privacy requirements may change, and so privacy requirements need to be reassessed at regular intervals [30]. Policy-based dynamic privacy design patterns may be a better technique for cloud computing. Cloud computing brings some novel attacks that have not figured in much of the security discussion to date. We need more research into this. Cloud computing systems for High-Performance Computing (HPC) are also a promising area for future provision. Cloud is not yet mature enough for HPC [31]. However, cloud computing helps save enterprise 30–60% of their technology expenditure, but owing to lack of agreement on common standards, many enterprises are losing opportunities. It is not so easy for cloud computing to achieve its aim of being a universally accessible application that is based on open standards. Amazon AWS Import/Export supports importing and exporting data into and out of Amazon S3 buckets in the USA, but still leaves complications in migration of data between clouds. A major challenge of moving applications to the cloud is the need to master multiple programming languages and operating environments [27]. Special attention is needed for government agencies to integrate their data from traditional to PaaS, a need to learn some new programming models residing in the cloud. Interoperability is another important issue for cloud. There is a need for data access interoperability, which is a unique programming interface to access diverse databases (such as JDBS, ODBC, Ado.NET). There are lots of standardization issues; in the race to standardization, many organizations and forums are working, but need to leverage the collaboration and discussions between them. Cloud Computing Interoperability Forum (CCIF) [16] was formed to define an organization that would enable interoperable enterprise class cloud computing platforms through application integration and stakeholder cooperation. Similarly, Microsoft's approach to interoperability principles [28] is a good starting point. Other organizations such as Open Cloud Consortium (OCC) [36], Open Grid Forum (OGF) [37], and Distributed Management Task Force (DMTF) [38] are also working on interoperability issues and open formats. Armbrust et al. [15] also identified many issues for future research. There are some complications with current programming frameworks and programming languages for cloud computing such as Google AppEngine with its SQL-like syntax called "GQL." Select statements in GQL can be performed on one table only. GQL does not support a join statement. The cloud developers will need more flexible query-oriented and API-oriented programming in future. Automated diagnosis is one of the problems in Hadoop. MapReduce is better for limited tasks like text searching or data mining, the things Google does on an epic scale. For tasks that require relational database capabilities at web scale, database sharing has become a favorite practice. The main problem of why several users do not use cloud computing yet is the lack of trust in the cloud itself (services, providers, etc.) and this lack is based on several issues (no acknowledgment of the policies applied for confidentiality of the user's information, privileges of the users in charge of the data, level of satisfaction in regard to compliance with the contract specifications, if the provider permits audits, technical support offered). The complexity will be there for developers to apply the disciplines of development across multiple platform technologies and computational models. The alignment of user needs with business strategy is also a challenging job for CIOs.

2.7 Conclusions

Cloud computing is a promising paradigm for delivering IT services as computing utilities. Clouds are designed to provide services to external users; providers need to be compensated for sharing their resources and capabilities. There are significant challenges and opportunities behind the ecosystem of cloud computing such as resource management, reliability, fault tolerance, security, SLA, utility model, and performance issues. There are many taxonomies, but they are vendor-concern oriented. The proposed taxonomy focused more on engineering approaches such as functional as well as structured aspects of cloud computing systems. We provided a consistent set of guidelines for clarity, and reusability, which is employed to classify a wide range of cloud computing systems. The value of the offered taxonomy lies in that it captures a given system's scope, scalability, generality, reusability, manageability, and flexibility. This chapter presented a different way of representing a taxonomy to classical approaches. This might be a new way to think about the components of taxonomy as layered services that can give a wide range of spectrum for flexibility and reusability. This taxonomy has been applied to the different cloud systems to find out the technical strengths and weaknesses. A survey of different cloud systems has been presented, and captures the different aspects of the taxonomy that provide an idea about functional and architectural view of the systems that they adopted. We concluded the chapter with a discussion of the considered systems, as well as directions for future research. It is hoped that this can provide stimulus to the researcher and ideas to the developer with respect to current cloud systems, hype, and challenges.

Acknowledgments This research was supported by the MKE (Ministry of Knowledge and Economy), Korea, under the ITRC (Information Technology Research Center) support program supervised by the NIPA (National IT Industry Promotion Agency) (NIPA-2009-C1090-0902-0026), and research program on Kookmin University.

References

1. Dean J, Ghemawat S (January 2008) MapReduce: simplified data processing on large clusters. Commun ACM 51(1):107–113
2. Sun Microsystems (2009). Virtualization for dummies
3. Software and Information Industry Association (2001, February). Software as a service: strategic backgrounder
4. Choudhary V (2009) Software as a service: implications for investment in software development. Proceedings of the 40th Hawaii international conference on system sciences
5. Kolakowski N (2009) Microsoft's cloud azure service suffers outage. Retrieved from, http://www.eweekeurope.co.uk/news/microsoft-s-cloud-azure-service-suffers-outage-396
6. Cruz A (2009) Gmail site reliability manager. Update in Gmail. Retrieved from, http://googleblog.blogspot.com/2009/02/update-on-gmail.html
7. Mayer M (2009) Search Products andUser Experience: This site may harm your computer on every search results. Retrieved from, http://googleblog.blogspot.com/2009/01/this-site-may-harm-your-computer-on.html

8. Jackson T (2008) Gmail product manager: we feel your pain, and we're sorry. Retrieved from, http://gmailblog.blogspot.com/2008/08/we-feel-your-pain-and-were-sorry.html
9. Pete, App Engine Team (2008) App engine outage today. Retrieved from, http://groups.google.com/group/google-appengine/
10. Allen Stern (2008) Update from Amazon Regarding Friday's S3 Downtime. Retrieved from, http://www.centernetworks.com/amazon-s3-downtime-update
11. AWS Service Health Dashboard (2008, July 20) Amazon S3 availability event. Retrieved from, http: //status.aws.amazon.com/s3-20080720.html
12. Tubanos A (2008) FlexiScale suffers 18-hour outage. Retrieved from, http://www.thewhir.com/
13. Amazon Web Services (AWS) (2008, Sept) Amazon web services: overview of security processes
14. Cavoukian A (2008, May 28) Privacy in the clouds: privacy and digital identity – implications for the Internet. Information and privacy commissioner of Ontario
15. Armbrust M et al (2009, February 10) Above the clouds: a berkeley view of cloud computing. EECS department, University of California, Berkeley, Technical Report No. UCB/EECS-2009-28
16. The Cloud Computing Interoperability Forum (CCIF) (2009) http://www.cloudforum.org/
17. Gathering Clouds of XaaS! (2008) Retrieved from, http://www.ibm.com/
18. http://www.roughtype.com (2008)
19. Apache Hadoop project (2009) Available from http://hadoop.apache.org/
20. Amazon Elastic Cloud Computing (EC2) (2009) Available from http://aws.amazon.com/ec2/
21. Crandell M (2008) Defogging cloud computing: a taxonomy. Available from http://gigaom.com/2008/06/16/defogging-cloud-computing-a-taxonomy/
22. Laird P (2009) Different strokes for different folks: a taxonomy of cloud offerings. Enterprise cloud submit, INTEROP
23. Cloud Computing Use Case Discussion Group (2009, August) Cloud computing use case. White Paper version 1.0. 5
24. Ried S (2009) Yet another cloud – how many clouds do we need? Retrieved from Forrester Research, http://www.forrester.com/
25. Gammage B, Shiffler III G (2007, August 8) Report highlight for dataquest insight: PC virtualization forecast scenarios. Gartner
26. Dayley A et al (2009, Jan 5) Dataquest insight: virtualization market size driven by cost reduction, resource utilization and management advantages. Gartner
27. Hayes, B (2008, July) Cloud computing. Commun ACM 51(7)
28. Microsoft's approach to interoperability (2009) Retrieved from, http://www.microsoft.com/interop/principles/default.mspx. Accessed 25 Sept 2009
29. Gottfrid D (2009) Self-service, prorated super computing fun! Retrieved from http://open.blogs.nytimes.com/
30. Pearson S (2009) Taking account of privacy when designing cloud computing services. Proceedings of the 2009 ICSE workshop on software engineering challenges of cloud computing, IEEE Comp Soc, pp 44–52
31. Napper J, Bientinesi P (2009) Can cloud computing reach the TOP500? Proceeding of the combined workshops on unconventional high performance computing workshop plus memory access workshop, ACM, pp 17–20
32. OASIS (Organization for the Advancement of Structured Information Standards) (2009) http://www.oasis-open.org/
33. GoGrid's prepaid cloud hosting plans (2009). http://www.gogrid.com/pricing/plans.php
34. Rainge E (2009, May) Worldwide telecom cloud billing 2009–2013 forecast. IDC Doc #217313
35. CFengine (2009) http://www.cfengine.org/
36. The Open Cloud Consortium (OCC) (2009) http://opencloudconsortium.org/
37. The Open Grid Forum (2009) http://www.ogf.org/
38. The Distributed management Task Force (DMTF) (2009) http://www.dmtf.org/about/

39. Buco MJ et al (2004, Jan) Utility computing SLA management based upon business objectives. IBM Syst J 43(1):159–178
40. The Official Google Blog (2008, Nov) Sorting 1 PB with MapReduce. Retrieved from http://googleblog.blogspot.com/
41. rPath (2009) http://www.rpath.com
42. Opscode (2009) http://www.opscode.com/
43. Sheehan M (2009) Message from GoGrid founders regarding denial of service attack. Retrieved from, GoGrid Official Blog, http://blog.gogrid.com/
44. Ristenpart T et al (2009) Hey, you, get off of my cloud: exploring information leakage in third-party compute clouds. Proceeding of ACM conference on computer and communications security
45. Linthicum DS, Morrison KS (2009) Value of SOA for cloud computing. Layer 7 technologies
46. Patterson D (2009) Recovery oriented computing. http://roc.cs.berkeley.edu
47. Ghemawat S, Gobioff H, Leung ST (2003) The google file system. Proceedings of the nine-teenth ACM symposium on operating systems principles, pp 29–43
48. Fielding RT (2000) Architectural styles and the design of network-based software architectures. Dissertation of doctor of philosophy, University of California, Irvine
49. RSA (2009, March) The role of security in trustworthy cloud computing. Continental Automated Building Association (CABA), Information Series, IS 2009-39
50. Thusoo A (2009, June 11) Hive-A petabyte scale data warehouse using hadoop. Retrieved from Facebook Engineering page, http://www.facebook.com
51. Hadoop/Hive (2009) http://wiki.apache.org/hadoop/Hive
52. Palankar M et al (2008) Amazon S3 for science grids: a viable solution? Proceedings of the 2008 international workshop on data-aware distributed computing workshop (DADC), pp 55–64
53. Carriero N, Gelernter D (1989) Linda in the context. Commun ACM 32(4):444–458
54. Gray J et al (1996) The dangers of replication and solution. Proceedings of the 1996 ACM SIGMOD international conference on management of data, pp 173–182

Chapter 3
Towards a Taxonomy for Cloud Computing from an e-Science Perspective

Daniel de Oliveira, Fernanda Araujo Baião, and Marta Mattoso

Abstract In the last few years, cloud computing has emerged as a computational paradigm that enables scientists to build more complex scientific applications to manage large data sets or high-performance applications, based on distributed resources. By following this paradigm, scientists may use distributed resources (infrastructure, storage, databases, and applications) without having to deal with implementation or configuration details. In fact, there are many cloud computing environments already available for use. Despite its fast growth and adoption, the definition of cloud computing is not a consensus. This makes it very difficult to comprehend the cloud computing field as a whole, correlate, classify, and compare the various existing proposals. Over the years, taxonomy techniques have been used to create models that allow for the classification of concepts within a domain. The main objective of this chapter is to apply taxonomy techniques in the cloud computing domain. This chapter discusses many aspects involved with cloud computing that are important from a scientific perspective. It contributes by proposing a taxonomy based on characteristics that are fundamental for scientific applications typically associated with the cloud paradigm.

3.1 Introduction

The evolution of computer science in the last decades enabled the advent of e-Science, which is entirely carried out in computational environments. The term "e-Science" is strictly related to those experiments based on computer simulations that are known as silico experiments [27].

The development of technologies such as grids [6] fostered the popularity of e-Science and consequently in silico experiments. In silico experiments are commonly found in many scientific domains, such as oil exploration [20]. An in silico

D. de Oliveira (✉)
COPPE, Federal University of Rio de Janeiro, 21945-970, Rio de Janeiro-RJ-Brazil
e-mail: danielcmo@gmail.com

N. Antonopoulos and L. Gillam (eds.), *Cloud Computing: Principles, Systems and Applications*, Computer Communications and Networks, DOI 10.1007/978-1-84996-241-4_3, © Springer-Verlag London Limited 2010

experiment is conducted by a scientist, who is responsible for managing the entire experiment, which comprises composing, executing, and analyzing it. Currently, most of the work of scientists during an in silico experiment is related to the execution of a sequence of programs. Each program produces a collection of data with certain semantics. These data are used as input to the next program to be executed in the chain sequence. The chaining of these programs may become unfeasible without systematic computational support. A scientific workflow may be defined as an abstraction that allows the structured composition of programs and data as a sequence of operations aiming at a desired result as defined by Mattoso et al. [16].

Simultaneously, in the last few years, cloud computing [28] emerged as a new computational paradigm where web-based services enabled different kinds of users to obtain a huge variety of capabilities, in infrastructure, software, and hardware, without having to deal with configuration and implementation details.

The programs and data (that are fundamental parts of scientific workflows) are moving from local environments to the cloud. Foster et al. [7] examined the differences between grid and cloud computing, offering a good foundation to categorize the existing cloud computing projects and/or services. They define cloud computing as "A large-scale distributed computing paradigm that is driven by economies of scale, in which a pool of abstracted, virtualized, dynamically-scalable, managed computing power, storage, platforms, and services are delivered on demand to external customers over the Internet."

The main advantage of cloud computing is that the average user is able to access a great variety of resources without having to acquire or configure the whole infrastructure. This is a fundamental need for scientific applications, since the scientists can be isolated from the complexity of the environment, focusing only on their in silico experiment.

The volume of published white papers and scientific papers evidences that cloud computing has both emerged and is already being adopted by some scientific projects [15]. Several technologies, platforms, applications, infrastructures, and standards have already been proposed. However, the concepts involved with cloud computing are not fully detailed or explained. Considering the growing interest in cloud computing and the difficulty in finding organized definitions of concepts associated to this paradigm, we present in this chapter a taxonomy for the cloud computing from an e-Science perspective.

Taxonomies [4] are a particular classification structure where concepts are arranged in a hierarchical way. The proposed cloud taxonomy provides an understanding of the domain and aims to help scientists when comparing different cloud computing environments. The cloud computing e-Science taxonomy presented in this chapter is useful for the scientific community to classify environments and to compare different cloud computing environments that are available for use. By consulting this taxonomy, they may consider the features that meet their needs, which may vary depending on the scientific experiment being conducted. The taxonomy considers a broad view of cloud computing, comprising all its major issues. Using the proposed taxonomy as a common vocabulary may facilitate scientists to find common characteristics of the existing environments and may help to choose the most adequate cloud environment.

3.2 Scientific Workflows and e-Science

This section presents the main definitions regarding e-Science and scientific workflow concepts. These concepts are presented along with some important aspects to be considered when modeling or executing scientific experiments using cloud computing. These aspects are used as a basis for elaborating the classes of the cloud computing taxonomy.

3.2.1 Scientific Workflows

According to the Workflow Management Coalition [31], a workflow may be defined as "the automation of a business process, in whole or part, during which documents, information or tasks are passed from one participant to another for action, according to a set of procedural rules." A workflow defines the order of task invocations or conditions under which tasks must be invoked and the task synchronization. This definition is related to business workflows; however, it can be exploited in the scientific domain [26], where tasks will be related to scientific applications instead of business ones. An example of scientific workflow is presented in Fig. 3.1. This workflow is part of a real deep water oil exploitation scientific experiment [20].

3.2.2 Scientific Workflow Management Systems

Scientific Workflow Management Systems (SWfMSs) are responsible for coordinating the invocation of programs, either locally or in remote environments. Many different SWfMSs can be found in the literature [1, 5]. Although current SWfMSs have many important characteristics and evolutions, according to Weske et al. [30], these SWfMSs need to offer adequate support for the scientist throughout the experimentation process, including: (i) designing the workflow through a guided interface; (ii) controlling several variations of workflows; (iii) executing the workflow in an efficient way; (iv) handling failures and; (v) accessing, storing, and managing data.

Most of this support can be achieved using the cloud computing paradigm. More specifically, efficient execution of scientific experiments, as well as management of

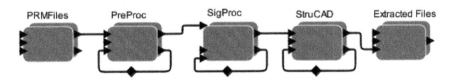

PRMFiles   PreProc   SigProc   StruCAD   Extracted Files

Fig. 3.1 Deep water oil exploitation scientific workflow [20]

the large amount of scientific data produced by the experiment, is provided by the computational infrastructure of cloud computing environments. The next section presents some important aspects for scientific experiments to be considered when choosing a cloud computing environment.

3.2.3 Important Aspects of In Silico Experiments

In silico experiments (that are usually modeled as scientific workflows) have some important aspects to be considered when being modeled or executed. Many of these aspects should be taken into account when choosing a supporting cloud computing environment. Cloud computing environments present some important characteristics that are related to those aspects and may influence when scientists choose a cloud environment to use. This section presents these aspects (business model, privacy, pricing, technological infrastructure, architecture, access, and standards) as they guide us to choose the classes of the proposed taxonomy.

One of the most important aspects for scientific experiments is reproducibility. To reproduce and validate an experiment, scientists must have all available information related to the experiment, including which parameter values were used in each instance of execution, the results (both final and intermediary) produced during its execution. This type of information is called provenance [8]. This data is stored in databases or via specialized services to store provenance, thus handling failures and retaining data integrity. Therefore, to achieve experiment reproducibility, the supporting cloud computing environment should provide two fundamental features, data storage and environment configuration. Data storage is required to store provenance data. Preferably, there should be a service that provides storage or database mechanisms to enable the scientist to access provenance data and track how the results of an experiment execution were obtained. Environment configuration is required since the whole environment used to execute the experiment should be able to be reconfigured. Those characteristics are related to the business model followed by a cloud computing environment.

Privacy is also a major issue for the scientific community. Usually, provenance data and programs related to a scientific experiment are considered intellectual property and because of that, they are not public until the research is published in a scientific paper. This way, the privacy aspect of cloud environments must be analyzed when dealing with scientific experiments.

Another important aspect to be considered is related to pricing. Scientists frequently use open-source and community environments. This type of programs and environments is freely available for general use, thus contributing to the reproducibility of experiment executions. The open-software culture of the scientific community must be considered, since most cloud environments are commercial, which means that the service is paid for. Thus, scientists should take into account the pricing of environments.

The architecture characteristics of the environment chosen to execute the experiment should also be taken into account. Scientific experiments need to be monitored and controlled by scientists. This way, the chosen cloud environment should provide characteristics such as monitoring, as well as individual control of an experiment execution independent from others' executions. Also, in many scenarios the execution of a whole experiment requires running programs in different technological platforms (operational systems, database servers), requiring that the cloud computing environment deals with heterogeneity.

Another important aspect is related to performance. These experiments usually need high-performance computational environments to run. Even using these environments, experiments may need days, weeks, or even months to finish. It is important to know (and classify) the technology infrastructure involved with the experiment to discover if this technology is able to offer the necessary computational resources to execute the entire experiment.

Another important topic is related to how scientists access the cloud environment to run experiments. The in silico scientific experiment must be able to access cloud environments in different ways. For example, in a specific experiment, results must be provided in a web page through a web browser; in another experiment, there must be an API to control the execution of the experiment, and so on.

In silico scientific experiments should be based on standards, ideally already used on the experiment domain or recommended by entities such as W3C [29]. These standards are important when modeling an in silico scientific experiment. Scientific experiments are usually based on open standards. The next section presents the proposed taxonomy for cloud computing that takes into account the aspects listed in this section.

3.3 A Taxonomy for Cloud Computing

A taxonomy [4] is a particular classification arranged in a hierarchical structure. It is typically organized by a parent–child relationship. Originally the term "taxonomy" referred only to the classification of living organisms. However, it has become popular in certain domains of science to apply the term in a wider, more general sense, where it may refer to a classification of things or concepts.

The cloud computing taxonomy presented in this chapter provides the classification of the components of the cloud computing domain into categories based on different aspects of this field and the requirements of a scientific experiment. This section describes a cloud computing taxonomy (presented in Fig. 3.2), which is decomposed into eight subtaxonomies.

The proposed taxonomy classifies the characteristics of cloud computing in terms of architectural characteristics, business model, technology infrastructure, privacy, standards, pricing, orientation, and access. Many of the classes of the taxonomy are interrelated. In Fig. 3.2, these relations are represented in orange arrows. Each one of these relations is explained throughout the chapter.

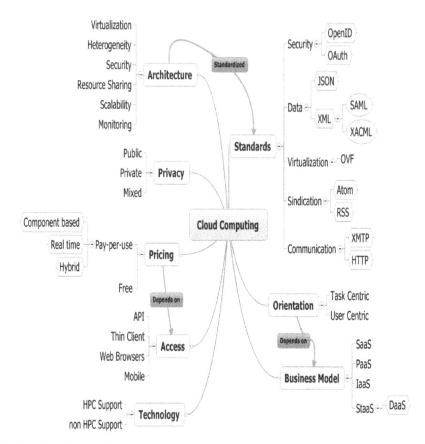

Fig. 3.2 Cloud computing taxonomy

3.3.1 Business Model

According to the business model adopted, clouds are usually classified into three major categories [18] (Fig. 3.3): Software as a Service (SaaS), Platform as a Service (PaaS), and Infrastructure as a Service (IaaS), creating a model named SPI [34].

In SaaS, the software is deployed by a service provider (just like an application to end-users) for commercial or free use as a service on demand. In IaaS, the provider delivers a computational infrastructure (such as a supercomputer) to the end-user on the web. In IaaS, the end-user is usually responsible for configuring the environment to use. PaaS is the delivery of a programming environment as a Service. The process of delivering platforms as services facilitates the deployment of applications into the cloud.

However, these three categories are too generic. More classification levels are indeed needed. For example, in the e-Science field, the generated data is one of the

Fig. 3.3 Business model
subtaxonomy

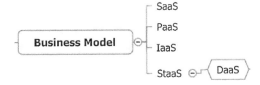

most valuable resources. This classification does not take into account services that
are based on storage or databases.

Thus, the business model subtaxonomy should include the following areas:
Storage as a Service (StaaS) and Database as a Service (DaaS), which are fundamental for e-Science and scientific workflows. We may define Storage as a
Service as a service that provides structured ways to access and maintain a storage facility that is remotely located. However, this kind of business model provides only the space and structure to store data. In scientific experiments, the
scientists usually need a database to store provenance data, because a database
provides features such as indexing and concurrency control, that a simple storage
does not provide.

This way, Database as a Service (DaaS) provides operations and functions of a
remotely hosted database, sharing it with other users, and having it logically function as if the database were local. This way, we may see the Database-as-a-Service
as one specialization of Storage-as-a-Service.

The business model directly influences the orientation of the cloud environment. For example, an IaaS business model allows a user-centric environment,
since the user is in control. On the other hand, an SaaS business model does not.
This class of the taxonomy is essential to guarantee the reproducibility of scientific experiments. The business model directly defines if the cloud environment
offers data, infrastructure, or application as a service, essential to guarantee reproducibility. For example, there should be a way to store provenance data to be
further analyzed, thus the cloud computing environment should follow DaaS to
allow data storage.

3.3.2 Privacy

According to the privacy aspect, we may classify cloud environments as private,
public, and mixed (Fig. 3.4). Public clouds may be considered as the most traditional of all types. In this kind of cloud, the various resources are dynamically
provided over the Internet, via web applications or web services, to any user.
Private clouds are environments that emulate cloud computing on private networks,
inside a corporation or a scientific institution.

A mixed cloud environment is one that is composed by multiple public and/or
private clouds. The concept of mixed cloud is still dubious. Some authors call a
mixed cloud also as hybrid [25]. Although this term is not wrong, it is also used to

Fig. 3.4 Privacy subtaxonomy

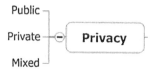

Fig. 3.5 Pricing subtaxonomy

define clouds that are implemented by different technologies [35], which may cause confusion.

This class of the taxonomy is important for e-Science because of the importance of privacy levels in scientific experiments. Programs and data are usually not public and scientists may prefer not to install programs or store data in public environments.

3.3.3 Pricing

Since it is important for the scientific experiments to deal with costs, we must classify cloud environment according to a pricing criterion. This subtaxonomy (Fig. 3.5) is composed of three main types of pricing. Free pricing is the pricing model applied when you are using your own cloud environment, where the resources are freely available for authorized users. The pay-per-use model is the one where the user pays a specific value related to his resource utilization. Also, it can be specialized to a component-based pricing, where each component (storage, CPU, and so on) has a different price and the real-time bill broken down by exact usage of components. These pay-per-use models are usually applied in both commercial clouds and scientific clouds. Science users pay for cloud usage in the same way as commercial users do. To our knowledge, there are no scientific institutions that share their resources at no cost.

Pricing is influenced by access characteristics. Since a cloud environment offers more access methods, each one of them is a component that can be priced by the provider.

3.3.4 Architecture

This subtaxonomy (Fig. 3.6) classifies the main architectural characteristics of a cloud computing environment. One fundamental architectural aspect of a cloud is heterogeneity. A cloud must support the aggregation of heterogeneous hardware and software resources, as it happens with scientific experiments. The concept of virtualization [2] is also a key aspect for clouds.

Through virtualization, many users may benefit from the same infrastructure using independent instances. Virtualization enables the first security [10] level in the clouds, since it allows the isolation of environments. In clouds, each user has unique access to its individual virtualized environment. Resource sharing is provided by clouds, since each resource is represented as a single artifact, giving the impression of a single dedicated resource. Scalability is mainly defined by increasing the number of working nodes. By definition, clouds offer the automatic resizing of virtualized hardware resources. Monitoring refers to the ability of watching the current status of virtual machines or services provided.

Each one of those architectural characteristics is standardized by specific standards (which are in another class of the taxonomy). Besides that, some architectural characteristics are important to scientific experiments, such as scalability and monitoring to control the execution.

3.3.5 Technology Infrastructure

The technological infrastructure subtaxonomy (Fig. 3.7) is responsible to classify a cloud environment according to the computational power provided by cloud environments. Particularly in commercial clouds, scientists have no access to the kind of technology that is used to implement it. In fact, in commercial cloud environments implementation details are hidden from the end-user (scientist). On the other hand, in academic or private clouds it is possible to obtain this information. This information may be quite useful in e-Science because many experiments need a powerful computational environment to run and if the cloud environment is not able to provide powerful resources, it will not be able to support these experiments. But, it is complicated to scientists to choose between those environments (clusters, blades, or grids) to run experiments, since they may not be computer experts. This way, we need to classify the environments using another classification.

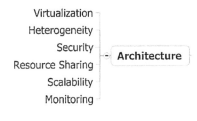

Fig. 3.6 Architecture subtaxonomy

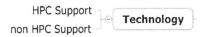

Fig. 3.7 Technology infrastructure subtaxonomy

This subtaxonomy provides a generic classification of cloud environments according to the support provided for high-performance computing (HPC). Since many experiments need HPC environments to run, cloud environments need to be classified according to these aspects. This way, cloud environments may be classified into HPC support and non-HPC support. HPC support cloud environments are those where multicore programming is allowed, and non-HPC support are those in which this kind of mechanism is not provided, for example.

3.3.6 Access

This subtaxonomy (Fig. 3.8) classifies cloud environments according to its access types. In most cases, we may find four types of accesses: web browsers, thin clients, mobile clients, and API. Browsers are the most common access way for cloud services. Many applications and infrastructures are accessible only on web browsers. It is intuitive since almost every computer has at least one browser installed and may access cloud services. Thin clients and mobile are types of access to clouds out of a desktop within handhelds or mobile phones. It has become popular to access services through phones instead of desktops. And finally, API is a fundamental way for accessing clouds.

API is a fundamental artifact for access through programming languages such as Java, Python, or C. By using an API, more complex applications may use cloud infrastructure in a native form. Since the scientific experiments modeled as scientific workflows are enacted using SWfMSs, one important need to connect SWfMSs to clouds is using an API because an API can be easily invoked by programmable components and most of the scientists follow this tendency.

3.3.7 Standards

This subtaxonomy (Fig. 3.9) presents some categories and standards found on literature for cloud computing. The Extensible Messaging and Presence Protocol (XMPP) [33] is an open technology for real-time communication, which powers a wide range of applications. Hyper Text Transfer Protocol (HTTP) is the most known standard for communication and it is intuitive to use it on the cloud, since it is used on basic web applications. OAuth [19] is a security protocol to publish and interact with protected data. In addition, it is an open protocol to allow secure

Fig. 3.8 Access subtaxonomy

Fig. 3.9 Standards subtaxonomy

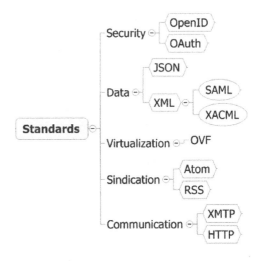

Fig. 3.10 Orientation subtaxonomy

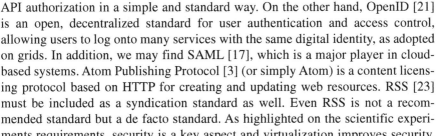

API authorization in a simple and standard way. On the other hand, OpenID [21] is an open, decentralized standard for user authentication and access control, allowing users to log onto many services with the same digital identity, as adopted on grids. In addition, we may find SAML [17], which is a major player in cloud-based systems. Atom Publishing Protocol [3] (or simply Atom) is a content licensing protocol based on HTTP for creating and updating web resources. RSS [23] must be included as a syndication standard as well. Even RSS is not a recommended standard but a de facto standard. As highlighted on the scientific experiments requirements, security is a key aspect and virtualization improves security. Virtualization is a key aspect of cloud computing and needs some standards. The OVF [22] is being considered as one of the de facto standards for virtualization. OVF enables flexible and secure distribution of software and data, facilitating the mobility of virtual machines. As happens in many web systems, data is usually represented and transferred using XML (and many more XML-based languages such as SAML [17], XACML [32], and JSON [11]). JSON is a lightweight data-interchange format.

3.3.8   Orientation

One important aspect of cloud computing for e-Science is the orientation (taxonomy represented in Fig. 3.10). Usually, the orientation changes as the type of service changes. For instance, when an application is provided on the cloud, we may consider it task-centric, because it is oriented to the task that will be executed. In other words, you need to transfer control to the application owners instead of having control of it. However, when the infrastructure is provided as a service, the user has control of the process. The programs, applications, and data are chosen by the user. Thus, the cloud may be user-centric.

3.4 Classifying Cloud Computing Environments Using the Taxonomy

In this section, we present a summarized survey of the main existing cloud computing environments according to the proposed taxonomy. Table 3.1 shows the selected cloud computing environments with their categorization based on the taxonomy. These cloud computing environments are the most commonly found in scientific literature [9, 14, 15, 24].

In Table 3.1, we may observe that none of the analyzed environments provides all functionalities and characteristics presented in the proposed taxonomy. Scientists will have to analyze their needs and verify in the classification the environment that is the most suitable. For example, suppose that scientific experiments require HPC support, API, and privacy as its main requirements. In a first analysis, scientists would choose between Nimbus and Eucalyptus. However, if a database service is also an important issue to be considered, they might trade between the available environments.

Table 3.1 Classification of cloud computing environments

	Cloud computing environments				
Categories	Amazon EC2[a]	Microsoft Azure[b]	Nimbus[c]	Eucalyptus[d]	IBM cloud[e]
Pricing	Real time	Real time	Free[f]	Free	Free[g]
Business model	IaaS, DaaS	PaaS, DaaS[h]	IaaS	IaaS	IaaS, DaaS
Orientation	User-centric	Task-centric	User-centric	User-centric	User-centric
Access	API, Browser	API, Browser	API	API	Browser
Privacy	Public	Public	Private	Private	Public
Virtualization	OVF	OVF	OVF	OVF	OVF
Monitoring	Yes	N/A[i]	N/A[i]	N/A[i]	N/A[i]
Technology	HPC support	Non-HPC support	HPC support	HPC support	HPC support

[a] http://aws.amazon.com/ec2/
[b] http://www.microsoft.com/windowsazure/
[c] www.nimbusproject.org/nimbus_cloud
[d] http://open.eucalyptus.com/
[e] http://www.ibm.com/ibm/cloud/
[f] Subject to acceptance
[g] Free for tests
[h] Microsoft Azure is composed by Windows Azure, Microsoft SWL Azure, and Windows Azure platform AppFabric
[i] Information not available

3.5 Taxonomies for Cloud Computing

There are some proposals in the literature related to cloud computing taxonomies. All presented taxonomies have focused mostly on the commercial aspect (e.g., business model), lacking on describing the domain according to important aspects for e-Science such as standards, privacy levels, and so on. Cloud computing providers adopt a specialized taxonomy to explain their approach, especially if they have to distinguish themselves from others. This section presents four taxonomies, already developed for the cloud computing domain.

Youseff [34] proposes a unified ontology for cloud computing. It presents a summary of cloud computing components, with a classification of these components, and their relationships. Even though this paper is a step forward, highlighting many technical challenges involved in building cloud components, it is not a real ontology, but a taxonomy that partially covers the cloud computing domain. In fact, this work classifies just the cloud computing components in five main layers. In addition, this ontology only takes the business model into account (classifying cloud computing as software as a service, hardware as a service, and so on). Many other aspects are needed to classify cloud computing environments, particularly for e-Science, such as pricing, access methods, and so on.

Leavitt [13], presents the whole cloud scenario with advantages and disadvantages, explaining the adoption of cloud by companies around the world and classifying cloud computing environments into four types that are equivalent to the business models presented in this paper. However, it proposes a type called "general services" that consider databases and storage provides as a service, differently from our taxonomy that created a new type named DaaS to designate this type of business model. This classification may be too generic since it groups in one class (general services) many important types for e-Science. Services for different purposes are classified as the same, and this may be not be desirable.

Laird [12] classifies cloud environments in a taxonomy that is composed by four main classes: Infrastructure, Platform, Service, and Applications. In each of these classes, it details some aspects and presents cloud environments that correspond to the classification. Many of the classes used in this work are present in our taxonomy. However, it is not focused on e-Science aspects and many important classes are not considered. Laird [12] is focused on commercial environments, and because of that, some classification is missing, such as HPC supporting. Since it is not a fundamental aspect for commercial applications that are executed in clouds, it was not considered.

The United States National Institute of Standards and Technology (NIST) recently provided definitions for cloud computing through an implicit taxonomy [18]. However, different from the taxonomy presented in this chapter, the NIST cloud computing taxonomy has focused on the business model aspect, lacking on describing the domain according to different aspects such as standards, privacy levels, and so on.

3.6 Conclusions and Final Remarks

In this chapter, we have introduced a taxonomy for cloud computing from an e-Science perspective. The authors believe that it will be useful for the scientific community in evaluating and comparing different cloud environments. By classifying environments using the proposed taxonomy, they may evaluate which environments meet their needs for executing scientific experiments in clouds. Different from the existing taxonomies, this taxonomy considers a broad view of cloud computing according to important aspects of scientific experiments and aims to explore the major properties of it.

This chapter highlights that despite the high interest about the topic, it is still a wide open field. New solutions for cloud computing are available, and many others are being announced, which makes the cloud computing field very fertile and hard to be understood and classified. It is fundamental that scientists are able to choose the best cloud environment for their experiments. The use of the taxonomy and its common vocabulary may facilitate scientists to find common characteristics of the existing environments and may help them to choose the most adequate one.

Acknowledgments The authors thank CNPq and CAPES for funding this research.

References

1. Altintas I, Berkley C, Jaeger E, Jones M, Ludascher B, Mock S (2004) Kepler: an extensible system for design and execution of scientific workflows. In: 16th SSDBM, Santorini, Greece, pp 423–424
2. Asosheh A, Danesh MH (2008) Comparison of OS level and hypervisor server virtualization. In: Proceedings of the 8th conference on systems theory and scientific computation, Rhodes, Greece, pp 241–246
3. Atom (2010) Atom Publishing Protocol. AtomEnabled.org – Atom Publishing Protocol. http://www.atomenabled.org/. Accessed 11 Jan 2010
4. Bruno D, Richmond H (2003) The true about taxonomies. Inform Manage J 37:44–46
5. Callahan SP, Freire J, Santos E, Scheidegger CE, Silva CT, Vo HT (2006) VisTrails: visualization meets data management. In: Proceedings of the 2006 ACM SIGMOD, Chicago, IL, pp 745–747
6. Foster I, Kesselman C (2004) The grid: blueprint for a new computing infrastructure. Morgan Kaufmann, Los Altos, CA
7. Foster I, Yong Zhao, Raicu I, Lu S (2008) Cloud computing and grid computing 360-degree compared. In: Grid computing environments workshop, 2008. GCE '08grid computing environments workshop, 2008. GCE '08, Auxtin, TX, pp 1–10
8. Freire J, Koop D, Santos E, Silva CT (2008) Provenance for computational tasks: a survey. Comput Sci Eng 10(3):11–21
9. Hoffa C, Mehta G, Freeman T, Deelman E, Keahey K, Berriman B, Good J (2008) On the use of cloud computing for scientific workflows. In: SWBES 2008SWBES 2008, Indianapolis, IN
10. Jensen M, Schwenk J, Gruschka N, Iacono LL (2009) On technical security issues in cloud computing. In: Proceedings of the 2009 IEEE international conference on cloud computing, Bangalore, India, pp 109–116
11. JSON (2010) JSON interchange format. JSON Interchange Format. http://json.org/. Accessed 11 Jan 2010

12. Laird P (2009) Cloud computing taxonomy. http://peterlaird.blogspot.com/2009/05/cloud-computing-taxonomy-at-interop-las.html. Accessed 11 Jan 2010
13. Leavitt N (2009) Is cloud computing really ready for prime time? Computer 42(1):15–20
14. Lizhe W, Jie T, Kunze M, Castellanos A, Kramer D, Karl W (2008) Scientific cloud computing: early definition and experience. In: Proceedings of HPCC '08, IEEE HPCC '08, pp 825–830
15. Matsunaga A, Tsugawa M, Fortes J (2008) CloudBLAST: combining MapReduce and virtualization on distributed resources for bioinformatics applications. In: Proceedings of the fourth IEEE international conference on eScience, e-Science'08, IEEE Computer Society, Washington, DC, vol 0, pp 222–229
16. Mattoso M, Werner C, Travassos GH, Braganholo V, Murta L, Ogasawara E, Oliveira D, Cruz S, Martinho W (2010) Towards supporting large scale in silico experiments life cycle. Int J Bus Process Integr Manage (IJBPIM), 5(1):79–92
17. Mishra P, Chopra D, Moreh J, Philpott R (2003) Differences between OASIS Security Assertion Markup Language (SAML) V1.1 and V1.0. OASIS Draft, Technical Report sstc-saml-diff-1.1-draft-01
18. NIST (2009) NIST.gov – computer security division – computer security resource center. NIST – cloud computing. http://csrc.nist.gov/groups/SNS/cloud-computing/index.html. Accessed 11 Jan 2010
19. OAuth (2010) OAuth – an open protocol to allow secure API authorization in a simple and standard method from desktop and web applications. http://oauth.net/. Accessed 11 Jan 2010
20. Oliveira D, Cunha L, Tomaz L, Pereira V, Mattoso M (2009) Using ontologies to support deep water oil exploration scientific workflows. In: IEEE international workshop on scientific workflows, Los Angeles, CA
21. OpenID (2010) OpenID Foundation website. http://openid.net/. Accessed 11 Jan 2010
22. OVF (2010) Open virtualization format (OVF) –virtual machines – virtualization. http://www.vmware.com/appliances/getting-started/learn/ovf.html. Accessed 11 Jan 2010
23. RSS (2010) RSS 2.0 specification (version 2.0.11). http://www.rssboard.org/rss-specification. Accessed 11 Jan 2010
24. Simmhan Y, Barga R, van Ingen C, Lazowska E, Szalay A (2008) On Building scientific workflow systems for data management in the cloud. In: Proceedings of the fourth IEEE international conference on eScience '08, eScience '08, IEEE Computer Society, Washington, DC, pp 434–435
25. Sotomayor B, Montero RS, Llorente IM, Foster I (2009) Virtual infrastructure management in private and hybrid clouds. IEEE Internet Comput 13(5):14–22
26. Taylor IJ, Deelman E, Gannon DB, Shields M (eds) (2007) Workflows for e-Science: scientific workflows for grids, 1st ed. Springer, London
27. Travassos GH, Barros MO (2003) Contributions of in virtuo and in silico experiments for the future of empirical studies in software engineering. In: Proceedings of 2nd workshop on empirical software engineering the future of empirical studies in software engineering, Fraunhofer IRB Verlag, Roman Castles, Italy
28. Vaquero LM, Rodero-Merino L, Caceres J, Lindner M (2009) A break in the clouds: towards a cloud definition. SIGCOMM Comput Commun Rev 39(1):50–55
29. W3C (2010) World Wide Web Consortium (W3C). http://www.w3.org/. Accessed 11 Jan 2010
30. Weske M, Vossen G, Medeiros CB (1996) Scientific workflow management: WASA architecture and applications, Universitat Munster, Germany
31. WfMC I (2009) Binding, WfMC Standards, WFMC-TC-1023. http://www. wfmc. org/. Accessed 11 Jan 2010
32. XACML (2010) OASIS eXtensible access control markup language (XACML). http://www.oasis-open.org/committees/tc_home.php?wg_abbrev=xacml. Accessed 11 Jan 2010
33. XMPP (2010) XMPP standards foundation. XMPP standards. http://xmpp.org/. Accessed 11 Jan 2010

34. Youseff L, Butrico M, Da Silva D (2008) Toward a unified ontology of cloud computing. In: Grid computing environments workshop, 2008. GCE '08grid computing environments workshop, 2008, GCE '08, pp 1–10
35. Zhang H, Jiang G, Yoshihira K, Chen H, Saxena A (2009) Intelligent workload factoring for a hybrid cloud computing model. In: Proceedings of the 2009 Congress on services – I, IEEE Computer Society, Washington, DC, pp 701–708

Chapter 4
Examining Cloud Computing from the Perspective of Grid and Computer-Supported Cooperative Work

Jinlei Jiang and Guangwen Yang

Abstract Cloud computing, which refers to services provisioning and consumption over the Internet, is the latest paradigm promising to deliver computing as a utility. Though it is still in its infancy and facing many challenges, cloud computing has drawn and is drawing more interest from both academia and industry. Taking grid computing as the baseline and using the findings in computer-supported cooperative work (CSCW) research, this chapter tries to answer such questions as why cloud computing is so attractive and how to make the vision of cloud computing really come true.

4.1 Introduction

Delivering computing as a utility was envisioned a way back by computing pioneer John McCarthy in 1961 as [17] – "If computers of the kind I have advocated become the computers of the future, then computing may someday be organized as a public utility just as the telephone system is a public utility... The computer utility could become the basis of a new and important industry.", and by Leonard Kleinrock in 1969 [10] – "As of now, computer networks are still in their infancy, but as they grow up and become sophisticated, we will probably see the spread of 'computer utilities' which, like present electric and telephone utilities, will service individual homes and offices across the country." Along the journey toward this dream, many computing paradigms have been proposed, including cluster computing, peer-to-peer (P2P) computing, services computing, and grid computing. Cloud computing, which refers to service (hardware such as CPU and storage, platform, and application) provisioning and consumption over the Internet in an on-demand approach, is the latest one joining this family. Though it is just an emerging

---

J. Jiang (✉)
Department of Computer Science & Technology, Tsinghua National Laboratory for Information Science & Technology, Tsinghua University, 100084, Beijing, P.R. China
e-mail: jjlei@tsinghua.edu.cn

N. Antonopoulos and L. Gillam (eds.), *Cloud Computing: Principles, Systems and Applications*, Computer Communications and Networks, DOI 10.1007/978-1-84996-241-4_4, © Springer-Verlag London Limited 2010

paradigm, more and more people [3,4,8,11] tend to think that cloud computing is the state-of-the-art practice and holds the promise to realize the long-held dream of "computing as a utility."

Nowadays, cloud computing has become a trend, drawing a lot of interest from both academia and industry. On the one hand, there are lots of hypes and columns available in the media, especially the IT-related ones. For example, using Google's exact search, the term "cloud computing" yields about 25,200,000 web pages, compared with 2,000,000 pages for "grid computing." Another result given by Google is also surprising – it only took 10 months for the cloud computing article by Berkeley [2] to get 138 citations. On the other hand, there are quite some products and services available on the market and still more products and services are coming. For example, besides Amazon's EC2 (Elastic Compute Cloud) and S3 (Simple Storage Service), other well-known cloud computing products and services include Salesforce's Force.com and SFA (Sales Force Automation), IBM's Blue Cloud, Google's App Engine and various Apps, and Microsoft's Windows Azure, to name but just a few. It is notable that AT&T and Verizon, two major telecom operators in the United States, also expanded their horizons into cloud computing by launching Synaptic Hosting and CaaS (computing-as-a-service), respectively, in 2009.

In spite of the facts above, cloud computing is still in its infancy with some debates on its concept and scope [3,8]. Some people think cloud computing is just another name given to utility computing. Others treat it as an upgrade to grid computing. Yet others argue that it is a revolution in computing architecture. Given the fact that cloud computing has a history of no more than 3 years, it is natural to see such a situation and it is also natural that the debates continue. In this chapter, we do not want to give another definition of cloud computing nor outline its boundary. Instead, our aim is to explore the following two questions:

- Why is cloud computing so attractive?
- What should we do to make the vision of cloud computing really come true?

To do so, we first examine the differences between cloud and grid computing in Section 2 with an aim to give a better understanding of the concept and scope of cloud computing. Afterwards, we turn to findings in computer-supported cooperative work (CSCW) research and try to give answers to the two questions. Our answers aim to give some hints for the development of cloud computing rather than solve all the challenges facing cloud computing.

4.2   Cloud and Grid: A Comparison

It is always effective to understand a new thing by comparing it with the existing ones. Here, grid computing is selected because it is the last computing paradigm before cloud computing along the journey toward "computing as a utility" and because it looks very much like cloud computing in many aspects. Figure 4.1 illustrates the paradigms of grid and cloud computing. As both grid and cloud computing

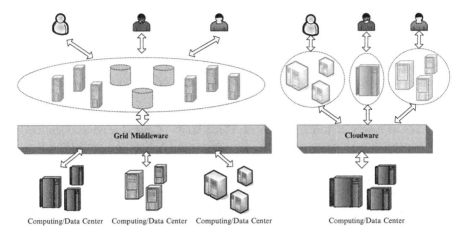

Fig. 4.1 A comparison of grid and cloud computing. Each computing/data center in the figure represents an administrative domain. The design of grid adopts a resource-centric approach with the focus to shield the heterogeneity of underlying resources and policies and to present various users with a vast yet uniform resource pool. All users of a grid face the same operating environment required by the grid middleware. On the contrary, cloud computing adopts a user- and task-centric design with an aim to deliver resources to users in their desired way. Each user in cloud computing has his/her own operating environment independent of the underlying resources

are of many shapes and colors, in the following we will concentrate our comparison on their origins, system design, and users.

4.2.1   A Retrospective View

Though cloud and grid look very similar in the sense that they both aim to provide enormous resources to their users in an on-demand manner, differences do exist between them. In this section, we explore their origins. The purpose is to identify the driving force behind grid and cloud computing and set a solid foundation for other comparisons.

Grid computing stems from academia, or more precisely the field of high-performance computing (HPC), in the 1990s with an aim to facilitate users to remotely utilize idle computing power within other computing centers when the local one is busy. This can be used to explain why the design of grid adopts a resource-centric approach. The grid at the early stage is termed compute grid. It was over nearly 10 years of development that grid technology became generally accepted as an effective way for "coordinated resource sharing and problem solving in dynamic, multi-institutional virtual organizations" [7]. As a result, compute grid evolved into grid computing, drawing much attention and funding from governments around the world. Along this transition, grid technology gets into the scope of enterprises. A milestone in the development of grid computing is the convergence of grid and service-oriented architecture (SOA) [13], resulting in first OGSA (Open Grid Services Architecture) and then WSRF (Web Service Resource Framework). It is since then that the potential of grid computing for business has fully unfolded. However, owing to a lack of explicit business model and many other factors that will be analyzed later, today there is still no widely accepted commercial-running grid service available on the market [12].

In contrast, cloud computing stems from the industry with an aim to sell resources as a service to its customers. Three kinds of cloud services identified are infrastructure as a service (IaaS, e.g., Amazon EC2 and S3, and IBM Blue Cloud), platform as a service (PaaS, e.g., Google App Engine, Microsoft Windows Azure, and Salesforce Force.com), and software as a service (SaaS, e.g., Salesforce SFA, Google Doc, and Microsoft Dynamic CRM). Before cloud computing was born, SOA has been prevalent for quite some time and much experience has been gained with grid operation. Cloud computing has a better starting point than any other computing paradigms mentioned in Section 1. Based on the lessons learned in the past, cloud computing adopts a user- and task-centric design as well as a "pay-as-you-go" business model. As a result, users' experiences with cloud services are enhanced greatly. Though cloud computing has a short history to now, many products and services are already available on the market.

4.2.2   Comparison from the Viewpoint of System

Different starting points lead to different systems. In this section, we will examine grid and cloud computing from a system point of view. Aspects covered are the technology behind the curtain and the system management.

In technical language, the purpose of grid computing is to integrate resources from different organizations forming a uniform resource pool, which can provide the ability that is impossible with a single computing/data center or that is beyond what a single organization can provide. Since these organizations are usually distributed geographically and have their own rights in determining vendors of their resources, the principal challenge facing grid computing is to shield the inherent heterogeneity and distribution of underlying resources. In contrast, the purpose of cloud computing is to divide resources into smaller pieces and deliver them to users in their desired way whenever needed. Resources in cloud computing are usually possessed or operated by a single organization and physically, they can be centralized within the same computing/data center or distributed across multiple computing/data centers, homogeneous or heterogeneous. In other words, resource heterogeneity and distribution is no longer a key problem in cloud computing. Instead, the principal challenge is to improve scalability, availability, and reliability.

Grid computing achieves its purpose through so-called grid middleware, a specific software product that provides necessary yet generic services for shielding the inherent underlying heterogeneity and distribution. Nowadays, there are well-established standards for grid middleware and quite some products and systems available, including Globus Toolkit (GT), Unicore, and gLite, to name but a few. Core services provided by the existing grid middleware are as follows:

- *Information Service*: maintains detailed up-to-date knowledge of all the resources or services in a grid environment. Based on the information service, suitable resources or services are identified. Information service, is also known as metadata service or directory service.
- *Security Service*: resources and users in grids are from multiple autonomous administrative domains. Security service is deployed to guarantee secure cross-organizational resource access that not only protects communications but also ensures no violation of the local administration policies.
- *Data Management*: provides some useful mechanisms for data access, data movement, data replication and location, and data integration. In GT4, data management related services include GridFTP, reliable file transfer (RFT), replica location service (RLS), data replication service (DRS), and data access and integration (OGSA-DAI) where OGSA-DAI is supplied by the third-party rather than the Globus team.
- *Execution Management*: deployed to fulfill a task using the resources provided, to track the progress of that task, and to manage the computing result. The key task of execution management is to determine where to run a given job according to the information provided by the information service.

Cloud computing also achieves its purpose by a middleware layer, which is called cloudware in this chapter. According to the type of service supplied (e.g., IaaS, PaaS, or SaaS), cloudware may provide various functionalities. In summary, the core functions of the cloudware are as follows:

- Maintains up-to-date information of the available physical resources (e.g., their capability, current load, and so on) as happens in grid computing. The purpose is to provide a basis for other functions such as virtual machine (VM) and application management. However, unlike in grid computing, this information is even transparent to developers.
- Create and manage VMs according to users' request. To utilize resources effectively, some algorithms or policies are deployed to determine where to create a VM, and when to start and stop a VM based on the information maintained. It is the duty of the hypervisor to keep the resource entitlement of a given VM.
- Application deployment, configuration, and execution. Meanwhile, the execution progress or status is also tracked.
- User management, pricing, and accounting. The purpose is to determine how users' requests are charged and maintain the actual usage of resources by a certain request or user.

Grid and cloud computing also show differences in system management as stated in the following.

In grid computing, since resources are owned and provided by different autonomous organizations, a heavy burden is raised to system management. For each node, besides routine maintenance work, system administrators must do much extra work to coordinate local administration policies with global ones. For example, they must make sure that resources are shared in a way fully compliant with local regulations. In addition, they must separate environments of local users from global ones to guarantee reliability and security. None of this work is trivial. Moreover, since there are quite some independent or interrelated components and services involved in a grid, installing and configuring the grid software itself implies a lot of work and presents some challenges even to experienced system administrators.

On the contrary, resources in cloud computing are usually possessed or operated by a single organization and as a result, there is no need to coordinate different administration policies. In addition, since each VM in cloud computing provides an isolated and independent running environment that is fully controllable by the user who creates it, there is also no need for system administrators to install and configure users' programs and to worry that they may interfere with each other and cause system disasters. Therefore, the burden of system management is greatly eased.

4.2.3 Comparison from the Viewpoint of Users

Different design philosophies lead to different systems, which in turn place different constraints on their users. This section compares grid and cloud computing from the viewpoint of users. Two kinds of users distinguished here are end-users who consume resources and services, and application developers who develop new applications or services using the resources and services supplied by a grid or a cloud.

Both grid and cloud computing provide two ways for end-users to consume resources supplied. The first involves using pre-installed software services through their own interfaces. Since these services are designed to support the needs of common users, in both cases end-users with special requirements or habits have to adapt themselves to the preset operation styles and instructions. Given the fact that grids are usually operated by computer scientists who know little about the domain needs, the problem is especially severe. The second involves running a task directly in a grid or a cloud. This shows quite some differences in operations and constraints as stated below.

To run a task in a grid, end-users need to specify the type and quantity of resources desired, information used for authentication, the program to be run and its arguments, sources of the input, and the output and its destination. This is an annoying procedure that often makes users stop. For example, *globusrun-ws*, the command supplied by GT4 for job submission and management, has 30 options for submitting a job and 15 options for monitoring a job. Though some tools have been provided as a help, much work is still needed, for example, to compose a job description file. Even if end-users have done all the work perfectly, there are still other risks that prevent their jobs getting done. One thing often ignored is that, because each grid middleware itself is a software system and has its special requirements on the running environment, the existing grids are very tightly bound to a specific operating system (OS), software libraries, or applications. For example, gLite presently can only run on Scientific Linux 4 and 5, and Debian 4. As a result, if the program corresponding to a job is not executable on the platform on top of which a grid middleware is running, or if one or more libraries needed by the program are unavailable, the job just could not get done even if there are enough resources available. Another depressing thing is that, because different grid systems in the real world deploy quite different ways for users to express their needs, the job description file prepared for one grid usually cannot be used in another one.

In contrast, running a task in clouds is much easier and faces fewer constraints. The only thing needed is to reserve the desired resources and configure them for the task to be run. Resource reservation can be done by several mouse clicks and resource configuration makes no difference when compared with the activity using local machines. Owing to the VM technology, users in cloud computing can always set up an environment capable of running their programs and thus the constraints laid by grids on the running programs as mentioned above no longer exist.

Grid and cloud computing also impose different requirements on application developers. Generally speaking, developing applications on a grid is a complex task. First, this implies that developers should know many details about the grid environment, for example, the way to stage data to and from the execution site, the way to find a specific service to be invoked, to name but a few. In addition, they must spend much time learning the related APIs (Application Programming Interfaces) – even the Simple API for Grid Applications (SAGA)[1] has a document of more than 300 pages. Second, since the grid is a highly dynamic environment, developers must pay more attention to such issues as exception handling, fault tolerance, scalability, performance, and so forth. Third, there are no mature tools for debugging and measuring the behavior of grid applications. Developers must struggle in their own ways (e.g., setting up an experimental grid of their own to monitor the behaviors of the application) to ensure the correctness of the application developed. It is easy to see from the statements above that programming on a grid raises a heavy burden on application developers.

As a comparison, programming in clouds is much easier. For IaaS, developers can always customize their working environments with their familiar tools and configurations, so there is almost no difference to programming on local machines. For PaaS, nearly every service provider supplies a platform SDK (Software Development Kit) and/or some debugging tool. For example, Google App Engine provides a fully featured local development environment with which developers can write, for example, standard Java applications. The Google plug-in for Eclipse provides an IDE (Integrated Development Environment) with application wizard and debug configuration for Google App Engine projects, making the development

---

[1] SAGA is an open standard defined and maintained by the Open Grid Forum (OGF). Its aim is to provide an interface for high-level grid application programming and enable application developers to write programs without knowing the detail of specific infrastructures.

process much easier and more efficient. Similarly, Visual Studio 2010 also provides a template for developers to write Windows Azure services. In this way, the complexity of the platform is shielded from developers and the pains of application development are greatly eased.

4.2.4   A Summary

Table 4.1 summarizes the differences between grid and cloud computing. The key points are highlighted below.

Grid computing adopts a resource-centric design and tries to meet various needs by a unified resource pool. As a result, many unnecessary details of the infrastructure are brought to both end-users and developers, making it difficult to use and hard to program. In addition, it also raises a heavy burden of system administration due to many administrative domains being involved. Cloud computing, on the contrary, adopts a user- and task-centric design and it meets diverse needs by different kinds of services, for example, infrastructure services, platform services, and software services. In cloud computing, the complexity is shielded from users. As a result, it is easy to use and program. In addition, managing a cloud is also easy since for most of the time there is only one administrative domain involved in it.

4.3   Examining Cloud Computing from the CSCW Perspective

In the previous section, we examined the differences between grid and cloud computing. In this section, we present some findings in CSCW research and utilize them to analyze the cloud.

Table 4.1 Grid and cloud computing fully compared

	Grid computing	Cloud computing
Origin	Academia, HPC field	Industry
Methodology	One-size-fit-all	Diversified services, e.g., IaaS, PaaS, and SaaS
Focus	Resource	User, task
Business model	No explicit one	Pay-as-you-go
Purpose	Resource integration	Resource partition
Technical challenge	Resource heterogeneity and distribution	Scalability, availability, and reliability
Administrative domain	Many	One
System management	Complex	Simple
Constraint	Many	Few
Usage	Complex	Simple
Programmability	Poor	Good

4.3.1 CSCW Findings

CSCW is a research field dealing with the issue of how to use computers, or more broadly information and communication technology (ICT), to facilitate a group of people to fulfill a common task [6]. Over 20 years of development since the term was first coined in 1984, people have gained much knowledge about this field. Cloud computing holds the promise to deliver computing as a utility, so it is a socio-technical system. It is in this sense that we think that the following findings of CSCW can also be used to answer the questions raised in Section 1 – why cloud computing is so attractive and how to make the vision of cloud computing really come true?

Finding 1: To derive the greatest benefit from CSCW, the supporting technology must infiltrate as widely as possible throughout the populace [16]. In this way, cooperative system designers can relieve themselves from hard work on such issues as heterogeneous resource management and interoperability and focus their efforts on more essential issues such as understanding and accounting for the characteristics of cooperative work and then devising proper mechanisms to support them.

Finding 2: Besides technical factors such as usability and functionality, the deployment of CSCW is affected by social factors such as various administrative and policy decisions [16]. Sometimes, the social factors function dominantly in making the decision on whether to adopt a certain technology or not.

Finding 3: A successful collaborative system must provide enough respect for the social habits of end-users [9]. Human is the most active and dynamic element in a collaborative environment, and providing respect for his/her habits means users can get better experiences during collaboration. This in turn implies that the collaborative system will be adopted by more and more users, and therefore, the critical mass problem [14] will easily be met.

Finding 4: Incentives are critical [1]. CSCW suffers from Grudin's inequality [9], which says that those who do additional work (capture and record the articulation work associated with collaboration) to make collaboration succeed may not be the ones who benefit most from the results, and thus it is necessary to provide some incentives or reward to those persons. In this way, more people will join the collaboration process and the contribution of people will also increase.

4.3.2 The Anatomy of Cloud Computing

The attractiveness of cloud computing can be accounted for using Finding 1, Finding 3, and Finding 4 as follows.

First, cloud computing, in general, presents no new technology. Virtualization technology, which is at the core of cloud computing, was first developed in the 1960s. Other technologies such as web services and Rich Internet Applications (RIA) also have a history of no less than 5 years. Today, all these technologies are well supported and popular. For example, Intel and AMD have released several processors with support for virtualization technology and there are many virtual machine monitors (VMMs) available on the market (e.g., ESXi and vSphere from VMware, Hyper-V from Microsoft, XEN and KVM from the open-source community). In addition, web services and RIA have become a must for the development of web applications. Thus, adopting these technologies sets up a good basis for the prosperity of this market because it makes entrance low. As a contrast, there was no prevalent integration technology at the beginning of grid computing and designers have to develop their own ways to integrate various resources. Though the convergence of grid computing and SOA provides new opportunities for resource integration, much work is still needed to reconcile various ways of information representation. Put simply, the entrance for grid computing is high. As a result, even after 10 years of development, grid computing today is still in its infancy in many aspects [12].

Next, cloud computing provides enough respect for the social habits of users because using a machine in the cloud is no different to using a local machine. As mentioned above, users of cloud computing can always work with their familiar tools and settings. In other words, users of cloud computing adapt the running environment to their applications rather than adapt the applications to the environment. Therefore, they do not need to change habits developed over years, which have a solid base. On the contrary, as we discussed in Section 2, users of grid computing, whether end-users or application developers, have limited, if any, control over the running environment, and have to bear many constraints being put on them. For developers, to take the full advantage of grid computing, they have to learn much for developing new applications or adapting the existing ones to the grid, which is a heavy burden to them. In addition, system administrators also face many new challenges in coordinating resource sharing and in guaranteeing the reliability, availability, and security of the running environment due to the involvement of multiple autonomous domains.

The last but the most important point, users of cloud computing need not do much, if any, additional work to use the services provided by the cloud. All the work they do is necessary and the same as what they do every day without cloud computing. For example, reserving a VM in clouds is an analog of buying a physical machine, but with much greater convenience. Installing software in a VM is no different to that in a physical machine. What's more, users can benefit from the advanced features of cloud computing such as unlimited resource being available on demand, no upfront commitment and pay-as-you-go usage of resources [2], and the great potentials for group collaboration as well as the universal access to information and services [15]. These features are especially attractive to small- and medium-sized businesses (SMBs) or start-ups that do not have enough resources for buying and maintaining servers and developing applications from scratch, for they imply a lot of savings of running costs. In contrast, things are quite different with grid computing. To use grid computing, much more should be paid on application development, system management, and so on. Particularly, since resource providers in grid computing receive no reward for sharing their resources, they are reluctant to help to solve various problems encountered.

In summary, compared with grid computing, cloud computing provides more benefits and rewards without changing the working way that people are familiar with.

Therefore, it is not strange at all that cloud computing is attractive. Indeed, cloud computing has accumulated a huge (potential) base of both service providers and consumers, and many market-research firms (e.g., IDC, Forrester, and Merrill Lynch) believe that cloud computing has enormous growth potential.

In spite of the facts above, cloud computing is still in its infancy and only has a limited adoption to now [11]. To make the vision of cloud computing really come true, we examine the obstacles to (rapid) growth of cloud computing. As with any other new paradigm, there are fears and concerns about cloud computing related to technology, social factors, or both. For example, Armbrust M et al. [2] listed the top ten obstacles as availability of service, data lock-in, data confidentiality and auditability, data transfer bottlenecks, performance unpredictability, scalable storage, bugs in large-scale distributed systems, scaling quickly, reputation fate sharing, and software licensing; Leavitt N [11] identified the challenges facing cloud computing as control, performance, latency, security and privacy, related bandwidth costs, vendor lock-in and standards, transparency, reliability, and others. In our opinion, issues such as performance, latency, scalability, and data transfer bottlenecks are related to technology and have been suffered for a long time before the emergence of cloud computing. Though they have some impact on the adoption of cloud computing, the impact is limited. It is the following issues that hinder the wide adoption of cloud computing.

4.3.2.1   Security and Privacy

According to a survey by IDC, security and privacy is the main concern of chief information officers and IT executives [11]. To us, such a concern arises from the violation or change of users' social habits – data and applications in cloud computing are usually stored or running on an external infrastructure outside a company's firewall, and users have to rely on service providers, NOT themselves, to protect their data and applications. Obviously, this may be quite different from what users are used to when using local machines. Since change of habit is a slow process, it is a natural result that only cloud computing has a very limited adoption just now according to Finding 2 and Finding 3. However security and privacy might be only a perceived risk as asserted by Armbrust M et al. [2]:

> We believe that there are no fundamental obstacles to making a cloud-computing environment as secure as the vast majority of in-house IT environments, and that many of the obstacles can be overcome immediately with well-understood technologies such as encrypted storage, Virtual Local Area Networks, and network middleboxes (e.g., firewalls, packet filters).

4.3.2.2   Data and/or Vendor Lock-In

This concern arises from the fact that there are currently no standards for IaaS, PaaS, and SaaS interfaces, and as a result, much work is needed for customers to port their data or programs from one cloud to another. While we admit that such concerns really matter it will become increasingly important as more and more cloud providers emerge, we also argue that its impact may not be as great as people think. On the one hand, people undergo such constraints in the real world. For example, designers have to make a choice between J2EE and .NET platform when developing new applications. When new hardware is bought, people have to install system and application software again to deliver their services. If we treat migrating an application from one infrastructure to another as the process of buying new hardware, the inconvenience caused by incompatible virtual image formats – a major problem with IaaS – would no more be a problem. On the other hand, people have recognized this problem and as a result, many standardization activities are in progress. Some of them are listed below. For more information, please refer to http://cloud-standards.org.

Cloud Security Alliance[2] was set up recently "to promote the use of best practices for providing security assurance within Cloud Computing, and provide education on the uses of Cloud Computing to help secure all other forms of computing." The Open Grid Forum (OGF) established the Open Cloud Computing Interface Working Group (OCCI-WG)[3] in March 2009 to develop a clean, open API for infrastructure clouds. The Storage Networking Industry Association (SNIA) has created a technical workgroup to develop the new Cloud Data Management Interface (CDMI).[4] The Open Cloud Consortium (OCC),[5] another newly established organization, aims to "support the development of standards for cloud computing and frameworks for interoperating between clouds." Finally, the Distributed Management Task Force (DMTF) has released the Open Virtualization Format (OVF) Specification [5] that "describes an open, secure, portable, efficient, and extensible format for the packaging and distribution of software to be run in virtual machines." Therefore, it is reasonable to believe that interoperation between clouds will get easier, making the concern about data/vendor lock-in less important.

4.3.2.3   Service Availability/Reliability

This concern ranked first in the list given by Armbrust M et al. [2]. It is a radical requirement of business continuity – users will not adopt a system that is unreliable and often unavailable to run their business. The reason why such a concern becomes so important lies in the change of operating mode – services are running outside a company's firewall and the quality of services relies not only on software vendors who develop services but also on providers who host services. No doubt, the well-known outages of Amazon S3, Google App Engine, and Salesforce.com make the

---

[2] http://www.cloudsecurityalliance.org/

[3] http://www.occi-wg.org/

[4] http://www.snia.org/cloud

[5] http://opencloudconsortium.org/

worry even much severe. However, as pointed out by Armbrust M et al. [2], the IT infrastructures of Amazon, Google, and Salesforce are better than their peers.

In summary, as a new paradigm, cloud computing does bring changes to business operation; that is, the operation is done remotely, out of the users' reach and full control. Since this differs from what users are used to, it is natural to see that much concern is raised according to the Findings 2 and 3. To address this, time matters. We need time to tackle technical challenges; we need time to cultivate application developers; we need time to build trust between customers and service providers; we need time to develop use cases to demonstrate the benefits of cloud computing. Once people get to know the reward of cloud computing over its risks, the wide adoption of cloud computing will come true as implied by Finding 4.

4.4   Conclusions

In this chapter, we first examined the differences between cloud and grid computing from their development and the viewpoint of system and users, respectively. Then, we analyzed the reasons why cloud computing is so attractive and some related concerns using the findings in CSCW research. Since cloud computing adopts a user- and task-centric design philosophy and shows enough respect for the social habits of users in using computers, its popularity is a natural result. At the same time, like any other new thing, cloud computing faces some challenges that slow its wide adoption. As time goes on and more and more experience is gained, cloud computing will eventually become an effective and efficient way to deliver computing as a utility. During this course, we researchers should address how to overcome the obstacles and demonstrate the real benefits and/or advantages of cloud computing.

Acknowledgments   The work reported here is co-sponsored by Natural Science Foundation of China (NSFC) under grant Nos. 60773145 and 60736020, and National High-Tech R&D (863) Program of China under grant Nos. 2006AA01A101, 2006AA01A108, 2006AA01A111, and 2006AA01A117.

References

1. Ackerman MS (2000) The intellectual challenge of CSCW: the gap between social requirements and technical feasibility. Hum-Comput Interact 15:179–203
2. Armbrust M, Fox A, Griffith R et al (2009) Above the clouds: a Berkeley view of cloud computing. Technical Report No. UCB/EECS-2009-28, University of California, Berkeley
3. Buyya R, Yeo CS, Venugopal S et al (2009) Cloud computing and emerging IT platforms: vision, hype, and reality for delivering computing as the 5th utility. Futur Gener Comp Syst 6:599–616
4. Dikaiakos MD, Katsaros D, Mehra P et al (2009) Cloud computing: distributed Internet computing for IT and scientific research. IEEE Internet Comput 5:10–13

5. DMTF (2009) Open Virtualization Format Specification. Document Number: DSP0243, http://www.dmtf.org/standards/published_documents/DSP0243_1.0.0.pdf. Accessed 4 January 2010
6. Ellis C, Gibbs S, Rein G (1991) Groupware: some issues and experiences. Commun ACM 2:38–58
7. Foster I, Kesselman C, Tuecke S (2001) The anatomy of the grid: enabling scalable virtual organizations. Int J High Perform Comput Appl 15:200–222
8. Foster I, Zhao Y, Raicu I et al (2008) Cloud computing and grid computing 360-degree compared. In: Proceedings grid computing environments workshop, IEEE Computer Society Press
9. Grudin J (1988) Why CSCW applications fail: problems in the design and evaluation of organization of organizational interfaces. In: Proceedings of CSCW'88, ACM Press, pp 85–93
10. Kleinrock L (2005) A vision for the Internet. ST J Res 1:4–5
11. Leavitt N (2009) Is cloud computing really ready for prime time? IEEE Comp 1:15–20
12. Lee CP, Dourish P, Mark G (2006) The human infrastructure of cyberinfrastructure. In: Proceedings of CSCW 2006, ACM Press, pp 483–492
13. Papazoglou MP, Heuvel W (2007) Service oriented architectures: approaches, technologies and research issues. VLDB J 16:389–415
14. Markus ML (1990) Toward a "Critical Mass" theory of interactive media. In: Fulk J, Steinfield C (eds) Organizations and communication technology. Sage, Newbury Park, CA
15. Miller M (2008) Cloud computing: web-based applications that change the way you work and collaborate online. Que Publishing, Indianapolis, USA
16. Mills KL (2003) Computer-supported cooperative work challenges. In: Drake M (ed) Encyclopedia of library and information science, 2nd edn. Taylor & Francis, New York
17. Wikipedia (2009) Utility Computing. http://en.wikipedia.org/wiki/Utility_computing. Accessed 4 Jan 2010

Chapter 5
Overview of Cloud Standards

Anand Govindarajan and Lakshmanan

Abstract Cloud computing is slowly transforming itself from a hype to reality. However, its maturity and further adoption depends on its ability to address concerns such as security, interoperability, portability and governance at the earliest opportunity. This can be accelerated by compliance to guidelines and standards defined in consensus by the cloud providers. Without addressing these concerns, users would be wary to tread this path in spite of its powerful economic model for business computing. This chapter will explore the readiness of various standards of interoperability, security, portability and governance for the cloud computing model. The market adoption of these standards will also be explored and gaps or opportunities for improvement will be discussed.

5.1 Overview – Cloud Standards – What and Why?

An IDC Survey [1] of senior Information Technology (IT) executives/CIOs shows that limited or lack of security, reliability, interoperability, portability and compliance in the cloud are some of the top concerns for its mainstream adoption.

The impact of these challenges and solution responsibility are not limited to the cloud providers, but span across all the players in the cloud ecosystem such as the service consumers, service providers and governing bodies. Hence, a solution or an approach to address these concerns should be built with consensus from all the players. Cloud Standardisation is the means to such solutions.

A. Govindarajan (✉)
Technical/Data Architect, Retail Banking Business Unit - UK EME
RBS Technology Services India Tower A, India Land Tech Park, Plot No.14,
3rd Main Street, Ambattur Industrial Estate, Ambattur, Chennai-600058 India
e-mail: ganandg@hotmail.com

Lakshmanan
Lead Principal, (IT Architecture Educator and Mentor)
Education & Research, Infosys Technologies Limited, Electronic City,
Bangalore 560 100 India

N. Antonopoulos and L. Gillam (eds.), *Cloud Computing: Principles,*
Systems and Applications, Computer Communications and Networks,
DOI 10.1007/978-1-84996-241-4_5, © Springer-Verlag London Limited 2010

Standardisation provides predictability for providers and consumers alike. It enables innovation, promotes vendor independence, interoperability, encourages repeatable processes and increases resources/skills availability.

IT has a fair share of standards that has lead to its maturity and faster adoption. Cloud computing can look at re-use/extension of the IT standards, restricting the creation of fresh ones to address unique scenarios and challenges of this model. For example, Amazon, a public cloud provider, could utilise the existing security standards for data centres like physical security, network security, etc., to protect its cloud environments. However, interoperability of a service between two public cloud environments would need fresh standards.

There needs to be cautious balance between the levels of standardisation so that it does not stifle innovation and enables early industry adoption. Hence, what will be some of the important standards that typical Enterprises look for before adoption? These are (restricting the definitions to IT):

- Interoperability/integration – interoperability enables products/software components to work with or integrate with each other seamlessly, in order to achieve a desired result. Thus, it provides flexibility and choice to use multiple products to achieve our need. This is enabled by either integrating through standard interfaces or by means of a broker that converts one product interface to another.
- Security – security involves the protection of information assets through various policies, procedures and technologies, which need to adhere to standards and best practices in order to achieve the desired level of security. For example, Payment Card Industry (PCI) data security standards from PCI SSC [2] define ways to secure credit card data to avoid fraud. This is applicable to all organisations that hold, process or pass credit cardholder information.
- Portability – as per Wikipedia [3], a software is said to be portable when the cost of porting the same from an existing platform for which it was originally developed, to a new platform, is less than the cost of re-writing it for the new platform. Software with good portability thus avoids vendor lock-in. This is typically achieved by adhering to standard interfaces defined between the software component and vendor platforms. For example, Java programs are set to be portable across operating systems (OS) that adhere to standard interfaces defined between the Java runtime environment and the OS.
- Governance, Risk Management and Compliance (GRC) – governance focuses on ensuring that the enterprise adheres to defined policies and processes. Risk management puts in controls to manage and mitigate risks as defined by the enterprise. Compliance ensures that the enterprise adheres to various legal/legislative as well as internal policies. Standards have been defined for IT systems to adhere to certain industry as well as legal standards such as Sarbanes–Oxley (SOX) [4], Health Insurance Portability and Accountability Act (HIPAA) [5], etc.

Having discussed the need for standards, the subsequent sections will present the various initiatives in this direction.

To understand the need for standards from the cloud perspective and the status of various initiatives better, a hypothetical company called Nimbus Corp is considered.

Nimbus is actively moving its IT systems to various cloud options. It started its journey into clouds with an IBM CloudBurst® private cloud for its marketing applications. Having been successful in its pilot, Nimbus started to move some of its data-processing-intensive applications to Amazon Web Services (public cloud) in time for handling Christmas volumes. It moved a couple of custom-built applications to Amazon EC2 and the Marketing data mart to Amazon's Oracle instance. The SaaS-based BI vendors, Birst or PivotLink, are being looked at for replacing its current marketing dashboard, having moved the data mart to the cloud. Nimbus is also considering using Force.com or Google App Engine (GAE) PaaS environments to build additional marketing applications. The standards are reviewed with this company in mind.

5.2 Deep Dive: Interoperability Standards

In using the new cloud setup for its applications, Nimbus faces the following interoperability challenges:

-   The SaaS-based marketing dashboard on one vendor cloud has to fetch the data from the Marketing data mart sitting on Amazon's infrastructure (IaaS)
-   The marketing applications built on Force.com or GAE (PaaS) needs to interact with the other applications running on Amazon EC2

Similarly, there could be many such scenarios between public and private cloud deployments as well as across various delivery models such as SaaS, PaaS and IaaS. What are the expectations from standards to address these challenges?

5.2.1 Purpose, Expectations and Challenges

Interoperability is typically achieved through APIs or brokers between the two interacting parties where the control and the data originating from the requestor is converted into a common format and then moved to the provider and vice versa. The purpose of the standards is thus to set guidelines for vendors, cloud providers and developers of these APIs/brokers to enable interoperability across various cloud resources and hence avoid vendor lock-in.

There are, however, additional challenges posed for interoperability in the cloud scenario when compared with that of the traditional IT environments, such as:

-   In addition to the interoperability of application control and data, other supporting aspects of policy management, security management and deployment/provisioning are also to be managed across all the interfacing environments.
-   In the infrastructure layer, cloud computing is supported by the concept of virtualisation. Interoperability heavily depends on the compatibility of these virtual machines (VM).

How do some of the current standardisation initiatives fare?

5.2.2   Initiatives – Focus, Sponsors and Status

Tables 5.1 and 5.2 show some of the key initiatives by industry bodies as well as by vendors towards interoperability standards.

5.2.3   Market Adoption

From Tables 5.1 and 5.2, except for industry initiatives like OVF, the standards are in very early stages of development. In addition, there are emerging cloud

Table 5.1 Interoperability – group initiatives

Standard name	Group/body	Focus	Readiness
Unified Cloud Interface [6]	Cloud Computing Interoperability Forum [7]	Vision is to build an API of all cloud APIs available from different vendors using RDF based on ontology language and thus enable interoperability	Draft Model defined
Open Cloud Computing Interface [8]	Open Grid Forum [9]	To provide an API specification for remote management of IaaS services across vendors	Draft API document ready
Open Virtualisation Format [10]	DMTF [11]	Build an industry standard format for portable virtual machines. VMs thus built can interoperate with any other VMs	Version 1.0 of OVF available
Standards and Interoperability of Large Data Clouds [12]	Open Cloud Consortium (OCC) [13]	To work on standards for large data clouds and interfaces between storage and compute clouds	Projects MalStone and Thriftstore in early releases

Table 5.2 Interoperability – vendor initiatives

Standard name	Group/body	Focus	Readiness
GoGrid API [14]	GoGrid [15]	To build a Public API to control their GoGrid Cloud infrastructure. The API is now open sourced	Available for use
Cloudware Open Architecture [16]	3Tera [17]	To build an Open Architecture/ framework for Cloud Computing for multiple players – subscribers, publishers, data-centre operators, etc. (entire ecosystem) to interoperate	Delivered in stages planned for the next 12–24 months

brokering/management vendors (such as RightScale, CloudKick and CloudSwitch) whose tools interoperate across cloud environments to provide management capabilities through a single interface. They eventually, as predicted by Gartner [18], could provide lot of additional services by building an abstraction layer across the clouds. Some of them are a part of the standard bodies driving these standards.

5.2.4   Gaps/Areas of Improvement

The mature initiatives are focused towards the infrastructure layer. The scenarios discussed earlier, such as:

1. Interoperability/integration between cloud delivery models (SaaS, PaaS and IaaS) is not addressed. Except for Unified Cloud Interface and Cloudware Arch, the rest primarily focus on the Infrastructure layer (IaaS).
2. Standards for interaction between private and public clouds are also not addressed. One such scenario is the usage of hybrid cloud.

Various vendors such as Amazon and other cloud brokers seem to have the required technology, but have to contribute by participating in the standardisation initiatives.

5.3   Deep Dive: Security Standards

Some of the scenarios of security that Nimbus would encounter, having adopted cloud computing, would be:

– Availability/Reliability – Amazon Web Services or Force.com could have outages that render Nimbus' marketing application unusable
– Data isolation/multi-tenancy – cloud providers, especially the SaaS vendors, enable multi-tenancy in their environment. This could lead to data isolation issues unless secured with proper access controls. Nimbus could have its data exposed to another client of Birst if the right controls are not in place.
– Data ownership – ideally Nimbus should own the data even if it resides with the cloud provider. However, the cloud provider also has access and could take ownership of some of the derived data such as platform usage patterns. This needs to be clarified between the parties.
– Trust – the relationship between Nimbus and the cloud provider runs on trust. Nimbus could have performed audits or been shown audit reports of, say, Amazon's environment, but it is a matter of trust to believe what has been shown is indeed active on Nimbus environment or its data are not misused by the provider's employees.

There are many more aspects of security such as service levels on data usage, data privacy, compliance, etc., that a cloud user would encounter. Are the reasons behind these unique challenges understood?

5.3.1 Purpose, Expectations and Challenges

Cloud computing brings in certain security challenges not seen in typical on-premise/enterprise infrastructure due to the nature of its model, such as:

- Distributed model – the data and services are spread across multiple data centres and infrastructures causing concerns of availability, ownership and compliance.
- Shared model – the cloud works on sharing code bases/services and infrastructure for data and services across multiple clients causing concerns of data isolation.
- Access ubiquity – cloud services are web-based and can be accessed from anywhere by means of any client type – secure or non-secure – causing concerns of hacking.

The focus is thus to ensure that security controls are effective to address these challenges. Broadly, the expectation from the standard would be to address:

- Cloud Data Security ensuring
  - Accountability (validating claim of identity by a user, user authentication and auditing of user actions)
  - Authorisation (access control to allow or deny user access based on privilege and confidentiality to prevent information disclosure to unauthorised parties)
  - Availability (data to be accessible whenever needed and with integrity)
- Cloud Service access security
  - To avoid Domain Name System (DNS) security threats during service access (e.g. IP hijacking, changing the path to destination IP)
  - To avoid Denial-of-Service(DoS) attacks on the cloud, impacting its availability
- Managing compliance due to issues such as data storage across geographies, etc. (this is extensively covered in the compliance section subsequently).

5.3.2 Initiatives – Focus, Sponsors and Status

Tables 5.3 and 5.4 show some of the key initiatives by industry bodies as well as by vendors towards security standards.

Table 5.3 Security – group initiatives

Standard name	Group/body	Focus	Readiness
Cloud Security Alliance Guidelines [19]	Cloud Security Alliance [20]	To outline areas of security concern and guidance for cloud providers to improve security of their service offerings	First version ready. Ver 2 expected in October 2009

Table 5.4 Security – vendor initiatives

Standard name	Group/body	Focus	Readiness
Amazon Virtual Private Cloud (VPC) [21]	Amazon Web Services (AWS) [22]	To enable enterprises to securely connect their existing infrastructure to AWS compute resources via a Virtual Private Network (VPN) connection	Available for use
Online Security Services and Compliance (OSSC) [23]	Microsoft [24]	To build a framework ensuring security, privacy, risk management, business continuity management, global criminal compliance and operational compliance of MS cloud infrastructure	Applied to MS cloud infrastructure

5.3.3 Market Adoption

Cloud Security Alliance is formed and backed by industry heavy weights such as HP, Verizon, VMware, McAfee, etc. This would speed up its adoption. Amazon [25] has put into practice several security measures to address all of the discussed issues.

5.3.4 Gaps/Areas of Improvement

Security is a very broad and most important concern to be addressed in cloud computing. Scenarios discussed are to be addressed before security is removed from the top concerns list of various user surveys.

5.4 Deep Dive: Portability Standards

Nimbus, having tried with an initial set of cloud providers, now decides to move some of its applications to other competitive/well-rated providers and some back to its on-premise environments. Portability here becomes a major concern and some relevant scenarios will be:

– The marketing applications built on Force.com need to be moved to the GAE or Microsoft Azure environment (PaaS) or even back to Nimbus data centre (application/service portability)
– Nimbus plans to consolidate its data marts into a centralised data warehouse. Hence, it wants its Marketing data mart to be moved back to Nimbus environment (data portability).

Do the current standards address these scenarios?

5.4.1 Purpose, Expectations and Challenges

The standards around portability are expected to enable smooth switch of cloud providers with minimal impact to cost and service quality. The purpose is thus to set guidelines for the cloud providers to build relevant layers of abstraction in their environments to help portability. Looking across the delivery models, the following are some of the challenges to address portability:

- SaaS – the content, data and metadata (application configurations) should be portable to a new environment for a smooth switch
- PaaS – the code base, application frameworks, data and metadata would be some things to port
- IaaS – the software runtime environments (configurations and APIs) would need to be ported. Typically, this would be the VM.

5.4.2 Initiatives – Focus, Sponsors and Status

Tables 5.5 and 5.6 show some of the key initiatives by industry bodies as well as by vendors towards portability standards.

5.4.3 Market Adoption

The current status shows that the portability using virtualisation (OVF standard) is the one in place. IBM has built an OVF toolkit and Citrix has Project Kensho OVF tool as a part of their Xenserver Virtualisation technology. Sun, Eucalyptus and few other vendors, however, are claiming portability by using open source-based platforms.

Table 5.5 Portability – group initiatives

Standard name	Group/body	Focus	Readiness
Open Virtualisation Format [10]	DMTF [11]	To build an industry standard format for portable virtual machines. Services running on VMs thus can be ported onto any virtualisation platform	Version 1.0 of OVF available
Cloud Storage Initiative [26]	SNIA [27]	To build a standard interface (CDMI) between the data and the cloud storage provider, indicating the data services to offer, thus enabling data portability across vendors	Cloud storage reference model and use cases drafts are ready to allow standards development

Table 5.6 Portability – vendor initiatives

Standard name	Group/body	Focus	Readiness
Cloud-Ready Server Templates [28]	RightScale [29]	To provide server deployment templates that allow portability of servers across multiple cloud environments	Available for use
Open Cloud Platform [30]	Sun [31]	To enable Open cloud based on open technologies such as Java, MySQL, OpenSolaris, Open Storage, etc., enabling portability on similar cloud platforms	Launched in March 2009

5.4.4   Gaps/Areas of Improvement

OVF standard addresses portability through movement of VMs, which is the typical technology basis for the cloud. This addresses the IaaS level portability. Standards/guidelines for portability of other models (SaaS, PaaS) as discussed earlier need to be addressed.

5.5   Deep Dive: Governance, Risk Management and Compliance Standards

Having placed several core and non-core systems on the cloud, Nimbus has a key dependency on the provider to ensure that these systems do not fail and impact its business. Several assessments and discussions with the provider were done and a contract signed up. Now, how does Nimbus ensure the contractual terms are being met on an on-going basis by the provider? What if there is a breach? How can this risk be managed? Nimbus has signed up for several regulatory measures. How far are these adhered to by the provider? What if there is a breach? These are some concerns handled by GRC function.

5.5.1   Purpose, Expectations and Challenges

GRC in cloud computing can be considered as an extension of the traditional model, but has to address several new challenges as this is applied to an environment external to the organisation. The governance requirements can be classified as:

1. Design-time governance covering
   (a) Service definition (e.g. design, build management, source code management, and QA)
   (b) Service deployment

2. Runtime governance covering
   (a) Service policy management (e.g. security, performance, reliability, etc.)
   (b) Service retirement
3. Change management for services, policies, processes, data and infrastructure

The governance spans across all the cloud service types, viz. software (SaaS), platform (PaaS) or infrastructure services (IaaS).

Risk management in a cloud will be relevant to managing all types of IT and business risks that ensue due to managing services in an external environment, such as operational risk (e.g. outages), security risks (both data and process), financial risk and legal risk (due to non-compliance of regulatory needs).

Lastly, compliance of cloud to various regulatory needs brings in typical requirements, such as:

1. Records management (ensuring records for all activities)
2. Auditing (audit of all transactions)
3. Legal and eDiscovery needs (support for any forensic investigation)
4. Data privacy (meeting privacy laws as per region)
5. Geography (restrictions on geography imposed by organisations/governments)

The expectation from the standards is to enable the cloud meet all the above-listed requirements.

5.5.2   Initiatives – Focus, Sponsors and Status

There are very few guidelines focused on GRC. The Cloud Security Alliance [19] discussed in Security standards also covers the aspects of GRC and is the only industry initiative. Table 5.7 shows the vendor initiatives only.

Table 5.7 Governance, risk and compliance – vendor initiatives

Standard/ product name	Group/body	Focus	Readiness
WebLayers Center 5.0 [32]	WebLayers [33]	To provide automated governance software with a central policy management feature to enforce policies and detect violations across all service life-cycle stages as well as across different infrastructures.	Available for use
Cloud-Ready Server Templates [28]	RightScale [29]	To provide server deployment templates for the cloud with the server configuration and policies pre-defined, thus ensuring governance and compliance	Available for use

5.5.3   Market Adoption

As seen from Table 5.7, there is only one initiative that is focused on GRC. This initiative also has not yet seen large-scale adoption. Furthermore, the initiatives from vendors are not yet standardised.

5.5.4   Gaps/Areas of Improvement

Given the importance of this focus area for an organisation to successfully and safely conduct its business with its system on the cloud, there seems to be a dearth of standards.

5.6   Deep Dive: Other Key Standards

5.6.1   Initiatives – Focus, Sponsors and Status

Apart from standards classified under interoperability, security, portability and governance and compliance, there are some key standards that are worth tracking. They focus either on other areas such as modelling, architecture frameworks or a broad support movement towards a cloud with open standards (Table 5.8).

Table 5.8 Other key standards – Group initiatives

Standard name	Group/body	Focus	Readiness
Open Cloud	Open Cloud Manifesto [34]	To support movement towards building a cloud with open standards	Initial Goals and Principles defined
OMG collaboration [35]	Object Management Group (OMG) [36]	To collaborate with other leading standards body to coordinate and communicate standards for cloud computing and storage	Formed in July 2009
Multiple standards	Organisation for the Advancement of Structured Information Standards (OASIS) [37]	Cloud as a natural extension of SOA. Standards already in place for security, interoperability, data import/export, etc. e.g., OASIS SAML, ebXML, SOA-RM	Available for use

5.7   Closing Notes

Standardisation historically has been a challenge. Getting competitors to agree on
standards or switch to another vendor's standards is tough. However, drive by powerful standards, organisations such as DMTF, SNIA, etc., with backing from industry
leaders, can definitely make it possible whilst avoiding excessive proliferation. The
aim should be to extend the IT standards to address the new scenarios that cloud
brings in and not create fresh standards making its definition and adoption tougher.

References

1. IT Cloud Services User Survey by IDC (2009) http://blogs.idc.com/ie/?p=210. Accessed 11
   Dec 2009
2. PCI Data Security Standard (2009) https://www.pcisecuritystandards.org/security_standards/
   pci_dss.shtml. Accessed 11 Dec 2009
3. Porting on Wikipedia (2009) http://en.wikipedia.org/wiki/Portability_(computer_science).
   Accessed 11 Dec 2009
4. Sarbanes-Oxley (SOX) on Wikipedia (2009) http://en.wikipedia.org/wiki/
   Sarbanes%E2%80%93Oxley_Act. Accessed 11 Dec 2009
5. HIPAA on Wikipedia (2009) http://en.wikipedia.org/wiki/HIPAA. Accessed 11 Dec 2009
6. Unified Cloud Interface (2009) http://code.google.com/p/unifiedcloud/. Accessed 11 Dec 2009
7. CCIF (2009) http://www.cloudforum.org/. Accessed 11 Dec 2009
8. OCCI (2009) http://www.occi-wg.org/doku.php. Accessed 11 Dec 2009
9. OGF (2009) http://www.ogf.org/. Accessed 11 Dec 2009
10. Open Virtualization Format Specification (2009) http://www.dmtf.org/standards/published_
    documents/DSP0243_1.0.0 .pdf. Accessed 11 Dec 2009
11. DMTF (2009) http://www.dmtf.org. Accessed 11 Dec 2009
12. Standards and Interoperability of Large Data Clouds (2009). http://opencloudconsortium.org/
    working-groups. Accessed 11 Dec 2009
13. Open Cloud Consortium (2009) http://opencloudconsortium.org/. Accessed 11 Dec 2009
14. GoGrid Moves API Specification to Creativecommons (2009) http://www.gogrid.com/com-
    pany/press-releases/gogrid-moves-api-specification-to-creativecommons.php. Accessed 11
    Dec 2009
15. GoGrid (2009) http://www.gogrid.com/. Accessed 11 Dec 2009
16. Cloudware Open Architecture (2009) http://www.3tera.com/Cloud-computing/. Accessed 11
    Dec 2009
17. 3Tera (2009) http://www.3tera.com/. Accessed 11 Dec 2009
18. Gartner Says Cloud Consumers Need Brokerages to Unlock the Potential of Cloud Services
    (2009) http://www.gartner.com/it/page.jsp?id=1064712. Accessed 11 Dec 2009
19. Cloud Security Alliance Guidelines (2009) http://www.cloudsecurityalliance.org/guidance/
    csaguide.pdf. Accessed 11 Dec 2009
20. Cloud Security Alliance (2009) http://www.cloudsecurityalliance.org/. Accessed 11 Dec 2009
21. Amazon VPC (2009) http://aws.amazon.com/vpc/. Accessed 11 Dec 2009
22. Amazon Web Services (2009) http://aws.amazon.com/. Accessed 11 Dec 2009
23. Securing Microsoft Cloud Infrastructure (2009) http://www.globalfoundationservices.com/
    security/index.html. Accessed 11 Dec 2009
24. Microsoft Cloud Computing (2009) http://www.microsoft.com/virtualization/cloud-computing/
    default.mspx. Accessed 11 Dec 2009

25. Amazon Web Services: Overview of Security Processes (2009) http://aws.amazon.com/. Accessed 11 Dec 2009
26. Cloud Storage Initiative (2009) http://www.snia.org/forums/csi/. Accessed 11 Dec 2009
27. Storage Networking Industry Assoc (SNIA) (2009) http://www.snia.org/. Accessed 11 Dec 2009
28. Cloud-Ready Server Templates (2009) http://www.rightscale.com/products/advantages/cloud-ready-servertemplates.php. Accessed 11 Dec 2009
29. RightScale website (2009) http://www.rightscale.com/. Accessed 11 Dec 2009
30. Open Cloud Platform (2009) http://www.sun.com/solutions/cloudcomputing/index.jsp. Accessed 11 Dec 2009
31. Sun Microsystems website (2009) http://www.sun.com/. Accessed 11 Dec 2009
32. WebLayers Center 5.0. (2009) http://www.weblayers.com/products/wl-center.shtml. Accessed 11 Dec 2009
33. WebLayers (2009) http://www.weblayers.com/. Accessed 11 Dec 2009
34. Open Cloud Manifesto (2009) http://www.opencloudmanifesto.org/. Accessed 11 Dec 2009
35. J. Nicholas Hoover (2009), Group Seeks Cloud Computing Standards (2009) http://www.informationweek.com/news/government/cloud-saas/showArticle.jhtml?articleID=218500732. Accessed 11 Dec 2009
36. Object Management Group (OMG) (2009) http://www.omg.org/. Accessed 11 Dec 2009
37. OASIS (2009) http://www.oasis-open.org/. Accessed 11 Dec 2009

Part II
Cloud Seeding

Chapter 6
Open and Interoperable Clouds: The Cloud@Home Way

Vincenzo D. Cunsolo, Salvatore Distefano, Antonio Puliafito, and Marco Scarpa

Abstract Cloud computing focuses on the idea of *service* as the elementary unit for building any application. Even though Cloud computing was originally developed in commercial applications, the paradigm is quickly and widely spreading in open contexts such as scientific and academic communities. Two main research directions can thus be identified: provide an *open* Cloud infrastructure able to provide and share resources and services to the community; and implement an *interoperable* framework, allowing commercial and open Cloud infrastructures to interact and interoperate. In this chapter, we present the *Cloud@Home* paradigm that proposes to merge *Volunteer* and Cloud computing as an effective and feasible solution for building open and interoperable Clouds. In this new paradigm, users' hosts are not passive interfaces to Cloud services anymore, but can interact (for free or by charge) with other Clouds, which therefore must be able to interoperate.

6.1 Introduction and Motivation

Cloud computing is a distributed computing paradigm that mixes aspects of *Grid computing, Internet computing, Autonomic computing, Utility computing,* and *Green computing.* Cloud computing is derived from the *service-centric perspective* that is quickly and widely spreading in the IT world. From this perspective, all capabilities and resources of a Cloud (usually geographically distributed) are provided to the users *as a service*, to be accessed through the Internet without any specific knowledge of, expertise with, or control over the underlying technology infrastructure that supports them.

Cloud computing offers a user-centric interface that acts as a unique, user friendly, point of access for users' needs and requirements. Moreover, it provides

---

V.D. Cunsolo (✉), S. Distefano, A. Puliafito, and M. Scarpa
University of Messina, Contrada di Dio, 98166, S. Agata, Messina, Italy
e-mail: vdcunsolo@unime.it; sdistefano@unime.it; apuliafito@unime.it;mscarpa@unime.it

N. Antonopoulos and L. Gillam (eds.), *Cloud Computing: Principles,*
Systems and Applications, Computer Communications and Networks,
DOI 10.1007/978-1-84996-241-4_6, © Springer-Verlag London Limited 2010

on-demand service provision, *QoS guaranteed offer*, and *autonomous system* for managing hardware, software, and data transparency to the users [25].

In order to achieve such goals, it is necessary to implement a level of abstraction of physical resources, uniforming their interfaces, and providing means for their management, adaptively, to user requirements. This is done through *virtualizations*, *service mashups* (Web 2.0), and *service-oriented architectures* (SOA). These factors make the Kleinrock outlook of computing as the fifth utility [13], following gas, water, electricity, and telephone.

Virtualization [4,23] allows execution of a software version of a hardware machine in a host system in an isolated way. It "homogenizes" resources: problems of compatibility are overcome by providing heterogeneous hosts of a distributed computing environment (the Cloud) using the same virtual machine software.

Web 2.0 [20] provides an interesting way to interface Cloud services, implementing service mashups. It is mainly based on an evolution of JavaScript with improved language constructs (late binding, closures, lambda functions, etc.) and AJAX interactions.

SOA is a paradigm for organizing and utilizing distributed capabilities that may be under the control of different ownership domains [14]. In SOA, *services* are the mechanism by which needs and capabilities are brought together. SOA defines standard interfaces and protocols that allow developers to encapsulate information tools as services that clients can access without the knowledge of, or control over, their internal workings [8].

An interesting attempt to fix Cloud concepts and ideas is provided in [26] through an ontology that demonstrates a dissection of the Cloud into the five main layers shown in Fig. 6.1. In this, higher layers services can be composed from the services of the underlying layers, which are:

1. *Cloud Application Layer:* provides interface and access-management tools (Web 2.0, authentication, billing, SLA, etc.), specific application services, services mashup tools, etc. to the Cloud end users. This model is referred to as Software as a Service (SaaS).

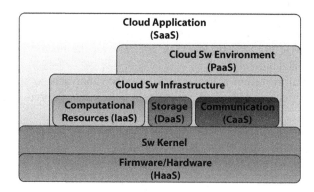

Fig. 6.1 The five main layers of Cloud

2. *Cloud Software Environment Layer*: providers of the Cloud software environments supply the users and Cloud applications' developers with a programming-language-level environment with a set of well-defined APIs. The services provided by this layer are referred to as Platform as a Service (PaaS).
3. *Cloud Software Infrastructure Layer*: provides fundamental resources to other higher-level layers. Services can be categorized into:

   (a) *Computational resources* – provides computational resources (VM) to Cloud end users. Often, such services are dubbed Infrastructure as a Service (IaaS).
   (b) *Data storage* – allows users to store their data at remote disks and access them anytime from any place. These services are commonly known as Data-Storage as a Service (DaaS).
   (c) *Communications* – provides some communication capabilities that are service-oriented, configurable, schedulable, predictable, and reliable. The concept of Communication as a Service (CaaS) emerged toward this goal, to support such requirements.

OAP and REST are examples of interface protocols used with some Cloud computational resources.

4. *Software Kernel*: provides the basic software management for the physical servers that comprise the Cloud. OS kernel, hypervisor, virtual machine monitor, clustering, grid middleware, etc.
5. Hardware and Firmware: form the backbone of the Cloud. End users directly interacting with the Cloud at this layer have huge IT requirements in need of subleasing Hardware as a Service (HaaS).

Great interest in Cloud computing has been manifested from both academic and private research centers, and numerous projects from industry and academia have been proposed. In commercial contexts, among the others, we highlight: Amazon Elastic Compute Cloud, IBM's Blue Cloud, Sun Microsystems Network.com, Microsoft Azure Services Platform, Dell Cloud computing solutions, etc. There are also several scientific activities driving toward Open Cloud-computing middlewares and infrastructures, such as: Reservoir [18], Nimbus-Stratus-Wispy-Kupa [22], OpenNebula [7], Eucalyptus [17], etc. All of them support and provide an on-demand computing paradigm, in the sense that a user submits his/her requests to the Cloud, which remotely, in a distributed fashion, processes them and gives back the results. This client–server model fits the aims and scope of commercial Clouds: the business. But, on the other hand, it represents a restriction for open/scientific Clouds, requiring great amounts of computing-storage resources usually not available from a single open/scientific community. This suggests the necessity to collect such resources from different providers and/or contributors who could share their resources with the specific community, perhaps by making "symbiotic" federations. In fact, one of the most successful paradigms in such contexts is *Volunteer computing*.

Volunteer computing (also called *Peer-to-Peer computing, Global computing,* or *Public computing*) uses computers volunteered by their owners as a source of computing power and storage to provide distributed scientific computing [2].

It is the basis of the *"@home"* philosophy of sharing/donating network connected resources for supporting distributed scientific computing.

We believe that the Cloud-computing paradigm is also applicable at lower scales, from the single contributing user who shares his/her desktop, to research groups, public administrations, social communities, and small and medium enterprises, who can make their distributed computing resources available to the Cloud. Both free sharing and pay-per-use models can be easily adopted in such scenarios.

From the utility point of view, the rise of the "techno-utility complex" and the corresponding increase in computing resource demands, in some cases growing dramatically faster than Moore's Law, predicted by the Sun CTO Greg Papadopoulos in the *red shift theory* for IT [15], could take us in a close future, toward an *oligarchy*, a lobby or a trust of few big companies controlling the whole computing resources market.

To avoid such a pessimistic but achievable scenario, we suggest addressing the problem in a different way: instead of building costly private *data centers* that the Google CEO, Eric Schmidt, likes to compare with the prohibitively expensive cyclotrons [3], we propose a more "democratic" form of Cloud computing, in which the computing resources of single users accessing the Cloud can be shared with others in order to contribute to the elaboration of complex problems.

As this paradigm is very similar to the Volunteer computing one, it can be named as *Cloud@Home*. Both hardware and software compatibility limitations and restrictions of Volunteer computing can be solved in Cloud computing environments, allowing to share both hardware and software resources and/or *services*.

The Cloud@Home paradigm could also be applied to commercial Clouds, establishing an *open computing-utility market* where users can both buy and sell their services. Since the computing power can be described by a "long-tailed" distribution, in which a high-amplitude population (Cloud providers and commercial data centers) is followed by a low-amplitude population (small data centers and private users) that gradually "tails off" asymptotically, Cloud@Home can catch the *Long Tail* effect [1], providing similar or higher computing capabilities than commercial providers' data centers, by grouping small computing resources from many single contributors.

In the following, we demonstrate how it is possible to realize all these aims through the Cloud@Home paradigm. In Section 2, we describe the functional architecture of the Cloud@Home infrastructure, and in Section 3, we characterize the blocks implementing the functions previously identified into the Cloud@Home core structure. Section 4 concludes the chapter by recapitulating our work and discussing challenges and future work.

6.2 Cloud@Home Overview

The idea behind Cloud@Home is to reuse *"domestic"* computing resources to build voluntary contributors' Clouds that are interoperable and, moreover, interoperate with other foreign, and also commercial, Cloud infrastructures. With Cloud@Home, anyone can experience the power of Cloud computing, both actively by providing his/her own resources and services, and passively by submitting his/her applications and requirements.

6.2.1 Issues, Challenges, and Open Problems

Ian Foster summarizes the computing paradigm of the future as follows [9]: "... we will need to support on-demand provisioning and configuration of integrated 'virtual systems' providing the precise capabilities needed by an end user. We will need to define protocols that allow users and service providers to discover and hand off demands to other providers, to monitor and manage their reservations, and arrange payment. We will need tools for managing both the underlying resources and the resulting distributed computations. We will need the centralized scale of today's Cloud utilities, and the distribution and interoperability of today's Grid facilities...."

We share all these requirements, but in a slightly different way: we want to actively involve users into such a new form of computing, allowing them to create their own interoperable Clouds. In other words, we believe that it is possible to export, apply, and adapt the *"@home"* philosophy to the Cloud-computing paradigm. In this way, by merging Volunteer and Cloud computing, a new paradigm can be created: *Cloud@Home*. This new computing paradigm gives back the power and control to users, who can decide how to manage their resources/services in a global, geographically distributed context. They can voluntarily sustain scientific projects by freely placing their resources/services at the scientific research centers' disposal, or can earn money by selling their resources to Cloud-computing providers in a pay-per-use/share context.

Therefore, in Cloud@Home, both the commercial/business and volunteer/scientific viewpoints coexist: in the former case, the end-user orientation of Cloud is extended to a collaborative two-way Cloud in which users can buy and/or sell their resources/services; in the latter case, the Grid philosophy of few but large computing requests is extended and enhanced to *open* Virtual Organizations. In both cases, QoS requirements could be specified, introducing in to the Grid and Volunteer philosophy (*best effort*) the concept of quality.

Cloud@Home can also be considered as a generalization and a maturation of the @home philosophy: a context in which users voluntarily share their resources without compatibility problems. This allows knocking down both hardware (processor bits, endianness, architecture, and network) and software (operating systems, libraries, compilers, applications, and middlewares) barriers of Grid and Volunteer computing. Moreover, Cloud@Home allows users to share not only physical resources, as in @home projects or Grid environments, but any kind of service. The *flexibility* and *extensibility* of Cloud@Home can allow to easily arrange, manage, and make available with significant computing resources (greater than those in Clouds, Grids, and/or @home environments) to everyone who owns a computer. Another significant improvement of Cloud@Home with regard to Volunteer computing paradigms is the QoS/SLA management: starting from the credit management system and other similar experiments on QoS, a mechanism for adequately monitoring, ensuring, negotiating, accounting, billing, and managing, in general, QoS and SLA will be implemented.

On the other hand, Cloud@Home can be considered as the enhancement of the Grid-Utility vision of Cloud computing. In this new paradigm, user's hosts are not passive interfaces to Cloud services, but can be actively involved in computing. At worst, single nodes and services could be enrolled by the Cloud@Home middleware to build own-private Cloud infrastructures that can with interact with other Clouds.

The Cloud@Home motto is: *heterogeneous hardware for homogeneous Clouds.* Thus, the scenario we prefigure is composed of several coexisting and interoperable Clouds, as depicted in Fig. 6.2. *Open Clouds* (yellow) identify open VO operating for free Volunteer computing; *Commercial Clouds* (blue) characterize entities or companies selling their computing resources for business; and *Hybrid Clouds* (green) can both sell or give for free their services. Both Open and Hybrid Clouds can interoperate with any other Clouds, as well as Commercial, while these latter can interoperate if and only if the Commercial Clouds are mutually *recognized*. In this way, it is possible to make *federations* of heterogeneous Clouds that can work together on the same project. Such a scenario has to be implemented transparently for users who do not want to know whether their applications are running in homogeneous or heterogeneous Clouds. The differences among homogeneous and heterogeneous Clouds are only concerned with implementation issues, mainly affecting the resource management: in the former case, resources are managed locally to the Cloud; in heterogeneous Clouds, interoperable services have to be implemented in order to support discovery, connectivity, translation, and negotiation requirements amongst Clouds.

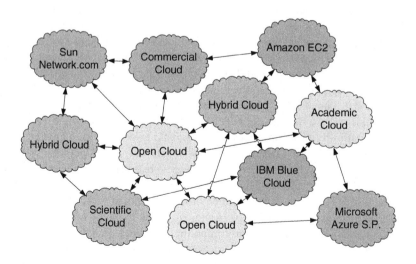

Fig. 6.2 Co-existing and interoperable Clouds anticipated for the Cloud@Home Scenario

The overall infrastructure must deal with the high dynamism of its nodes/resources, allowing to move and reallocate data, tasks, and jobs. It is therefore necessary to implement a lightweight middleware, specifically designed to optimize migrations. The choice of developing such middleware on existing technologies (as done in Nimbus-Stratus starting from Globus) could be limiting, inefficient, or not adequate from this point of view. This represents another significant enhancement of Cloud@Home against Grid: a lightweight middleware allows to involve limited resources' devices into the Cloud, mainly as consumer hosts accessing the Cloud through "thin client" but also, in some specific applications, as contributing hosts implementing (light) services according to their availabilities. Moreover, the Cloud@Home middleware does not influence code writing as Grid and Volunteer computing paradigms do.

Another important goal of Cloud@Home is *security*. Volunteer computing has security concerns, while the Grid paradigm implements complex security mechanisms. Virtualization in Clouds implements isolation of services, but does not provide any protection from local access. With regard to security, the specific goal of Cloud@Home is to extend the security mechanisms of Clouds to the protection of data from local access. As Cloud@Home is composed of an amount of resources potentially larger than commercial or proprietary Cloud solutions, its *reliability* can be compared with Grid or the Volunteer computing and should be greater than other Clouds.

Lastly, *interoperability* is one of the most important goals of Cloud@Home. This is an open problem in Grid, Volunteer, and Cloud computing, which we want to address in Cloud@Home.

The most important issues that should be taken into account in order to implement such a form of computing can be listed as follows:

- *Resources and Services management* – a mechanism for managing resources and services offered by Clouds is mandatory. This must be able to enroll, discover, index, assign and reassign, monitor, and coordinate resources and services. A problem to face at this level is the compatibility among resources and services and their portability.
- *Frontend* – abstraction is needed in order to provide users with a high-level service-oriented point of view of the computing system. The frontend provides a unique, uniform access point to the Cloud. It must allow users to submit functional computing requests, only providing requirements and specifications, without any knowledge of the system-resources deployment. The system evaluates such requirements and specifications, and translates them into physical resource demands, deploying the elaboration process. Another aspect concerning the frontend is the capability of customizing Cloud services and applications.
- *Security* – effective mechanisms are required to provide authentication, resources and data protection, data confidentiality, and integrity.
- *Resource and service accessibility, reliability, and data consistency* – it is necessary to implement redundancy of resources and services, and hosts' recovery policies because users voluntarily contribute to the computing, and therefore, can asynchronously, at any time, log out or disconnect from the Cloud.

- *Interoperability among Clouds* – it should be possible for Clouds to interoperate.
- *Business models* – for selling Cloud computing, it is mandatory to provide QoS and SLA management for both commercial and open-volunteer Clouds (traditionally best effort) to discriminate among the applications to be run.

6.2.2   Basic Architecture

A possible Cloud@Home architecture that could address the issues listed earlier is shown in Fig. 6.3, which has been adapted to the ontology provided in [26] and reported in Fig. 6.1. Two types of users are distinguished in such an architecture according to the role that they assume in the Cloud: *end users*, if they only interface the Cloud for submitting requests, and/or *contributing users* if they make available their resources and services for building up and supporting the Cloud. According to this point of view, the Cloud is composed of several *contributing hosts* offered by the corresponding contributing users to end users who interact with the Cloud and submit their requests through their *consumer hosts*. To access a Cloud, both contributing and end users must authenticate themselves into the system. One of the main enhancements of Cloud@Home is that a user/host can be contributing and/or end user/consumer host, establishing a symbiotic mutual interaction with the Cloud.

Such an architecture will be described below by identifying and detailing tasks and functions of each of the five layers characterized in the Cloud ontology presented in Section 1.

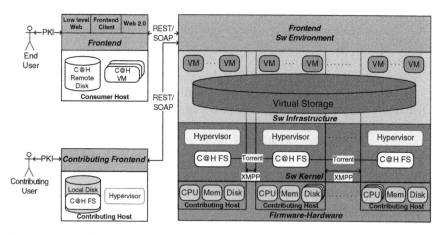

Fig. 6.3   Basic architecture of Cloud@Home

6.2.2.1 Software Environment

The Cloud@Home software environment implements the user-infrastructure frontend interface. It is responsible for the resources and services management (enrolling, discovery, allocation, coordination, monitoring, scheduling, etc.) from the global Cloud system's perspective. It also provides tools, libraries, and APIs for translating user requirements into physical resource demands. Moreover, in commercial Clouds, it must be able to negotiate the QoS policy to be applied (SLA), thus monitoring for its fulfillment and, in case of unsatisfactory results, adapting the computing workflow to such QoS requirements.

If the Cloud's available resources and services do not satisfy the requirements, the frontend provides mechanisms for requesting further resources and services from other Clouds, both open and/or commercial. In other words, the Cloud@ Home frontend implements the interoperability among Clouds, also checking for service reliability and availability. To improve reliability and availability of services and resources, especially if QoS policies and constraints have been specified, it is necessary to replicate services and resources by introducing redundancy.

The Cloud@Home software environment is split into two parts, as shown in Fig. 6.3: the server side, implementing resource management and related problems, and the client side, providing mechanisms and tools for authenticating, enrolling, accessing, and interacting with the Cloud services and resources. The client frontend is distinguished according to the role assumed by the user/host: for end users, only a *thin* client able to interact with the frontend server and to submit requests to the Cloud must be installed into the consumer hosts; for contributing users, contributing hosts must provide the software for interfacing with the Cloud@Home frontend server and for supporting the Cloud (C@H FS library, storage space, and/or hypervisor according to the service supported).

In a widely distributed system that is globally spread, the knowledge of resource accesses and uses assumes great importance. To access and/or use the Cloud services, a generic user first authenticates him/herself and then specifies whether he/she wants to make available his/her resources and services for sharing, or he/she only uses the Cloud resources for computing. The frontend provides means, tools, and policies for managing users. The best mechanism to achieve secure authentication is the *Public Key Infrastructure* (PKI) [21], better if combined with smartcard devices that, through a trusted certification authority, ensure user identification. In order to avoid multiple authentications, a mechanism of authentication management and credential delegation, such as *single sign-on* (SSO), must be provided by the server frontend.

Referring to Fig. 6.3, three alternative solutions can be offered to end users by the software environment for accessing a Cloud: (a) Cloud@Home frontend client, (b) Web 2.0 user interface, and (c) low-level Web interface (directly specifying REST or SOAP queries). These also provide mechanisms for customizing user applications by composing (service mashup and SOA) and submitting own services.

6.2.2.2 Software Infrastructure

The virtualization of physical resources offers a homogeneous view of Cloud's services and resources to end users. Two basic services are provided by the software infrastructure to the software environment, and consequently, to end users: *execution* and *storage* services.

The execution service, implementing the computational resources sublayer of Fig. 6.1, allows to create and manage virtual machines. A user, sharing his/her resources within a Cloud@Home, allows the other users of the Cloud to execute and manage virtual machines locally at his/her node, according to policies and constraints negotiated and monitored through the software environment. In this way, a Cloud of virtual machine's executors is established, where virtual machines can migrate or can be replicated in order to achieve reliability, availability, and QoS targets. As shown in Fig. 6.3, from the end user's point of view, an execution Cloud is seen as a set of virtual machines available and ready-to-use. The virtual machines' *isolation* implements protection and therefore security. This security is ensured by the hypervisor that runs the virtual machine's code in an isolated scope, similarly to a sandbox, without affecting the local host environment.

The storage service implements a storage system distributed across the storage hardware resources composing the Cloud, highly independent of them because data and files are replicated according to QoS policies and requirements to be satisfied. From the end user's point of view, a storage Cloud appears as a locally mounted remote disk, similar to a Network File System or a Network Storage. Tools, libraries, and API for interfacing to storage Clouds are provided by the frontend client to end users, while the service is implemented by the Cloud@Home software infrastructure and software kernel.

In a distributed environment where any user can host a part of private data, it is necessary to protect such data from unauthorized accesses (data security). A way to obtain data *confidentiality* and *integrity* could be cryptography, as better explained in the software kernel description.

6.2.2.3 Software Kernel

The software kernel provides infrastructure, mechanisms, and tools to the software for locally managing the physical resources of the Cloud in order to implement execution and storage services.

Cloud@Home negotiates with users who want to join a Cloud about his/her contribution. This mechanism involves the software kernel that provides tools for reserving execution and/or storage resources for the Cloud, and monitors these resources so that constraints, requirements, and policies specified are not violated. This ensures reliability and availability of the resources, avoiding overloading of the local system and therefore reducing the risk of crashes.

To implement the execution service in a generic device or to enroll it into an execution Cloud, the device must have a hypervisor ready to allocate and run virtual machines, as shown in Fig. 6.3 . If a storage service is installed into the device, a portion of the local storage system must be dedicated for hosting the Cloud data. In such cases, the Cloud@Home file system is installed into the devices' shared storage space.

The software kernel also implements data security (integrity and confidentiality), ensuring that stored data cannot be accessed by those who physically host them (*insider attacks, identity thefts, account hijacking*, etc.). We propose an approach that combines the inviolability of the Public Key Infrastructure asymmetric cryptography and the speed of symmetric cryptography (details in [6]). Data are first encrypted by the symmetric key and then stored into the selected host with the symmetric key encrypted by the user private key. This ensures that only authorized users can decrypt the symmetric key and consequently access the data.

In order to implement secure and reliable connections amongst nodes, we choose the *Extensible Messaging and Presence Protocol* (XMPP) protocol [19]. XMPP is an open technology for real-time communication, which powers a wide range of applications including instant messaging, presence, multi-party chat, voice and video calls, collaboration, lightweight middleware, content syndication, and generalized routing of XML data, also supporting security features. However, as the data stored in a Cloud@Home storage are encrypted, it is not necessary to use a secure channel for data transfers, and hence, a more performant protocol, such as BitTorrent [5] can be used. The XMPP secure channel is required for sending and receiving nonencrypted messages and data to/from remote hosts.

6.2.2.4 Firmware/Hardware

The Cloud@Home firmware/hardware layer is composed of a *"cloud"* of generic contributing nodes and/or devices geographically distributed across the Internet. They provide the physical-hardware resources to the upper layers for implementing the execution and storage services.

6.2.3 *Application Scenarios*

Several possible application scenarios can be imagined for Cloud@Home:

- *Research centers, public administrations, and communities* – the Volunteer computing inspiration of Cloud@Home provides means for the creation of open, interoperable Clouds for supporting scientific purposes, overcoming the portability and compatibility problems highlighted by the @home projects. Similar benefits could be experienced in public administrations and open communities (social networks, peer-to-peer, gaming, etc). Through Cloud@ Home, it could be possible to implement resources and service management policies with QoS requirements (characterizing the scientific project importance) and specifications (QoS classification of resources and services available). A new deal for Volunteer computing, since this latter does not take into consideration QoS, follows a best effort approach.

- *Enterprises* – planting a Cloud@Home computing infrastructure in business-commercial environments can bring considerable benefits, especially in small and medium, as well as big enterprises. Usually, in every enterprise, there exists a capital of stand-alone computing resources dedicated to a specific task (office automation, monitoring, designing, and so on). Since such resources are only (partially) used in office hours, through Internet connectivity, it becomes possible to build up a Cloud@Home data center, in which shared services are allocated (web server, file server, archive, database, etc.) without any compatibility constraints or problems.

- The interoperability amongst Clouds allows to buy computing resources from commercial Cloud providers if needed or, otherwise, to sell the local Cloud computing resources to the same or different providers. This allows reducing and optimizing business costs according to QoS/SLA policies, improving performances and reliability. For example, this paradigm allows dealing with the *peaks economy*: data centers could be sized for managing the medium case, and worst cases (peaks) could be managed by buying computing resources from Cloud providers. Moreover, Cloud@Home drives towards resource rationalization: all the business processes can be securely managed over the web, allocating resources and services where needed. In particular, this can improve marketing and trading (E-commerce), making available a lot of customizable services to sellers and customers. The interoperability could also point to another scenario, in which private companies buy computing resources in order to resell them (*subcontractors*).

- *Ad-hoc networks, wireless sensor networks, and home automation* – the Cloud-computing approach, in which both software and computing resources are owned and managed by service providers, eases the programmers' efforts in facing device heterogeneity problems. Mobile application designers should start to consider that their applications, besides needing to be usable on a small device, will need to interact with the Cloud. Service discovery, brokering, and reliability are important issues, and services are usually designed to interoperate. In order to consider the arising consequences related to the access of mobile users to service-oriented grid architecture, researchers have proposed new concepts such as mobile dynamic virtual organizations [24].

- An open research issue is whether or not a mobile device should be considered as a service provider of the Cloud itself. The use of modern mobile terminals, such as smart-phones, not just as Web service requestor but also as mobile hosts that can themselves offer services in a true mobile peer-to-peer setting, is also discussed in [16]. Context-aware operations involving control and monitoring, data sharing, synchronization, etc, could be implemented and exposed as Cloud@Home Web services. Cloud@Home could be a way to implement *Ubiquitous* and *Pervasive* computing: many computational devices and systems can be engaged simultaneously for performing ordinary activities, and may not necessarily be aware of the fact that they are doing so.

6.3 Cloud@Home Core Structure

Once the functional architecture of Cloud@Home has been introduced, it is necessary to characterize the blocks implementing the functions thus identified. These blocks are pictorially depicted in the layered model of Fig. 6.4 that reports the core structure of the overall system implementing the Cloud@Home server-side. As done for the functional architecture, the core structure is also specified by following the Cloud ontology characterized in Fig. 6.1. Moreover, the Cloud@Home core structure is subdivided into two subsystems: *management* and *resource subsystems*. Such subsystems are strictly interconnected: the management subsystem implements the upper layer of the functional architecture, while the resource subsystem implements the lower level functionalities.

Figure 6.5 pictorially depicts the deployment of the Cloud@Home core structure into the physical infrastructure. Such implementation highlights the hierarchical-distributed approach of Cloud@Home. On top of the hierarchy, there are the blocks implementing the management subsystem that can be deployed into different servers/nodes, one for each block, or can be grouped into the same node. Nevertheless, in order to achieve reliability and availability goals, it is necessary to adequately

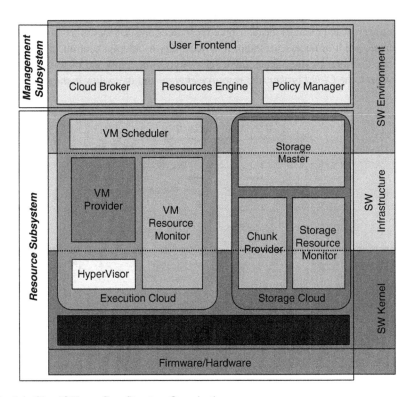

Fig. 6.4 Cloud@Home Core Structure Organisation

replicate such nodes, in particular if all the management subsystem blocks are deployed into the same unique node.

VM schedulers and storage masters manage smaller groups (grid, clusters, multi-core nodes, etc.) of resources. They can be designated both globally by the management subsystem and/or locally by applying self-organizing/autonomic algorithms such as election mechanisms. A VM scheduler and a storage master can be deployed into the same node/server, while, obviously, two or more VM schedulers/storage masters cannot coexist in the same node. For reliability/availability purpose, they can also be replicated and/or hierarchically organized.

At the bottom of the hierarchy, there are the contributing hosts. Each contains the software for supporting the specific service for what was enrolled into the Cloud. Thus, a node contributing to the execution Cloud has a hypervisor, a VM provider, and a VM resource monitor, while a storage Cloud contributing host has a chunk provider and a storage resource monitor. As shown in Fig. 6.4 and also stated earlier, it is possible that the same host contributes to both execution and storage Clouds, and therefore, has both execution and storage components.

6.3.1   Management Subsystem

In order to enroll and manage the distributed resources and services of a Cloud, providing a unique point of access for them, it is necessary to adopt a centralized approach that is implemented by the management subsystem. It is composed of four parts: the *user frontend*, the *Cloud broker*, the *resource engine,* and the *policy manager*.

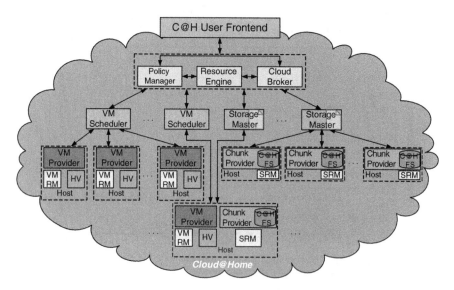

Fig. 6.5 Cloud@Home Core Structure Infrastructure Deployment.

The user frontend provides tools for Cloud@Home-user interactions. It collects and manages the users' requests issued by the Cloud@Home clients. All such requests are transferred to the blocks composing the underlying layer (resource engine, Cloud broker, and policy manager) for processing.

An important task carried out by the user frontend is the Clouds interoperability, implemented point-to-point, connecting the interface of the Clouds wishing to interoperate. If one of the Clouds does not have the Cloud@Home core structure of Fig. 6.3, it is necessary to translate the requests between Cloud@Home and foreign Clouds formats, a task delegated by the user frontend to the Cloud broker. The Cloud broker collects and manages information about the available Clouds and the services they provide (both *functional* and *non-functional* parameters, such as QoS, costs, and reliability, *request formats' specifications* for Cloud@Home-foreign Cloud translations, etc.).

The policy manager provides and implements the Cloud's access facilities. This task falls into the security scope of identification, authentication, authorization, and permissions management. To achieve this target, the policy manager uses an infrastructure based on PKI, smartcard devices, Certification Authority, and SSO. The policy manager also manages the information about users' QoS policies and requirements.

The resource engine is the heart of Cloud@Home. It is responsible for the resources' management, the equivalent of a Grid *resource broker* in a broader Cloud environment. To meet this goal, the resource engine applies a hierarchical policy. It operates at a higher level, in a centralized way, indexing all the resources of the Cloud. Incoming requests are delegated to *VM schedulers* or *storage masters* that, in a distributed fashion, manage the computing or storage resources, respectively, coordinated by the resource engine.

The management subsystem is implemented as a centralized subsystem managing the whole infrastructure. Although this solution introduces a single point of failure into the architecture, this is the only possible way to manage resource QoS, SLA, dynamic provisioning, and monitoring because there has to be a subsystem that aggregates information and has to know the condition of the whole infrastructure, there needs to be a coordinator. Reliability, availability, and fault-tolerance issues can be achieved by replicating the management subsystem and its components, adequately managing the consistency of redundant replicas.

6.3.2   Resource Subsystem

The resource subsystem contains all the blocks implementing the local and distributed management functionalities of Cloud@Home. This subsystem can be logically split into two parts offering different software infrastructure services: the *execution Cloud* and the *storage Cloud*. The management subsystem is also able to merge them, providing a unique Cloud that can offer both execution and/or storage services.

The execution Cloud provides tools for managing virtual machines according to users' requests and requirements coming from the management subsystem. It is composed of four blocks: *VM scheduler, VM provider, VM resource monitor,* and *hypervisor.*

The VM Scheduler is a peripheral resource broker of the Cloud@Home infrastructure, to which the resource engine delegates the management of computing/execution resources and services of the Cloud. It establishes which, what, where, and when to allocate a VM; moreover, it is responsible for moving and managing VM services. From the end user's point of view, a VM is allocated somewhere on the Cloud; therefore, its migration is transparent for the end user that is not aware of any VM migration mechanism. However, some problems can affect VM migrations into the Cloud@Home environment. As the nodes implementing the Cloud are, generally, widely distributed across the Internet, for migrating a VM with its entire context from one node to another (remote) node, great transfer delays are introduced. In a highly dynamic environment, where VM migrations could be highly frequent, this could become a serious problem.

A possible solution to such a problem is the introduction of technique-based difference algorithms, similar to the one implemented in the *union file system* (UnionFS) [27]. In each node contributing to the execution Cloud of the Cloud@ Home infrastructure, redundant basic VM images must be available (if possible). Thus, in case of migration, starting from the selected data/files comparison algorithm (diff), instead of transferring the whole VM with its context, a lighter (diff) file only containing the differences between a new VM and the one to migrate is sent to the destination host, which recomposes the original VM starting from a new VM instance and runs it. This technique can considerably reduce the amount of data to transfer, and consequently the corresponding transfer times.

Differentiation techniques might be appropriate for moving VM disk images (although they would require some fundamental restrictions to be placed on the images that could be used), but they do not address the problem of migrating VM memory state. Such a problem could be addressed by exploiting specific and advanced live migration techniques implementing reduced bandwidth usage, just-in-time live migration behavior, and live migration across WAN, mainly based on compression algorithms [11,12].

The VM provider, the VM resource monitor, and the hypervisor are responsible for managing a VM locally to a physical resource. A VM provider exports functions for allocating, managing, migrating, and destroying a virtual machine on the corresponding host. The VM resource monitor allows taking the local computing resources under control, according to requirements and constraints negotiated in the setup phase with the contributing user. If during a virtual machine execution, the local resources crash or become insufficient to keep the virtual machine running, the VM resource monitor asks the scheduler to migrate the VM elsewhere.

In order to implement the storage Cloud, we specify the *Cloud@Home file system* (FS), adopting an approach similar to the Google FS [10]. The Cloud@Home FS splits data and files into *chunks* of fixed or variable size, depending on the storage resources available. The architecture of the storage file system is hierarchical: data chunks are physically stored on *chunk providers* and corresponding *storage masters* index the chunks through specific *file indexes* (FI). The storage master is the directory server, indexing the data stored in the associated chunk providers. It directly interfaces with the resource engine to discover the resources storing data. In this context, the resource engine can be considered, in its turn, as the directory server indexing all the storage masters. To improve the storage Cloud reliability, storage masters must be replicated. Moreover, a chunk provider can be associated to more than one storage master.

In order to avoid a storage master becoming a bottleneck, once the chunk providers have been located, data transfers are implemented by directly connecting end users and chunk providers. Similar techniques to the ones discussed about VM schedulers can be applied to storage masters for improving performance and reliability of the storage Clouds.

Chunk providers physically store the data that, as introduced earlier, are encrypted to achieve the confidentiality goal. Data reliability can be improved by replicating data chunks and chunk providers, consequently updating the corresponding storage masters. In this way, a corrupted data chunk can be automatically recovered and restored through the storage masters, without involving the end user.

In order to achieve QoS/SLA requirements in a storage Cloud, it is necessary to periodically monitor its storage resources, as done in the execution Cloud for VM. For this reason, in the Cloud@Home core structure of Fig. 6.3, we have introduced a specific storage resource monitor block. As it monitors the state of a chunk provider, it is physically located and deployed into each chunk provider composing the storage Cloud. The choice of replicating the resource monitor in both execution and storage Clouds is motivated by the fact that we want to implement two different, separated, and independent services.

6.4   Conclusions

In this chapter, we have discussed an innovative computing paradigm merging volunteer contributing and Cloud approaches into Cloud@Home. This proposal represents a solution for building Clouds, starting from heterogeneous and independent nodes, not specifically conceived for this purpose. Cloud@Home implements a generalization of both Volunteer and Cloud computing by aggregating the computational potentialities of many small, low-power systems, exploiting the long-tail effect of computing.

In this way, Cloud@Home opens the Cloud computing world to scientific and academic research centers, as well as to public administration and communities, and potentially single users: anyone can voluntarily support projects by sharing his/her resources. On the other hand, it opens the utility computing market to the single user who wants to sell his/her computing resources. To realize this broader vision, several issues must be adequately taken into account: reliability, security, portability of resources and services, interoperability among Clouds, QoS/SLA, and business models and policies.

It is necessary to have a common understanding regarding an ontology that fixes concepts, such as resources, services, virtualization, protocol, format, interface, and corresponding metrics, including Clouds' functional and nonfunctional parameters (QoS, SLA, and so on), which must be translated into specific interoperable standards.

References

1. Anderson C. (2006) The long tail: how endless choice is creating unlimited demand. Random House Business Books, London
2. Anderson DP, Fedak G (2006) The computational and storage potential of volunteer computing. In: CCGRID '06, pp 73–80
3. Baker S (2008, December 24) Google and the wisdom of clouds. BusinessWeek. http://www.businessweek.com/magazine/content/07_52/b4064048925836.htm
4. Barham P, Dragovic B, Fraser K, Hand S, Harris T, Ho A, Neugebauer R, Pratt I, Warfield A (2003) Xen and the art of virtualization. In: Proceedings of the nineteenth ACM symposium on operating systems principles (SOSP '03), ACM, pp 164–177
5. Cohen B (2008) The BitTorrent protocol specification. BitTorrent.org. http://www.bittorrent.org/beps/bep_0003.html
6. Cunsolo VD, Distefano S, Puliafito A, Scarpa M (2009) Implementing data security in grid environment. Enabling technologies, IEEE international workshops on 0, pp 177–182
7. Distributed Systems Architecture Research Group: OpenNEbula Project [URL]. Universidad Complutense de Madrid (2009). http://www.opennebula.org/
8. Foster I (2005) Service-oriented science. Science 308(5723)
9. Foster I (2008) There's grid in them thar clouds. Ian Foster's blog. http://ianfoster.typepad.com/blog/2008/01/theres-grid-in.html
10. Ghemawat S, Gobioff H, Leung ST (2003) The google file system. SIGOPS Oper Syst Rev 37(5):29–43
11. Hacking S, Hudzia B (2009) Improving the live migration process of large enterprise applications. In: Proceedings of the 3rd international workshop on virtualization technologies in distributed computing (VTDC '09), ACM, pp 51–58
12. Jin H, Deng L, Wu S, Shi X, Pan X (2009) Live virtual machine migration with adaptive, memory compression. In: IEEE cluster computing and workshops (CLUSTER '09), pp 1–10
13. Kleinrock L (2005) A vision for the internet. ST J Res 2(1):4–5
14. MacKenzie CM, Laskey K, McCabe F, Brown PF, Metz R, Hamilton BA (2006) Reference model for service oriented architecture 1.0. http://docs.oasis-open.org/soa-rm/v1.0/
15. Martin R (2007, August 20) The red shift theory. InformationWeek. http://www.informationweek.com/news/hardware/showArticle.jhtml?articleID=201800873
16. Narayana SS, Jarke M, Prinz W (2006) Mobile web service provisioning. In: AICT-ICIW '06, IEEE Computer Society, p 120
17. Nurmi D, Wolski R, Grzegorczyk C, Obertelli G, Soman S, Youseff L, Zagorodnov D (2008) The eucalyptus open-source cloud-computing system. In: Proceedings of cloud computing and its applications (2008)
18. Reservoir Consortium: Reservoir Project [URL] (2009). http://www-03.ibm.com/press/us/en/pressrelease/23448.wss/
19. Saint-Andre P, Tronçon R, Smith K (2008) XMPP: the definitive guide: building real-time applications with jabber technologies, rough cuts version edn. O'Reilly
20. Tim O'Reilly: What is WEB 2.0 (2005). http://www.oreillynet.com/pub/a/oreilly/tim/news/2005/09/30/what-is-web-20.html

21. Tuecke S, Welch V, Engert D, Pearlman L, Thompson M (2004) Internet X.509 Public Key Infrastructure (PKI) proxy certificate profile
22. University of Chicago-University of Florida-Purdue University-Masaryk University: Nimbus-Stratus-Wispy-Kupa Projects [URL] (2009). http://workspace.globus.org/clouds/nimbus.html/, http://www.acis.ufl.edu/vws/, http://www.rcac.purdue.edu/teragrid/resources/#wispy, http://meta.cesnet.cz/cms/opencms/en/docs/clouds
23. VMWare: Understanding Full Virtualization, Paravirtualization, and Hardware Assist (2007). White Paper
24. Waldburger M, Stiller B (2006) Toward the mobile grid: service provisioning in a mobile dynamic virtual organization. In: IEEE international conference on computer system and application, pp 579–583
25. Wang L, Tao J, Kunze M, Castellanos AC, Kramer D, Karl W (2008) Scientific cloud computing: early definition and experience. In: HPCC '08, pp 825–830
26. Youseff L, Butrico M, Da Silva D (2008) Toward a unified ontology of cloud computing. In: Grid computing environments workshop (GCE '08), pp 1–10
27. Zadok E, Iyer R, Joukov N, Sivathanu G, Wright CP (2006)) On incremental file system development. ACM Trans Storage 2((2):161–196

Chapter 7
A Peer-to-Peer Framework for Supporting MapReduce Applications in Dynamic Cloud Environments

Fabrizio Marozzo, Domenico Talia, and Paolo Trunfio

Abstract MapReduce is a programming model widely used in Cloud computing environments for processing large data sets in a highly parallel way. MapReduce implementations are based on a master-slave model. The failure of a slave is managed by re-assigning its task to another slave, while master failures are not managed by current MapReduce implementations, as designers consider failures unlikely in reliable Cloud systems. On the contrary, node failures – including master failures – are likely to happen in dynamic Cloud scenarios, where computing nodes may join and leave the network at an unpredictable rate. Therefore, providing effective mechanisms to manage master failures is fundamental to exploit the MapReduce model in the implementation of data-intensive applications in those dynamic Cloud environments where current MapReduce implementations could be unreliable. The goal of our work is to extend the master-slave architecture of current MapReduce implementations to make it more suitable for dynamic Cloud scenarios. In particular, in this chapter, we present a Peer-to-Peer (P2P)-MapReduce framework that exploits a P2P model to manage participation of intermittent nodes, master failures, and MapReduce job recovery in a decentralized but effective way.

7.1 Introduction

Cloud computing is gaining increasing interest both in science and industry for its promise to deliver service-oriented remote access to hardware and software facilities in a highly reliable and transparent way. A key point for the effective implementation of large-scale Cloud systems is the availability of programming models that support a wide range of applications and system scenarios. One of the most successful programming models currently adopted for the implementation of data-intensive Cloud applications is MapReduce [1].

F. Marozzo (✉)
Department of Electronics, Computer Science and Systems (DEIS),
University of Calabria, Rende, Italy
e-mail: fmarozzo@deis.unical.itomenico

N. Antonopoulos and L. Gillam (eds.), *Cloud Computing: Principles,*
Systems and Applications, Computer Communications and Networks,
DOI 10.1007/978-1-84996-241-4_7, © Springer-Verlag London Limited 2010

MapReduce defines a framework for processing large data sets in a highly parallel way by exploiting computing facilities available in a large cluster or through a Cloud system. In MapReduce, users specify the computation in terms of a *map* function that processes a key/value pair to generate a list of intermediate key/value pairs, and a *reduce* function that merges all intermediate values associated with the same intermediate key.

MapReduce implementations (e.g., Google's MapReduce [2] and Apache Hadoop [3]) are based on a master-slave model. A job is submitted by a user node to a master node that selects idle workers and assigns each one a map or a reduce task. When all map and reduce tasks have been completed, the master node returns the result to the user node. The failure of a worker is managed by re-executing its task on another worker, while current MapReduce implementations do not cope with master failures, as designers consider failures unlikely in large clusters or reliable Cloud environments.

On the contrary, node failures – including master failures – can occur in large clusters and are likely to happen in dynamic Cloud environments such as an Intercloud, a Cloud of clouds, where computing nodes may join and leave the system at an unpredictable rate. Therefore, providing effective mechanisms to manage master failures is fundamental to exploit the MapReduce model in the implementation of data-intensive applications in large dynamic Cloud environments where current MapReduce implementations could be unreliable. The goal of our work is to study how the master-slave architecture of current MapReduce implementations can be improved to make it more suitable for dynamic Cloud scenarios such as Interclouds.

In this chapter, we present a Peer-to-Peer (P2P)-MapReduce framework that exploits a P2P model to manage participation of intermittent nodes, master failures, and MapReduce job recovery in a decentralized but effective way. An early version of this work, presenting a preliminary architecture of the P2P-MapReduce framework, has been presented in [4]. This chapter extends the previous work by describing an implementation of the P2P-MapReduce framework and a preliminary performance evaluation.

The remainder of this chapter is organized as follows. Section 2 provides a background to the MapReduce programming model. Section 3 describes the P2P-MapReduce architecture, its current implementation, and preliminary evaluation of its performance. Finally, Section 4 concludes the chapter.

7.2 MapReduce

As mentioned earlier, MapReduce applications are based on a master-slave model. This section briefly describes the various operations that are performed by a generic application to transform input data into output data according to that model.

Users define a *map* and a *reduce* function [1]. The *map* function processes a (key, value) pair and returns a list of intermediate (key, value) pairs:

$$map\ (k1,v1) \rightarrow list(k2,v2).$$

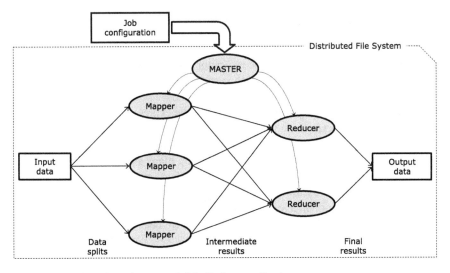

Fig. 7.1 Execution phases in a generic MapReduce application

The *reduce* function merges all intermediate values having the same intermediate key:

$$reduce\ (k2,\ list(v2)) \rightarrow list(v2).$$

The whole transformation process can be described through the following steps (see Fig. 7.1):

1. A master process receives a "job configuration" describing the MapReduce job to be executed. The job configuration specifies, amongst other information, the location of the input data, which is normally a directory in a distributed file system.
2. According to the job configuration, the master starts a number of mapper and reducer processes on different machines. At the same time, it starts a process that reads the input data from its location, partitions that data into a set of splits, and distributes those splits to the various mappers.
3. After receiving its piece of data, each mapper process executes the *map* function (provided as part of the job configuration) to generate a list of intermediate key/value pairs. Those pairs are then grouped on the basis of their keys.
4. All pairs with the same keys are assigned to the same reducer process. Hence, each reducer process executes the *reduce* function (defined by the job configuration), which merges all the values associated with the same key to generate a possibly smaller set of values.
5. The results generated by each reducer process are then collected and delivered to a location specified by the job configuration, so as to form the final output data.

Besides the original MapReduce implementation by Google [2], several other MapReduce implementations have been realized within other systems, including Hadoop [3], GridGain [5], Skynet [6], MapSharp [7], and Disco [8]. Another system sharing most of the design principles of MapReduce is Sector/Sphere [9], which has been designed to support distributed data storage and processing over large Cloud systems. Sector is a high-performance distributed file system, and Sphere is a parallel data processing engine used to process Sector data files. In [10], a distributed data mining application developed using such system has been described.

Several applications of the MapReduce paradigm have been demonstrated. In [11], some examples of interesting applications that can be expressed as MapReduce computations, including: performing a distributed grep, counting URL access frequency, building a reverse Web-link graph, building a term-vector per host, and building inverted indices, performing a distributed sort. In [3], many significant types of applications that have been (or are being) implemented by exploiting the MapReduce model, including machine learning and data mining, log file analysis, financial analysis, scientific simulation, image retrieval and processing, blog crawling, machine translation, language modeling, and bioinformatics have been mentioned.

7.3 P2P-MapReduce

The objective of the P2P-MapReduce framework is twofold: (i) handling master failures by dynamically replicating the job state on a set of backup masters; (ii) supporting MapReduce applications over dynamic networks composed by nodes that join and leave the system at unpredictable rates.

To achieve these goals, P2P-MapReduce exploits the P2P paradigm by defining an architecture in which each node can act either as a master or slave. The role assigned to a given node depends on the current characteristics of that node, and hence, it can change dynamically over time. Thus, at each time, a limited set of nodes is assigned the master role, while the others are assigned the slave role.

Moreover, each master node can act as a backup node for other master nodes. A user node can submit the job to one of the master nodes, which will manage it as usual in MapReduce. That master will dynamically replicate the entire job state (i.e., the assignments of tasks to nodes, the locations of intermediate results, etc.) on its backup nodes. In case those backup nodes detect the failure of the master, they will elect a new master among them that will manage the job computation using its local replica of the job state.

The remainder of this section describes the architecture of the P2P-MapReduce framework, its current implementation, and a preliminary evaluation of its performance.

7.3.1 Architecture

The P2P-MapReduce architecture includes three basic roles, shown in Fig. 7.2: user (*U*), master (*M*), and slave (*S*). Master nodes and slave nodes form two logical P2P networks called *M-net* and *S-net*, respectively. As mentioned earlier, computing nodes are dynamically assigned the master or slave role, and hence, *M-net* and

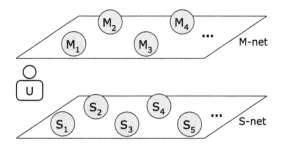

Fig. 7.2 Basic architecture of a P2P-MapReduce network

S-Net change their composition over time. The mechanisms used for maintaining this infrastructure are discussed in Section 3.2.

In the following, we describe, through an example, how a master failure is handled in the P2P-MapReduce architecture. We assume the initial configuration represented in Fig. 7.2, where *U* is the user node that submits a MapReduce job, nodes *M* are the masters, and nodes *S* are the slaves.

The following steps are performed to submit the job and recover from a master failure (see Fig. 7.3):

1. *U* queries *M-net* to get the list of the available masters, each one characterized by a workload index that measures how busy the node is. *U* orders the list by ascending values of workload index and takes the first element as a primary master. In this example, the chosen primary master is M_1; thus, *U* submits the MapReduce job to M_1.
2. M_1 chooses *k* masters for the backup role. In this example, assuming that *k=2*, M_1 chooses M_2 and M_3 for this role. Thus, M_1 notifies M_2 and M_3 that they will act as backup nodes for the current job (in Fig. 7.3, the apex "*B*" to nodes M_2 and M_3 indicates the backup function). This implies that whenever the job state changes, M_1 backs up it on M_2 and M_3, which in turn will periodically check whether M_1 is alive.
3. M_1 queries *S-net* to get the list of the available slaves, choosing (part of) them to execute a map or a reduce task. As for the masters, the choice of the slave nodes to use is done on the basis of a workload index. In this example, nodes S_1, S_3, and S_4 are selected as slaves. The tasks are started on the slave nodes and managed as usual in MapReduce.
4. The primary master M_1 fails. Backup masters M_2 and M_3 detect the failure of M_1 and start a distributed procedure to elect a new primary master among them.
5. The new primary master (M_3) is elected by choosing the backup node with the lowest workload index. M_2 continues to play the backup function, and to keep *k* backup masters active, another backup node (M_4, in this example) is chosen by M_3. Then, M_3 proceeds to manage the MapReduce job using its local replica of the job state.
6. As soon as the MapReduce job is completed, M_3 returns the result to *U*.

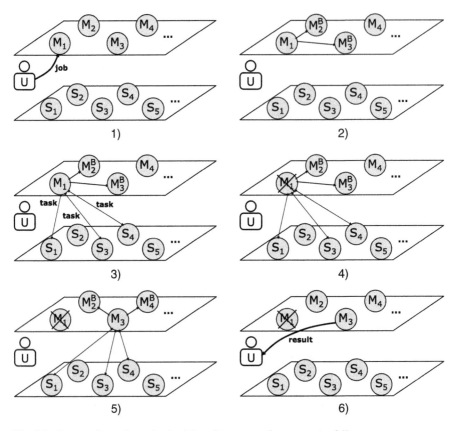

Fig. 7.3 Steps performed to submit a job and to recover from a master failure

It is worth noticing that the master failure and the subsequent recovery procedure are transparent to the user. It should also be noted that a master node may simultaneously play the role of primary master for one job and that of backup master for another job.

7.3.2   Implementation

We implemented a prototype of the P2P-MapReduce framework using the JXTA framework [12]. JXTA provides a set of XML-based protocols that allow computers and other devices to communicate and collaborate in a P2P fashion. Each peer provides a set of services made available to other peers in the network. Services are any type of programs that can be networked by a single or a group of peers.

In JXTA, there are two main types of peers: *rendezvous* and *edge*. The rendezvous peers act as routers in a network, forwarding the discovery requests submitted by edge peers to locate the resources of interest. Peers sharing a common set of interests are organized into a *peer group*. To send messages to each other, JXTA peers use asynchronous communication mechanisms called *pipes*. Pipes can be either point-to-point or multicast, so as to support a wide range of communication schemes. All resources (peers, services, etc.) are described by *advertisements* that are published within the peer group for resource-discovery purposes.

In the following, we briefly describe how the JXTA components are used in the P2P-MapReduce system to implement basic mechanisms for resource discovery, network maintenance, job submission, and failure recovery. Then, we describe the state diagram that steers the behavior of a generic node and the software modules provided by each node in a P2P-MapReduce network.

7.3.2.1   Basic Mechanisms

Resource Discovery

All master and slave nodes in the P2P-MapReduce system belong to a single JXTA peer group called *MapReduceGroup*. Most of these nodes are edge peers, but some of them also act as rendezvous peers, in a way that is transparent to the users. Each node exposes its features by publishing an advertisement containing basic information, such as its `Role` and `WorkloadIndex`.

An edge peer publishes its advertisement in a local cache and sends some keys identifying that advertisement to a rendezvous peer. The rendezvous peer uses those keys to index the advertisement in a distributed hash table called Shared Resource Distributed Index (SRDI), managed by all the rendezvous peers of *MapReduceGroup*. Queries for a given type of resource (e.g., master nodes) are submitted to the JXTA Discovery Services that uses SRDI to locate all the resources of that type without flooding the entire network.

Note that *M-net* and *S-net*, represented in Fig. 7.2, are "logical" networks in the sense that queries to *M-net* (or *S-net*) are actually submitted to the whole *MapReduceGroup,* but restricted to nodes having the attribute `Role` set to "`Master`" (or "`Slave`") using the SRDI mechanisms.

Network Maintenance

Network maintenance is carried out cooperatively by all nodes on the basis of their role. The maintenance task of each slave node is to periodically check the existence of at least one master in the network. In case no masters are found, the slave promotes itself to the master role. In this way, the first node joining the network always assumes the master role. The same happens to the last node remaining into the network.

The maintenance task of master nodes is to ensure the existence of a given percentage p of masters on the total number of nodes. This task is performed periodically by one master only (referred to as *coordinator*), which is elected for this purpose among all the masters using a variation of the "bully" election algorithm. The coordinator has the power of changing slaves into masters, and vice versa. During a maintenance operation, the coordinator queries all nodes and orders them by ascending values of workload index: the first p percent of nodes must assume (or maintain) the master role, while the others will become or remain slaves. Nodes that have to change their role are notified by the coordinator in order to update their status.

Job Submission and Failure Recovery

To describe the JXTA mechanisms used for job submission and master-failure recovery, we take the six-point example presented in Section 3.1 as reference:

1. The user node invokes the Discovery Service to obtain the advertisements of the master nodes published in *MapReduceGroup*. Based on the `WorkloadIndex`, it chooses the primary master for its job. Then, it opens a bidirectional pipe (called *PrimaryPipe*) to the primary master and submits the job configuration.
2. The primary master invokes the Discovery Service to choose its backup masters and opens a multicast pipe (*BackupPipe*) to the backup masters. The *BackupPipe* has two goals: replicating job state information to the backup nodes and allowing backup nodes to detect a primary master failure in case the *BackupPipe* connection times out.
3. The primary master invokes the Discovery Service to select the slave nodes to be used for the job. Slave nodes are filtered on the basis of `WorkloadIndex` attribute. The primary master opens a bidirectional pipe (*SlavePipe*) to each slave and starts a map or a reduce task on it.
4. The backup masters detect a primary master failure (i.e., a timeout on the *BackupPipe* connection) and start a procedure to elect the new primary master (to this end, they connect each other with a temporary pipe and exchange information about their current `WorkloadIndex`).
5. The backup master with the lowest `WorkloadIndex` is elected as the new primary master. This new primary master binds the pipes previously associated with the old primary master (*PrimaryPipe*, *BackupPipe* and *SlavePipes*), chooses (and connect to) a substitute backup master, and then continues to manage the MapReduce job using its replica of the job state.
6. The primary master returns the result of the MapReduce job to the user node through the *PrimaryPipe*.

The primary master detects the failure of a slave by getting a timeout to the associated *SlavePipe* connection. If this event occurs, a new slave is selected and the failed map or reduce task is assigned to it.

7.3.2.2 State Diagram and Software Modules

The behavior of a generic node is modeled as a state diagram that defines the different states that a node can assume, and all the events that determine the transitions

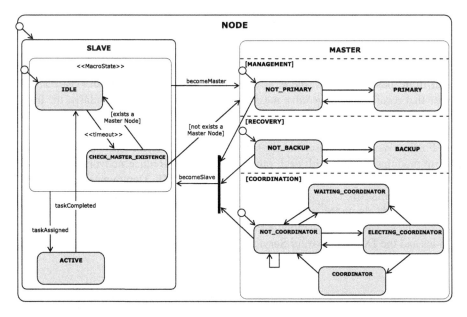

Fig. 7.4 UML state diagram describing the behavior of a generic node in the P2P-MapReduce framework

from one state to another one. Figure 7.4 shows such a state diagram modeled using the UML State Diagram formalism.

The state diagram includes two macro-states, SLAVE and MASTER, which describes the two roles that can be assumed by each node. The SLAVE state has three states, IDLE, CHECK_MASTER_EXISTENCE, and ACTIVE, which represent a slave waiting for task assignment, a slave checking the existence of a master, and a slave executing a given task, respectively.

The MASTER state is modeled with three parallel macro-states, which represent the different roles that a master can perform concurrently: possibly acting as a primary master for one or more jobs (MANAGEMENT), possibly acting as a backup master for one or more jobs (RECOVERY), and coordinating the network for maintenance purposes (COORDINATION).

The MANAGEMENT macro-state contains two states: NOT_PRIMARY, which represents a master node currently not acting as a primary master for any job, and PRIMARY, which in contrast, represents a master node currently managing at least one job as a primary master.

Similarly, the RECOVERY macro-state includes two states: NOT_BACKUP (the node is not managing any job as a backup master) and BACKUP (at least one job is currently being backed up on this node).

The COORDINATION macro-state includes four states: NOT_COORDINATOR (the node is not acting as coordinator), COORDINATOR (the node is acting as coordinator), WAITING_COORDINATOR, and ELECTING_COORDINATOR for nodes currently participating in the election of the new coordinator, as mentioned in Section 3.2.1.

The combination of the concurrent states [NOT_PRIMARY, NOT_BACKUP, NOT_COORDINATOR] represents the abstract state MASTER.IDLE. The transition from master to slave role is allowed only to masters in the MASTER.IDLE state that receive a *becomeSlave* message from the coordinator. Similarly, the transition from slave to master role is allowed to slaves that receive a *becomeMaster* and are not in ACTIVE state.

Finally, we briefly describe the software modules inside each node and how those modules interact with each other in a P2P-MapReduce network. Figure 7.5 shows such modules and interactions using the UML Deployment/Component Diagram formalism.

Each node includes three software modules/layers: *Network, Node,* and *MapReduce.* The Network module is in charge of the interactions with the other nodes and the JXTA Discovery Service. The Node module controls the lifecycle of

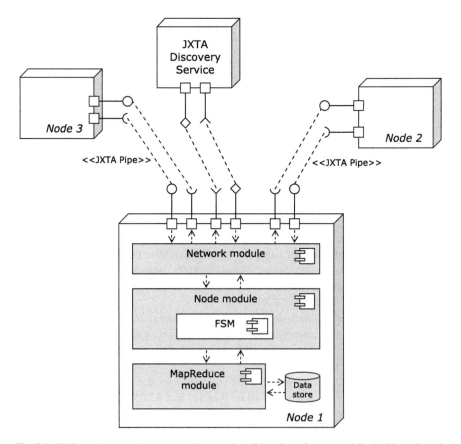

Fig. 7.5 UML deployment/component diagram describing the software modules inside each node and the interactions among nodes

the node in its various aspects, including network maintenance, job management, and so on; its core is represented by the FSM component that implements the logic of the finite state machine described in Fig. 7.4. The MapReduce module manages the local execution of jobs (when the node is acting as a master) or tasks (when the node is acting as a slave).

7.3.3   Evaluation

We carried out a preliminary set of experiments to evaluate the behavior of the P2P-MapReduce framework when compared with a centralized implementation of MapReduce, in the presence of dynamic-nodes participation. The experimental results demonstrate that by using a P2P approach, it is possible to extend the MapReduce architectural model making it suitable for highly dynamic Cloud environments where failure must be managed to avoid a critical loss of computing resources and time.

The evaluation has been carried out by implementing a simulator of the system in which each node is represented by an independent thread. Each thread executes the algorithms specified by the state diagram in Fig. 7.4, and communicates with the other threads by invoking local routines having the same interface of the JXTA pipes. Our simulation analyzes the system in steady state, that is, when *M-net* and *S-net* are formed and the desired ratio between the number of masters and slaves is reached.

The network includes 1,000 nodes. To simulate dynamic-nodes participation, a joining rate R_J and a leaving rate R_L are defined. On average, for every $1/R_J$ s, one node joins the network, while for every $1/R_L$ another node abruptly leaves the network so as to simulate an event of failure (or a disconnection). In our simulation, $R_J = R_L$ in order to keep the total number of nodes and the master/slave ratio approximately constant during the whole simulation. In particular, we considered the following values for R_J and R_L: 0.05, 0.1, and 0.2, which correspond to the join/failure of one node (out of 1,000 nodes)–every 20, 10, and 5 s, respectively.

For every 120 s (mean value), a user entity submits one job to the system. The average sequential duration of a job is 20 h that are distributed, on an average, to 100 nodes. On the basis of the actual number of slaves, the system determines the amount of time each slave will be busy to complete its task. Every node, other than managing a job or a task, executes the network-maintenance operations described earlier (election of the coordinator, choice of backup masters, etc.).

The main task performed by the simulator is evaluating the number of jobs failed versus the total number of jobs submitted to the system. For the purpose of our simulations, a "failed" job is a job that does not complete its execution, that is, it does not return a result to the submitting user. The failure of a job is always caused by an unmanaged failure of the master responsible for that job. The failure of a slave, on the contrary, never causes a failure of the whole job because its task is re-assigned to another slave.

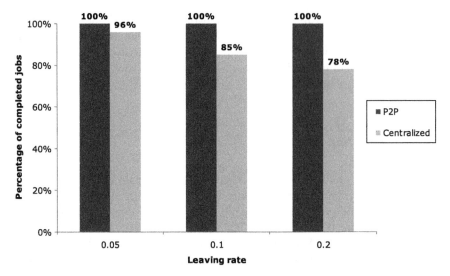

Fig. 7.6 Percentage of completed jobs in centralized and P2P scenarios for a leaving rate ranging from 0.05 to 0.2

The system has been evaluated in two scenarios: (i) *centralized*, where there is only one primary master and there are no backup masters; (ii) *P2P*, where there are ten masters and each job is managed by one master that periodically replicates the job state on one backup master. Figure 7.6 presents the percentage of completed jobs in centralized and P2P scenarios after the submission of 100 jobs.

As expected, in the centralized scenario the number of failed jobs increases as the leaving rate increases. In contrast, the P2P-MapReduce scenario is able to complete all the jobs for all the considered leaving rates, even if we used just one backup per job. It is worth noticing that when a backup master becomes primary master as a consequence of a failure, it chooses another backup in its place to maintain the desired level of reliability.

The percentages given in Fig. 7.6 can be translated into lost CPU hours, by multiplying the average job duration to the average number of failed jobs. In the centralized scenario, the absolute number of failed jobs is 4, 15, and 22 for leaving rates of 0.05, 0.1, and 0.2, respectively. Hence, with an average sequential duration of 20 h per job, the total number of lost computing hours equals, in the worst case, 80, 300, and 440 h.

We can further estimate the amount of resources involved in a typical MapReduce job by taking the statistics about a large set of MapReduce jobs run at Google, presented in [1]. In March 2006, the average completion time per job was 874 s, using 268 slaves on average. By assuming that each machine is fully assigned to one job, the overall machine time is 874 × 268 s (about 65 h). In September 2007, the average job completion time was 395 s using 394 machines, with an overall machine time of 43 h.

From the statistics reported earlier, and from the results generated by our experiments, we see that a master failure causes loss of dozens of CPU hours for a typical MapReduce job. Moreover, when the number of available machines per user is limited (as in a typical Cloud systems where resources are shared among thousands of users), a master failure also produces a significant loss of time because the job completion time increases as the number of machines decreases.

7.4   Conclusions

Providing effective mechanisms to manage master failures, job recovery, and participation of intermittent nodes is fundamental to exploit the MapReduce model in the implementation of data-intensive applications in dynamic Cloud environments or Cloud of clouds scenarios where current MapReduce implementations could be unreliable.

The P2P-MapReduce model presented in this chapter exploits a P2P model to perform job state replication, manage master failures, and allow participation of intermittent nodes in a decentralized but effective way. Using a P2P approach, we extended the MapReduce architectural model, making it suitable for highly dynamic environments where failure must be managed to avoid a critical loss of computing resources and time.

References

1. Dean J, Ghemawat S (2008) MapReduce: simplified data processing on large clusters. Commun ACM 51(1):107–113
2. Google's Map Reduce (2009). http://labs.google.com/papers/mapreduce.html (Visited: September 2009)
3. Hadoop (2009) http://hadoop.apache.org (Visited: September 2009)
4. Marozzo F, Talia D, Trunfio P (2008) Adapting MapReduce for dynamic environments using a peer-to-peer model. Workshop on cloud computing and its applications, Chicago, USA
5. Gridgain (2009) http://www.gridgain.com (Visited: September 2009)
6. Skynet (2009) http://skynet.rubyforge.org (Visited: September 2009)
7. MapSharp (2009) http://mapsharp.codeplex.com (Visited: September 2009)
8. Disco (2009) http://discoproject.org (Visited: September 2009)
9. Gu Y, Grossman R (2009) Sector and sphere: the design and implementation of a high performance data cloud. Philos Tr S A 367(1897):2429–2445
10. Grossman R, Gu Y (2008) Data mining using high performance data clouds: experimental studies using sector and sphere. SIGKDD 2008, Las Vegas, USA
11. Dean J, Ghemawat S (2004) MapReduce: simplified data processing on large clusters. Symposium on Operating Systems Design and Implementation (OSDI), San Francisco, USA
12. Gong L (2001) JXTA: a network programming environment. IEEE Internet Comput 5(3): 88–95

Chapter 8
Enhanced Network Support for Scalable Computing Clouds

Francesco Pamieri and Silvio Pardi

Abstract We introduce the concept of network resource visibility and performance awareness in the cloud control logic, aiming at optimizing the transport layer activities within the cloud, and thus coping with the scalability problems experienced in traditional Internet-based clouds by large-scale data processing applications. With the aid of new dynamic "network on demand" facilities complementing the existing cloud services portfolio, we can gain some form of control on the underlying transport layer, bypassing the actual locality constraints in resource allocation and allowing the flexible orchestration of resources available in different sites and belonging to different administrative domains.

8.1 Introduction

Sharing of computer and storage resources has become a popular solution for a number of key enterprise applications, including resolving complicated simulation tasks, distributing high workloads between several sites, and dispersing critical data and/or information technology assets among several locations to minimize the risk of catastrophic failures. During times of limited budgets, resource sharing has also become a popular means to reduce cost. Traditionally, this approach was limited to data center infrastructures, but the latest trends such as virtualization and broadband interconnects have pushed resource-sharing concepts even further. The emerging cloud-computing paradigm allows us to locate computing and storage resources anywhere in the world. No longer does the computer (whether it is a PC or supercomputer) have to be co-located with its users or funding institution. More precisely, cloud computing is referred to as an information service that is available to an end-user out of a "transparent" cloud, whereby the cloud is an abstract model for the end-user, which has no specific physical location. The cloud is generally a conglomerate of interconnected, redundant data centers built to provide certain services. Originally starting with Internet-related services such as search

F. Pamieri (✉)
Università degli Studi di Napoli Federico II, CSI, Via Cinthia, 5, 80126 Napoli, Italy
e-mail: fpalmier@unina.it

N. Antonopoulos and L. Gillam (eds.), *Cloud Computing: Principles,*
Systems and Applications, Computer Communications and Networks,
DOI 10.1007/978-1-84996-241-4_8, © Springer-Verlag London Limited 2010

engines, more traditional services, applications, and tasks that used to reside on an end-user's terminal or computer get transferred to the cloud. The only requirement to gain access to them is a broadband connection. With the available high bandwidth optical networks, it is now possible to locate the available resources on the cloud within properly equipped sites in remote locations throughout the world. A move towards clouds signals a fundamental shift in how we handle information. At the most basic level, it is the computing equivalent of the evolution in electricity a century ago when farms and businesses shut down their own generators and bought power instead from efficient industrial utilities. Unfortunately, the best-effort delivery system of the Internet, often used as the underlying transport network for most of the existing cloud infrastructures, imposes severe constraints on the transfer of massive amounts of data, and thus restricts the deployment of the above-mentioned applications on wide-area scales. Besides the lack of bandwidth, the inability to provide dedicated links makes the current network technology not well suited for performance-critical Grid computing. A solution is needed for providing dedicated end-to-end connections, dynamically allocable on-demand or by scheduled reservation, to critical data-intensive applications. Accordingly, in this chapter, we introduce the concept of network resource visibility and network performance awareness into the cloud control logic for coping with the severe scalability limits (with respect to the more demanding data-intensive application) of cloud infrastructures operating in a network-oblivious fashion. We present the benefits of such an extended cloud by proposing a new service and resource management model, where each service is associated with specific performance requirements to be enforced by considering both the needed runtime resources available and the end-to-end communication features of the connections between them. We focus our efforts on the transport facilities located at the "lowest" layer of the cloud systems, because here we can provide a solid foundation on top of which language-, service-, and application-level cloud-computing systems can be explored and developed. By introducing some form of control of the underlying transport layer, we bypass the usual locality constraint in computation and storage resource allocation needed to ensure acceptable performances within the cloud runtime system, allowing the flexible orchestration of resources available in different sites and belonging to different administrative domains. Also, by adopting proven circuit switched network concepts with modern wavelength-routed networks as an improved hybrid transport facility within clouds, we address the "missing link" in the cloud networking "big picture", i.e. the concept of dynamic "network on demand" services complementing the existing cloud resource-sharing and computing-services portfolio.

8.2   The Cloud Evolution

The upcoming evolution of cloud computing is a major change in our computing technology. One of the most important parts of that evolution is the advent of the first production platforms based on the cloud paradigm. Such platforms promise real gains in terms of performance scalability and agility to their users. By leveraging cloud computing, an organization can rapidly deploy applications where the underlying technological components can expand and contract with the natural ebb and flow of the involved business lifecycle. Traditionally, once an application was deployed, it was bound to a particular infrastructure until the infrastructure was upgraded/improved. The result was low efficiency, poor utilization, and limited flexibility. Cloud enablers such as virtualization and grid computing allow applications to be dynamically deployed onto the most suitable infrastructure at runtime. Cloud computing takes these concepts further, by allowing more automated resource and workload management practices. This elastic aspect of cloud computing allows applications to scale and grow without needing traditional "fork-lift" upgrades. Like any new paradigm, Cloud computing represents an architectural shift from the traditional distributed computing approaches. Such a shift is best described by the addition of a new and as transparent as possible middleware layer on top of the existing computer and device operating systems that we can call a Cloud Operating System (COS). It can be considered as a network operating system running atop a cloud, i.e. a hyper network of computers. As its name suggests, this kind of runtime platform lets users write applications that run in the cloud, or to use services provided from the cloud, or both. But the transformation that cloud computing makes possible goes beyond simply running applications on a virtualized platform built on someone else's hardware. It extends the computing model with the transparent utilization of a platform that the provider has created, and which, to some degree, abstracts the essence of scalability and distributed processing. More generally, the concept of cloud computing can incorporate various computer technologies including web infrastructure, Web 2.0, and many other emerging technologies. People may have different perspectives from different views. For example, from the view of the end-user, the cloud-computing service moves the application software and operation system from desktops to the cloud side, which enables users to plug-in anytime from anywhere and utilize large-scale storage and computing resources. On the other hand, the cloud-computing service provider may focus on how to distribute and schedule the computer resources. Nevertheless, storage and computing on massive data are the key issues for a cloud infrastructure.

8.3 Improved Network Support for Cloud Computing

The promise of cloud computing is ubiquitous access to a broad set of applications and services, which are delivered over the network to multiple customers. Such services are essentially offered through interfaces available within the "clouds," rather than spread over the single computers connected through the Internet. On the other hand, such cloud infrastructures, because of their high degree of abstraction, have the potential to introduce unpredictable performance behaviours. In fact, while sharing the resources available on a large distributed infrastructure can average out the variability of individual workloads, it is extremely difficult to predict the exact performance characteristics of your application at any particular time. Like in any shared infrastructure, varying individual workloads, resource demands, of and network load conditions, can result in unpredictable performance behaviour of the combined applications. Furthermore, as cloud computing enables users and applications to store all their data on the network, handling and moving large volumes of data within the cloud or between the users and the cloud may become a challenging issue. Consequently, cloud-service providers must guarantee that data are processed automatically and transferred transparently when and where they are needed. Also important to the notion of cloud is the automation of these tasks. An environment in which the system requires human intervention to allocate bandwidth on communication links or resources to processes is not a cloud: it is simply a data center. Integrating an accurate network view into the cloud management in order to support these types of services would make the cloud more flexible and also increase the efficient use of the available resources and communication infrastructure. The underlying network architecture building the foundation for cloud computing consists of interconnected server farms within the data centers and a high-speed transport network providing connectivity to remote and backup sites. These high-speed connections form the backbone of the cloud network and are required to run at highest bandwidth with lowest transmission latency, and in general, according to a properly defined QoS degree. Cloud-computing resources can be made accessible through the public Internet, private high-performance networks, and often through a hybrid mixing of the two. Providers and users of cloud services must understand the performance, redundancy, and cost associated with all the available options, because not all the applications that have to be run on the cloud have the same features: some will only require the basic capabilities available on the public Internet or traditional public connection services, while others may require the enforcing of specific network performance constraints.

8.3.1 Why the Internet is Not Enough?

The public Internet is the simplest choice for delivering cloud-based services. In this model, the cloud provider simply purchases Internet connectivity and its customers access the services via their own Internet connections. However, modern high-performance applications are raising communication and bounded-time execution requirements that the public Internet cannot meet neither at the present nor even in the foreseeable future. In fact, the traditional Internet-shared network paradigm is based on the best-effort packet-forwarding service that is a proven efficient technology for transporting burst transmission of short data packets, e.g., for remote login, consumer-oriented email, and web applications. Unfortunately, this is not enough to meet the challenge of the large-scale data transfer and connectivity requirement of the modern cloud-based collaborations. More precisely, the traditional packet-forwarding paradigm, based on statistical multiplexing, is not scalable in its ability to rapidly move very large data quantities. Making forwarding decisions every 1,500 bytes is sufficient for emails or 10–100 KB web pages. This is not the optimal mechanism if we have to cope with data size of six to nine orders larger in magnitude. For example, copying 1.5 TB of data using packet switching requires making the same forwarding decision about one billion times, over many routers along the path. Internet-based cloud infrastructures lack the scalability features required by modern data-transfer-intensive applications in several aspects: network resources cannot be reserved in advance, bandwidth is too low, QoS is not guaranteed, and hence, neither application success nor a bounded completion time can be ensured to the users. Particularly, reservation of connectivity resources is needed to facilitate the transportation of enormous datasets between distant sites within the cloud in predictable times. Clearly, this cannot be easily achieved in traditional packet-switched networks, where the resource needs are usually not known and hence cannot be planned in advance.

8.3.2   Transparent Optical Networks for Cloud Applications: The Dedicated Bandwidth Paradigm

Creating a dedicated circuit over several available high-speed links will be a much more effective multiplexing technique for large data transfers. Consequently, there is the need to develop new architectures and services that support cloud infrastructures in association with emerging networks technologies, having the potential to always provide in advance the available large bandwidth pipes with a capacity of several orders of magnitude beyond that of today's communication infrastructures. Only a modern optical transport network provides the capacity and bandwidth needed to support these demanding cloud-computing applications. Accordingly, in order to achieve connectivity resources in terms of bandwidth and quality of service (QoS) when and where the applications need, it is necessary to perform advanced provisioning of end-to-end dedicated optical "virtual circuits" through the network, implemented on properly reserved wavelengths on the available Wavelength Division Multiplexing (WDM)-based optical transport infrastructures. In detail, according to the WDM paradigm, the optical transmission spectrum can be carved up into a number of non-overlapping wavelength bands, each supporting a single communication channel operating at whatever protocol or rate one desires (protocol and bit-rate transparency). Thus, by allowing multiple independent channels to coexist on a single fiber, we can make the most of the available optical infrastructures, with the corresponding challenges being the design and development of appropriate network architectures, control-plane protocols, and algorithms that make these connectivity resources available to cloud applications. As such network control plane provides an advance reservation capability to the circuit, the data-intensive applications can be guaranteed to achieve certain bandwidth and QoS in specific time slots. This can be considered the most promising mechanism to meet all the future data transfer demands from applications running on the cloud through the provisioning of huge amounts of cheap bandwidth through dedicated end-to-end connections fulfilling the proper QoS requirements.

8.4 Architecture and Implementation Details

The solution to all the above-mentioned issues will result in a flexible and evolutionary architecture that supports cooperation between different entities (computing
systems/clusters, storage, scientific instruments, etc.) within the cloud, based on a
scalable framework for dynamic and transparent configuration and interconnection
of multiple types of resources for high-performance cloud-computing services over
globally distributed optical network systems. To achieve this, we have to abstract
and encapsulate the available network resources into manageable and dynamically
provisioned entities within the cloud in order to meet the complex demand patterns
of the applications and to optimize the overall network utilization. More precisely,
we need to conceive a new cloud architecture considering the network resources as
key resources that can be managed and controlled like any other resource by the
cloud middleware/distributed operating system services. In such architecture, the
cloud system is modeled by using a three-layer hierarchical schema:

- The *infrastructure layer*, providing a virtualized interface to hardware resources,
  such as CPU, memory, connectivity/bandwidth, and storage, and aggregating
  and allocating them on a totally distributed basis
- The *platform layer* including the components that implement the cloud basic
  services and runtime environment, such as the cloud operating system kernel, a
  distributed file system (DFS), cloud input/output (I/O) facilities, computing and
  virtualization engine, network management, and interface modules
- The *application layer* hosting domain-specific application and realizing the
  cloud service abstraction through specific interfaces

The interfaces provided at the infrastructure layer make the platform layer almost
totally independent from the underlying hardware resources, and thus ensure high
scalability and flexibility benefits to the whole cloud architecture. Accordingly, the
infrastructure layer can be implemented by using a public service such as Amazon
EC2/S3 [1,2] or another private-owned infrastructure or solution such as a computing cluster or a grid.

Analogous to the operating system that manages the complexity of an individual
machine, the COS handles the complexity at the platform layer and aggregates the
resources available in all the data centers participating in the cloud. In particular, it
runs applications on a highly unified, reliable, and efficient virtual infrastructure
made up of distributed components, automatically managing them to support
pre-defined service-level agreements (SLAs) in terms of availability, security, and
performance assurance for the applications. It also dynamically moves the applications with the same service-level expectations across on-premise or off-premise
sites within the clouds for the sake of highest operational efficiency.

A DFS platform provides a consistent view of the data seen by all the clients
named in a hierarchical name space among multiple naming/directory servers, and
ensures their distribution across the cloud to handle heavy loads and reliability in
case of failures.

The I/O subsystem provides data-exchange services in the same infrastructure or among different clouds by using several protocols and facilities. Such services are implemented within the network control logic that has the role of collective broker for network connectivity requirements, keeps track of the resources and interfaces available on the cloud, and copes with all the necessary network operations by hiding the complexity of the resource-specific allocation tasks. These functions are implemented in the cloud middleware platform by relying on information models responsible for capturing structures and relationships of the involved entities. To cope with the heterogeneity of the network infrastructure resources, we propose a new technology-independent network resource abstraction: the Traffic Engineered end-to-end virtual circuit that can be used for virtual-connection transport. Such virtual circuit mimics a direct point-to-point connection or pipe with specific bandwidth and QoS features. The network control logic handles each connectivity request; it then coordinates the setting up of the needed tunnels between the nodes on the cloud hosting the requesting applications. This schema guarantees access to dedicated circuits, which may be requested on-demand or by advance reservation to deliver more reliable and predictable network performance.

Finally, the user interface supports administrators and clients to monitor and manage the cloud platform and the applications running on it through specific user-friendly interfaces. It includes configuration, accounting, performance, and security-management facilities. In this domain, many open-source technologies can be considered. The web services technology is a good candidate to play a role in building such user interface, which makes the cloud easily accessible through the network by delivering desktop-like experience to the users (Fig. 8.1).

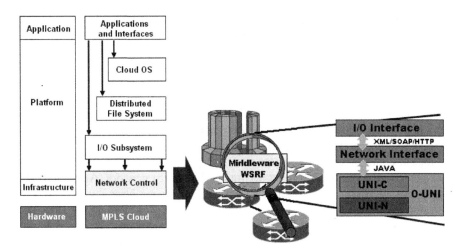

Fig. 8.1 The cloud-reference architecture

8.4.1 Traffic Management and Control Plane Facilities

In our proposed architectural framework, an application program running on a cloud has the view of a virtualized communication infrastructure unifying all the needed computational and storage resources into a common "virtual site" or "virtual network" abstraction, and should be able to dynamically request some specific service levels (bandwidth/QoS, protection, etc.) on it. The fulfilment of the above-mentioned requests triggers the on-demand construction of one or more dedicated point-to-point or multipoint "virtual" circuits or pseudo-wires between the cloud sites hosting the application's runtime resources, and is accomplished co-operatively by the network devices on the end-to-end paths between these sites. The above-mentioned circuits can either be dedicated layer-2 channels, realizing the abstractions of a transport network behaving as a single virtual switching device, or traffic engineered paths with guaranteed bandwidth, delay, etc. All the involved network resources have to be defined in advance at the "virtual network" configuration time. Control-plane protocols define the procedures for handling such traffic engineering operations, i.e., immediate requests for connectivity at a guaranteed rate. The transparency and adaptability features of cloud infrastructures make support for these operations absolutely necessary in a suitable transport network, which may be a mesh of private or public shared networks, owned and managed by some co-operating service providers and/or enterprises. The underlying network must be as transparent as possible with respect to the cloud infrastructure, so that all the necessary network operations are almost totally hidden to the applications and/or Virtual Machines running on it. Traffic management in our model should work on a pure "peer-based" model based on MPLS/GMPLS [3,4] technology that introduces a circuit-switching paradigm on top of the basic IP packet-switching framework. We consider a network built on label switching routers (LSR), optical wavelength switches, and communication links that may be under the administrative control of several cooperating NSP, realizing a common transport infrastructure. The optical devices implement an intelligent all-optical core where packets are routed through the network without leaving the optical domain. The optical network and the surrounding IP networks are independent of each other, and an edge LSR interacts with its connected switching nodes only over a well-defined User-Network Interface (UNI). A subset of the routers are known to be ingress and egress points for the network traffic within the cloud and these are typically the customer edge (CE) devices directly attached to the NSP's point-of-presence locations or Provider Edge (PE) devices. There are no requirements for CE devices in order to map the logical connections to the remote sites – they have to be configured as if they were connected to a single bridged network or local area network. Also, the NSP edge nodes and the optical switches within the core do not have any information related to the cloud, and only transfer the tagged packets or cross-connect optical ports/wavelengths from one LSR to another in a transparent way. The key idea in such architecture is to realize a strict separation between the network control and forwarding planes. The space of all possible forwarding options in a network domain is partitioned into "Forwarding Equivalence Classes" (FECs). The packets are labelled at the ingress depending on the FEC they belong to. Here, the FEC concept clearly resembles that of a point-to-point or multipoint dedicated logical connection or virtual circuit. Each of the intermediate nodes uses the label (or the incoming transport wavelength in the optical core) of each incoming packet to determine its next hop. Labels can be pushed, swapped, and popped by the LSRs and a specific label distribution protocol (such as LDP [5] or RSVP [6]) is used for label information exchange between all the nodes. All the network intelligence is located in the edge nodes, where the virtual connection originates and terminates, and where all the necessary tunnels are set up to connect to all the other NSP nodes. The main advantage of such a circuit-switching paradigm is that it enables performance isolation between traffic streams that belong to different virtual connections – something that packet switching alone cannot guarantee. By performance isolation, we mean that we can prevent the performance of a virtual connection from being affected by a traffic stream belonging to another one. All the above-mentioned facilities need pre-determined "conduits" or label switched paths (LSPs) to be established to specific destinations. Traffic is steadily mapped onto them according to the dynamic needs of the involved users and their capabilities. More precisely, LSPs can be characterized by optional properties, such as the amount of bandwidth, type of packet treatment, or class of service. The former parameter is used at a set-up time in a traffic engineering capable network to select LSP routes with an amount of available bandwidth sufficient to satisfy the LSP request. This attribute can also be used for subsequent LSP route optimizations. On the other hand, the class of service can be used to identify the MPLS packets that belong to the same traffic aggregate and have to be forwarded according to the same behaviour. In this way, the LSP can be regarded as a Differentiated Service Path. The LSPs can thus be used to implement explicit virtual connections on the underlying transport network, supporting precise reservations on a service-level basis and obeying traffic-isolation constraints. Such virtual connections are long-lived ones, possibly lasting for several months at a stretch. At the network control plane level, for each virtual connection between two CE nodes, at least a couple of reserved LSPs must be set up through the underlying network to carry a service-guaranteed traffic stream from the ingress router to the egress one where the CE nodes are attached.

8.4.2   Service Plane and Interfaces

In the proposed scenario, the network turns out to be a resource as important as computation and/or storage. As such, the cloud operating system requires the same level of control towards the subsets of well-defined amounts of network resources for the entire execution of a specific task. A chief goal of this control is to turn the network into a virtualized resource that can be acted upon and controlled by other layers of software, realizing a service plane available to applications and virtual machines. Such a service plane is typically concerned with dedicated end-to-end optical channel/circuit allocation, optimization, monitoring, and restoration across the network that becomes the fundamental architectural "glue" unifying all the distributed resources into a "virtual site" and "virtual computing system" abstraction, so that they can be made available to the applications as if they were in the same Server Farm/data center and LAN. The service plane must be designed to be extensible from the ground up. It should allow adaptation of the above-mentioned control plane interfaces and abstract their network view, or element set, into its service portfolio. In other words, the network becomes a resource managed by the cloud as much as computation or storage, and the service virtualization is layered upon the available network control plane technology in the IP/optical environment.

8.4.2.1 Providing Network Services to Cloud-Computing Infrastructures

When network connections are considered as resources to be managed and shared within the cloud framework, one needs to exactly specify what is meant by network resources, how to encapsulate them into the cloud-services paradigm, and how to manage these services. A specific cloud service is a self-contained, self-described application that can be published, located, and invoked over a network. By this definition, capacities offered by a network endpoint do not constitute a service offered by the cloud. Multiple endpoints must co-operate to establish a network service for the cloud. By comparison, other resources, such as storage capacity or processing capacity, can be offered by a node without co-operation with other nodes. For this reason, we believe that a different abstraction is required to model network resources as a cloud service.

8.4.2.2 The Cloud Operating System–Network Interface

A natural choice for modeling this interface is the Web Service Resource Framework (WSRF) [7] aiming at providing specialized web services enhanced for cloud users and applications. Implementing each high-level system component as a stand-alone web service has the following benefits: first, each web service exposes a well-defined language-agnostic API in the form of a WSDL document containing both operations that the service can perform and I/O data structures. Second, we can leverage the existing web-service features such as WS Security policies for secure communication between the components. The Interface's WS service can advertise a single multiprotocol endpoint for authenticating and consuming user requests, while also translating the request to an internal protocol. Communication with the top-level service interface may take place via SOAP/http eventually secured by SSL and some authentication mechanisms, such as X509 or HMAC signatures. This can be achieved through the introduction and utilization of pluggable request-handling interfaces in the supporting web services stack software. All the offered web service interfaces need to be stateless and persistent, where data is not retained among invocations and services outlive their clients. The internal services must be unconcerned with the details of the outward-facing interfaces utilized by users while benefitting from enforcement of message-validation requirements. The network control logic must support these basic service functions within the cloud middleware by relying on information models responsible for capturing structures and relationships of the involved entities. Access to the optical transport network control plane may be realized through an optical user-network interface (O-UNI) standardized by the Optical Internetworking Forum (OIF) [8]. The optical network services can be made available to the upper middleware layers through an O-UNI compliant programmatic interface library interfacing the client-side middleware services with the underlying edge routers. Every interface function can be in turn mapped to a set of UNI primitives for network resource setting. Each network resource or node has to be described by a set of XML interface elements, and the main interface methods should allow the management and monitoring of the available LSPs and relative traffic and performance parameters. Thus, every connection created will be characterized by the virtual channel or LSP (identified by the addresses engaged) that in turn is characterized by a set of attributes (service class, bandwidth available and utilized). In detail, the proposed abstractions, supporting the connectivity services, concern:

- The creation of a virtual point–to-point or multipoint network that transparently allows the connection between its endpoints with specific performance attributes (bandwidth, latency, and protection)
- The deletion/release function that allows an existing virtual network to be deleted and its resource released for further usage
- The modification of a virtual point-to-point or multipoint network by adding or removing some participants or changing its service-level requirements

8.5 Proof of Concept Implementation and Performance Analysis

We proved the main concepts beyond the presented model and analyzed its performance by using a very simple cloud prototype testbed, implemented on the existing Federico II University high-performance network and scientific computing infrastructure. In particular, the infrastructure-layer services have been implemented on top of the distributed grid infrastructure that unifies all the main computing and storage resources belonging to the SCoPE (Italian acronym for high Performance, Cooperative and distributed System for scientific Elaboration) project. Such grid infrastructure is based on the gLite [9] middleware and spans several data centers geographically distributed in the Naples urban area. Its connectivity is supported by a metropolitan optical fiber network that offers high-performance communication facilities to all the involved research sites.

8.5.1 The Prototype Details

The architecture of the cloud prototype matches the three-layer paradigm presented in the previous sections (see Fig. 8.2).

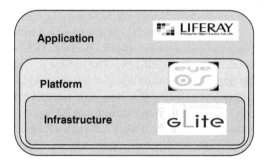

Fig. 8.2 The prototype architecture

The main technological choices underlying our prototype implementation are:

- gLite at the infrastructure layer. Such solution realizes a resource-virtualization facility based on the traditional gLite core and collective services, specifically conceived for e-science applications. gLite provides computing and storage facilities through a web services based interface by using the CREAM and SRM protocols, and implements data-movement services, resource brokering, work-load management, and accounting. The gLite middleware can be integrated with other infrastructure management facilities, such as VM-based runtime environments (i.e. OpenNebula [10]) and map-and-reduce [11] services (i.e. Hadoop [12]). For our testbed, we extended the gLite middleware by introducing the support of some basic network control services and interfaces.
- The platform layer is implemented by using the eyeOS [13], a Cloud Operating System. EyeOS offers Web 2.0 like tools, available through a flexible and powerful Web Desktop interface for the creation of new cloud applications, simply by using a meta-language based on PHP/AJAX. EyeOS manages user profiles and interacts with the underlying infrastructure layer.
- Finally, the application interface has been implemented through a portlet container that guarantees the seamless integration of different technologies and exposes the cloud prototype user interface, monitoring facilities, and Wiki pages. The product of choice is LifeRay, an open-source solution based on a Service Oriented Architecture (SOA) that supports Single Sign-On (SSO) for simplifying user authentication and authorization tasks.

The above-mentioned software stack guaranteed the abstraction and virtualization services needed at each layer of the cloud architecture, and offered simple and effective mechanisms for creating new applications and making them available to the final users throughout the cloud infrastructure.

8.5.1.1   The Underlying Network Infrastructure

The physical transport infrastructure, on which our prototype is based (see Fig. 8.3), is approximately 50-km long, consists of 156 single-mode fibers connecting, in a

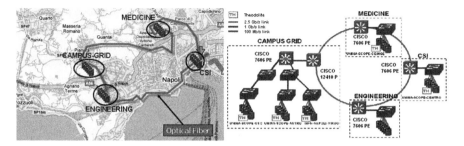

Fig. 8.3 The prototype network

multi-ring shape with multiple differentiated ways, four ring-to-ring interchange and service aggregation centers strategically placed on the metro area, which realizes the main transport and access distribution infrastructure. The backbone is built on a fully meshed core realized between four high-performance Cisco routers (a 12410 GSR and three 7606 OSRs), each acting as an access aggregation point (POP) in the metropolitan area. On the multi-ring backbone, we deployed an MPLS-based control plane architecture capable of establishing, managing, and tearing down bandwidth and QoS-guaranteed end-to-end connections.

8.5.1.2   The Prototype Cloud Network Control Logic and its Services

The network control logic has been implemented within our prototype testbed, by integrating a set of Perl scripts realizing some simple interface services at the gLite middleware layer, with the eyeOS interface. Such simple kernel of network services interacts with other cloud services/applications at different levels of the cloud stack, and enables location-independent data transfer and replication, together with bandwidth on demand and virtual-switch implementation through the user-interface facilities. The basic functions provided are reserving, releasing, and querying or modifying the status of end-to-end virtual circuits between different sites of the underlying distributed computing infrastructure. They have been made available through a web-service interface, in which every basic operation is characterized by a set of user-layer attributes (i.e. service class, bandwidth, and traffic-flow identifier) that in turn is implemented at the control-plane layer by a couple of unidirectional traffic-engineered LSP tunnels, together with some flow-specific routing policies. Every basic service function is in turn mapped to a set of Cisco CLI commands for network resource configuration, submitted to the network elements within the MPLS core using the Net::Telnet::Cisco standard Perl interface. Each invocation of specific function triggers the execution of a Perl script using a dedicated CLI session for the duration of its execution. When triggering the creation of pseudo-wire connections between the nodes, the requiring application needs to supply detailed information about all the physical nodes and ports involved to the network control logic. These data can be obtained on each node through the Cisco CDP protocol using a simple Perl interface agent (based on the Net::CDP standard class/module).

The interaction with the network control logic is realized by a new set of cloud services created on top of eyeOS web-desktop. The authentication/authorization process is based on x509 proxy certificates with the Virtual Organization Membership Services (VOMS)-extension, in the gLite-style. A user with the proper privileges can ask for a virtual circuit operation through the eyeOS network interface.

8.5.2 Performance Evaluation and Results Discussion

In this section, we present some simple performance evaluation experiences done on our Cloud prototype to show how an application working on large data volumes distributed in the different sites within the cloud can greatly benefit from the introduction of the above-mentioned network control facilities in the cloud stack, and to demonstrate the effectiveness of the implemented architecture in providing QoS or bandwidth guarantees. To better emphasize the above-mentioned benefits and improvements to application behaviour, we performed our tests under real-world extreme traffic load conditions, by working between the Monte S. Angelo Campus site, actually the largest data center in the SCoPE infrastructure, and the Medicine Campus site, currently hosting the other largest storage repository available to the university's research community. More precisely, the presented results have been obtained by analyzing the throughput associated to the transfer of 1-GB datasets between two EMC2 Clarion CX-3 storage systems located in the above-mentioned sites.

Both the involved storage area networks are connected to their respective access switches through dedicated resource manager nodes equipped with 1 Gbps full-duplex Ethernet interfaces. Here, for simplicity sake, we considered several sample-transfer sessions moving more than 2 TB of experimental data. During the first data transfer, performed on the cloud without any kind of network resource reservation, the underlying routing protocol picks the best but most crowded route between the two sites (owing to the strong utilization of the involved links in peak hours) through the main branch of the metro ring, so that we were able transfer 500 GB of data in 4 h (average 30 s/file) with an average throughput of 33 MB/s (about 270 Mbit/s) and a peak rate of 86 MB/s. We also observed a standard deviation equal to 12.0 owing to the noise present on the link, as it can be appreciated from the strong oscillation illustrated in the picture in Fig. 8.4. During the second test, we created a virtual point-to-point network between the two storage sites by reserving a 1-Gbps bandwidth channel to the above-mentioned data-transfer operation. Such action triggered the creation of a pair of dynamic end-to-end LSPs (one for each required direction) characterized with the required bandwidth on the involved PE nodes. In the presence of background traffic saturating the main branch, such LSPs were automatically re-routed through the secondary (and almost unused) branch to support the required bandwidth commitment. In this case, we observed that the whole 500-GB data transfer was completed in 1 h and 23 min (9.9 s/file) with an average throughput of 101 MB/s and a peak of 106 MB/s. We also observed an improvement in standard deviation achieving an acceptable value of 2.8 against the 12.5 of the best-effort case. We also evidenced a 20-MB/s loss with respect to the theoretical

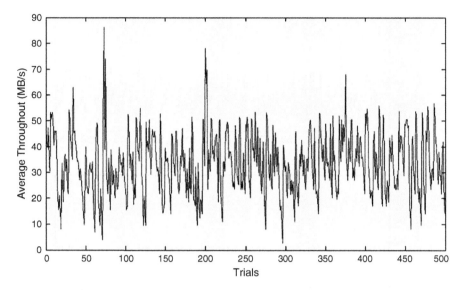

Fig. 8.4 The best effort transfer behaviour

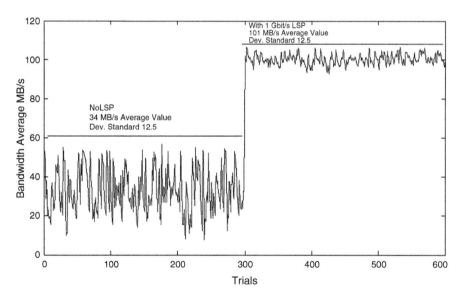

Fig. 8.5 The gain achieved through a virtual connection

achievable maximum bandwidth, due to the known TCP and Ethernet overhead and limits. This simple test evidences how the above-mentioned facility can be effective in optimizing the data-transfer performance within the cloud, and the results are more impressive when expressed in graphical form, as presented in Fig. 8.5, showing the gain achieved by concatenating a sequence of 300 file transfers in the best effort network with the other 300 transfers on the virtual 1-Gbps point-to-point network.

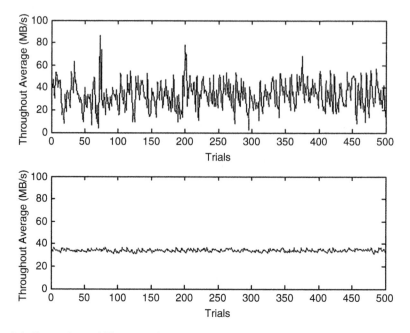

Fig. 8.6 Connection-stability comparison

We also examined the end-to-end connection stability by copying the same data volumes (500 GB) between the SANs, both in the presence of a virtual connection and without it. In the following graphs (Fig. 8.6), we have compared the average throughput observed in the first best-effort transfer operation (where an average throughput of 300 Mbps is achieved) and when the same bandwidth is reserved across the cloud sites. In both the sessions, we were able to transfer the whole 500 GB of data in approximately the same time (about 4 h) with an average throughput of 34 MB/s (about 272 Mbit/s versus the theoretical 300 Mbit/s), but with a standard deviation equal to 1.13 against a value of 12.0 of the best-effort case.

This demonstrated the much higher stability of the virtual circuit arrangement exhibiting a guaranteed bandwidth within a 10% range.

8.6 Related Work

To the best of our knowledge, few experiences about network-empowered cloud infrastructures can be found in the literature. One of the most interesting approaches [14] focuses on the migration of virtual machines and proposes a scheduling model to minimize the migration-related risks of network congestions with respect to bandwidth-demand fluctuations. A more experimental approach is presented in [15], where an effective large-scale cloud testbed called the Open Cloud Testbed (OCT) is proposed. In contrast with other cloud testbeds spanning small geographic areas and communicating through commodity Internet services, the OCT is a wide-area testbed based on four data centers that are connected with a high-performance 10-Gbps network, based on a foundation of dedicated lightpaths. However, such an infrastructure, even if empowered by a high-performance network, does not provide dynamic bandwidth allocation mechanisms driven by the application requirements, and its network-management facilities are limited to basic monitoring. Other interesting issues regarding the benefits of a network-aware approach can be found in [16], where the authors present the performance improvements obtained through network resource engineering in running bioinformatics application such as Lattice-Boltzmann simulations and DNA analysis. Other examples of the introduction of a network-aware philosophy in high-performance distributed computing systems are described in [17–21]. Finally, there is an active open discussion about "End-to-end Network Service Level agreements (SLAs)" within the EGEE project [22] exploring several strategies for advanced network-services provision and analyzing the benefits of using specific SLAs for the most demanding applications.

8.7 Conclusions

We introduced a new network-centric cloud architecture in which the traditional resource-management facilities can be extended with enhanced end-to-end connectivity services that are totally under the control of the cloud control logic. Such framework enables simple and affordable solutions that facilitate vertical and horizontal communication, achieved through proper interfaces and software tools between the existing network control plane and provisioning systems and the applications requiring dynamic provisioning of high bandwidth and QoS. Accordingly, we proposed and developed a new service-oriented abstraction based on the existing web services architecture and built on the WSRF framework,which introduces a new network control layer between the cloud customers and the network infrastructure, decoupling the connection service provisioning from the underlying network implementation. Such a control layer provides the necessary bridge between the cloud and its data-transfer facilities so that the capabilities offered by the combination of the features of modern network and distributed computing systems greatly enhance the ability to deliver cloud services according to specific SLAs and strict QoS requirements.

References

1. Amazon: Amazon elastic compute cloud. http://aws.amazon.com/ec2/. Accessed Dec 2009
2. Amazon: Amazon simple storage service. http://aws.amazon.com/s3/. Accessed Dec 2009
3. Rosen E, Viswanathan A, Callon R (2001) Multiprotocol label switching architecture. IETF RFC 3031
4. Mannie E (2004) Generalized multi-protocol label switching (GMPLS) architecture. IETF RFC 3945
5. Jamoussi B et al (2002) Constraint-based LSP setup using LDP. IETF RFC 3212

6. Berger L (2003) Generalized multi-protocol label switching signaling resource ReserVation Protocol-Traffic Engineering (RSVP-TE) extensions. IETF RFC 3473
7. Czajkowski K, Ferguson DF, Foster I, Frey J, Graham S, Maguire T, Snelling D, Tuecke S (2004) From open grid services infrastructure to WS-resource framework: refactoring & evolution. http://www-106.ibm.com/ developerworks/library/ws-resource/ogsi_to_wsrf_1.0.pdf. Accessed Dec 2009
8. Rajagopalan B et al (ed) (2000) User Network Interface (UNI) 1.0 signaling specification. OIF2000.125.3
9. gLite: Lightweight middleware for grid. http://glite.web.cern.ch/glite/. Accessed Dec 2009
10. OpenNebula: The open source toolkit for cloud computing. http://www.opennebula.org/. Accessed Dec 2009
11. Dean J, Ghemawat S (2004) MapReduce: simplified data processing on large clusters. Proceedings of 6th symposium on operating system design and implementation (OSDI), pp 137–150
12. Hadoop: The Hadoop Project. http://hadoop.apache.org/core/. Accessed Dec 2009
13. eyeOS: The open source cloud's web desktop. http://eyeos.org/. Accessed Dec 2009
14. Stage A, Setze T (2009) Network-aware migration control and scheduling of differentiated virtual machine workloads, Proceedings of the ICSE workshop on software engineering challenges of cloud computing, IEEE Comsoc
15. Grossman RL, Gu Y, Michal Sabala M, Bennet C, Seidman J, Mambretti J (2009) The open cloud testbed: a wide area testbed for cloud computing utilizing high performance network services. CoRR abs/0907.4810
16. Coveneya PV, Giupponia G, Jhab S, Manosa S, MacLarenb J, Picklesc SM, Saksenaa RS, Soddemannd T, Sutera JL, Thyveetila M, Zasadaa SJ (2009) Large scale computational science on federated international grids: the role of switched optical networks. Future Gen Comput Syst 26(1):99–110
17. Hao F, Lakshman TV, Mukherjee S, Song H (2009) Enhancing dynamic cloud-based services using network virtualization. Proceedings of VISA '09: the 1st ACM workshop on Virtualized infrastructure systems and architectures, Barcelona, Spain
18. Bradley S, Burstein F, Gibbard B, Katramatos D et al. (2006) Data sharing infrastructure for peta-scale computing research. Proceedings of CHEP, Mumbai, India
19. Nurmi D, Wolski R, Grzegorczyk C, Obertelli G, Soman S, Youseff L, Zagorodnov D (2008) Eucalyptus: a technical report on an elastic utility computing architecture linking your programs to useful systems. UCSB CS Technical Report #2008–2010
20. Palmieri F (2006) GMPLS-based service differentiation for scalable QoS support in all-optical GRID applications, Elsevier. Future Gen Comp Syst 22(6):688–698
21. Palmieri F (2009) Network-aware scheduling for real-time execution support in data-intensive optical Grids. Future Gen Comp Syst 25(7):794–803
22. The EGEE Project: Advanced Services: End-to-end Network Service Level agreements (SLAs). http://technical.eu-egee.org/index.php?id=352. Accessed Dec 2009

Chapter 9
YML-PC: A Reference Architecture Based on Workflow for Building Scientific Private Clouds

Ling Shang, Serge Petiton, Nahid Emad, and Xiaolin Yang

Abstract Cloud computing platforms such as Amazon EC2 provide customers flexible, on-demand resources at low cost. However, while the existing offerings are useful for providing basic computation and storage resources, they fail to consider factors such as security, custom, and policy. So, many enterprises and research institutes would not like to utilize those public Clouds. According to investigations on real requirements from scientific computing users in China, the project YML-PC has been started to build private Clouds and hybrid Clouds for them. In this paper, we will focus on the first step of YML-PC to present a reference architecture based on the workflow framework YML for building scientific private Clouds. Then, some key technologies such as trust model, data persistence, and schedule mechanisms in YML-PC are discussed. Finally, some experiments are carried out to testify that the solution presented in this paper is more efficient.

9.1 Introduction

Cloud computing, as a term for internet-based services, was launched by famous IT enterprises (e.g. Google, IBM, Amazon, Microsoft, Yahoo, etc.). It promises to provide on-demand computing power in the manner of services with quick implementation, little maintenance, and lower cost. Clouds aim at being dynamically scalable and offer virtualized resources to end-users through the internet. Solutions deployed in Clouds can be characterized as easy-to-use, pay-by-use, less time to solution, and lower cost. Clouds can be divided into three types: public Clouds, private Clouds, and hybrid Clouds. Generally speaking, public Clouds refer to entities that can provide services to external parties, such as Amazon and Google. Private Clouds are used to provide services to internal users who would not like to

L. Shang (✉)
MAP Team, Lifl, Laboratoire d'Informatique Fondamentale de Lille (LIFL),
University of Sciences and Technology of Lille, France
e-mail: ling.shang@lifl.fr

N. Antonopoulos and L. Gillam (eds.), *Cloud Computing: Principles,*
Systems and Applications, Computer Communications and Networks,
DOI 10.1007/978-1-84996-241-4_9, © Springer-Verlag London Limited 2010

utilize public Clouds for some issues that span over security, custom, confidence, policy, law, and so on. Hybrid Clouds share resources between public Clouds and private Clouds through a secure network.

Scientific computing requires an ever-increasing number of computing resources to deliver for growing sizes of problems in a reasonable time frame, and cloud computing holds promise for the performance-hungry scientific community [1]. Several evaluations have shown that better performance can be achieved at lower cost using Clouds and cloud technology than based on previous technologies. For example, papers [2, 3] make an evaluation of cloud technology on public Clouds (e.g. EC2). Papers [4, 5] evaluate cloud technology based on private Clouds (e.g. clusters in internal research institute). Paper [6] shows the potential to utilize volunteer computing resources to form Clouds. Papers [7–9] present methods to improve the performance of a Desktop Grid platform. Paper [10] analyzes the cost-benefit of cloud computing versus Desktop Grids. Papers [11–13] introduce some Clouds solutions based on volunteer computing resources.

An investigation is made into requirements for building scientific computing environments for non-large enterprises and research institutes in China. Those issues can be summarized as follows: First, most of the enterprises and research institutes have their computing environment, but they suffer from shortage of computing resources. Second, they would not like to spend a lot of money to expand their computing resources. On the other hand, they hope that they can make full use of wasted CPU cycle of individual PCs in labs and offices. Third, they need a high-level programming interface to decrease their costs (time, money) in developing applications that suit computing environments. Last but not least, they would like to utilize their own computing environments for addressing the importance and security of their data. After all, these data are bought from other corporates with high cost and they are required to keep those data secret. To meet these requirements, a project has been started between the University of Science and Technology of Lille, France, and Hohai University, China. Its general goal is to build a private Cloud environment that can provide end-users with a high-level programming interface, and users can utilize computing resources they need without considering where these computing resources come from (i.e. the layer of program interface is independent of the layer of computing resources).

YML [14–16] is a large-scale workflow programming framework, developed by PRiSM laboratories at the university of Versailles and Laboratoire d'Informatique Fondamentale de Lille (LIFL, Grand Large Team, INRIA Futurs) at the University of Science and Technology of Lille. The aim of YML is to provide users with an easy-to-use method to run parallel applications on different distributed computing platforms. The framework can be divided into three parts: end-users interface, YML frontend, and YML backend. End-users interface is used to provide an easy-to-use and intuitive way to submit applications, and applications, can be developed using a workflow-based language, YvetteML. YML frontend is the main part of YML, which includes compiler, scheduler, data repository, abstract component, and implementation component. The role of this part is to parse parallel programs, into executable tasks and schedule these tasks to appropriate computing resources. YML backend is the layer to connect different Grid and Desktop Grid middleware through different special interfaces, and users can develop these interfaces very easily. The YML is a component-based framework in which components can interact with each other through well-defined interfaces and researchers can add/modify one or several interfaces for other middleware to YML very easily.

Paper [18] presents a method of resource management in Clouds through a grid middleware. Here, we will extend YML to build scientific private Clouds for non-big enterprises and research institutes. We call this project "YML-PC." Three steps are needed to make this project a reality. The first step is to integrate volunteer computing resources into dedicated computing resources through YML and make them work in co-ordination. Volunteer computing resources can be a supplement to dedicated computing resources and a volunteer computing resources-based platform has the ability to expand computing resource pools dynamically by nature. If dedicated computing resources are not enough for users, volunteer computing resources can be utilized to implement their tasks. But users do not know whether their tasks are run on dedicated computing resources or volunteer computing resources, and they need not know. The key issue of this step is how to allocate tasks to different kinds of computing resources more reasonably and make those computing resources work with high efficiency. The second step is to develop an interface for Hadoop and integrate it into YML. Then, some evaluations will be made on cluster environment + Hadoop. The third step is to try to build a hybrid Clouds environment through combining step one with step two. The solution is that step one can stand for a kind of private Clouds and step two can be deployed on public Clouds, then YML as a workflow-based framework can harness private Clouds and public Clouds.

In this paper, our work focuses on the first step. To do that, our research-in-progress on YML focuses on the following aspects:

- Data flows. Added in the application file. Through adding this flow, data persistence and data replication mechanisms can be realized in YML-PC. Also, it can help to improve the efficiency of the platform greatly.
- Monitor and Trust model. Introduced to monitor the available status of non-dedicated computing resources and predict their future status. Also, a method to evaluate expected execution time based on standard virtual machine is adopted. Through this method, heterogeneous computing resources can be changed into homogeneous computing resources and then can be evaluated. According to this evaluation and prediction, tasks can be allocated to appropriate computing resources.

The remainder of this paper is organized as follows: Section 2 is the general introduction of YML. Section 3 describes the design and implementation of the YML-based private Clouds in detail. In Section 4, some evaluations are made and some related works are discussed. Section 5 gives conclusions and describes future work.

9.2   Overview of YML

YML is a workflow-based framework dedicated to execution of parallel applications on various middleware. Now it can support two middlewares: OmniRPC [19] and XtremWeb[20]. OmniRPC can harness dedicated computing resources in cluster and grid environments, while XtremWeb can collect volunteer computing resources in Desktop Grid. Condor is on the way to being integrated into YML. Figure 9.1 shows us the overview of YML.

There are four parts in the Fig. 9.1, which are CLIENT, Data Repository, YML, and YML workers.

CLIENT provides the end-users an intuitive way to express parallel applications by means of a workflow. The description language of YML is called YvetteML and can express several execution structures of parallel programs, such as sequential execution, parallel execution, and conditional branch and event notification/reception (event signals are used to control when an operation can be executed). A simple example can be presented through Fig. 9.2. What we want to emphasize here is that end-users just use YvetteML to describe the workflow and he/she must not know how to program using special programming languages (e.g. Java, C, C++, Fortune, MPI). The parallel program described using YvetteML can be run on different platforms without any change. We will explain this point in the part of YML workers in detail.

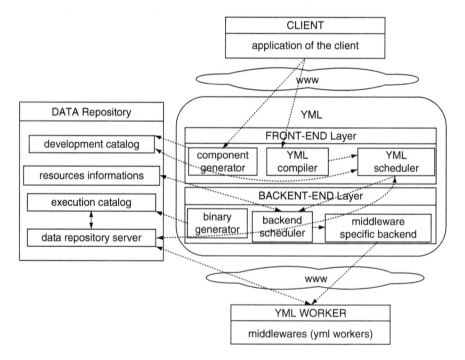

Fig. 9.1 Overview of YML framework [17]

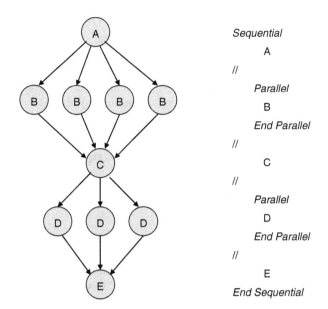

Sequential

A

//

Parallel

B

End Parallel

//

C

//

Parallel

D

End Parallel

//

E

End Sequential

Fig. 9.2 Sketch of high-level program interface

Data Repository contains four parts, which are Development catalog, Resources information, Execution catalog, and Data server. Development catalog has functions (e.g. function A, B in Fig. 9.2.) developed using C or C++. These functions can be reused in other applications. For example, application 1 and application 2 both need "function A" and if you develop "function A" for application 1, you can reuse it in application 2 without any change. After "function A" in Development catalog is registered in YML, "function A" will become the executable function in the Execution catalog. Resources information is information about which computing nodes can be utilized. The information is dynamically changed according to the availability of computing resources. As well known to us all, the key characteristic of volunteer computing resources is volatility. So, accurate prediction of volunteer computing resources is very important and it is also the key research point of this paper. Data server is used to store data, and its transport model is based on server/worker. So, adopting server/worker-based data transport model is another key research point of this paper.

YML is the core of the "sandwich" architecture of YML framework. It can hide the complexity and heterogeneity of the underlying computing platforms and provide a unique programming interface to end-users. YML has two layers, which are Front-end and Back-end. Front-end can parse the pseudocode-based program in CLIENT and invoke executable functions accordingly to form an executable graph. According to this graph, YML scheduler will allocate tasks to Back-end scheduler. Then, Back-end scheduler allocates those tasks to different computing resources according to Resources information. Back-end provides different interfaces to different middleware.

YML workers is the interface layer for middleware. Different middleware can be used to harness different kinds of computing resources. For example, XtremWeb can be used to collect volunteer computing resources and OmniRPC can harness dedicated computing resources such as clusters and Grids. Here, what we want to emphasize is that whatever kinds of middleware are used to harness computing resources, the program in CLIENT can be run without any change.

9.3   Design and Implementation of YML-PC

9.3.1   Concept Stack of Cloud Platform

This section presents a detailed design for how to build the environment of cloud computing based on previous work from papers [21–24]. As shown in Fig. 9.3, generally speaking, cloud computing can have four main layers. The base is the layer of "computing resources" and above this layer, "Operating system" and "Grid middleware" can be used to harness those different kinds of computing resources.

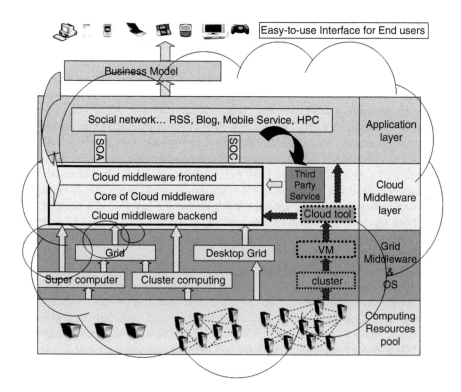

Fig. 9.3 Concept stack of cloud platform

Then, "cloud middleware" layer can help users compose applications without considering the underlying infrastructure; this layer hides different interfaces from different platforms/systems/middleware and provides a uniform, high-level abstraction and easy-to-use interface for end-users. The top layer is "application layer" and cloud platform will provide different interfaces according to different requirements. Business model helps to support "pay-by-use" model, and users can get the best services within their budget through "bidding mechanism."

Next, detailed explanation will be made on those layers one by one:

- Computing Resource pool: this layer consists of different kinds of computing resources, which can be clusters, supercomputer, large data center, volunteer computing resources, and some devices. It aims at providing end-users with on-demand computing power.
- Grid middleware and OS: the role of this layer is to harness all kinds of computing resources in the computing resource pool. Some virtual machines can be generated through virtual technology based on cluster (perhaps also based on volunteer computing resources).
- Cloud middleware layer: in the cloud platform, cloud middleware can be divided into three parts according to their roles. *Cloud middleware backend* aims to monitor all kinds of computing resources and encapsulate those heterogeneous computing resources into homogeneous computing resources. *Cloud middleware frontend* is used to parse application programs into executable subtasks. Cloud platform always provides end-users with higher-level abstract interfaces. Through parsing the application program, this layer can generate a file in which some necessary services (executable functions, computing resources, third-party service library) are listed. *The core of cloud middleware* includes a "matchmaker factory" in which appropriate matches can be made based on business models between tasks and computing resources according to their requirements and properties. Then, scheduler allocates those "executable functions" and "third-party services" to appropriate computing resources.
- Application layer: this layer is generated according to real requirements by end-users based on SOA. And SOA can make sure that all the interfaces from different service providers are common and easy to invoke.
- Business model: this model can support a pay-by-use model to end-users. It can also help end-users get the best services within their budget.
- End-user interface: The interface must be a high-level abstraction and easy to use. It is very helpful for nonexpert computer users to utilize Cloud platform.

9.3.2   Design of YML-PC

The detailed design of YML-PC is made based on a concept stack of cloud platform (see Fig. 9.4). As mentioned earlier, the development on YML-PC can be divided into three steps. The components with dashed border will be developed in the second

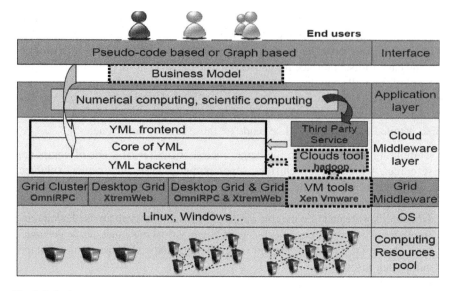

Fig. 9.4 Reference architecture of YML-PC

step. In this paper, we are focussed on the first step. So, the detailed description will also focus on the design and implementation of first step of YML-PC. YML-PC is designed to build private Clouds for scientific computing based on workflow. Some features of YML-PC can be summarized as:

- YML-PC can harness two kinds of computing resources at the same time and this can help to improve computing power greatly through integrating volunteer computing resources. At the same time, no extra cost is needed to do that and volunteer computing resources can also help YML-PC to scale in a dynamic way.
- YML-PC shields the heterogeneity of program interfaces of underlying middleware/system/platform and provides a high-level abstraction, unique interface for end-users.
- YML-PC can make full use of different kinds of computing resources according to their properties. To improve the efficiency of YML-PC, prescheduling and "data persistence" mechanisms are introduced into YML-PC.

Computing resource pool: The computing resource pool of YML-PC consists of two different kinds of computing resources: dedicated computing resources (servers or clusters) and non-dedicated computing resources (PCs). As well known to us all, a cluster is too expensive to scale up for non-big research institutes and enterprises. At the same time, there are a lot of PCs in which a lot of CPU cycles are wasted. So, it is appealing (from the viewpoint of both economy and feasibility) to harness these two kinds of computing resources together. Computing resource pool with a lot of PCs has features like being low cost, and scalabile by nature; these features are key points of Clouds.

OS: Operating system is the base for installing other software. Now YML-PC and OmniRPC (used to harness dedicated computing resources) only support Linux OS. XtremWeb, used to collect volunteer computing resources, can support Windows OS and Linux OS.

Grid middleware: The construction of a computing resource pool in YML-PC is based on state-of-the-art technology: Grid and Desktop Grid technology. For YML-PC, we utilize gird middleware OmniRPC to harness cluster-based computing resources and Desktop Grid middleware XtremWeb to manage volunteer computing resources. Also, we can utilize these two middleware at the same time to form a computing resource pool consisting of two kinds of computing resources. As well known to us all, traditional scientific computing mostly runs based on cluster or supercomputer and it is necessary to make full use of this kind of computing resource. At the same time, the power of volunteer computing is huge and it has been proved by existing volunteer platforms such as Seti@home. It is very meaningful to make volunteer computing resources be the supplement/extension of traditional computing resources.

Application layer and Interface: The main design goal of YML-PC is for scientific computing and numerical computing. So, to make scientific computing more easy, a pseudocode-based high-level interface is provided to end-users.

YML frontend, YML backend and the core of YML will be described in the next section.

9.3.3 Core Design and Implementation of YML-PC

Fig. 9.5 will show us the core design and implementation of YML-PC. We will explain these components in Fig. 9.5 one by one.

YML frontend: This provides end-users with an easy-to-use interface and allows them to focus only on the design of the algorithm. Users need not take low-level software/hardware into consideration when they develop their application programs. For the program interface of YML-PC, we still adopt the interface of YML. For those "reusable services" (functions described in Fig. 9.2), two ways exist the first is that users can develop those "reusable services" by themselves or with computer engineers; the second way is to invoke those functions from a common library (e.g. LAPACK, BLAS; we also call these "third-party services"). Here, what we want to emphasize is that both the pseudocode-based program and those functions developed are reusable and both are platform-independent and system-independent. System independence means that users need not know what kinds of operating system/middleware are utilized. Platform independence means that code can be run on any platform (cluster, grid, Desktop Grid) without any change. That is, these codes developed by users can be reused without caring about the middleware, system, and platform. You can use OmniRPC on a grid/cluster platform or XtremWeb on a Desktop Grid platform or both, but users' code can be reused without change.

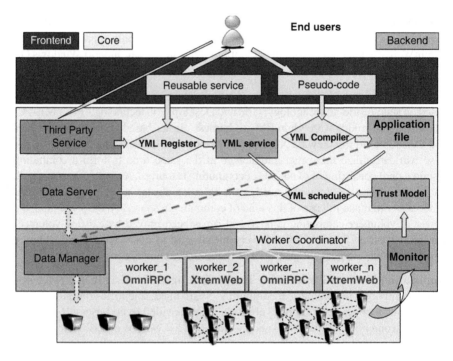

Fig. 9.5 Core part of YML-PC

The core of YML: Three components are included in this layer: YML register, YML compiler, and YML scheduler.

YML register is used to register reusable services and third-party services. Once registered, these services can be invoked by YML scheduler automatically.

YML compiler is composed of a set of transformation stages that lead to the creation of an application file from pseudocode-based program. The application file consists of a series of events and operations. Events are in charge of sequences of operations. In other words, which operation can be executed in parallel/sequence is decided by the events table. Operations refer to those services registered by YML register. One important work made in this paper is that a data flow table is generated in the application file. Through the data flow table, data dependence between operations can be found (see "data flow table" in Fig. 9.6). As well known to us all, these data dependencies determine the execution (in parallel/sequence) of different operations. According to these data dependencies, prescheduling mechanisms can be realized (see column "node" in "IP address table" of Fig. 9.6). Then, collaborating the "IP address table" (in Fig. 9.6), data persistence and data replication mechanisms can be realized. The general idea of this part of work can be described using Fig. 9.6.

YML scheduler is a just-in-time scheduler. It is in charge of allocating the executable YML services to appropriate computing resources shielded by

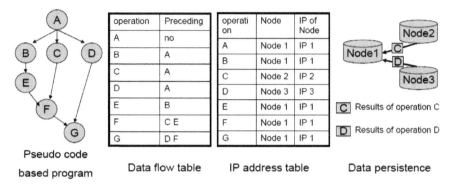

Fig. 9.6 General idea of "Data Persistence" in YML-PC

YML back-end layer. YML scheduler is always executing two main operations sequentially. First, it checks for tasks ready for execution. This is done each time a new event is introduced and leads to allocating tasks to the YML back-end. The second operation is to monitor those tasks currently being executed. Once tasks have started to execute, the scheduler regularly checks whether these tasks have changed to the finished state. The scheduler will push new tasks with its input data set and related YML services to an underlying computing node when the node's state is completion or unexpected error.

To make the process presented above a reality, two parts of this work are in mentioned this paper. The first is to introduce monitoring and a prediction model for volunteer computing resources. It is well known that volatility is the key characteristic of volunteer computing resources and if we do not know any regularity of volunteer computing resources, the problem with data dependence between operations means that it cannot run on a Desktop Grid platform. The reason is that frequent task migration will render the program incomplete forever. We call this a "deadlock of tasks." To avoid this situation, we introduce a monitor and prediction model TM-DG [25]. TM-DG is used to predict the probability of availability of computing nodes in the Desktop Grid during a certain time slot. The time slot depends on users' daily behaviors. For example, the availability of computing nodes in the lab has relation to students' school timetable. If students go to classes, computers in the lab can be utilized for scientific computing. So the choice of time slot is related to time slots of classes. It is because 2 h is needed for each class that the time slot in [25] is set as 2 h. TM-DG collects two bodies of independent evidence: (1) percentage of completion of the allocated task, and (2) an active probe by a special test node, based on the time slot. Considering the "recommendation evidence" from other users, Dempster-Shafer's theory [26] is used to combine these bodies of evidence to get the degree of node trustworthiness. The result of TM-DG can be expressed by a four-tuple <I, W, H, m(T)>, in which I represents the identity of computation node, W represents the day of the week, H represents a time interval in a day, and m represents the probability of node availability. The four-tuple

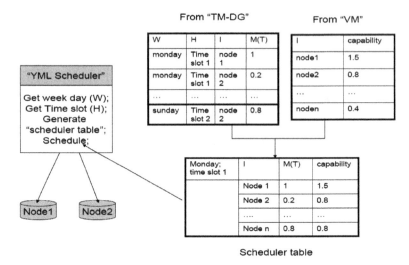

Fig. 9.7 Description of YML scheduler

<node I, Monday, 1, 0.6> represents that the time slot is from 0 to 2 a.m. on Monday, and the probability of successful execution on node I during this time slot is 0.6. So in this paper, monitor component in YML-backend and schedule component in Core of YML are based on the time slot.

The second part involves making full use of computing resources, so evaluation of capability of heterogeneous computing nodes has to be made. So, a standard virtual machine (VM) is proposed in this paper. The standard VM can be set in advance. For example, the VM is set through a series of parameters (Ps, Ms, Ns, Hs), in which Ps stands for CPU power of VM (2.0 MHz CPU), Ms represents memory of VM (1 G Memory), Ns means network bandwidth of VM (1G), and Hs stands for disk storage space required (10 G). Users can adapt the number of parameters according to real situation. A real computing node 'Rm' can be described as (Pr, Mr, Nr, Hr). The capacity (Crm) of 'Rm' can be presented as follows: Crm= a1 * Pr/Ps + a2 * Mr/Ms + a3 * Nr/Ns + a4 * Hr/Hs, in which a1 + a2 + a3 + a4 = 1. The value of ax (x = 1, 2, 3, 4) can be set according to different influences on final results from different parameters in real situations. We can set an appropriate value to ax (x = 1...n) based on historic information. Through the VM, expected execution times of tasks on a computing node can be estimated.

Scheduler can choose appropriate computing nodes according to predictions of availability of computing resources (from TM-DG) and time needed to execute a task on this node (from VM). Scheduler will get the detail time and form the scheduler table and then schedule tasks to appropriate computing nodes. The YML scheduler mechanism can be described using Fig. 9.7. When a fault is generated, the task will be rescheduled. Future research about fault tolerance in YML-PC will focus on: (1) allocating the same task to three or more volunteer computing nodes; (2) preemptive scheduling based on multi-queue scheduling mechanisms.

YML backend: YML backend encapsulates different underlying middleware and provides a consistent executable environment to tasks from the layer "core of YML." Concurrently, it permits to utilize one or several middleware through a specific interface for each middleware. The back-end layer consists of three parts named *Monitor, worker coordinator,* and *data manager.* In general, YML backend sends requests for executing a task on a computing node and if the task finishes, it also notifies the scheduler that the task is terminated successfully. *Data manager* is a component for managing all data exchanges between nodes and data server. This component provides two services: distributing appropriate data to workers and retrieving the final results. *Worker coordinator* maintains a list of active requests and a list of finished requests. The status can change dynamically according to the status of computing nodes. It will allocate those tasks from YML scheduler to appropriate computing nodes in computing resource pools. *Monitor* component is used to monitor the status of computing nodes. The monitoring mechanism is based on users' daily behavior, which is adopted to predict the available time of computing resources and make prediction for data migration.

9.4 Primary Experiments on YML-PC

In this section, three kinds of primary experiments (emulations) are made to show that: (1) the computing resource pool can be scaled very easily; (2) great improvements on platform efficiency can be made through emulating the data persistence; (3) great improvements on platform efficiency can be made through emulating appropriate task distribution between different virtual organizations.

Here, inter-iterative parallel-based block-based Gauss-Jordan algorithm [27, 28] is used. According to the algorithm, q^2 is the number of block-counts of matrix. The number of total tasks the algorithm will generate is q^3. All these experiments are based on YML+OmniRPC, YML+XtremWeb, YML+OmniRPC/XtremWeb, and Grid 5,000 platform [29]. In our experiments, the computational resources can be described as follows (Table 9.1):

Table 9.1 Parts of computing resources in Grid'5000 platform

Site	Cluster	Nodes	CPU/memory
Nancy	Grelon	120	2 × Inter xeon, 1.6 GHz/2 GB
Rennes	Paravent	99	2 × AMD opteron, 2 GHz/2 GB
Lyon	Sagittaire	70	2 × AMD opteron, 2.4 GHz/2 GB
Bordeaux	Bordereau	93	2 × AMD opteron, 2.6 GHz/2 GB

9.4.1 YML-PC Can Be Scaled Up Very Easily

In this experiment, we set the block-size of submatrix to 1,500 * 1,500, and the middleware is YML+Xtremweb. The reason is that XtremWeb can be easily scaled up for its "pull model" based task allocation mechanism. "R-B" represents that the computing resource pool has ten computing nodes, while "R-A" implies that the computing resources have scaled up to 20 computing nodes. Scale up occurs during the process of program execution.

Figure 9.8 shows that when the block-count is less than 3^2, there is little influence on the elapsed time whether computing resource pool scales up or not. But when the block-count is more than 3^2, scalability of computing resource pool has an important influence on the elapsed time. The reason stems from the algorithm itself. When the block-count is small, tasks generated are few; ten computing resources can be enough for generated tasks. So, the influence on the elapsed time is small. With the increase in block-count of matrix, the generated tasks increase greatly. More computing resources are needed. So, the influence on elapsed time becomes more obvious. In a word, from Fig. 9.8, we can conclude that, whether the block count is small or large, scalability of a computing pool can improve the efficiency of the platform. At the same time, this experiment testifies that YML-PC has the ability to scale.

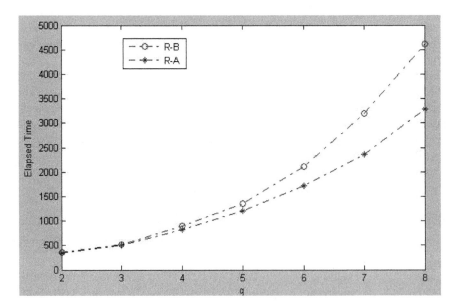

Fig. 9.8 Feature of scalability of YML-PC

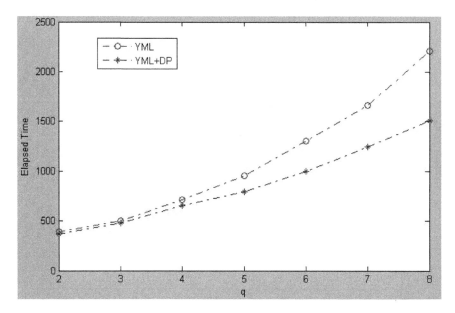

Fig. 9.9 Data persistence in YML-PC

9.4.2 Data Persistence in YML-PC

The efficiency of YML-PC can be improved with the help of data persistence technology. In this experiment, we set block-size of submatrix as 1,500 * 1,500. The middleware is YML+OmniRPC. YML in Fig. 9.9 represents that the platform does not support data persistence, while YML+DP stands for the YML-PC supporting data persistence.

Figure 9.9 shows that data persistence is very important for scientific computing especially for scientific computing with substantial data. It can save a lot of time and thus improve the efficiency of the platform. With increase in block-counts of matrix, more tasks are generated and therefore a lot of data transfers between data server and workers are generated. If we take data persistence technology in cloud computing platform, less communication overhead is generated and the efficiency of cloud platform can be improved.

9.4.3 Schedule Mechanism in YML-PC

Appropriate selection of computing resources based on trust model in YML-PC is very important. In this experiment, we set block-size as 1,500 * 1,500, and the middleware is YML+Xtremweb. 'No fault' in Fig. 9.10 represents the no

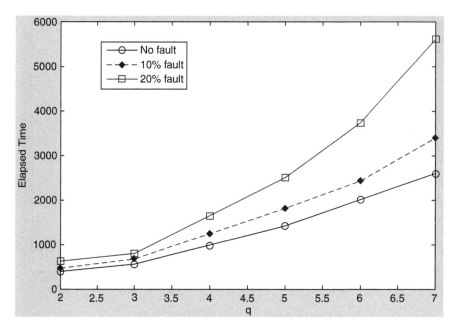

Fig. 9.10 Schedule mechanism in YML-PC

faults happen on the computing nodes. In other words, the trust model is totally correct. '10% faults' stands for 10% of computing nodes in cloud platform fail during the process of program execution. In other words, the accurate rate of trust model is 90%. '20% faults' stands for 20% of computing nodes in cloud platform failing during program execution. In other words, the accurate rate of trust model is 80%.

Figure 9.10 tells us that choosing appropriate computing resources to execute tasks is very important. Improper match-making between computing resources and tasks will decrease efficiency greatly. So, monitoring the computing resources in cloud computing is very important and we had better find the regularity behind its appearance through monitoring. Trust model in paper [25] can be utilized in cloud platform and it can be improved by adopting a better behavior model to describe users' behavior regularity.

9.5 Conclusion and Future Work

Cloud computing has gained great success for search engines, social e-networks, e-mail, and e-commercial. Amazon can provide different levels of computing resources to users by the way of pay-by-use. Many research institutes, such as the University of Berkeley, Delft University of Technology, and so on, have made evaluations on Amazon cloud platform. At the same time, Kondo et al try to evaluate the cost-benefits of public Clouds and Desktop Grid platform and conclude that Desktop Grid platform is promising and can be the base of cloud platform. So, based on the research mentioned above and real situation of non-big enterprises and research institutes in China, this paper extended the YML framework and presented YML-PC, which is a workflow-based framework for building scientific private Clouds. The project YML-PC will be divided into three steps: (1) Build private Clouds based on YML through harnessing dedicated computing resources and volunteer computing resources and make them work together with high efficiency. (2) Extend YML to support Hadoop and run Hadoop on cluster-based virtual machines. (3) Combining step 1 and step 2, build a hybrid Cloud based on YML. This paper focused on step 1. To improve the efficiency of YML-PC, "trust model" and "data persistence mechanism" are introduced in this paper. Simulations demonstrate that our idea is appropriate for building YML-PC.

Future work will focus on developing components to make YML-PC a reality. Then, more users' behavior models will be researched to improve the accuracy of prediction on available "time slot" of volunteer computing nodes. Fault-tolerant-based schedule mechanism is another key issue of our future work. A new idea, which is to deploy virtual tool (Xen, VMware for example) on volunteer computing resources and form several virtual machines on volunteer computing node, is also to be evaluated.

References

1. Ostermann S et al Early cloud computing evaluation. http://www.pds.ewi.tudelft.nl/_iosup/
2. Armbrust M, Fox A, Griffith R, Joseph A, Katz R, Konwinski A, Lee G, Patterson D, Rabkin A, Stoica I, Zaharia M (2009, Feb 10) Above the clouds: a Berkeley view of cloud computing. Technical Report, University of California, Berkley, USA
3. Garfinkel SL (Aug 2007) An evaluation of Amazon's grid computing services: EC2, S3 and SQS. Technical Report TR-08-07, Harvard University
4. de Assuncao MD, di Costanzo A, Buyya R (2009) Evaluating the cost-benefit of using cloud computing to extend the capacity of clusters. HPDC '09, ACM, pp 141–150
5. Ibrahim S, Jin H, Lu L, Qi L, Wu S, Shi X (2009) Evaluating MapReduce on virtual machines: The Hadoop case. CloudCom 2009, pp 519–528
6. David P (2006) Anderson, Gilles Fedak: the computational and storage potential of volunteer computing. CCGRID 2006, pp 73–80
7. Heien EM, Anderson DP (2009) Computing low latency batches with unreliable workers in volunteer computing environments. J Grid Comput 7(4):501–518
8. Javadi B, Kondo D, Vincent JM, Anderson DP (Sept 2009) Mining for statistical models of availability in large scale distributed systems: an empirical study of SETI@home. 17th IEEE/ACM MASCOTS 2009, London, UK
9. Ma X, Vazhkudai SS, Zhang Z (December 2009) Improving data availability for better access performance: a study on caching scientific data on distributed desktop workstations. J Grid Comput 7(4):419–438
10. Kondo D, Javadi B, Malecot P, Cappello F, Anderson DP (2009) Cost-benefit analysis of Cloud Computing versus desktop grids. ipdps, pp 1–12
11. Andrzejak A, Kondo D, Anderson DP (2010) Exploiting non-dedicated resources for cloud computing. In the 12th IEEE/IFIP (NOMS 2010), Osaka, Japan, 19–23 April 2010

12. Domingues P, Araujo F, Silva L (2009) Evaluating the performance and intrusiveness of virtual machines for desktop grid computing, IPDPS, 23–29 May 2009, pp 1–8

13. Vincenzo D (2009) Cunsolo, Salvatore Distefano, Antonio Puliafito, Marco Scarpa: Cloud@ Home: bridging the gap between volunteer and cloud computing. ICIC (1):423–432

14. Delannoy O, Emad N, Petiton SG (2006) Workflow global computing with YML. In: The 7th IEEE/ACM international conference on grid computing, pp 25–32

15. Delannoy O (Sept 2008) YML: a scientific workflow for high performance computing. Ph.D. thesis, Versailles

16. Delannoy O, Petiton S (2004) A peer to peer computing framework: design and performance evaluation of YML. In: third international workshop on HeterPar 2004, IEEE Computer Society Press, pp 362–369

17. Choy L, Delannoy O, Emad N, Petiton SG (2009) Federation and abstraction of heterogeneous global computing platforms with the YML framework, cisis, pp 451–456. In: The international conference on complex, intelligent and software intensive systems, 2009

18. Caron E, Desprez F, Loureiro D, Muresan A (2009) Cloud computing resource management through a grid middleware: a case study with DIET and eucalyptus. Cloud, pp 151–154

19. Sato M, Boku T, Takahashi D (2003) OmniRPC: a Grid RPC system for parallel programming in cluster and grid environment. In: the 3rd IEEE international symposium on cluster computing and the grid, pp 206–213

20. Germain C, eri VN', Fedak G, Cappello F (2000) Xtremweb: building an experimental platform for global computing. In: Buyya R, Baker M (eds) GRID, ser. lecture notes in Computer Science, vol 1971. Springer, Heidelberg, pp 91–101

21. Wang L, Tao J, Kunze M, Castellanos AC, Kramer D, Karl W (2008) Scientific cloud computing: early definition and experience. In the 10th IEEE international conference on HPCC, pp 825–830

22. Foster I, Zhao Y, Raicu I, Lu S (2008) Cloud computing and grid computing 360-degree compared. In Grid computing environments workshop, pp 1–10

23. Vecchiola C, Pandey S, Buyya R (2009) High-performance cloud computing: a view of scientific applications. In the 10th international symposium on pervasive systems, algorithms and networks (I-SPAN 2009), Kaohsiung, Taiwan, December 2009

24. Jha S, Merzky A, Fox G (June 2009) Using clouds to provide grids with higher levels of abstraction and explicit support for usage modes. Concurr Comput Pract Exper 21(8): 1087–1108

25. Shang L, Wang Z, Zhou X, Huang X, Cheng Y (2007) Tm-dg: a trust model based on computer users' daily behavior for desktop grid platform. In CompFrame '07: proceedings of the 2007 symposium on component and framework technology in high-performance and scientific computing, ACM, New York, USA, pp 59–66

26. Smets P (1990) The transferable belief model and other interpretations of Dempster-Shafer's model. In the proceedings of the sixth annual conference on uncertainty in artificial intelligence, pp 375–384, 27–29 July 1990

27. Shang L, Wang Z, Petiton SG (2008) Solution of large scale matrix inversion on cluster and grid. In proceedings of the 2008 seventh international conference on grid and cooperative computing (GCC), 24–26 October 2008, pp 33–40

28. Shang L, Petiton S, Hugues M (2009) A new parallel paradigm for block-based Gauss-Jordan algorithm (gcc). In the eighth international conference on grid and cooperative computing, pp 193–200

29. Cappello F et al (2005) Grid'5000: a large scale and highly reconfigurable grid experimental testbed. In the 6th IEEE/ACM international conference on grid computing, pp 99–106

Chapter 10
An Efficient Framework for Running Applications on Clusters, Grids, and Clouds

Brian Amedro, Françoise Baude, Denis Caromel, Christian Delbé, Imen Filali, Fabrice Huet, Elton Mathias, and Oleg Smirnov

Abstract Since the appearance of distributed computing technology, there has been a significant effort in designing and building the infrastructure needed to tackle the challenges raised by complex scientific applications that require massive computational resources. This increases the awareness to harness the power and flexibility of Clouds that have recently emerged as an alternative to data centers or private clusters. We describe in this chapter an efficient high-level Grid and Cloud framework that allows a smooth transition from clusters and Grids to Clouds. The main lever is the ability to move application infrastructure-specific information away from the code and manage them in a deployment file. An application can thus easily run on a cluster, a grid, or a cloud, or any mix of them without modification.

10.1 Introduction

Traditionally, HPC relied on supercomputers, clusters, or more recently, computing grids. With the rise of cloud computing and effective technical solutions, questions such as "is cloud computing ready for HPC" or "does a computing cloud constitute a relevant reservoir of resources for parallel computing" are around. This chapter gives some concrete answers to such questions. Offering a suitable middleware and associated programming environment to HPC users willing to take advantage of cloud computing is also a concern that we address in this chapter. One natural solution is to extend a grid computing middleware in such a way that it becomes able to harness cloud computing resources. A consequence is that we end up with a middleware that is able to unify resource acquisition and usage of grid and Cloud resources. This middleware was specially designed to cope with HPC computation and communication requirements, but its usage is not restricted to this kind of application.

B. Amedro (✉)

OASIS Research Team, INRIA Sophia Antipolis, 2004 route des lucioles – BP 93, 06902 Sophia-Antipolis, France

e-mail: brian.amedro@sophia.inria.fr

N. Antonopoulos and L. Gillam (eds.), *Cloud Computing: Principles, Systems and Applications*, Computer Communications and Networks, DOI 10.1007/978-1-84996-241-4_10, © Springer-Verlag London Limited 2010

This chapter explores in detail the relevance of using hybrid grid/Cloud environments and the technical challenges that such mixing raises at the middleware level. In particular, this chapter provides and analyzes performance results that we obtained on Amazon Elastic Cloud computing (EC2) running some of the NAS parallel benchmarks. Then, we provide some insight into two complementary and relevant concepts: Cloud bursting and seeding: (1) *Cloud bursting* is relevant whenever the amount of available resources on a cluster or grid is not sufficient to face a required level of computing power, and hence must be augmented with some Cloud resources, be it in a static and anticipated way or dynamically in an on-demand way; and (2) *Cloud seeding* is relevant whenever some specific kinds of resources are not available within the computing cloud, and hence must be acquired from outside.

The remainder of this chapter is organized as follows: Section 2 presents some existing Cloud frameworks and our position in relation to them. Section 3 gives some benchmarks and proposes solutions to deploy applications in a Cloud, through the proposed framework. Section 4 details the application deployment in a unified environment mixing grids, cluster, and Clouds. Section 5 deals with the deployment process under Cloud bursting and Cloud seeding scenarios. Lastly, Section 6 concludes this chapter and outlines future directions.

10.2   Related Work

10.2.1   *General View of Cloud Computing frameworks*

Cloud services are mainly divided into three service delivery models: Software as a Service (SaaS), for example, Google Mail; Platform as a Service (PaaS), for example, Google AppEngine; and, Infrastructure as a Service(IaaS), for example, Amazon EC2. As the work presented in this chapter is strongly related to the *IaaS* model, in this section, we only focus on this category of service. *IaaS* providers aim to offer resources to users in a pay-as-you-go manner. A key provider of such a service is Amazon through its Elastic Cloud Computing (EC2) and Simple Storage Service (S3).

Some services or tools have been proposed to ease the use of Clouds or enhance their functionalities. enStratus[6] provides a set of tools for managing Cloud infrastructure and handling the "confidence" questions about moving an application into a Cloud. The user does not need to change a line of code for enStratus. Scalr[11] is a hosting environment for Amazon EC2. It provides services such as load balancing, fault tolerance, and self-scaling. Vertebra [12] is a Cloud computing framework for the orchestration of complex processes. It takes into consideration security, fault tolerance, and portability aspects. The OpenNebula Toolkit [2] is a virtual infrastructure engine that allows a dynamic deployment and reallocation of virtual machines. It leverages existing virtualization platforms to come up with a new virtualization layer between the service and the physical infrastructure. It supports private, public, and hybrid Cloud deployment models. Nimbus [1] is a set of open source tools that provide an *IaaS* Cloud computing solution. It allows users to lease remote resources by deploying virtual machines on those resources. Using the Nimbus Cloud, the requested resources can be dynamically adjusted as a function of the application needs.

10.2.2   Cloud Computing Middleware

In order to run applications on a Cloud, one needs a flexible middleware that eases the development and the deployment process. GridGain [8] provides a middleware that aims to develop and run applications on both public and private Clouds without any changes in the application code. It is also possible to write dedicated applications based on the map/reduce programming model. Although GridGain provides mechanism to seamlessly deploy applications on a grid or a Cloud, it does not support the deployment of the infrastructure itself. It does, however, provide protocols to discover running GridGain nodes and organize them into topologies (*Local Grid*, *Global Grid*, etc.) to run applications on only a subset of all nodes.

Elastic Grid [7] infrastructure provides dynamic allocation, deployment, and management of Java applications through the Cloud. It also offers a Cloud virtualization layer that abstracts specific Cloud computing provider technology to isolate applications from specific implementations.

10.3   Deploying Applications in the Cloud

In the rest of our study, we will focus on the Amazon EC2 Web Service. Initially, we seek to determine the performance that can be expected. Then, we propose solutions to facilitate the deployment of applications in this context and to enable the usage of hybrid grid/Cloud environments. To reach this goal, we will use the *ProActive Parallel Suite* [3]. This framework is composed of three parts: (1) *ProActive Programming* offers a Java API for parallel and distributed computing, (2) *ProActive Resource Manager* gathers heterogeneous computing resources (parallel machines, clouds, grids, etc.) into an unified access mechanism (further details are given in Sections 3 and 5.1). *ProActive Scheduler* runs any kind of tasks (native, Java, Matlab, etc.) on a set of nodes acquired by the resource manager.

10.3.1   Benchmarking the Cloud

In order to assess the worthiness of using Amazon EC2 cloud as an HPC platform, we have deployed a series of benchmarks well known in the world of HPC, the MPI NAS Parallel Benchmarks. We have launched them on four different architectures, described in Table 10.1: a private cluster and three types of Amazon EC2 instances. To provide consistent and predictable CPU capacity, Amazon describes the CPU

Table 10.1 Deployment architectures

	Private cluster		
Processors	2 QuadCore Opteron 2356 (2.3 GHz)/64 bits		
Memory	32 GB		
Hard drive	2 × 73 GB SAS 15,000 rpm		
I/O Performance	Gigabit Ethernet		
	Small	*High-CPU medium*	*High-CPU XLarge*
EC2 compute units	1/32 bits	5 (2 × 2.5)/32-bits	20 (8 × 2.5)/64 bits
Memory	1.7 GB	1.7 GB	7 GB
Hard drive	160 GB	350 GB	1690 GB
I/O Performance	Moderate	Moderate	High

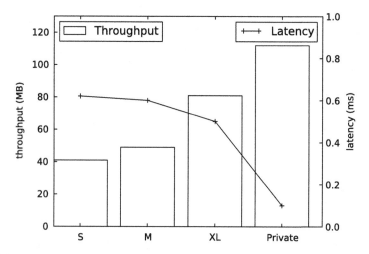

Fig. 10.1 I/O performance comparison between a private cluster and EC2 instances

capacity of its instances in terms of an *EC2 Compute Unit,* and claims that it is the equivalent CPU capacity of a 1.0–1.2 GHz 2007 Opteron.

The chart presented in Fig. 10.1 shows that the *Small* and the *Medium* instances share the same throughput and latency, describing *Moderate* EC2 I/O performance, while the *XLarge* instance reflects *High* EC2 I/O performance. When compared with the Gigabit Ethernet connectivity provided by our own private cluster, there is a large gap, especially for latency.

Figure 10.2 shows the performance (Mflops) of three of the NAS Parallel Benchmarks on each architecture by varying the number of processes. Results average ten runs, and variation does not exceed 6%. Up to 32 processes, we run one process per machine; and then we increase the number of processes per machine.

- EP is an embarrassingly parallel problem that involves almost no communication between the processes. It is a strong test for pure computational speed. This test clearly shows the speed difference between all the instances. The XL instance is

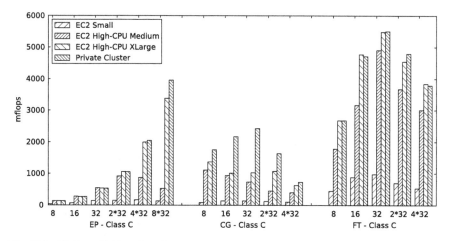

Fig. 10.2 NAS parallel benchmarks

roughly equivalent to our private architecture (eight cores at 2.3 GHz), whereas the medium instance runs at the same rate, but with only two cores. Similarly, we see that the small instance is about 2.5–3 times slower than the others.

- CG computes a conjugate gradient involving a large number of small messages, and is a strong test for communication performance. It confirms the results shown in Fig. 10.1. Amazon EC2 performance is well below what we get with our private cluster.
- FT is a Fourier transformation benchmark. It is a test for both computation and communication speed involving large data transfers. With such a problem, the gap between our private architecture with medium and XL instances narrows.

As shown by the previous experiments, EC2 does not offer good performance for communication-intensive applications when compared with a local cluster. However, CPU-intensive application do not present a significant performance hit. When dealing with a complex application mixing communications and computations, it might be interesting to have a part on a Cloud and another on a cluster, depending on the application characteristics and the possibility to decompose the application in such a way. This, however, makes deploying such application more complex.

We now present different mechanisms that simplify the execution of applications over heterogeneous environments.

10.3.2   The ProActive GCM Deployment

The ProActive middleware provides an abstract descriptor-based deployment model and framework [4], giving users the capability to deploy an application on different platforms without changing the source code. The idea behind the ProActive GCM Deployment is to perform the discovery of resources, creation of remote processes, and data-handling externally to the application, completely

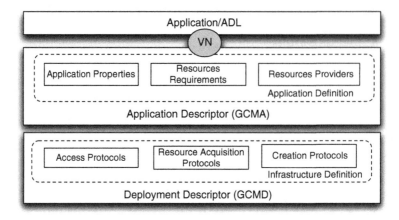

Fig. 10.3 GCM descriptor based deployment model

separating the business code and deployment. In addition to these activities, the definition of the deployment can also encompass security, tunneling of communications, fault tolerance, and support of portable file transfer operations.

The whole deployment process (Fig. 10.3) and environment configuration is defined by means of XML descriptors that depict the application requirements and deployment process. The deployment of ProActive/GCM applications depends on two types of descriptors:

- GCM Application Descriptors (GCMA): the GCMA descriptors define application-related properties, such as localization of libraries, file transfer, application parameters, and nonfunctional services (logging, security, checkpoint, and fault tolerance). GCMA descriptors expose the resulting physical environment as a logical network of virtual nodes (VNs) that are used by applications as an abstract representation of computing nodes. The GCMA also defines with or multiple resource providers.
- GCM Deployment Descriptors (GCMD): the GCMD descriptors define access protocols to reach the resources (e.g. SSH, RSH, GSISSH, etc.), acquisition protocols and tools which are required to access the resources (e.g. Amazon EC2, PBS, LSF, Sun Grid Engine, OAR, etc.), creation protocols that have a relation with how to launch processes (e.g. SSH, OAR, gLite, Globus), and communication protocols (e.g. RMI, RMISSH, HTTP, SOAP, etc.).

The advantages of this model are clear: on one side, if the users want to add a new resource provider (e.g. a private cluster, production grid, or Cloud), the application code does not change and a single line is enough to add the resource provider to the application descriptor (GCMA). On the other side, the definition of the deployment process happens just once for each resource and can be reused for different applications.

10.3.3   Technical Solutions for Deployment over Heterogeneous Infrastructures

In the best possible scenario, all the machines involved in one computation are externally accessible through a public IP without any network restriction. In practice, this rarely occurs and machines are usually isolated by firewall and NAT. Hence, we must explore more sophisticated strategies to make the communication possible among processes located in different domains.

10.3.3.1   Virtual Private Network (VPN)

A *Virtual Private Network (VPN)* is an overlay network built on top of an existing larger one. It is often installed to provide a secure extension of a private network into an insecure environment such as the Internet. Thus, communication between nodes is *tunneled* through the underlying network, bypassing firewalls.

In order to *expose* a private network to the Internet to allow some external machines to connect, a *VPN Gateway*, which will be the entry point of the network, must be configured. This gateway will be a part of the private network, but also has access to the Internet. Then, each client machine wishing to join the VPN will connect to the gateway. Regarding firewalls, client and gateway must be defiltered for both input and output VPN traffic.

A VPN can thus offer a way to add external resources to an IaaS, or add IaaS resources to a private infrastructure.

10.3.3.2   Amazon Virtual Private Cloud (VPC)

Amazon Virtual Private Cloud (VPC) service provides a private subnetwork within the Amazon Cloud. All EC2 nodes, composing this Amazon VPC, are isolated and can only be reached through a VPN connection from a private network. This allows seamless extension of an existing infrastructure and EC2 resources can be managed as private ones.

This service allows extending existing security and management policies of a private IT infrastructure to the VPC. By doing so, it allows applications to be seamlessly executed in multi-domain environments.

10.3.3.3   Message Forwarding and Tunneling

The ProActive middleware also offers a solution to address network restrictions such as firewalls and NAT, which is built-in and lightweight, based on SSH. This solution also provides a seamless integration of forwarding and tunneling, but at the application level (i.e. no need to configure routing at the OS and network levels).

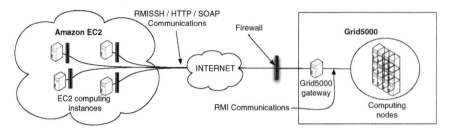

Fig. 10.4 Tunneling and forwarding communications on a heterogeneous Cloud-grid environment

It only requires a configuration of entry points of each involved domain and uses communication protocols such as SSH.

Figure 10.4 depicts a scenario where a single application runs over a set of nodes distributed in Amazon EC2 and Grid5000[1]. In this scenario, all the nodes located in Amazon EC2 offer inbound and outbound communication, but nodes located on Grid5000 are isolated from the external network. ProActive, however, enables the usage of these resources as if every node is accessible by every other node by forwarding incoming and outgoing messages through the Grid5000 gateway.

In a more protected environment, nodes might be isolated on both sides. The ProActive built-in tunneling/forwarding can be configured through a double-forwarding mechanism to handle such a situation. In any case, applications remain unchanged and the execution in different scenarios only requires the modification of configuration files associated with the ProActive Runtime. The communication process may involve a multi-protocol approach.

10.3.4 Conclusion and Motivation for Mixing

We have seen that the deployment of an application in a heterogeneous environment can be simplified with tools such as the ProActive GCM Deployment. Technical solutions such as VPN and SSH tunneling are used to manage the characteristics of a network while securing connections. We have also seen that an IaaS, such as Amazon EC2, offers a range of instances with features and performance that can match user needs.

Thus, we can consider setting up different usage strategies to mix resources with different goals. Strategies could be geared to a full transition phase towards full cloud outsourcing of computing, an optimization of costs by fitting the choice of computing resources to the needs of the application, or by temporarily extending an infrastructure to meet a special need.

---

[1]Grid5000 is a French national Grid distributed over nine sites for a total of about 5,000 cores

10.4 Moving HPC Applications from Grids to Clouds

It is not yet clear how much impact Clouds will have on HPC in the future. In fact, it is very unlikely that highly optimized clusters will be replaced by Cloud resources in a near future. Considering that most enterprises and public institutes that require them already have in-house HPC resources, which could provide processing power at lower costs, the notion of private Clouds or a mix between Clouds and cluster/grids resources seems more cost-effective to solve the problem of providing resources.

Scientific applications require sophisticated middleware because they usually present complex multi-point interactions and strong processing and network requirements, which necessitate performance. Porting such applications to heterogeneous environments increases the importance of middleware support.

In this section, we present a versatile GCM/ProActive-based lightweight framework that supports distributed and parallel scientific applications, so that porting of legacy applications is possible and easy for any kind of distributed computing environment or even a mixture of them. To illustrate this, we also present performance results obtained with a scientific PDE-based application in different contexts, including an experimental Grid, a public Cloud, and the mixture of these infrastructures.

10.4.1 HPC on Heterogeneous Multi-Domain Platforms

From the development point of view, the usage of resources spread across multi-domain platforms as if it were a single infrastructure requires an integrated middleware. Such middleware should provide users with clear abstractions to develop applications that could be easily adapted to be deployed with different resource providers, despite different underlying characteristics of resources.

In the next section, we present in more detail a component-based integrating middleware, which emphasizes a clear separation between application development and the execution platform. This middleware eases the transition from clusters to grids and Clouds by providing seamless deployment and multi-protocol point-to-point and multi-point communication in multi-domain environments.

10.4.2 The Hierarchical SPMD Concept and Multi-level Partitioning of Numerical Meshes

The traditional way of designing domain decomposition-based simulations is to adopt an SPMD technique combining mesh-partitioning and the message-passing programming model. The hierarchical SPMD is an evolution of the traditional flat SPMD parallel programming paradigm toward a heterogeneous hierarchical approach. The hierarchical SPMD concept consists in assigning hierarchical identifiers to processes and treating collective communications in a topology-aware manner.

Heterogeneity in network and resources is a challenging issue for domain decomposition based scientific applications. The main reason comes from the fact that these applications rely upon a bulk synchronous iterative approach and applications loop at the pace of the slowest process. The hierarchical network topology and computing power heterogeneity must therefore be considered in the mesh-partitioning and communication process.

We propose a multi-level partitioning approach to balance load among processors and optimize the communication process. The multi-level partitioner is capable of taking into account the characteristics of the resources (CPU power and amount of memory) and their topology to partition a global mesh in a way such that each process presents an equivalent processing time, yet minimizing communication through slower links [9]. The different levels defining the physical hierarchy are mapped into the communication process, which is configured depending on the effective location of communicating processes and the available communication protocols. The runtime also takes topology into account to stage the communication operations so that communication over slower networks (e.g. Internet) is avoided.

10.4.3   The GCM/ProActive-Based Lightweight Framework

The GCM/ProActive-based lightweight framework takes the form of a component-based infrastructure that offers support to multi-protocol communication. This infrastructure is composed according to the hierarchy of resources and gives the applications a view of a unique global computing infrastructure, despite the localization and access restrictions of resources.

Figure 10.5 shows an example of such composition, which reflects a single global application deployed upon a resources set onto two separate but interconnected administrative domains. On the left, we run a standalone MPI application on a Cloud (e.g. a set of Amazon EC2 instances) and on the right, another standalone MPI application runs over a multi-cluster based grid (e.g. the Grid5000). Each of the MPI processes is wrapped by a GCM primitive component that is connected to the external

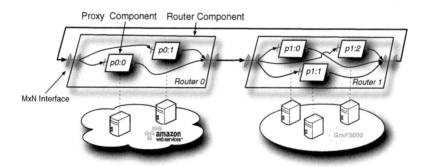

Fig. 10.5 Typical GCM/ProActive based multidomain runtime support for HPC

router component representing the next level up in the infrastructure. Owing to the hierarchical composition and the routing interfaces associated with higher levels, all the nodes are logically connected, even if indirectly, to every other in the multi-domain. Hence, the independent MPI executions are coupled to form a single parallel application along the Hierarchical SPMD concept.

Collective communications profit from the topology, enabling them to be staged and parallelized. Besides, and whenever possible, for optimization purposes we can create on-demand direct bindings to perform point-to-point communications, thus bypassing the hierarchy.

10.4.4   Performance Evaluation

We evaluate the component-based framework and the hierarchical SPMD model through a nontrivial simulation of electromagnetic-wave propagation in three-space dimensions. This simulation is based on a finite element method working on arbitrarily unstructured tetrahedral meshes for solving a system of Maxwell equations.

From the computational point of view, the execution is characterized by two types of operations: purely local operations on the tetrahedra for computing integral values and a calculation involving neighbor subdomains, which involves a *gather-compute-scatter* sequence. Formulations are described in more detail in [5].

In [9], we highlighted performance improvements for applications developed along the Hierarchical SPMD concept when compared with pure "flat" MPI implementations including grid-aware ones (as Grid-MPI). The experimental results we present here focus on the comparison among three scenarios: a multi-cluster grid, Amazon EC2, and a multi-domain environment that couple both setups.

The experiments we present here were conducted in one cluster (grelon, located in Nancy, France) of the Grid5000 testbed and the Amazon EC2 platform with two instance sizes: Small instances and High-CPU Extra Large instances. Grid5000 resources present Dual Core Intel Xeon 5110 (1.6 GHz) with 2 GB of memory and Gigabit Ethernet interconnection. Small Amazon EC2 instances represent one compute unit with 1 GB of memory, and High-CPU Extra Large represent 20 compute units (eight virtual cores with 2.5 EC2 Compute Units each) with 7 GB of memory. The software involved in these experiments are Java Sun SDK v1.6.0_07, ProActive v3.91, and GridMPI v2.1.1.

Figure 10.6 presents the overall execution times and MFlops/s obtained in the different scenarios. With the application being network- and CPU-intensive, both CPU and network affect the overall performance. On average, Small Amazon EC2 instances present a performance four times smaller than one using the standard cluster of Grid5000. High-CPU Extra Large instances present a better CPU performance than Grid5000 machines, but provide a slower network interconnection which results in a comparable global performance. A mix of Grid5000 resources and Small Amazon EC2 does not perform well when compared with single-site

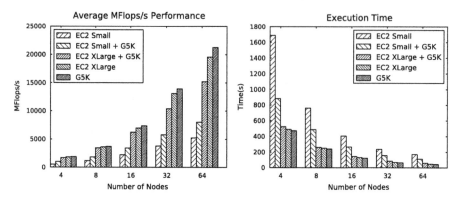

Fig. 10.6 Performance over Grid5000, Amazon EC2, and resource mix

execution over Grid5000; even with the balance of load by the partitioner, processes running on EC2 presented lower performance. Using both Grid5000 resources and Extra Large EC2 instances has proved to be more advantageous, presenting, on average, only 15% of overhead for such inter-domain execution when compared with the average of the best single domain ones. This is mainly due to high-latency communication and message tunneling, but this overhead could be further softened because of the possibility of adding extra resources to/from the grid/Cloud.

From a cost-performance point of view, previous performance evaluations of Amazon EC2 [10] showed that MFlops obtained per dollar spent decreases exponentially with increasing computing cores, and the cost for solving a linear system increases exponentially with the problem size. Our results indicate the same when using Cloud resources exclusively. Mixing resources, however, seems to be more feasible since a trade-off between performance and cost can be reached by the inclusion of in-house resources in computation.

10.5 Dynamic Mixing of Clusters, Grids, and Clouds

As we have seen, mixing Cloud and private resources can provide performance close to that of a larger private cluster. However, doing so in a static way can lead to a waste of resources if an application does not need the computing power during its complete lifetime. We will now present a tool that enables the dynamic use of Cloud resources.

10.5.1 The ProActive Resource Manager

The ProActive Resource Manager is a software for resource aggregation across the network, developed as a ProActive application. It delivers compute units represented by ProActive nodes (Java Virtual Machines running the ProActive Runtime) to a scheduler that is in charge of handling a task flow and distributing tasks or accessible resources. Owing to the deployment framework, presented in the Section 3.2, it can retrieve computing nodes using different standards such as SSH, LSF, OAR, gLite, EC2, etc. Its main functions are:

- Deployment, acquisition, and release of ProActive nodes to/from an underlying infrastructure
- Supplying ProActive Scheduler with nodes for task executions, based on required properties
- Maintaining and monitoring the list of resources and managing their states

Resource Manager is aimed at abstracting the nature of a dynamic infrastructure and simplifying effective utilization of multiple computing resources, enabling their exploitation from different providers within a single application. In order to achieve this goal, the Resource Manager is split into multiple components.

The core is responsible for handling all requests from clients and delegating them to other components. Once the request for getting new nodes for computation is received, the core "redirects it to a selection manager." This component finds appropriate nodes in a pool of available nodes based on criteria provided by clients, such as a specific architecture or a specific library.

The pool of nodes is formed by one or several node aggregators. Each aggregator (node source) is in charge of node acquisition, deployment, and monitoring from a dedicated infrastructure. It also has a policy defining conditions and rules of acquiring/releasing nodes. For example, a time slot policy will acquire nodes only for a specified period of time.

All platforms supported by GCMD are automatically supported by the ProActive Resource Manager. When exploiting an existing infrastructure, the Resource Manager takes into account the fact that it could be utilized by local users, and provides fair resource utilization. For instance, Microsoft Compute Cluster Server has its own scheduler and the ProActive deployment process has to go through it instead of contacting cluster nodes directly. This behavior makes possible the coexistence of ProActive Resource Manager with others without breaking their integrity.

As we mentioned earlier, the node source is a combination of infrastructure and a policy representing a set of rules driving the deployment/release process. Among several such predefined policies, two have to be mentioned. The first addresses a common scenario when resources are available for a limited time. The second is a balancing policy – the policy that holds the number of nodes depending on the user's needs. One such balancing policy is implemented by the Proactive Resource Manager, which acquires new nodes dynamically when the scheduler is overloaded and releases them as soon as there is no more activity in the scheduler.

Using node sources as building blocks helps to describe all resources at your disposal and the way they are used. Pluggable and extensible policies and infrastructures make it possible to define any kind of dynamic resource aggregation scenarios. One of such scenario is Cloud bursting.

10.5.2 Cloud Bursting: Managing Spike Demand

Companies or research institutes can have a private cluster or use Grids to perform their daily computations. However, the provisioning of these resources is often done based on average usage for cost management reasons. When a sudden increase in computation arises, it is possible to offload some of them to a Cloud. This is often referred to as *Cloud bursting*.

Figure 10.7 illustrates a *Cloud bursting* scenario. In our example, we have an existing *local network* that is composed of a *ProActive Scheduler* with a *Resource Manager*. This resource manager handles *computing resources* such as desktop machines or clusters. In our figure, these are referred to as *local computing nodes*.

A common kind of application for a scheduler is a bag of independent tasks (no communication between the tasks). The scheduler will retrieve a set of free *computing nodes* through the resource manager to run pending tasks. This *local network* is protected from Internet with a firewall that filters connections.

When the scheduler experiences an uncommon load, the resource manager can acquire new computing nodes from Amazon EC2. This decision is based on a *scheduling loading policy*, which takes into account the current load of the scheduler and the Service Level Agreement provided. These parameters are directly set in the resource manager administrator interface. However, when *offloading* tasks to the Cloud, we have to pay attention to the *boot delay* that implies a waiting time of few minutes between a node request and its availability for the scheduler.

The Resource Manager is capable of bypassing firewalls and private networks by any of the approaches presented in Section 3.3.3.

10.5.3 Cloud Seeding: Dealing with Heterogeneous Hardware and Private Data

In some cases, a distributed application, composed of dependent tasks, can perform a vast majority of its tasks on a Cloud, while running some of them on a local

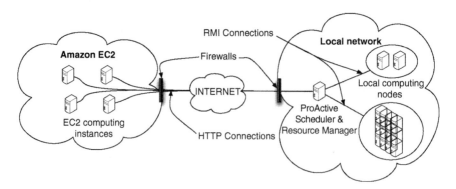

Fig. 10.7 Example of a Cloud bursting scenario

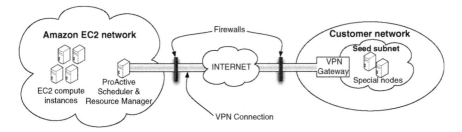

Fig. 10.8 Example of a simple Cloud seeding scenario

infrastructure in order to have access to computing resources with a specific configuration such as GPU equipment. This type of requirement can also happen in cases where some tasks use software protected by a license, and use some private data or algorithms which should never get out to an untrusted environment such as a Cloud.

Cloud Seeding aims at providing a solution to such problems by extending the capabilities of a Cloud with specific external resources.

Figure 10.8 shows a simple Cloud seeding example. In this scenario, most parts of the application are hosted in the Cloud. The ProActive Scheduler and the Resource Manager are hosted on an Amazon EC2 instance, as well as the computing nodes that are used by the scheduler. However, some tasks need a particular resource configuration in order to be executed, such as a GPU processor. The resource manager can handle, in addition to the Amazon EC2 nodes, a set of *special nodes* from the *customer network* gathered in a *seed subnet*.

As seen in Section 3.3, multiple technical solutions can be used to build such a configuration. In our example, we used a VPN-based solution. To enable the scheduler and the resource manager to communicate with these special nodes, we gather them in a *seed subnet* that hosts a VPN gateway and connects the scheduler and the resource manager to this VPN gateway. However, this type of configuration does not allow Amazon EC2 instances to communicate directly with these special nodes. If we want to permit such communication, one solution is for each Amazon EC2 instance to create a VPN connection with the VPN gateway. Another solution is to build an Amazon VPC, as described in Section 3.3.2, to connect the *seed* and the *VPC* subnets together, thus creating a virtual network authorizing communication between any nodes in this network.

10.6   Conclusion

In this paper, we have evaluated the benefits of Cloud computing for scientific applications. Although the performance can be similar to a dedicated cluster for computationally-intensive code, it drops when running communication-intensive code. This observation motivates the need for mixing Cloud and traditional computing platforms. Hybrid platforms require mechanisms adapted to gather resources, deploy applications, and ensure efficient communications.

Although a low-level solution such as VPN may be useful, these solutions are limited because they hide the heterogeneity and prevent the adaptation of the deployment and applications to the environment. Using ProActive and the ProActive/GCM deployment allows specifying how resources are acquired and how the communication should be performed (through simple protocols or message tunneling and forwarding).

We have shown that these mechanisms are powerful enough to build a modular grid/Cloud middleware to support scientific domain-decomposition applications. We illustrated this through adaptating a complex communication- and network-intensive HPC application to run efficiently over a mix of Cloud resources and dedicated ones, without much overhead. Finally, we have also shown how ProActive Resource Manager enables dynamic mixing of Cloud and grid platforms, allowing both Cloud bursting and Cloud seeding within a single framework. These mechanisms also offer a solution to smoothly migrating applications from clusters and grids to Clouds.

Experiments presented in this paper were carried out using the Grid'5000 experimental testbed, developed under the INRIA ALADDIN development action with support from CNRS, RENATER, and several French Universities, as well as other funding bodies (see https://www.grid5000.fr). The authors would also like to thank Amazon Web Services and the PacaGrid CPER for providing computing resources.

References

1. Nimbus toolkit. http://workspace.globus.org/
2. Opennebula project. http://www.opennebula.org/
3. Proactive parallel suite. http://proactive.inria.fr.
4. Baude F, Caromel D, Mestre L, Huet F, Vayssière J (2002) Interactive and descriptor-based deployment of object-oriented grid applications. Proceedings of the 11th IEEE international symposium on high performance distributed computing
5. Bernacki M, Lanteri S, Piperno S (2006) Time-domain parallel simulation of heterogeneous wave propagation on unstructured grids using explicit non-diffusive, discontinuous Galerkin methods. J Comp Acoustics 14(1):57–81
6. enStratus. The enstratus framework for amazon ec2, http://www.enstratus.com/
7. E. Grid. Elastic grid. http://www.elastic-grid.com/
8. GridGain. Grid grain: The open cloud platform. http://www.gridgain.com/
9. Mathias E, Cavé V, Lanteri S, Baude F (2009) Grid-enabling spmd applications through hierarchical partitioning and a component-based runtime. In: Proceedings of the 15th international euro-par conference on parallel processing (Euro-Par '09), Springer-Verlag, Berlin, Heidelberg, pp 691–703
10. Napper J, Bientinesi P (2009) Can cloud computing reach the top500? In: Proceedings of the combined workshops on UnConventional high performance computing workshop plus memory access workshop (UCHPC-MAW '09), ACM, New York, USA, pp 17–20
11. Scalr. The scalr framework for cloud computing, http://www.scalr.net/
12. Vertebra. Easy to manage framework for orchestrating complex processes in the cloud. http://www.engineyard.com/vertebra.

Chapter 11
Resource Management for Hybrid Grid and Cloud Computing

Simon Ostermann, Radu Prodan, and Thomas Fahringer

Abstract From its start of using supercomputers, scientific computing constantly evolved to the next levels such as cluster computing, meta-computing, or computational Grids. Today, Cloud Computing is emerging as the paradigm for the next generation of large-scale scientific computing, eliminating the need for hosting expensive computing hardware. Scientists still have their Grid environments in place and can benefit from extending them using leased Cloud resources whenever needed. This paradigm shift opens new problems that need to be analyzed, such as integration of this new resource class into existing environments, applications on the resources, and security. The virtualization overheads for deployment and starting of a virtual machine image are new factors, which will need to be considered when choosing scheduling mechanisms. In this chapter, we investigate the usability of compute Clouds to extend a Grid workflow middleware and show on a real implementation that this can speed up executions of scientific workflows.

11.1 Introduction

In the last decade, Grid computing gained became popular in the field of scientific computing through the idea of distributed resource sharing among institutions and scientists. Scientific computing is traditionally a high-utilization workload, with production Grids often running at over 80% utilization [1] (generating high and often unpredictable latencies), and with smaller national Grids offering a rather limited amount of high-performance resources. Running large-scale simulations in such overloaded Grid environments often becomes latency-bound or suffers from well-known Grid reliability problems [2].

S. Ostermann (✉)
Institute of Computer Science, University of Innsbruck, Technikerstraße 21a,
6020, Innsbruck, Austria
e-mail: simon@dps.uibk.ac

N. Antonopoulos and L. Gillam (eds.), *Cloud Computing: Principles,
Systems and Applications*, Computer Communications and Networks,
DOI 10.1007/978-1-84996-241-4_11, © Springer-Verlag London Limited 2010

Today, a new research direction, coined by the term Cloud computing, proposes an alternative that could prove attractive to scientific computing scientists because of four main advantages. First, Clouds promote the concept of leasing remote resources rather than buying hardware, which frees institutions from permanent maintenance costs and eliminates the burden of hardware deprecation following Moore's law. Second, Clouds eliminate the physical overhead costs of adding new hardware, such as compute nodes to clusters or supercomputers and the financial burden of permanent over-provisioning of occasionally needed resources. Through "scaling-by-credit-card," Clouds promise to immediately scale up or down an infrastructure according to the temporal needs in a cost-effective fashion. Third, the concept of hardware virtualization can represent a significant breakthrough for the automatic and scalable deployment of complex scientific software, and can also significantly improve the shared resource utilization. Fourth, the provisioning of resources through business relationships pushes specialized data center companies to offer reliable services, which existing Grid infrastructures fail to deliver.

Despite the existence of several integrated environments for transparent programming and high-performance use of Grid infrastructures for scientific applications [3], there are no results yet published in the community that report on extending them to enjoy the benefits offered by Cloud computing. While there are several early efforts that investigate the appropriateness of Clouds for scientific computing, they are either limited to simulations [4], do not address the highly successful workflow paradigm [5], or do not attempt to extend Grids with Clouds as a hybrid-combined platform for scientific computing.

In this chapter we extend a Grid workflow application development and computing environment to harness resources leased by Cloud computing providers. Our goal is to provide an infrastructure that allows the execution of workflows on conventional Grid resources which can be supplemented on-demand with additional Cloud resources, if necessary. We concentrate our presentation on the extensions we brought to the resource management service to consider Cloud resources, comprising new Cloud management, software (image) deployment, and security components. We present experimental results using a real-world application in the Austrian Grid environment, extended with an academic Cloud constructed using Eucalyptus middleware [6] and Xen virtualization technology [7].

The chapter continues in Section 2 with a background on the ASKALON Grid environment and a short introduction to several Cloud computing terms. Section 3 presents the architecture of the Grid resource management service enhanced for Cloud computing, which is evaluated in Section 4 for a real application executed in a real Grid environment enhanced with a Cloud testbed. Section 5 compares our approach with the most relevant related work, and Section 6 concludes the chapter.

11.2   Background

While there are several workflow execution middlewares for Grid computing [3], none is known to support the new type of Cloud infrastructure.

11.2.1   ASKALON

ASKALON [8] is a Grid application development and computing environment developed at the University of Innsbruck with the goal of simplifying the development and optimization of applications that can harness the power of Grid and Cloud (see Section 2.2) computing. Figure 11.1 shows the main components of ASKALON. The user composes workflow applications at a high level of abstraction using an UML graphical modeling tool. Workflows are specified as a directed graph of *activity types* representing an abstract semantic description of the computation, such as a Gaussian elimination algorithm, a Fast Fourier Transform, or an N-body simulation. The activity types are interconnected in a workflow through control-flow and data-flow dependencies. The abstract workflow representation is given in an XML form (AGWL [9]) to the ASKALON middleware services for transparent execution onto the Grid. This task is mainly accomplished by a fault-tolerant *enactment engine*, together with a *scheduling* service in charge of computing optimized mappings of workflow activities onto the available Grid resources.

To achieve this task, the scheduler employs a *resource management* service that consists of two main components: GridARM for discovery and brokerage of hardware resources by interfacing with a Grid information service [10], and GLARE for registration and provisioning of software resources. An important component of GLARE is the automatic provisioning of *activity deployments* on remote Grid sites, which are properly configured installations of the legacy software and services implementing the activity types. Once an activity deployment has been installed, we say that the remote resource has been *provisioned,* and can be used by the scheduler and enactment engine for the workflow execution. This execution can be monitored using graphical tools [11] or via the engine's event system.

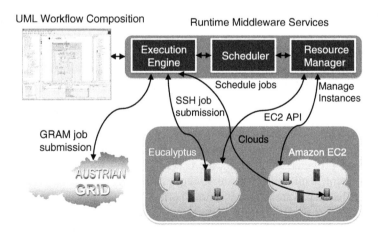

Fig. 11.1 Simplified ASKALON architecture extended for computational clouds

11.2.2   Cloud Computing

The term Cloud computing is being increasingly used for provisioning various services through the Internet, which are billed like utilities.

From a scientific point of view, the most popular interpretation of Cloud computing is *Infrastructure as a Service (IaaS)*, which provides generic means for hosting and provisioning access to raw computing infrastructure and its operating software. IaaS are typically provided by data centers renting modern hardware facilities to customers that only pay for what they use, which frees them from the burden of hardware maintenance and deprecation. IaaS is characterized by the concept of resource *virtualization,* which allows customers to deploy and run their own guest operating system on top of the virtualization software (e.g. [7]) offered by the provider. Virtualization in IaaS is also a key step toward distributed, automatic, and scalable deployment, installation, and maintenance of software.

To deploy a guest operating system showing to the user another abstract and higher-level emulated platform, the user creates a virtual machine image, in short *image*. In order to use a Cloud resource, the user needs to copy and boot an image on top, called virtual machine instance, in short *instance*. After an instance has been started on a Cloud resource [12], we say that the resource has been *provisioned* and can be used. If a resource is no longer necessary, it must be *released* such that the user no longer pays for its use.

Commercial Cloud providers typically offer customers a selection of *resource classes* or *instance types* with different characteristics including CPU type, number of cores, memory, hard disk, and I/O performance.

11.3   Resource Management Architecture

To enable the ASKALON Grid environment use Cloud resources from different providers, we extended the resource management service to three new components: Cloud management (see Section 3.1), image catalog (see Section 3.2), and security mechanisms (see Section 3.3).

Whenever the high-performance Grid resources are exhausted, the ASKALON scheduler has the option of supplementing them with additional ones leased from Cloud providers to complete the workflow faster. A limit for the maximum number of leased resources that are requested is set for each cloud in their credential properties. This limit helps to save money and stay within the resource limits given by the cloud provider. EC2 allows the users to request up to 20 instances on a normal account, while bigger resource requests require contacting Amazon. Our Eucalyptus-based private cloud (dps.cloud) offers 12 cores and any further requests can not be served, so the limit for resource requests was set to 12. When a deployment request for a new Cloud resource arrives from the scheduler, the resource manager arranges its provisioning by performing the following steps (see Fig.11.2):

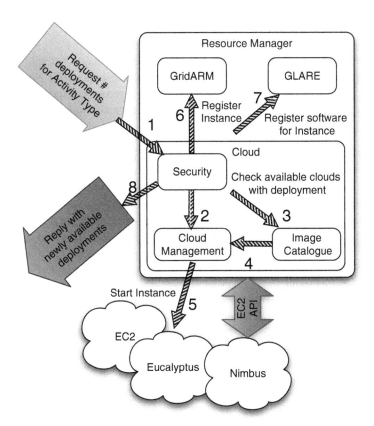

Fig. 11.2 The cloud-enhanced resource management architecture

1. Retrieves a signed request for a certain number of activity deployments needed to complete the workflow.
2. The security component checks the credential of the request, and which Clouds are available for the requesting user (see Section 3.3).
3. The image catalog component retrieves the predefined registered images for the accessible Clouds (see Section 3.2).
4. The images are checked to see whether they include the requested activity deployment or if they have the capability to auto-deploy.
5. The instances are started using the Cloud management component, and the image boot process is monitored until a (SSH) control connection is possible to the new instance. If the instance does not contain the requested activity deployment, an optional auto-deployment process using GLARE takes place.
6. A new entry is created in GridARM with all information required by the new instance, such as identifier, IP address, and number of CPUs.
7. All the activity deployments contained in the booted image are registered in GLARE.
8. The resource manager replies to the scheduler with the new deployments for the requested activity types.

11.3.1 Cloud Management

In terms of functionality, the Cloud-enabled resource manager extends the Grid resource manager with two new runtime functions: the request for new deployments for a specific activity type and the release of a resource after its use ended. The Cloud management component is responsible for provisioning, releasing, and checking the status of an instance.

Figure 11.3 shows a generic instance state transition diagram, which we constructed by analyzing the instance states in different Cloud implementations [12,13]. Upon a *request* for additional resources, the Cloud management component selects the resources (instance types) with the best price/performance[1] ratio, matching the request to which it transfers an image containing the required activity deployments, or enabled with auto-deployment functionality (state *starting*). In the *running* state, the image is booted, while in the *accessible* state, the instance is ready to be used. In the *resizing* phase, the underlying hardware is reconfigured, for example by adding more cores or memory, while in the *restarting* phase, the image is rebooted, for example, upon a kernel change. The release of an image upon *shut down* is signaled by the *terminated* state. The *failed* state indicates any error that automatically releases the resource.

Upon a resource release, the instance and all the deployments registered are removed from GridARM and GLARE. However, if there are pending requests for an existing instance containing the required deployments, the resource manager can optimize the provisioning by reusing the same instance for the next user if they share the same Cloud credential (or if other trust mechanisms allow it).

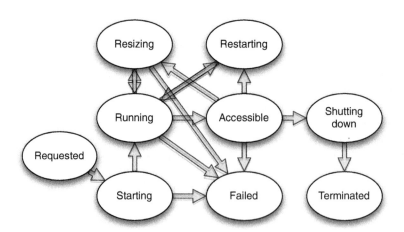

Fig. 11.3 Cloud instance state transition diagram

---

[1]Using the Linpack benchmark results for the different Cloud instance types, as shown in Table 11.6.

Table 11.1 Characteristics of the resource classes offered by four selected clouds as of December 2009

Cloud	Name	Cores (ECUs)	RAM [GB]	Arch. [bit]	I/O Perf.	Disk [GB]	Cost [$/h]
Amazon EC2	m1.small	1 (1)	1.7	32	Medium	160	0.085
	m1.large	2 (4)	7.5	64	High	850	0.34
	m1.xlarge	4 (8)	15.0	64	High	1,690	0.68
	c1.medium	2 (5)	1.7	32	Medium	350	0.17
	c1.xlarge	8 (20)	7.0	64	High	1,690	0.68
	m2.2xlarge	4 (13)	34.2	64	High	850	1.2
	m2.4xlarge	8 (26)	68.4	64	High	1,690	2.4
GoGrid	GG.small	1	1.0	32	–	60	0.19
	GG.large	1	1.0	64	–	60	0.19
	GG.xlarge	3	4.0	64	–	240	0.76
ElasticHosts[14]	EH.small	1	1.0	32	–	30	£0.042
	EH.large	1	4.0	64	–	30	£0.09
Mosso[15]	Mosso.small	4	1.0	64	–	40	0.06
	Mosso.large	4	4.0	64	–	160	0.24

The Cloud manager also maintains a registry of the available resource classes (or instance types) offered by different Cloud providers containing the number of cores, the amount of memory and hard disk, I/O performance, and cost per unit of computation. For example, Table 11.1 contains the resource class information offered by four Cloud providers, which need to be entered by the resource manager admin in the Cloud management registry due to the lack of a corresponding API.

Today, different commercial and academic Clouds provide different interfaces to their services, as no official standard has yet been defined. We are using, in the Cloud management component, the Amazon API [16] defined by EC2, which is also implemented by Eucalyptus [6] and Nimbus (previously known as Globus Workspaces [17]) and used for building "academic Clouds." To support more Clouds, plug-ins to other interfaces or use of metacloud software [18] is required. Table 11.2 shows an overview of Cloud providers that are currently offering API access to provision and release their resources, and which could therefore be integrated into an automatic resource management system. This overview also shows the difference in the available hardware configurations of the selected providers. There is also a wide range of Cloud providers that do not offer an API to control the instances and therefore are not listed.

11.3.2 Image Catalog

Each Cloud infrastructure provides a different set of images offered by the provider or defined by the users, which need to be organized in order to be of use. For example, the Amazon EC2 API provides built-in functionality to retrieve the list of

Table 11.2 Feature summary of selected cloud providers supporting automatic resource management as of December 2009

Property/provider	Agathon [19]	Amazon EC2 [12]	FlexiScale [20]	GoGrid [13]	dps.cloud
Bus size	64	32, 64	32, 64	32, 64	64
operating system	Linux	Linux Windows	Linux Windows	Linux Windows	Linux
Number of images	1	4105 1 (Windows)	5 3 (Windows)	14 11 (Windows)	3
Hardware configs	32	5	40	5	3
Auth. service	Login password	X.509 certificate	Login password	Key, MD5 signature	X.509 certificate
Auth. instance	Login password	RSA keypair	Login password	Login password	RSA keypair
Middleware	AppLogic [21]	Proprietary	Proprietary	Proprietary	Eucalyptus [6]

available images, while other providers only offer plain text HTML pages listing their offers. A few providers even have the lists of possible images hidden in their instance start API documentation. The information about the images provided by different Cloud providers is in all cases limited to simple string names, and lacks additional semantic descriptions of image characteristics, such as the supported architecture, operating system type, embedded software deployments, or support for auto-deployment functionality. The task of the image catalog is to systematically organize this missing information, which is registered manually by the resource manager administrator.

Figure 11.4 shows the hierarchical image catalog structure where each provider has an assigned set of images, and for each image, there is a list of embedded activity deployments, or which can be automatically deployed. Custom images with embedded deployments have reduced the provisioning overhead, as the deployment part is skipped.

Images are currently not interoperable between Cloud providers that generate a large image catalog that needs to be managed. As Table 11.2 demonstrates, the variety of offers between different providers is high. For example, Amazon EC2 has by far the most images available, also due to the fact that users can upload their custom or modified images and make them available to the community. At the other extreme, Agathon [19] only provides one standard instance for its users. The bus size of the different images may create additional problems with the activity deployments on the started instances. For example, Amazon EC2 only offers 32-bit architectures on their two cheapest instance types, while the others are 64 bit.

11.3.3 Security

Security is a critical topic in Cloud computing with applications running and producing confidential data on remote unknown resources that need to be protected. Several

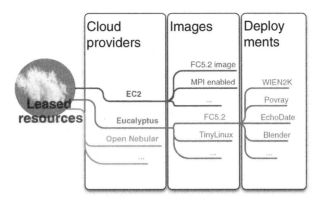

Fig. 11.4 The image catalogue hierarchical architecture

issues need to be addressed, such as authentication to the Cloud services and the started instances, as well as securing user credit card information. Authentication is supported by existing providers either through a key pair and certificate mechanism or by using login and password combinations (see Table 11.2).[2]

One can distinguish between two types of credentials in Cloud environments:

- *User credential* is a persistent credential associated with a credit card number used for provisioning and releasing Cloud resources.
- *Instance credential* is a temporary credential used for manipulating an instance through the SSH protocol.

As these credentials are issued separately by the providers, users will have different credentials for each Cloud infrastructure, in addition to their Grid Security Infrastructure (GSI) certificate. The resource manager needs to manage these credentials in a safe manner, while granting secure access to the deployed Cloud resources to the other services and application.

The security mechanism of the resource manager is based on GSI proxy delegation credentials, which we extended with two secured repositories for Cloud access:

- A *MyCloud* repository that similar to a MyProxy repository [22], stores copies of the user credentials which can only be accessed by authenticating with a GSI credential associated with it.
- A *MyInstance* repository for storing temporary instance credentials generated for each started instance.

The detailed security procedure upon an image deployment request is as follows (see Fig.11.5):

---

[2]Some Cloud providers [19] require the configuration of virtual private networks (VLAN) to authenticate with the Cloud that requires the automatic creation of SSH tunnels using port forwarding; we plan to explore this in future work.

Fig. 11.5 Combined
grid-cloud security
architecture

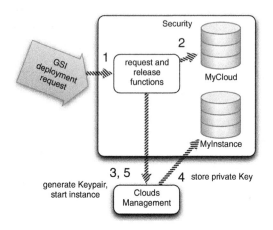

1. A GSI-authenticated request for a new image deployment is received.
2. The security component checks in the MyCloud repository for the Clouds for which the user has valid credentials.
3. A new credential is generated for the new instance that needs to be started. In case multiple images need to be started, the same instance credential can be used to reduce the credential generation overhead (about 6–10 s in our experiments, including the communication overhead).
4. The new instance credentials are stored in the MyImage repository, which will only be accessible to the enactment engine service for job execution after proper GSI authentication.
5. A start instance request is sent to the Cloud using the newly generated instance credential.
6. When an instance is released, the resource manager deletes the corresponding credential from the MyInstance repository.

11.4 Evaluation

We extended the ASKALON enactment engine to consider our Cloud extensions by transferring files and submitting jobs to Cloud resources using the SCP/SSH provider of the Java CoG kit [23]. Some technical problems with these providers of the CoG kit required us to change the source code and create a custom build of the library to allow seamless and functional integration into the existing system.

For our experiments, we selected a scientific workflow application called Wien2k [24], which is a program package for performing electronic structure calculations of solids using density functional theory based on the full-potential (linearized) augmented plane-wave ((L)APW) and local orbital (lo) method. The Wien2k Grid workflow splits the computation into several course-grain activities, the work distribution being achieved by two parallel loops (second and fourth) consisting of a large number of independent activities calculated in parallel.

The number of sequential loops is statically unknown. We have chosen a problem case (called atype) that we solved using 193 and 376 parallel activities, and a problem size of 7.0, 8.0, and 9.0, which represents the number of planewaves that is equal to the size of the eigenvalue problem (i.e. the size of the matrix to be diagonalized) referenced as problem complexity in this work.

Figure 11.6 shows on the left the UML representation of the workflow that can be executed with ASKALON, and on the right, a concrete execution directed acyclic graph (DAG) showing one iteration of the while loop and four parallel activities in the parallel sections. The workflow size is determined at runtime as the parallelism is calculated by the first activity, and the last activity generates the result, which helps decide if the main loop is executed again or the result reaches the specified criteria.

We executed the workflow on a distributed testbed summarized in Table 11.3, consisting of four heterogeneous Austrian Grid sites [25] and 12 virtual CPUs from an "academic Cloud" called dps.cloud built using the Eucalyptus middleware [6] and the XEN virtualization mechanism [7]. We configured the dps.cloud resource classes to use one core, while multi-core configurations were prohibited by a bug in the Eucalyptus software (planned to be fixed in the next released). We fixed the

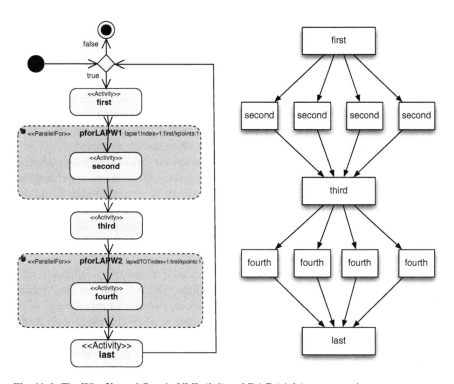

Fig. 11.6 The Wien2k workflow in UML (*left*) and DAG (*right*) representation

Table 11.3 Overview of resources used from the grid and the private cloud for workflow execution

Grid site	Location	Cores used	CPU type	GHz	Mem/core
karwendel	Innsbruck	12	Opteron	2.4	1,024 mb
altix1.uibk	Innsbruck	12	Itanium	1.4	1,024 mb
altix1.jku	Linz	12	Itanium	1.4	1,024 mb
hydra.gup	Linz	12	Itanium	1.6	1,024 mb
dps.cloud	Innsbruck	12	Opteron	2.2	1,024 mb

Table 11.4 Wien2K execution time and cost analysis on the Austrian grid with and without cloud resources for different number of parallel activities and problem sizes

Parallel activities	Problem complexity	Grid execution	Grid + cloud execution	Speedup using Cloud	Used instances Hours	$	Paid instances Hours	$	$/T $/min
193	Small (7.0)	874.66	803.66	1.09	2.7	0.54	12	2.04	1.72
193	Medium (8.0)	1,915.41	1218.09	1.57	4.1	0.82	12	2.04	0.18
193	Big (9.0)	3,670.18	2193.79	1.67	7.3	1.46	12	2.04	0.08
376	Small (7.0)	1,458.92	1275.31	1.14	4.3	0.86	12	2.04	0.67
376	Medium (8.0)	2,687.85	2020.17	1.33	6.7	1.34	12	2.04	0.18
376	Big (9.0)	5,599.67	4228.90	1.32	14.1	2.81	24	4.08	0.17

machine size of each Grid site to 12 cores to eliminate the variability in the resource availability and make the results across different experiments comparable.

We used a just-in-time scheduling mechanism that tries to map each activity onto the fastest available Grid resource. Once the Grid becomes full (because the size of the workflow parallel loops is larger than the total number of cores in the testbed), the scheduler starts requesting additional Cloud resources for executing, in parallel, the remaining workflow activities. Once these additional resources are available, they will be used to link Grid resources with different job submission methods.

Our goal was to compare the workflow execution for different problem sizes on the four Grid sites, with the execution using the same Grid environment supplemented by additional Cloud resources from dps.cloud. We executed each workflow instance five times and reported the average values obtained. The runtime variability in the Austrian Grid was less than 5%, because the testbed was idle during our experiments and each CPU was dedicated to running its activity with no external load or other queuing overheads.

Table 11.4 shows the workflow execution times for 376 and 193 parallel activities in six different configurations. The small, medium, and big configuration values represent a problem size parameter that influences the execution time of the parallel activities. The improvement in using Cloud resources when compared with using only the four Grid sites increases from a small 1.08 speedup for short workflows with 14-min execution time, to a good 1.67 speedup for large workflows with 93-min execution time. The results show that a small and rather short workflow does not benefit much from the Cloud resources due to the high ratio between the smaller computation and the high provisioning and data transfer overheads. The main bottleneck when using Cloud resources is that the provisioned single core instances use separate file systems that require separate file transfers to start the computation. In contrast, Grid sites are usually parallel machines that share one file system across a larger number of cores, which significantly decreases the data transfer overheads. Nevertheless, for large problem sizes, the Cloud resources can help to significantly shorten the workflow completion time in case Grids become overloaded.

Table 11.5 gives further details on the file transfer overheads and the distribution of activity instances between the pure Grid and the combined Grid-Cloud execution. The file transfer overhead can be reduced by increasing the size of a resource class (i.e. number of cores underneath one instance, which share a file system and the input files for execution), which may result in a lower resource allocation efficiency as the resource allocation granularity increases. We plan to investigate this tradeoff in future work.

To understand and quantify the benefit and the potential costs of using commercial Clouds for similar experiments (without running the Wien2k workflows once again because of cost reasons), we executed the LINPACK benchmark [26] that measures the GFlop sustained performance of the resource classes offered by three Cloud providers: Amazon EC2, GoGrid (GG), and our academic dps.cloud (see Table 11.1). We configured LINPACK to use the GotoBLAS linear algebra library (one of the fastest implementations on Opteron processors in our experience) and MPI Chameleon [27] for instances with multiple cores. Table 11.6 summarizes the results that show the m1.large EC2 instance as being the closest to the dps.cloud, assuming that the two cores are used separately, which indicates an approximate realistic cost of $0.20 per core hour. The best sustained performance is offered by GG; however, it has extremely large resource provisioning latencies

Table 11.5 Grid versus cloud file transfer and activity instance distribution to grid and cloud resources [t]

Parallel activities	File transfers			Activities run	
	Total	To grid	To cloud	Total	On cloud
376	2,013	1,544	469 (23%)	759	209 (28%)
193	1,127	778	349 (31%)	389	107 (28%)

Table 11.6 Average LINPACK sustained performance and resource provisioning latency results of various resource classes (see Table 11.1)

Instance	dps. cloud	m1.small	m1.large	m1.xl	c1.medium	c1.xl	GG.1gig	GG.4gig
Linpack (GFlops)	4.40	1.96	7.15	11.38	3.91	51.58	8.81	28.14
Number of cores	1	1	2	4	2	8	1	3
GFlops per core	4.40	1.96	3.58	2.845	1.955	6.44	8.81	9.38
Speedup to dps	1	0.45	1.63	2.58	0.88	11.72	2.00	6.40
Cost [$ per hour]	0 (0.17)	0.085	0.34	0.68	0.17	0.68	0.18	0.72
Provisioning time [s]	312	83	92	65	66	66	558	1,878

(see next paragraph). The c1.xlarge (c1.xl) resource class provides the best per-core sustained performance from the Amazon EC2 instances; however, it aggregates eight cores and therefore has an increased cost per hour.

We also measured the resource provisioning time in the three Clouds, that is, the time elapsed from when resources are requested until they are accessible (see Fig. 11.3). The dps.cloud has an average provisioning time of about 5 min because of the slower hard-drive available. Amazon EC2 is the fastest and needs about 74 s, while GG is surprisingly slow and needs 20 min on an average. The dps.cloud provisioning time could be improved through faster storage hardware, while future versions of Eucalyptus also promise an improvement in image management and caching.

A characteristic of all Clouds that we surveyed is that they charge the resource consumption based on hourly billing increments, and not based on 1s billing increments, as assumed by the simulations performed in two recent related works [4,5]. Table 11.4 shows that for our relatively short workflows below 2 h, there can be a significant difference between the hourly and the 1s billing increment policies. This ratio is decreasing with the growing problem size from 4.4 for the smallest workflow to 1.64 for the largest workflow.

Finally, we define a new metric called $ per unit of saved time ($/T) as the ratio between the time gained by using Cloud resources and total cost of these resources. The results show that the medium and big workflows are the most convenient to be scaled on additional Cloud resources and cost between \$0.08 and \$0.18 per saved minute, while the small workflows exhibit high costs of up to \$1.72 per minute because of the hourly billing increments.

11.5 Related Work

Deelman et al. [4] analyzed the cost of Cloud storage for an image mosaic workflow and a possible on-demand calculation of the results. The work is based on an Amazon EC2 and S3 simulation rather than the real execution. The computation cost model is based on 1s billing increment and the storage cost model on a byte-per-second billing increment, in contrast to the real Cloud providers that are charged based on hourly, gigabyte-per-month billing increments.

Assuncao et al. [5] described an approach of extending a local cluster with Cloud resources using two schedulers, one for the cluster and one for the Cloud, applying different strategies. The possible benefit of not violating deadlines and achieving higher cluster throughput is analyzed. The system concentrates on clusters and does not extend its scope to Grids or multiple Cloud providers. Their results are generated using simulation and do not take the real speed of Cloud resources into account.

Gropp et al. [28] check the usability of Cloud computing for scientific applications using several benchmarks, and shows that Cloud computing can be useful to scientific computing in general.

Yigitbasi et al. [29], present a framework to analyze the performance of Clouds and the results encourage the usability of Clouds for loosely-coupled jobs such as in workflows.

11.6   Conclusions and Future Work

In this chapter, we extended a Grid workflow development and computing environment to use on-demand Cloud resources in Grid environments offering a limited amount of high-performance resources. We presented extensions to the resource-management architecture to consider Cloud resources comprising three new components: Cloud management for automatic image management, image catalog for management of software deployments, and security for authenticating with multiple Cloud providers. We presented experimental results of using a real-world application in the Austrian Grid environment, extended with an academic Cloud. Our results demonstrate that workflows with large problem sizes can significantly benefit from being executed in a combined Grid and Cloud environment. Similarly, the cost of using Cloud resources is more convenient for large workflows due to the hourly billing increment policies applied.

Our environment currently supports providers offering Amazon EC2-compliant interfaces, which we plan to extend for other Cloud providers. We also plan to investigate more sophisticated multi-criteria scheduling strategies, such as the effect of the resource class granularity (i.e. number of underlying cores) on the execution time, resource allocation efficiency, and the overall cost. In addition, we also intend to use the Cloud simulation framework presented in [30] for validating various scheduling and optimization strategies at a larger scale.

References

1. Iosup A, Dumitrescu C, Epema D, Li H, Wolters L (2006) How are real grids used? The analysis of four grid traces and its implications. In international conference on grid computing, IEEE Computer Society, pp 262–269
2. Costa GD, Dikaiakos MD, Orlando S (2007) Analyzing the workload of the south-east federation of the egee grid infrastructure, CoreGRID Technical Report, Tech. Rep. TR-0063, 2007
3. Yu J, Buyya R (2005) A taxonomy of scientific workflow systems for grid computing. ACM SIGMOD Rec 34(3):44–49
4. Deelman E, Singh G, Livny M, Berriman JB, Good J (2008) The cost of doing science on the cloud: the montage example. In proceedings of the ACM/IEEE conference on high performance computing, SC 2008. IEEE/ACM, Austin, Texas, USA, p 50
5. Assuncao ACM, Buyya R (2009) Evaluating the cost-benefit of using cloud computing to extend the capacity of clusters. In: Kranzlmüller D, Bode A, Hegering H.-G, Casanova H, Gerndt M (eds) 11th IEEE international conference on high performance computing and communications (HPCC 2009), ACM
6. Nurmi D, Wolski R, Grzegorczyk C, Obertelli G, Soman S, Youseff L, Zagorodnov D (2008) Eucalyptus: a technical report on an elastic utility computing architecture linking your programs to useful systems. UCSB Computer Science Technical Report, Tech. Rep. 2008–10, 2008
7. Chisnal D (2007) The definitive guide to the Xen hypervisor. Prentice-Hall, New Jersey
8. Fahringer T, Prodan R, Duan R, Nerieri F, Podlipnig S, Qin J, Siddiqui M, Truong HL, Villazón A, Wieczorek M (2005, November 13–14) Askalon: a grid application development and computing environment. In proceedings of the 6th IEEE/ACM international conference on grid computing (GRID 2005). IEEE, Seattle, Washington DC, pp 122–131

9. Fahringer T, Qin J, Hainzer S (2005) Specification of grid workflow applications with agwl: an abstract grid workflow language. In CCGRID. IEEE Computer Society, pp 676–685
10. Czajkowski K, Fitzgerald S, Foster I, Kesselman C (2001) Grid information services for distributed resource sharing. In 10th international symposium on high performance distributed computing. IEEE Computer Society Press
11. Ostermann S, Plankensteiner K, Prodan R, Fahringer T, Iosup A (2008) "Workflow monitoring and analysis tool for ASKALON", in Grid and Services Evolution. Barcelona, Spain, pp 73–86
12. Amazon (2009) Elastic compute cloud (EC2). http://aws.amazon.com/ec2/. Accessed January 2009
13. GoGrid (2009) Cloud hosting: Instant windows and linux cloud servers. http://www.gogrid.com/. Accessed January 2009
14. "Elastichosts: Cloud hosting and cloud computing that's flexible and easy to use. http://www.elastichosts.com/
15. Mosso (2009) The cloud, cloud computing, cloud hosting, cloud services @ mosso. http://www.mosso.com/. Accessed January 2009
16. Amazon Inc. (2009) Amazon ec2 api. http://developer.amazonwebservices.com/connect/kbcategory.jspa?categoryID=87. Accessed April 2009
17. Keahey K, Freeman T, Lauret J, Olson D (2007) Virtual workspaces for scientific applications. In Scientific discovery through advanced computing. Boston, MA
18. Buyya R, Yeo CS, Venugopal S (2008, 25–27 Sept) Market-oriented cloud computing: Vision, hype, and reality for delivering it services as computing utilities. In 10th IEEE international conference on high performance computing and communications (HPCC 2008). IEEE, Dalian, China, pp 5–13
19. Agathon Group (2009) https://www.agathongroup.com/. Accessed January 2009
20. FlexiScale (2009) Utility computing on demand. http://flexiscale.com/. Accessed January 2009
21. 3tera (2009) Applogic - grid operating system for web applications. http://www.3tera.com/AppLogic/. Accessed January 2009
22. Novotny J, Tuecke S, Welch V (2001) An online credential repository for the Grid: MyProxy. In proceedings of the tenth international symposium on high performance distributed computing (HPDC-10), IEEE Computer Society Press
23. von Laszewski G, Foster I, Gawor J (2000) CoG kits: a bridge between commodity distributed computing and high-performance grids. In Java Grande Conference. ACM Press, pp 97–106
24. Blaha P, Schwarz K, Luitz J (2001) *WIEN2k,* a full potential linearized augmented plane wave package for calculating crystal properties. TU Wien ISBN 3-9501031-1-2, 2001
25. Volkert J (2006, July 6–9) Austrian grid: Overview on the project with focus on parallel applications. In 5th international symposium on parallel and distributed computing (ISPDC 2006). IEEE Computer Society, Timisoara, Romania, p 14
26. Dongarra JJ, Luszczek P, Petitet A (2003) The LINPACK benchmark: past, present and future. Concurr Comput Prac Exp 15(9):803–820
27. Gropp W, Lusk E, Ashton D, Buntinas D, Butler R, Chan A, Ross R, Thakur R, Toonen B (2005) Mpich2 user's guide, version 1.0.3, Mathematics and computer science division, Argonne national laboratory. Technical Report. http://www-unix.mcs.anl.gov/mpi/mpich/
28. Rehr JJ, Gardner JP, Prange M, Svec L, Vila F (2009) Scientific computing in the cloud. Computing Research Repository vol. abs/0901.0029, 2009
29. Yigitbasi N, Iosup A, Ostermann S, Epema D (2009) C-meter: A framework for performance analysis of computing clouds. In International Workshop on Cloud Computing (Cloud 2009)
30. Calheiros RN, Ranjan R, Rose CAFD, Buyya R (2009) Cloudsim: a novel framework for modeling and simulation of cloud computing infrastructures and services. Computing Research Repository, vol. abs/0903.2525, 2009

Chapter 12
Peer-to-Peer Cloud Provisioning: Service Discovery and Load-Balancing

Rajiv Ranjan, Liang Zhao, Xiaomin Wu, Anna Liu, Andres Quiroz, and Manish Parashar

Abstract Clouds have evolved as the next-generation platform that facilitates creation of wide-area on-demand renting of computing or storage services for hosting application services that experience highly variable workloads and requires high availability and performance. Interconnecting Cloud computing system components (servers, virtual machines (VMs), application services) through peer-to-peer routing and information dissemination structure are essential to avoid the problems of provisioning efficiency bottleneck and single point of failure that are predominantly associated with traditional centralized or hierarchical approaches. These limitations can be overcome by connecting Cloud system components using a structured peer-to-peer network model (such as distributed hash tables (DHTs)). DHTs offer deterministic information/query routing and discovery with close to logarithmic bounds as regards network message complexity. By maintaining a small routing state of O (log n) per VM, a DHT structure can guarantee deterministic look-ups in a completely decentralized and distributed manner.

This chapter presents: (i) a layered peer-to-peer Cloud provisioning architecture; (ii) a summary of the current state-of-the-art in Cloud provisioning with particular emphasis on service discovery and load-balancing; (iii) a classification of the existing peer-to-peer network management model with focus on extending the DHTs for indexing and managing complex provisioning information; and (iv) the design and implementation of novel, extensible software fabric (*Cloud peer*) that combines public/private clouds, overlay networking, and structured peer-to-peer indexing techniques for supporting scalable and self-managing service discovery and load-balancing in Cloud computing environments. Finally, an experimental evaluation is presented that demonstrates the feasibility of building next-generation Cloud provisioning systems based on peer-to-peer network management and information

R. Ranjan (✉)
SA Project, CRC Smart Services, Service Oriented Computing Research Group,
School of Computer Science and Engineering, University of New South Wales, Australia
e-mail: rajivr@cse.unsw.edu.au

N. Antonopoulos and L. Gillam (eds.), *Cloud Computing: Principles,*
Systems and Applications, Computer Communications and Networks,
DOI 10.1007/978-1-84996-241-4_12, © Springer-Verlag London Limited 2010

dissemination models. The experimental test-bed has been deployed on a public cloud computing platform, Amazon EC2, which demonstrates the effectiveness of the proposed peer-to-peer Cloud provisioning software fabric.

12.1 Introduction

Cloud computing [1–3] has emerged as the next-generation platform for hosting business and scientific applications. It offers infrastructure, platform, and software as services that are made available as on-demand and subscription-based services in a pay-as-you-go model to users. These services are, respectively, referred to as Infrastructure as a Service (IaaS), Platform as a Service (PaaS), and Software as a Service (SaaS). Adoption of Cloud computing platforms [4–9] as an application provisioning environment has the following critical benefits: (i) software enterprises and startups with innovative ideas for new Internet services are no longer required to make large capital outlays in the hardware and software infrastructures to deploy their services or human expense to operate it; (ii) government agencies and financial organizations can use Cloud services as an effective means for cost cutting by leasing their IT service hosting and maintenance from external cloud providers; (iii) organizations can more cost-effectively manage peak-load by using the cloud, rather than planning and building for peak load, and having under-utilized servers sitting there idle during off peak time; and (iv) failures due to natural disasters or regular system maintenance/outage may be managed more gracefully as services may be more transparently managed and migrated to other available cloud resources, hence enabling improved service-level agreement (SLA).

The process of deploying application services on publically accessible clouds (such as Amazon EC2 [8]) that expose their capabilities as a network of virtualized services (hardware, storage, database) is known as Cloud provisioning. The Cloud provisioning process consists of two key steps [10]: (i) VM provisioning, involving instantiation of one or more VMs on physical servers hosted within public or private Cloud computing environments – the selection of a physical server for hosting VMs in a cloud is based on a number of mapping requirements including available memory, storage space, and proximity of the parent cloud; and (ii) application service provisioning, with mapping and scheduling of requests to the services that are hosted within a VM or on a set of VMs. In this chapter, we mainly focus on the second step, which involves dynamically distributing the incoming requests among the services in a load-balanced and decentralized manner, given a set of VMs that are hosting different types of application services.

Cloud provisioning from a business services point of view involves deriving cloud-based application component deployments driven by expected performance (Quality of Service (QoS)). Clouds offer an unprecedented pool of software and hardware resources, which gives businesses a unique ability to handle the temporal variation in their service demands through dynamic provisioning or deprovisioning of capabilities. Whenever there is a variation in temporal and spatial locality of workload such as number of concurrent users, total users, and load conditions, each application component must dynamically scale (application service elasticity) to offer good quality of experience to users, and maintain an optimal usage of cloud resources. Cloud-enabling any class of application service would require developing models for service placement, computation, communication, and storage, with emphasis on important scalability requirements.

Currently, one of the prominent Cloud service providers Amazon EC2 offers two services, namely CloudWatch [11] and Elastic Load Balancer [12]. Fundamentally, CloudWatch and Elastic Load Balancer are centralized web services that can be associated with numerous EC2 instances. However, centralized approaches have several critical design limitations including: (i) single point of failure; (ii) lack of scalability; (iii) high network communication cost at links leading to the service; (iv) requirement of high computational power to serve a large number of resource look-up and updated queries on the server running the central service.

As Clouds become ready for mainstream acceptance, scalability [13] of services will come under more severe scrutiny due to the increasing number of online services in the Cloud, and massive numbers of global users. To overcome the aforementioned limitations, fundamental Cloud services for discovery, monitoring, and load-balancing should be decentralized by nature and different service components (VM instances and application elements) must interact to adaptively maintain and achieve the desired system wide connectivity and behaviour.

The rest of this chapter is organized as follows: First, a layered approach to architecting peer-to-peer Cloud provisioning system is presented. This is followed by some survey results on Cloud provisioning capabilities in leading commercial public clouds. The finer details related to architecting peer-to-peer Cloud service discovery and load-balancing techniques over DHT overlay is then presented, followed by a discussion of the design and implementation of peer-to-peer Cloud provisioning (Cloud peer) software fabric. Lastly, we present the analysis and experimental results of the peer-to-peer Cloud provisioning implementation across a public Cloud (Amazon EC2) environment (Table 12.1).

Table 12.1 Summary of provisioning capabilities exposed by public Cloud platforms

Cloud platforms	Load balancing	Provisioning	Autoscaling
Amazon Elastic Compute Cloud	√	√	√
Eucalyptus	√	√	×
Microsoft Windows Azure	√	√ (Fixed templates so far)	√ (Manually at the moment)
Google App Engine	√	√	√
GoGrid Cloud Hosting	√	√	√ (Programmatic way only)

12.2   Layered Peer-to-Peer Cloud Provisioning Architecture

This section presents information on various architectural elements that form the basis for peer-to-peer Cloud provisioning architecture. It also presents an overview of the applications that would benefit from the architecture, which envisages a hosting infrastructure consisting of multiple geographically distributed private and public clouds owned by one or more service providers. Figure 12.1 shows the layered design of the peer-to-peer Cloud provisioning architecture. Physical Cloud servers, along with core middleware capabilities, form the basis for delivering IaaS. The user-level middleware aims at providing PaaS capabilities. The top layer focuses on application services (SaaS) by making use of services provided by the lower layers. PaaS/SaaS services are often developed and provided by third-party service providers, who are different from IaaS providers.

Cloud Applications (SaaS): Popular Cloud applications include Business to Business (B2B) applications, traditional eCommerce type of applications, enterprise business applications such as CRM and ERP, social computing such as Facebook and MySpace, and compute, data intensive applications and content delivery networks (CDNs). These applications have radically different application characteristics and workload profiles, and hence, to cope with the variation in temporal and spatial locality of service request, the application services must be supported by a Cloud provisioning infrastructure that dynamically scales the deployed

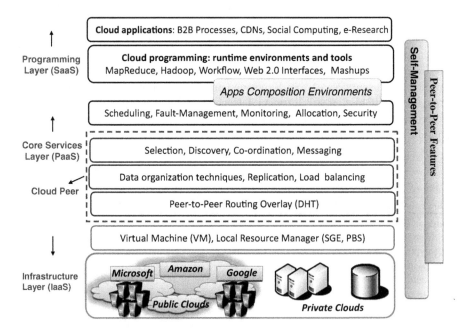

Fig. 12.1 A layered peer-to-peer Cloud provisioning architecture

services in order to achieve good performance, optimal resource usage, and hence offer quality experience to its end-users.

Development Framework Layer: This layer includes the software frameworks such as Web 2.0 Interfaces (Ajax, IBM Workplace, and Visual Studio.net Azure plug-in) that help developers in creating rich, cost-effective, user-interfaces for browser-based applications. The layer also provides the data-intensive, parallel programming environments (such as MapReduce, Hadoop, Dryad) and composition tools that ease the creation, deployment, and execution of applications in Clouds.

Core Services Layer (PaaS): This layer implements the platform-level services that provide run-time environment-enabling Cloud computing capabilities to application services built using User-Level Middleware. Core services at this layer include scheduling, fault-management, monitoring, dynamic SLA management, accounting, billing, and pricing. Further, the services at this layer must be able to provide support for decentralized co-ordinated interaction, scalable selection, and messaging between distributed Cloud components. Some of the existing services operating at this layer are Amazon EC2's CloudWatch and Load-balancer service, Google App Engine, Microsoft Azure's fabric controller, and Aneka [14].

To be able to provide support for decentralized service discovery [15] and load-balancing between cloud components (VM instances, application services), novel distributed hash table (DHT)-based PaaS layer services, techniques, and algorithms need to be developed at this layer for supporting complex interactions with guarantees on dynamic management. In Fig. 12.1, this component of PaaS layer is shown as Cloud peer service. Architecting Cloud services based on decentralized network models or overlays (such as DHTs) is significant since DHTs are highly scalable, can gracefully adapt to the dynamic system expansion (new host/VM/service instantiation) or contraction (host/VM/service instance destruction) and outage, and are not susceptible to single point of failure in massive scale, internetworked private and public cloud environments.

Infrastructure Layer (IaaS): The computing power in Cloud computing environments is supplied by a collection of data centers that are typically installed with many thousands of servers. At the IaaS layer, there exist massive physical servers (storage servers and application servers) that power the data centers. These servers are transparently managed by the higher-level virtualization services and toolkits that allow sharing of their capacity among virtual instances of servers. These virtual machines (VMs) are isolated from each other, which aids in achieving fault-tolerant behaviour and the isolation of security contexts.

Another trend in Cloud usage is combination of private clouds with public clouds, in order to attend unexpected or periodic peaks in local demand without investing in acquiring new equipment for the local infrastructure. Resources from the data center may be either available for public in general (public clouds) or may be restricted to users belonging to the organization that owns the data center (private clouds). It is also possible to have hybrid models, in which resources are leased from the public cloud whenever the private cloud cannot cope with the incoming demand.

12.3 Current State-of-the-Art and Practice in Cloud Provisioning

Key players in public Cloud computing, including Amazon, Microsoft, Google App Engine, Eucalyptus [16], and GoGrid, offer a variety of prepackaged services for monitoring, managing, and provisioning resources. However, the techniques implemented in each of these Clouds vary.

The three Amazon Web Services (AWS), Elastic Load Balancer [12], Auto Scaling [17], and CloudWatch [11], together expose functionalities that are required for undertaking provisioning of application services on Amazon EC2. Elastic Load Balancer service automatically provisions incoming application workload across available Amazon EC2 instances. Auto-scaling service can be used to dynamically scale-in or scale-out the number of Amazon EC2 instances for handling changes in service demand patterns. And finally, the CloudWatch service can be integrated with the above services for strategic decision-making based on collected real-time information.

Eucalyptus is an open source Cloud computing platform. It is composed of three controllers. Among the controllers, the cluster controller is a key component to application service provisioning and load balancing. Each cluster controller is hosted on the head node of a cluster to interconnect outer public networks and inner private networks together. By monitoring the state information of instances in the pool of server controllers, the cluster controller can select the available service/ server for provisioning incoming requests. However, when compared with AWS, Eucalyptus still lacks some of the critical functionalities, such as autoscaling for built-in provisioner.

Fundamentally, Windows Azure Fabric has a weave-like structure, which is composed of nodes (servers and load balancers), and edges (power, Ethernet, and serial communications). The fabric controller manages a service node through a built-in service, the Azure fabric controller agent, which runs in the background tracking the state of the server and reporting these metrics to the controller. If a fault state is reported, the controller can manage a reboot of the server or a migration of services from the current server to other healthy servers. Moreover, the controller also supports service provisioning by matching the services/VMs that meet the required demands.

GoGrid Cloud Hosting offers developers F5 Load Balancers [18] for distributing application service traffic across servers, as long as IPs and specific ports of these servers are attached. The load balancer provides the Round Robin algorithm and Least Connect algorithm for routing application service requests. Also, the load balancer is able to sense a crash of the server, redirecting further requests to other available servers. But currently, GoGrid Cloud Hosting only gives developers programmatic APIs to implement their custom autoscaling service.

Unlike other Cloud platforms, Google App Engine offers developers a scalable platform in which applications can run, rather than providing access directly to a customized virtual machine. Therefore, access to the underlying operating system is restricted in App Engine. Load-balancing strategies, service provisioning, and autoscaling are all automatically managed by the system behind the scenes.

In addition, no single Cloud infrastructure provider has its data centers at all possible locations throughout the world. As a result, Cloud application service (SaaS) providers will have difficulty in meeting QoS expectations for all their users. Hence, they would like to logically construct hybrid Cloud infrastructures (mixing multiple public and private clouds) to provide better support for their specific user needs. This kind of requirement often arises in enterprises with global operations and applications such as Internet service, media hosting, and Web 2.0 applications. This necessitates building technologies and algorithms for seamless integration of Cloud infrastructure service providers for provisioning of services across different Cloud providers.

12.4   Cloud Service Discovery and Load-Balancing Using DHT Overlay

12.4.1   Distributed Hash Tables

Structured systems such as DHTs offer deterministic query search results within logarithmic bounds on network message complexity. Peers in DHTs such as Chord, CAN, Pastry, and Tapestry maintain an index for O (log n) peers where n is the total number of peers in the system. Inherent to the design of a DHT are the following issues [19]: (i) generation of node-ids and object-ids, called keys, using cryptographic/randomizing hash functions such as SHA-1 [19–22] – the objects and nodes are mapped on the overlay network depending on their key value and each node is assigned responsibility for managing a small number of objects; (ii) building up routing information (routing tables) at various nodes in the network – each node maintains the network location information of a few other nodes in the network; and (iii) an efficient look-up query resolution scheme.

Whenever a node in the overlay receives a look-up request, it must be able to resolve it within acceptable bounds such as in O (log n) routing hops. This is achieved by routing the look-up request to the nodes in the network that are most likely to store the information about the desired object. Such probable nodes are identified by using the routing table entries. Though at the core various DHTs (Chord, CAN, Pastry, and Tapestry, etc.) are similar, still there exist substantial differences in the actual implementation of algorithms including the overlay network construction (network graph structure), routing table maintenance, and node join/ leave handling. The performance metrics for evaluating a DHT include fault-tolerance, load-balancing, efficiency of look-ups and inserts, and proximity awareness [23]. In Table 12.2, we present the comparative analysis of Chord, Pastry, CAN, and Tapestry based on basic performance and organization parameters. Comprehensive details about the performance of some common DHTs under churn can be found in [24].

Table 12.2 Summary of complexity of distributed hash table overlays

DHT system	Overlay structure	Look-up protocol	Network parameters	Routing table size	Routing complexity	Join/ leave overhead
Chord	Circular identifier space	Matching key and server-id	n =number of servers	$O (\log n)$	$O (\log n)$	$O ((\log n)^2)$
Pastry	Plaxton style mesh	Matching key and prefix in server-id	n =number of servers in the network, b= base of the identifier	$O (\log_b n)$	$O (b \log_b n) + b$	$O (\log n)$
CAN	Multidimensional space	Key, value pair map to a point in space	n =number of servers in the network, d = dimensions	$O (2\ d)$	$O (d\ n^{1/d})$	$O (2\ d)$
Tapestry	Plaxton style mesh	Matching suffix in server-id	n =number of servers in the network, b = base of the identifier	$O (\log_b n)$	$O (b \log_b n) + b$	$O (\log n)$

Other classes of structured peer-to-peer systems such as Mercury [25] do not apply randomizing hash functions for organizing data items and nodes. The Mercury system organizes nodes into a circular overlay and places data contiguously on this ring. As Mercury does not apply hash functions, data partitioning among nodes is not uniform. Hence, it requires an explicit load-balancing scheme. In recent developments, new-generation P2P systems have evolved to combine both unstructured and structured P2P networks. We refer to this class of systems as hybrid. Structella [26] is one such P2P system that replaces the random graph model of an unstructured overlay (Gnutella) with a structured overlay, while still adopting the search and content placement mechanism of unstructured overlays to support complex queries. Other hybrid P2P design includes Kelips [27] and its variants. Nodes in Kelips overlay periodically gossip to discover new members of the network, and during this process nodes may also learn about other nodes as a result of look-up communication. Other variants of Kelips allow routing table entries to store information for every other node in the system. However, this approach is based on the assumption that the system experiences low churn rate [24]. Gossiping and one-hop routing approach has been used for maintaining the routing overlay in the work [28].

12.4.2   Designing Complex Services over DHTs

Limitations of Basic DHT Implementations and Query Types: Traditionally, DHTs have been efficient for single-dimensional queries such as "finding all resources that match the given attribute value." Since Cloud computing IaaS and PaaS level services such as servers, VMs, enterprise computers (private cloud resources), storage devices, and databases are identified by more than one attribute, a search query for these services is always multidimensional. These search dimensions or attributes can include service type, processor speed, architecture, installed operating system, available memory, and network bandwidth.

Based on recent information published by Amazon EC2 CloudWatch service, each Amazon Machine Image (AMI) instance has seven performance metrics (see Table 12.3) and four dimensions (see Table 12.4) associated with it. Additionally, these AMIs can host different application service types, including web hosting,

Table 12.3 Performance metrics associated with an Amazon EC2 AMI instance

CPU Utilization	Network Incoming Traffic	Network Outgoing Traffic	Disk Write Operations	Disk Read Operations	Disk Write Bytes	Disk Read Bytes

Table 12.4 Performance dimensions associated with an Amazon EC2 AMI instance

Image ID	Autoscaling group name	Instance ID	Instance type

social networking, content-delivery, and high-performance computing, that have varying request invocation, access, and distribution patterns. The type of application services hosted by an AMI instance is dependent on the business needs and scientific experiments. In these cases, a Cloud service discovery query (which can be issued by provisioning software) will combine the aforementioned attributes related to AMI instances and application service types and therefore can have the following semantics:

> Cloud Service Type = "web hosting" && Host CPU Utilization < "50%" && Instance OSType = "WinSrv2003" && Host Processor Cores > "1" && Host Processors Speed > "1.5 GHz" && Host Cloud Location = "Europe"

On the other hand, VM instances deployed on the Cloud hosts needs to publish their information so that provisioning software can search and discover them. VM instances update their software and hardware configuration and the deployed services' availability status by sending *update query* to the DHT overlay. An update query has the following semantics:

> Cloud Service Type = "web hosting" && Host CPU Utilization = "30%" && Instance OSType = "WinSrv2003" && Host Processor Cores = "2" && Host Processors Speed = "1.5 GHz" && Host Cloud Location = "Europe"

Extending DHTs to support indexing and matching of multidimensional range (service discovery query) or point (update query) queries, to index all resources whose attribute value overlaps a given search space, is a complex problem. Multidimensional range queries are based on ranges of values for attributes rather than on specific values. Compared to single-dimensional queries, resolving multidimensional queries is far more complicated, as there is no obvious total ordering of the points in the attribute space. Further, the query interval has varying size, aspect ratio, and position such as a window query. The main challenges involved in enabling multidimensional queries in a DHT overlay include designing efficient service attribute data: (i) distribution or indexing techniques; and (ii) query routing techniques.

Data Indexing Techniques for Mapping Multidimensional Range and Point Queries: A data indexing technique partitions the multidimensional attribute space over the set of VMs in a DHT network. Efficiency of the distribution mechanism directly governs how the query processing load is distributed among the Cloud peers. A good distribution mechanism should possess the following characteristics [29]: (i) locality: data points nearby in the attribute space should be mapped to the same Cloud peer, hence limiting the distributed lookup complexity; (ii) load balance: the number of data points indexed by each Cloud peer should be approximately the same to ensure uniform distribution of query processing; (iii) minimal metadata: prior information required for mapping the attribute space to the overlay space should be minimal; and (iv) minimal management overhead: during VM instantiation and destruction operation, update policies such as the transfer of data points to a newly joined Cloud peer should cause minimal network traffic. Note that the assumption here is that every VM instance hosts a Cloud peer service, which is responsible for managing activities related to overlay network.

There are different kinds of database indices [30] that can handle mapping of multidimensional objects such as the space filling curves (SFCs) (including the Hilbert curves, Z-curves), k-d tree, MX-CIF Quad tree, and R*-tree in a DHT overlay. In literature, these indices are referred to as spatial indices [31]. Spatial indices are well suited for handling the complexity of multidimensional queries. Although some spatial indices can have issues as regards to routing load-balance in case of a skewed attribute/data set, all the spatial indices are generally scalable in terms of the number of hops traversed and messages generated while searching and routing multidimensional/spatial service discovery and update queries. However, there are different tradeoffs involved with each of the spatial indices, but basically they can all support scalability and Cloud service discovery. Some spatial index would perform optimally in one scenario but the performance could degrade if the attribute/data distribution changed significantly.

Routing Techniques for Handling Multidimensional Queries in DHT Overlay: DHTs guarantee deterministic query look-up with logarithmic bounds on network message cost for single-dimensional queries. However, Cloud's service discovery and update query are multidimensional (as discussed in previous sections). Hence, the existing DHT routing techniques need to be augmented in order to efficiently resolve multidimensional queries. Various data structures that we discussed in the previous section effectively create a logical multidimensional index space over a DHT overlay. A look-up operation involves searching for an index or set of indexes in a multidimensional space. However, the exact query routing path in the multidimensional logical space is directly governed by the data distribution mechanism (i.e. based on the data structure that maintains the indexes). In this context, various approaches have proposed different routing/indexing heuristics.

Efficient query routing algorithms should exhibit the following characteristics [29]: (i) routing load balance: every peer in the network should route forward/route approximately the same number of query messages; and (ii) low routing state per Cloud peer: each Cloud peer should maintain a small number of routing links hence limiting new Cloud peer (VM) join and Cloud peer (VM) state update cost. In the current peer-to-peer literature, multidimensional data distribution mechanisms based on the following structures have been proposed: (i) space filling curves; and (ii) tree-based structures. Resolving multidimensional queries over a DHT overlay that utilizes SFCs for data distribution consists of two basic steps [10]: (i) mapping the multidimensional query onto the set of relevant clusters of SFC-based index space; and (ii) routing the message to all VMs that fall under the computed SFC-based index space. On the other hand, routing multidimensional query in a DHT overlay that employs tree-based structures for data distribution requires routing to start from the root. However, the root VM presents a single point of failure and load imbalance. To overcome this, the authors introduced the concept of fundamental minimum level. This means that all the query processing and the data storage should start at that minimal level of the tree rather than at the root. There are a number of techniques available for distributed routing in multidimensional space. The performance of techniques varies depending on the distribution of data in the multidimensional space, and VM in the underlying DHT overlay.

12.5   Cloud Peer Software Fabric: Design and Implementation

The Cloud peer implements services for enabling decentralized and distributed discovery supporting status look-ups and updates across the internetworked Cloud computing systems, enabling inter-application service co-ordinated provisioning for optimizing load-balancing and tackling the distributed service contention problem. The dotted box in Fig. 12.1 shows the layered design of Cloud peer service over DHT based self-organizing routing structure. The services built on the DHT routing structure extends (both algorithmically and programmatically) the fundamental properties related to DHTs including deterministic look-up, scalable routing, and decentralized network management. The Cloud peer service is divided into a number of sublayers (see Fig. 12.1): (i) higher level services for discovery, co-ordination, and messaging; (ii) low level distributed indexing and data organization techniques, replication algorithms, and query load-balancing techniques; (iii) DHT-based self-organizing routing structure. A Cloud peer undertakes the following critical tasks that are important for proper functioning of DHT-based provisioning overlay.

12.5.1   Overlay Construction

The overlay construction refers to how Cloud peers are logically connected over the physical network. The software implementation utilizes (the open source implementation of Pastry DHT known as the FreePastry) Pastry [32] as the basis for creation of Cloud peer overlay. A Pastry overlay interconnects the Cloud peer services based on a ring topology. Inherent to the construction of a Pastry overlay are the following issues: (i) Generation of Cloud peer IS and query (discovery, update) ids, called keys, using cryptographic/randomizing hash functions such as SHA-1. These IDs are generated from 160-bit unique identifier space. The ID is used to indicate a Cloud peer's position in a circular ID space, which ranges from 0 to $2^{160} - 1$. The queries and Cloud peers are mapped on the overlay network depending on their key values. Each Cloud peer is assigned responsibility for managing a small number of queries; and (ii) building up routing information (leaf set, routing table, and neighborhood set) at various Cloud peers in the network. Given the Key K, the Pastry routing algorithm can find the Cloud peer responsible for this key in $O(\log_b n)$ messages, where b is the base and n is the number of Cloud Peers in the network.

Each Cloud peer in the Pastry overlay maintains a routing table, leaf set, and neighborhood set. These tables are constructed when a Cloud peer joins the overlay, and it is periodically updated to take into account any new joins, leaves, or failures. Each entry in the routing table contains the IP address of one of the potentially many Cloud peers whose id have the appropriate prefix; in practice, a Cloud peer is chosen, which is close to the current peer, according to the proximity metric. Figure 12.2 shows a hypothetical Pastry overlay with keys and Cloud peers distributed on the circular ring based on their cryptographically generated IDs.

12.5.2   Multidimensional Query Indexing

To support multidimensional query indexing (Cloud service type, Host utilization, Instance OS type, Host Cloud location, Host Processor speed) over Pastry overlay, a Cloud peer implements a distributed indexing technique [33], which is a variant of peer-to-peer MX-CIF Quad tree [34] data structure. The distributed index builds a multidimensional attribute space based on the Cloud service attributes, where each attribute represents a single dimension. An example of a two-dimensional attribute space that indexes service attributes including speed and CPU type is shown in Fig. 12.2. The first step in initializing the distributed index is the process called minimum division (f_{min}). This process divides the Cartesian space into multiple index cells when the multidimensional distributed index is first created. As a result of this process, the attribute space resembles a grid-like structure consisting of multiple index cells. The cells resulting from this process remain constant throughout the life of the indexing domain and serve as entry points for subsequent service discovery and update query mapping. The number of cells produced at the minimum division level is always equal to $(f_{min})^{dim}$, where *dim* is dimensionality of the attribute space. Every Cloud peer in the network has basic information about the attribute space co-ordinate values, dimensions, and minimum division level. Cloud peers can obtain this information (cells at minimum division level, control points) in a configuration file from the bootstrap peer. Each index cell at f_{min} is uniquely identified by its centroid, termed as the control point. In Fig. 12.2, $f_{min} = 1$, dim = 2. The Pastry overlay hashing method (DHash (co-ordinates)) is used to map these control points so that the responsibility for an index cell is associated with a Cloud peer in the overlay. For example in Fig. 12.2, DHash(x_1, y_1) = $k10$ is the location of the control point A (x_1, y_1) on the overlay, which is managed by Cloud peer 12.

12.5.3   Multidimensional Query Routing

This action involves the identification of the index cells at minimum division level f_{min} in the attribute space to map a service discovery and update query. For a mapping service discovery query, the mapping strategy depends on whether it is a multidimensional point query (equality constraints on all search attribute values) or multidimensional range query. For a multidimensional point service discovery query, the mapping is straightforward since every point is mapped to only one cell in the attribute space. For a multidimensional range query, mapping is not always singular because a range look-up can cross more than one index cell. To avoid mapping a multidimensional service discovery query to all the cells that it crosses (which can create many unnecessary duplicates), a mapping strategy based on diagonal hyperplane of the attribute space is utilized. This mapping involves feeding the service discovery query's spatial dimensions into a mapping function, *IMap*(query).

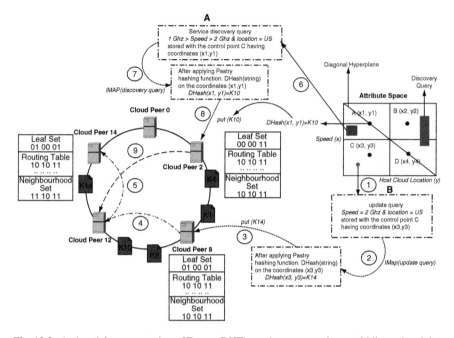

Fig. 12.2 A pictorial representation of Pastry (DHT) overlay construction, multidimensional data indexing, and routing: (1) a service hosted within a VM publishes an update query; (2) Cloud peer 8 computes the index cell, $C(x_3,y_3)$, to which the update query maps by using mapping function *IMap*(query); (3) next, distributed hashing function, $DHash(x_3, y_3)$, is applied on the cell's co-ordinate values, which yields an overlay key, K14; (4) Cloud peer 8 based on its routing table entry forwards the request to peer 12; (5) similarly, peer 12 on the overlay forwards the request to Cloud peer 14; (6) a provisioning service submits a service discovery query; (7) Cloud peer 2 computes the index cell, $C(x_1, y_1)$, to which the service discovery query maps; (8) $DHash(x_1, y_1)$ is applied that yields an overlay key, K10; (9) Cloud peer 2 based on its routing table entry forwards the mapping request to peer 12

This function returns the IDs of index cells to which given query can be mapped (refer to step 7 in Fig. 12.2). Distributed hashing (*DHash*(cells)) is performed on these IDs (which returns keys for Pastry overlay) to identify the current Cloud peers responsible for managing the given keys. A Cloud peer service uses the index cell(s) currently assigned to it and a set of known base index cells obtained at the initialization as the candidate index cells. Similarly, mapping of the update query also involves the identification of the cell in the attribute space using the same algorithm. An update query is always associated with an event region [35] and all cells that fall fully or partially within the event region would be selected to receive the corresponding objects. The calculation of an event region is also based on the diagonal hyperplane of the attribute space. Giving in-depth information here is out of the scope for this chapter; however, the readers who would like to have more information can refer the paper [15, 30, 33] that describes the index in detail.

12.5.4 Designing Decentralized and Co-ordinated Load-Balancing Mechanism

A co-ordinated provisioning of requests between virtual machine instances deployed in Clouds is critical, as it prevents the service provisioners from congesting the particular set of VMs and network links, which arises due to lack of complete global knowledge. In addition, it significantly improves the Cloud user Quality of Service (QoS) satisfaction in terms of response time. The Cloud peer service in conjunction with the Pastry overlay and multidimensional indexing technique is able to perform a decentralized and co-ordinated balancing of service provisioning requests among the set of available VMs. The description of the actual load-balancing mechanism follows next.

As mentioned in previous section, both service discovery query (issued by service provisioner) and update query (published by VMs or Services hosted within VMs) are spatially hashed to an index cell i in the multidimensional attribute space. In Fig. 12.3, a service discovery query for provisioning request P1 is mapped to an index cell with control point value A, while for P2, P3, and P4, the responsible cell has control point value C. Note that these service discovery queries are posted by service provisioners. In Fig. 12.3, a provisioning service inserts a service discovery query with Cloud peer p, which is mapped to index cell i. The index cell i is spatially hashed through IMap(query) function to an Cloud peer s. In this case, Cloud peer s is responsible for co-ordinating the provisioning of services among all the service discovery queries that are currently mapped to the cell i. Subsequently, VM u issues a resource ticket (see Fig. 12.3) that falls under a region of the attribute space currently required by the provisioning requests P3 and P4. Next, the Cloud peer s has to decide which of the requests (either P3 or P4 or both) is allowed to claim the update query published by VM u. The load-balancing decision is based on the principle that it should not lead to over-provisioning of service(s) hosted within VM u. This mechanism leads to co-ordinated load-balancing across VMs in Clouds and aids in achieving system-wide objective function.

The examples in Table 12.5 are service discovery queries that are stored with a Cloud peer service at time $T = 700$ s. Essentially, the queries in the list arrived at a time ≤700 and waited for a suitable update query that could meet their provisioning requirements (software, hardware, service type, location). Table 12.6 depicts an update query that arrived at $T = 700$. Following the update query arrival, the Cloud peer service undertakes a procedure that allocates the available service capacity with VM (that published the update query) among the list of matching service discovery queries. Based on the updating VM's attribute specification, only service discovery query 3 matches. Following this, the Cloud peer notifies the provisioning services that posted the query 3. Note that queries 1 and 2 have to wait for the arrival of update queries that can match their requirements.

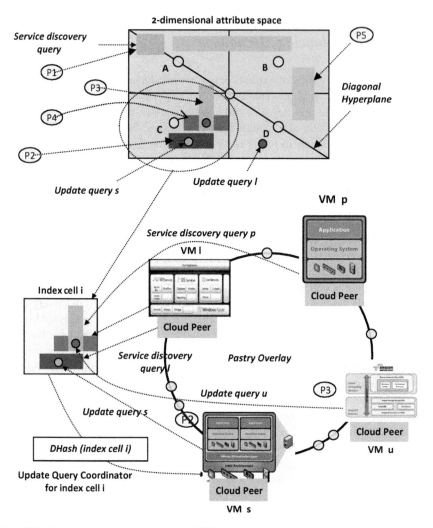

Fig. 12.3 Co-ordinated provisioning across VM instances: multidimensional service provisioning requests {P1, P2, P3, P4}, index cell control points {A, B, C, D}, multidimensional update queries {l, s}, and some of the spatial hashing to the Pastry overlay, i.e. the multidimensional (spatial) coordinate values of a cell's control point is used as the Pastry key. For this figure, f_{min} =2, dim = 2

Table 12.5 Service discovery query stored with a Cloud Peer service at time T

Time	Discovery query ID	Service type	Speed (GHz)	Cores	Location
300	Query 1	Web hosting	>2	1	USA
400	Query 2	Scientific simulation	>2	1	Singapore
500	Query 3	Credit card authenticator	>2.4	1	Europe

Table 12.6 Update query published with a Cloud Peer service at time T

Time	VM ID	Service type	Speed (GHz)	Processors	Type
700	VM 2	Credit card authenticator	2.7	One (available)	Europe

12.6   Experiments and Evaluation

In this section, we evaluate the performance of the proposed peer-to-peer Cloud provisioning concept by creating a service and VM pool that consists of multiple virtual machines that are hosted within the Amazon EC2 infrastructure. We assume unsaturated server availability for these experiments, so that enough capacity can always be allocated to a VM for any service request. Next, we describe the various details related to Cloud peer (peer-to-peer network, multidimensional index structure, and network configuration parameters), PaaS layer provisioning software, and application characteristics related to this experimental evaluation.

12.6.1   Cloud Peer Details

A Cloud peer service operates at PaaS layer and handles activities related to decentralized query (discovery and update) routing, management, and matching. Additionally, it also implements the higher-level services such as publish/subscribe-based co-ordinated interactions and service selections. Every VM instance, which is deployed on a Cloud platform, hosts a Cloud peer service (see Figs. 12.2 and 12.3) that loosely glues it to the overlay. Next follows the details related to Cloud peer configuration.

FreePastry[1] *Network Configuration*: Both Cloud Peers' nodeIDs and discovery/ update queries' IDs are randomly generated from and uniformly distributed in the 160-bit Pastry identifier space. Every Cloud peer service is configured to buffer a maximum of 1,000 messages at a given instance of time. The buffer size is chosen to be sufficiently large such that the FreePastry does not drop any messages. Other network parameters are configured to the default values as given in the file freepastry.params. This file is provided with the FreePastry distribution.

Multidimensional Index Configuration: The minimum division f_{min} of logical multidimensional index is set to 3, while the maximum height f_{max} of the distributed index tree is constrained to 3. In other words, the division of the multidimensional attribute space is not allowed beyond f_{min} for simplicity. The index space has provision for defining service discovery and update queries that specify the VM characteristics in four dimensions including number of application service type being hosted, number of processing cores available on the server hosting the VM, hardware architecture of the processor(s), and their processing speed. The aforementioned multidimensional index configuration results into $81(3^4)$ index cells at f_{min} level.

---

[1] An open source pastry DHT implementation. http://freepastry.rice.edu/FreePastry

Service Discovery and Update Query's Multidimensional Extent: Update queries, which are posted by VM instances, express equality constraints on service, installed software environments, and hardware configuration attribute values (e.g. =).

12.6.2 Aneka: PaaS Layer Application Provisioning and Management Service

At PaaS layer, we utilize the Aneka [14] software framework that handles activities related to application element scheduling, execution, and management. Aneka is a .NET-based service-oriented platform for constructing Cloud computing environments. To create a Cloud application provisioning system using Aneka, a developer or application scientist needs to start an instance of the configurable Aneka container hosting required services on each selected VM.

Services of Aneka can be clearly characterized into two distinct spaces: (i) Application Provisioner, a service that implements the functionality that accepts application workload from Cloud users, performs dynamic discovery of application management services via the Cloud peer service, dispatches workload to application management service, monitors the progress of their execution, and collects the output data, which returned back to the Cloud users. An Application Provisioner need not be hosted within a VM, it only needs to know the end-point address (such as web service address) of a random Cloud peer service in the overlay to which it can connect and submit its service discovery query; and (ii) Application Management Service, a service, hosted within a VM, which is responsible for handling execution and management of submitted application workloads. An application management service sits within a VM and updates its usage status, software, and hardware configurations by sending update queries to the overlay. One or more instance of application management service can be connected in a single-level hierarchy to be controlled by a root-level Aneka Management Co-ordinator. This kind of service integration is aimed at making application programming flexible, efficient, and scalable.

12.6.3 Test Application

The PaaS layer software service, Aneka, supports composition and execution of application programs that are composed using different service models to be executed within the same software environment. The experimental evaluation in this chapter considers execution of applications programmed using a multithreaded programming model. The Thread programming model [14] defines an application as a collection of one or more independent work units. This model can be successfully utilized to compose and program embarrassingly-parallel programs (parameter sweep applications). The Thread model fits better for implementing and architecting new applications and algorithms on Cloud infrastructures since it gives finer degree of control and flexibility as regards to runtime control.

To demonstrate the feasibility of architecting Cloud provisioning services based on peer-to-peer network models, we consider composition and execution of Mandelbrot Set computation. Mathematically, the Mandelbrot set is an ordered collection of points in the complex plane, the boundary of which forms a fractal. The Application Provisioner service implements and cloud enables the Mandelbrot fractal calculation using a multithreaded programming model. The application submission interface allows the user to configure a number of horizontal and vertical partitions into which the fractal computation can be divided. The number of independent thread units created is equal to the horizontal x vertical partitions. For evaluations, we vary the values for horizontal and vertical parameters over the interval 5 × 5, 10 × 10, and 15 × 15. This configuration results in observation points.

12.6.4   Deployment of Test Services on Amazon EC2 Platform

To test the feasibility of the aforementioned services with regard to the provisioning of application services on Amazon EC2 cloud platform, we created Amazon Machine Images (AMIs) packaged with a Cloud peer, Application Management, and Aneka Management Co-ordinator services. The image that hosts the Aneka Management Co-ordinator is equipped with Microsoft Windows Server 2003 R2 Datacenter edition, Microsoft SQL Server 2005 Express, and Internet Information Services 6, while the AMI hosts only the Management Service and has Microsoft Windows Server 2003 R2 Datacenter system installed. For every AMI, we installed only the essential software including mandatory Cloud peer service, which is hosted within a Tomcat 6.0.10, Axis2 1.2 container. Cloud peer is exposed to the provisioning and management services through WS* interfaces. Later, we built our customized Amazon Machine Images from the two instances, creating and starting up more management co-ordinator and application management services by using customized images. We configured three management co-ordinators and nine management services. The management service is divided into groups of three that connect with a single co-ordinator resulting in a hierarchical structure. The management co-ordinator services communicate and internetwork through the Cloud peer fabric service. Figure 12.4 shows the pictorial representation of the experiment setup.

12.7   Results and Discussions

To measure the performance of peer-to-peer Cloud provisioning technique in regard to response time, co-ordination delay, and Pastry overlay network message complexity, we consider simultaneous provisioning of test applications at Application Provisioner A and B (see Table 12.7). The *response time* for an application is calculated by subtracting the output arrival time of the last thread in the submission

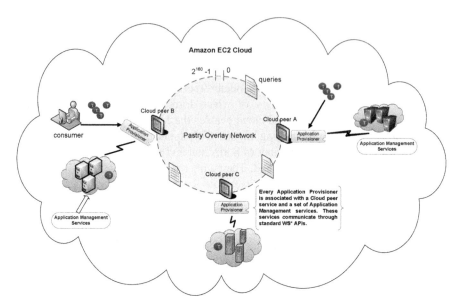

Fig. 12.4 Experiment Setup in Amazon EC2

Table 12.7 Response time, co-ordination delay, message count versus complexity

Problem complexity	5×5		10×10		15×15	
Provisioner	A	B	A	B	A	B
Response time (s)	27	27	107	104	245	229
Coordination delay (s)	5.58	7.13	26.08	24.97	60.06	48.09
Update message	3,203		3,668		3,622	
Discovery message	75		400		450	
Total message count	5,760		7,924		8,006	

list from the time at which the application is submitted. The metric *co-ordination delay* sums up the latencies for: (i) a service discovery query to be mapped to a Cloud peer, (ii) waiting time till an update query matches the discovery query; and (ii) notification delay from the Cloud peer to the Application Provisioner that originally posted the service discovery query. Pastry overlay message complexity measures the details related to the number of messages that flow through the network in order to: (i) initialize the multidimensional attribute space, (ii) map the discovery and update queries, (iii) maintain overlay, and (iv) send notifications.

Table 12.7 (response time vs. complexity) shows the results for response time in seconds with increasing complexity/problem size for the test application. Cloud consumers submit their applications with provisioner A and B. The initial experimental results reveal that with increase in problem complexity (number of horizontal and vertical partitions), the Cloud consumers experience increase in response times. The basic reason behind this behaviour of the provisioning system is related to the fixed number Application Management services, i.e. 9, available to the Application Provisioners. With increase in the problem complexity, the number of job threads (a job thread represents a single work unit, e.g. for a 5 × 5 Mandelbrot configuration, 25 job threads are created and submitted with the Application Provisioner) that are to be executed with management services increase, hence leading to worsening queuing and waiting delays. However, this behaviour of the provisioning system can be fixed through implementation of reactive provisioning of new VM instances to reflect the sudden surge in application workload processing demands (problem complexity). In our future work, we want to explore how to dynamically provision or de-provision VMs and associated Application Management services driven by workload processing demands.

Table 12.7 (coordination delay vs. complexity) presents the measurements for average co-ordination delay for each discovery query with respect to increase in the problem complexity. The results show that at higher problem complexity, the discovery queries experience increased co-ordination delay. This happens because the discovery queries of the corresponding job threads have to wait for a longer period of time before they are matched against an update query object. However, the job thread processing time (CPU time) is not affected by the co-ordination delay; hence, the response time in Table 12.7 shows a similar trend to delay.

In Table 12.7 (message count vs. complexity), we show the message overhead involved with management of multidimensional index, routing of discovery and update query messages, and maintenance of Pastry overlay. We can clearly see that as application size (problem complexity) increase, the number of messages required for mapping the query objects and maintenance of the overlay network increase. The number of discovery and update messages produced in the overlay is a function of the multidimensional index structure that indexes and routes these queries in a distributed fashion. Hence, the choice of the multidimensional data indexing structure and routing technique governs the manageability and efficiency of the overlay network (latency, messaging overhead). Hence, there is much work required in this domain as regards to evaluating the performance of different types of multidimensional indexing structures for mapping the query messages in peer-to-peer settings.

12.8 Conclusions and Path Forward

Developing provisioning techniques that integrate application services in a peer-to-peer fashion is critical to exploiting the potential of Cloud computing platforms. Architecting provisioning techniques based on peer-to-peer network models (such as DHTs) is significant; since peer-to-peer networks are highly scalable, they can gracefully adapt to the dynamic system expansion (join) or contraction (leave, failure), and are not susceptible to a single point of failure. To this end, we presented a software fabric called Cloud peer that creates an overlay network of VMs and application services for supporting scalable and self-managing service discovery and load-balancing. The functionality exposed by the Cloud peer service is very powerful and our experimental results conducted on Amazon EC2 platform confirm that it is possible to engineer and design peer-to-peer Cloud provisioning systems and techniques.

As part of our future work, we would explore other multidimensional data indexing and routing techniques that can achieve close to logarithmic bounds on messages and routing state, balance query (discovery, load-balancing, coordination) and processing load, preserve data locality, and minimize the metadata. Another important algorithmic and programming challenge in building robust Cloud peer services is to guarantee consistent routing, look-up, and information consistency under concurrent leave, failure, and join operations by application services. To address these issues, we will investigate robust fault-tolerance strategies based on distributed replication of attribute/query subspaces to achieve a high level of robustness and performance guarantees.

References

1. Armbrust M, Fox A, Griffith R, Joseph A, Katz R, Konwinski A, Lee G, Patterson D, Rabkin A, Stoica I, Zaharia M (2009) Above the clouds: a Berkeley view of cloud computing. University of California at Berkley, USA. Technical Rep UCB/EECS-2009-28
2. The Reservoir Seed Team (2008) Reservoir – an ICT infrastructure for reliable and effective delivery of services as utilities. IBM Res Rep H-0262
3. Buyya R, Yeo C, Venugopal S, Broberg J, Brandic I (2009) Cloud computing and emerging IT platforms: vision, hype, and reality for delivering computing as the 5th utility. Future Gen Comput Syst 25:599–616
4. Google (2009) Google App Engine. https://appengine.google.com/. Accessed 16 Dec 2009
5. Ultra Serve Internet Pty Ltd (2009) Rejila On Demand Cloud Computing Servers. http://www.rejila.com/. Accessed 14 Dec 2009
6. Rackspace US, Inc. (2009) The Rackspace Cloud. http://www.rackspacecloud.com. Accessed 12 Dec 2009
7. Microsoft (2009) Windows Azure Platform, http://www.microsoft.com/windowsazure/. Accessed 12 Dec 2009
8. Amazon Web Services LLC (2009) Amazon Elastic Compute Cloud, http://aws.amazon.com/ec2/. Accessed 16 Dec 2009
9. Salesforce.com (2009) Application Development with Force.com's Cloud Computing Platform http://www.salesforce.com/platform/. Accessed 16 Dec 2009
10. Quiroz A, Kim H, Parashar M, Gnanasambandam N, Sharma N (2009) Towards autonomic workload provisioning for enterprise grids and clouds. In: Proceedings of the 10th IEEE/ACM international conference on grid computing, Banf, Alberta, Canada, 13–15 Oct 2009, IEEE Computer Society Press
11. Amazon Web Services LLC (2009) Amazon CloudWatch. http://aws.amazon.com/cloudwatch/. Accessed 22 Sept 2009
12. Amazon Web Services LLC (2009) Elastic Load Balancer http://aws.amazon.com/elasticload-balancing/. Accessed 22 Sept 2009
13. Rochwerger B, Breitgand D, Levy E, Galis A, Nagin K, Llorente L, Montero R, Wolfsthal Y, Elmroth E, Caceres J, Ben-Yehuda M, Emmerich W, Galan F (2009) The reservoir model and architecture for open federated cloud computing. IBM Syst J 53
14. Chu X et al (2007) Aneka: next-generation enterprise grid platform for e-Science and e-Business applications. In: Proceedings of the 3rd IEEE international conference on e-Science and grid computing, Bangalore, India

15. Ranjan R, Chan L, Harwood A, Karunasekera S, Buyya R (2007) Decentralised resource discovery service for large scale federated grids. In: Proceedings of the 3rd IEEE international conference on eScience and grid computing (eScience'07), Bangalore, India, IEEE Computer Society, Los Alamitos, CA
16. Eucalyptus Systems Inc (2009) Eucalyptus Systems. http://www.eucalyptus.com/. Accessed 22 Sept 2009
17. Amazon Web Services LLC (2009) Auto Scaling. http://aws.amazon.com/autoscaling/. Accessed 22 Sept 2009
18. GoGrid Cloud Hosting (2009) F5 Load Balancer. GoGrid Wiki. http://wiki.gogrid.com/wiki/index.php/(F5)_Load_Balancer. Accessed 21 Sept 2009
19. Bakhtiari S, Safavi-Naini R, Pieprzyk J (1995) Cryptographic Hash Functions: A Survey. http://citeseer.ist.psu.edu/bakhtiari95cryptographic.html. Accessed 22 Sept 2009
20. Balakrishnan H, Kaashoek MF, Karger D, Morris R, Stoica I (2003) Looking up data in peer-to-peer systems. Commun ACM 46(2):43–48
21. Karger D, Lehman E, Leighton T, Panigrahy R, Levine M, Lewin D (1997) Consistent hashing and random trees: distributed caching protocols for relieving hot spots on the World Wide Web. In: Proceedings of the 29th annual ACM symposium on theory of computing (STOC '97), New York. ACM Press, pp 654–663
22. Preneel B (1999) The state of cryptographic hash functions. In: Lectures on data security. Modern cryptology in theory and practice. Springer, London, pp 158–182
23. Lua K, Crowcroft J, Pias M, Sharma R, Lim S (2005) A survey and comparison of peer-to-peer overlay network schemes. IEEE Commun Surv Tutorials 7(2), IEEE Communications Society Press, Washington DC, USA
24. Li J, Stribling J, Gil TM, Morris R, Frans Kaashoek M (2004) Comparing the performance of distributed hash tables under churn. In: Proceedings of the 3rd international workshop on peer-to-peer systems (IPTPS04), San Diego, CA
25. Bharambe A, Agarwal M, Seshan S (2004) Mercury: supporting scalable multi-attribute range queries. In: Proceedings of SIGCOMM 2004 (SIGCOMM'04). ACM, Portland, OR
26. Castro M, Costa M, Rowstron A (2004) Should we build Gnutella on a structured overlay? SIGCOMM Comput Commun Rev 34(1):131–136
27. Linga P, Demers A, Gupta I, Birman K, van R (2003) Kelips: building an efficient and stable peer-to-peer DHT through increased memory and background overhead. In: Proceedings of the 2nd international workshop on peer-to-peer systems (IPTPS03), Berkeley, CA
28. Spence D, Crowcroft J, Hand S, Harris T (2005) Location based placement of Whole Distributed Systems. In: Proceedings of the 2005 ACM conference on Emerging network experiment and technology (CoNEXT'05). ACM Press, New York, pp 124–134
29. Ganesan P, Yang B, Garcia-Molina H (2004) One torus to rule them all: multi-dimensional queries in peer-to-peer systems. In: Proceedings of the 7th International Workshop on the Web and Databases (WebDB '04). ACM Press, New York, pp 19–24
30. Ranjan R, Harwood A, Buyya R (2008) Peer-to-peer based resource discovery in global grids: a tutorial. IEEE Commun Surv Tutorials 10(2):6–33
31. Samet H (1989) The design and analysis of spatial data structures. Addison–Wesley, Reading, MA
32. Rowstron A, Druschel P (2001) Pastry: scalable, decentralized object location, and routing for large-scale peer-to-peer systems. In: IFIP/ACM international conference on distributed system platforms, Heidelberg
33. Ranjan R (2007) Coordinated resource provisioning in federated grids. Ph.D. thesis, The University of Melbourne
34. Tanin E, Harwood A, Samet H (2007) Using a distributed quadtree index in peer-to-peer networks. VLDB J 16(2):165–178, Springer, New York
35. Gupta A, Sahin OD, Agrawal D, Abbadi AEl (2004) Meghdoot: content-based publish/subscribe over peer-to-peer networks. In: Proceedings of the 5th ACM/IFIP/USENIX international conference on Middleware (Middleware '04), New York. Springer, New York, pp 254–273

Chapter 13
Mixing Grids and Clouds: High-Throughput Science Using the Nimrod Tool Family

Blair Bethwaite, David Abramson, Fabian Bohnert, Slavisa Garic,
Colin Enticott, and Tom Peachey

Abstract The Nimrod tool family facilitates high-throughput science by allowing researchers to explore complex design spaces using computational models. Users are able to describe large experiments in which models are executed across changing input parameters. Different members of the tool family support complete and partial parameter sweeps, numerical search by non-linear optimisation and even workflows. In order to provide timely results and to enable large-scale experiments, distributed computational resources are aggregated to form a logically single high-throughput engine. To date, we have leveraged grid middleware standards to spawn computations on remote machines. Recently, we added an interface to Amazon's Elastic Compute Cloud (EC2), allowing users to mix conventional grid resources and clouds. A range of schedulers, from round-robin queues to those based on economic budgets, allow Nimrod to mix and match resources. This provides a powerful platform for computational researchers, because they can use a mix of university-level infrastructure and commercial clouds. In particular, the system allows a user to pay money to increase the quality of the research outcomes and to decide exactly how much they want to pay to achieve a given return. In this chapter, we will describe Nimrod and its architecture, and show how this naturally scales to incorporate clouds. We will illustrate the power of the system using a case study and will demonstrate that cloud computing has the potential to enable high-throughput science.

13.1 Introduction

Traditionally, university research groups have used varying sources of infrastructure to perform computational science, from clusters owned by individual departments to high-end facilities funded by federal governments. While these are priced differently,

B. Bethwaite (✉)
Faculty of Information Technology, Monash University, Clayton, Australia
e-mail: blair.bethwaite@infotech.monash.edu.au

N. Antonopoulos and L. Gillam (eds.), *Cloud Computing: Principles,*
Systems and Applications, Computer Communications and Networks,
DOI 10.1007/978-1-84996-241-4_13, © Springer-Verlag London Limited 2010

they have rarely been provided on a strict commercial basis. Local clusters, for example, are usually funded by recurrent university funding or by one-off grants. Further, access to these machines is controlled by the users themselves. With regard to high-end facilities, such as the Australian National Compute Infrastructure (http://www.nci.org.au) or the US TeraGrid (http://www.teragrid.org), it is often necessary to apply for a peer reviewed grant, and the quality of the application is assessed by a resource-allocation committee. However, these grants are usually made in terms of CPU hours rather than dollars.

Cloud computing represents a major shift in the provisioning and delivery of computing infrastructure and services. It enables a shift from distributed, unmanaged resources to a variety of scalable, centralised services managed in professional data-centres with rapid elasticity of resource and service provisioning to users. Most importantly, commercial cloud services have appeared in which users can pay for access on an hourly basis. These resources open the opportunity for university researchers to buy compute time on an ad-hoc basis – shifting university funding models from capital expenditure to recurrent costs.

This transition poses many policy issues as well as a range of technical challenges. Existing resources that are free will not disappear; there is clearly a role for continued investment in university infrastructure. On the other hand, commercial clouds could provide an overflow, or elastic, capability for individual researchers. One could easily imagine a research group performing much of their base-load computations on 'free' resources, but resorting to pay-as-you-go services to meet peak demand. To date, very few tools can support both styles of resource provisioning.

Many years ago, we introduced the idea of a computational economy as a mechanism to enable resource sharing on an open basis [1]. In this model, resource providers charged for time and users paid. At that time, we only envisaged a pseudo unit of currency to allow different users to compete for scarce resources. A user willing to pay more has more chance of achieving a deadline, and will complete more work than one who is only prepared to pay less. We implemented this scheme in the Nimrod tool family [2], though the lack of global infrastructure based on this model made it more of an academic proposal.

However, the Nimrod computational economy provides an ideal mechanism for mixing free and pay-as-you-go commercial cloud services. Interestingly, the same algorithms that we proposed for the computational economy can be used to trade-off resources in such a mixed grid.

In this chapter, we discuss the Nimrod tool family and describe the kind of high-throughput problems that it solves. We discuss the scheduling system that Nimrod uses to balance time and cost-based deadlines, and show that these can be used on a mixed test-bed consisting of grid and cloud resources. We then illustrate the power of the system to achieve scientific outcomes. Our case study shows that a user has the ability to decide how much money they are prepared to pay for improved science outcomes. Specifically, the case study explores the basic science that can be delivered from a typical university department cluster, and shows how the Amazon Elastic Cloud (EC2) (http://aws.amazon.com/ec2/) can augment this to improve the science outcomes. The chapter also discusses some of the issues that arise in the implementation of our Amazon specific adapters and some of the open challenges for Nimrod and similar tools.

13.2 High-Throughput Science with the Nimrod Tools

While computation is now widely used in scientific research, we frequently see studies that report on just a few simulations or the analysis of a small quantity of data. Such studies may be suggestive, but they are typically not robust in the sense of quantifying sensitivity to factors such as initial conditions, parameter choices and data used for parameter estimation.

The commodity parallel computing revolution promises to make such limitations unnecessary. Continued Moore's Law growth in transistor counts in microprocessors, combined with physical limits on circuit size, is spurring the development of multi-core processors, which may be used alone or within larger multiprocessor systems to run large numbers of computational studies in parallel. Further, the emergence of commercial computing clouds means that researchers can access large amounts of computing power cheaply and quickly. Similarly, many fields that were once data poor now have access to multi-terabyte datasets, with commodity parallel disk arrays providing for low-cost storage and commodity parallel computers enabling rapid analysis.

While the availability of suitable commodity hardware is pushing high-throughput computing (HTC) into the realms of everyday science, such science would not be possible without the considerable tool support necessary to effectively leverage and orchestrate the data and processing resources. To gain the throughput necessary to obtain results in a timely fashion, it is often necessary to use multiple distributed resources, which comprise varied hardware, and typically run different software stacks. In some cases, the computational effort required dwarfs the resources provided by a researcher's home institution and/or state and national initiatives, indicating that the researcher must either source the capacity elsewhere, compromise on accuracy or scope, or possibly abort their plans.

Resources for high-throughput science are typically commodity clusters managed by batch queuing systems or idle-cycle harvesting pools (e.g. Condor [3] pools), made available remotely through grid middleware interfaces, such as Globus [4], UNICORE [5] and GLITE [6]. These middleware stacks and the development efforts around them have focused on exposing and standardising the task/job and data-oriented services typical of the requirements of HTC and HPC workloads. There are a number of successful production grid initiatives operating worldwide, such as OSG, EGEE, TeraGrid and PRAGMAGrid. However, grid computing has not had a widespread adoption outside of scientific HTC, most likely because it has been specifically tailored for that application domain. There also remain significant technological barriers that slow adoption, such as interoperability [7,8] and application deployment [9].

The low cost, abundance and increasing performance of virtualisation technology, which is being exploited to consolidate computing infrastructure, promises to ease and promote novel solutions to the deployment problem. This will also have a positive influence on interoperability between systems and HTC applications by allowing the same software stack from operating system to scientific application, to be built, hosted and run on one infrastructure, and relatively easily transferred to and run on another – whether it is a grid or cloud system.

13.2.1   The Nimrod Tool Family

Over the past 15 years, we have built, maintained and improved the Nimrod tool family. These tools automate parameter sweeps and searches using distributed computing resources. A user typically provides Nimrod with a *plan* file that contains information about the parameters and their values, and a description on how to execute the applications. *Plan* files are declarative and deliberately similar to the job scripts used by batch queue systems; however, they also expose file transfer and parameter substitution functionality.

Users specify the input files to copy to the computational node, the tasks necessary to execute the application for a single parameter combination, and the output files to copy back. Thus, the task syntax used in the *plan* file is intuitive, because it is declarative and mimics how a user might run the application on their machine or a local cluster.

Using Nimrod significantly decreases the effort required to scale-up the level of parallelism in a computational experiment. Users are able to add computational resources and associated credentials to Nimrod and choose any combination in order to create a logical high-throughput engine for each experiment. In this way, Nimrod provides meta-scheduling functionality by distributing jobs across multiple underlying resource schedulers.

The Nimrod tools have been successfully used in various research involving high-throughput science – with recent work in fields such as molecular biology [10], cardiology [11], chemistry [12] and climatology [13]. We actively pursue collaborations with specialists who have challenging and novel applications for parametric distributed computing.

Table 13.1 lists the major, actively developed, components of Nimrod. When we refer to Nimrod services or just 'Nimrod' without qualifying a particular variant or group, we are referring to Nimrod/G components.

13.2.2   Nimrod and the Grid

Nimrod targets different types of computational resources, ranging from local batch schedulers to distributed Condor [3] pools and Globus-enabled [4] grid resources. The latter leverages Globus functions that support remote job execution, file transport, security and resource discovery.

Table 13.1 Components of the Nimrod tool family (non-exhaustive)

Tool	Purpose	Utilises
Nimrod/G [1]	Provides distributed parameter sweep and single task execution via grid and cloud mechanisms, plus economic and deadline scheduling of jobs across multiple compute resources. Importantly, Nimrod/G operates either as a tool (usually via a web portal) or a middleware layer in its own right, serving as a job management system for other software, including the other members of the Nimrod family.	
Nimrod/O [14]	Supports design optimisation rather than complete enumeration. Computational models are treated as functions that accept input parameters and return an objective cost value. Nimrod/O incorporates a number of different search heuristics ranging from gradient descent to genetic algorithms. Used in conjunction with Nimrod/G, it can exploit parallelism in the search algorithm.	Nimrod/G[a]
Nimrod/E [15]	Provides experimental design techniques (e.g. fractional factorial analysis) for analysing parameter effects on an applications output. The outcome is a Nimrod/G style sweep that explores only those parameter combinations likely to influence the experiment's results, reducing the number of runs required to achieve useful scientific outcomes.	Nimrod/G[a]
Nimrod/K [16]	Integrates the above Nimrod tools into the Kepler workflow engine; along with a novel dataflow mechanism, this provides dynamic parallelism for Kepler workflows.	Nimrod/G[a], Kepler

[a] The other tools utilise Nimrod/G as a distributed computing middleware, but can also operate independently by using the local machine as a compute resource

Nimrod's Globus support began prior to the release of the widely adopted pre-web services Globus Toolkit 2, and has continued with more recent releases of the web services-based Globus Toolkit 4. As a result, it supports resources using both variants of the toolkit through the *globus* or *gt4 actuator*.

Recently, we used Nimrod/G to run a large experiment in protein crystallography, made particularly significant by its use of over 20 high-end clusters from several grids worldwide to provide the half-a-million CPU hours required for the experiment within 2 months [7]. Cloud computing has the potential to significantly increase throughput for such science, while decreasing the human effort involved in coordinating interoperability and deployment between resources.

13.2.3 Scheduling in Nimrod

Nimrod supports a pluggable scheduling architecture that allows it to use a range of different scheduling techniques. The simplest, a first-come-first-served approach, places jobs on resources in order to maximise throughput. This default approach allows a user to leverage as many resources as possible. A range of schedulers also support a computational economy in which resource providers charge, and users pay, for service. This allows a user to express the importance of their experiment in terms of a deadline, combined with a computational budget. Nimrod/G pioneered this approach in 2000 [1] when no such infrastructure existed.

Originally, the idea of a computational economy was to provide a common language in which different users could compare their resource requests. Within a finite economy, users who were prepared to expend more of their *grid dollar* (G$) budget were more likely to complete computations within their deadlines. This approach was expanded into an architecture in which users paid for services, and service providers charged [17].

Commercial clouds now form the first publicly accessible computational economy, making economic computational and data scheduling especially significant and topical. In commercial clouds, service providers charge 'real' money based on the cost of provision. Importantly, in this work, we have merged these two different uses of currency, and have leveraged the earlier work in a computational economy to embrace commercial clouds.

The existing *job scheduler* has been designed for space-shared batch-queued systems, as is typical on a computational grid. It was envisaged that these resources would charge for some absolute atomistic measure of computing used (e.g. MIPS), rather than in time-slice as is the case with EC2. This means that the scheduler will underestimate the budget used and will not recognise the time already purchased. However, as we have shown in Section 4, the current implementation is still applicable; implementing a time-slice scheduler will be a subject of future work.

As a consequence of the Nimrod tools specialising in parameter study applications, the *job scheduler* is able to make reasonable assumptions about job execution times, resource performance and job throughput. Many modelling applications have low variance in their processing requirements between the parameter sets (e.g. the case study in Section 4), though there are certainly exceptions, for example, the case study in [7]. Nimrod's economic and deadline-scheduling algorithms exploit this property of the workload to provide soft deadline and budget guarantees. Much theoretical and practical work has been devoted to the area of scheduling, with wildly varying approaches. Some strive to meet hard deadlines on an inherently unreliable distributed infrastructure by using task-replication algorithms [18], others mandate an omniscient super-scheduler; some assume historical data to predict non-deterministic events, and still others employ statistical inference and machine learning to predict and adjust reliability [19].

Nimrod takes a practical, adaptive, approach by requiring no extra information or service. This is important because, from our experience, we observed that users often have little idea of the computational requirements of their models across varying hardware or inputs. Also, for the typical workload (with low job run-time variation and an order of magnitude greater number of jobs than parallel processing units), this produces results very close to optimal, and for the typical user, near enough is good enough.

Table 13.2 Adaptive scheduling algorithms in Nimrod/G

Scheduling strategy	Execution time (not beyond deadline)	Execution cost (not beyond budget)
Time	Minimise	Limited by budget
Time optimal	Minimise	Unlimited budget
Cost	Limited by deadline	Minimise
None	Limited by deadline	Limited by budget

Nimrod implements four different adaptive scheduling strategies (listed in Table 13.2) [20] that attempt to meet deadline and/or budget constraints, possibly while minimising execution time or cost. Over the duration of the experiment, the scheduler refines a profile for each computational resource and alters the job allocation accordingly.

As commercial clouds enable researchers to easily expand their computational test-beds beyond the confines of university-level infrastructure, it is likely that they will wish to do so while continuing to utilise their local resources and minimising expenditure on cloud time. For this reason, the experiment we present in Section 4 uses the cost-minimisation strategy.

13.3   Extensions to Support Amazon's Elastic Compute Cloud

Recently, we developed a new *actuator* and associated components capable of interfacing Nimrod with compute clouds offering EC2-compatible APIs. In addition to allowing Nimrod jobs to be run on EC2, it also supports Eucalyptus [21] and OpenNebula [22] clouds. In this section, we discuss the extension and provide a discussion of issues involved in writing applications for such clouds.

The EC2 service provides one of the most generic and low-level interfaces to Infrastructure as a Service (IaaS) utility computing. At its most basic, it simply allows clients to start an instance of a particular virtual machine image on one of a handful of virtual hardware configurations. Further use of that instance is afforded via Secure Shell (SSH) access, which EC2 supports by providing a service for generating and managing SSH cryptographic key-pairs. Instances are then pre-configured with a key of the client's choice when a virtual machine is booted.

In contrast to IaaS, grid middleware typically provides a Platform as a Service (PaaS) to some representation of a computational job – usually an invocation of some program, optionally staged into the remote machine as part of the job and potentially specifying a number of options relevant to the local resource manager (LRM) or batch queuing system.

Developing or adapting an application to use EC2 can be challenging, and often requires writing code for tasks peripheral to the main purpose of the application such as machine provisioning and management. Grid clients, such as Nimrod, typically deal with middleware interfaces at the level of job management and file-transfer services without concern for the lifecycle of the machine on which the jobs might run. Typically, Nimrod only needs to know (or discover) the resource type and contact details, along with the architecture of the platform, in order to use it as a computational resource. No explicit management of the underlying computational resource is normally required. Hence, management of the virtual infrastructure is the largest part of the extension.

Rather than using a higher-level IaaS or PaaS built on top of EC2, we opted to use the basic core interface – the EC2 web service for provisioning and SSH for interaction. This means that the EC2 extension can accommodate a broad range of uses, and importantly for deployment it can utilise almost any virtual machine image suitable for running within the cloud. It is important to note that the extension provides an EC2 cloud execution mechanism for Nimrod, and that many of the higher level AWS services (such as Elastic Load Balancer) are not applicable to Nimrod because it is not a cloud-hosted service. We are simply interested in utilising the compute capacity.

To define a Nimrod EC2 resource requires a label, the service URL, the access and secret key file locations, a machine (and optionally, kernel and initial ramdisk) image identifiers, an instance type, and limits on the number of instances to run in parallel. There are further options, such as whether the use of a proxy or tunnelling is required, and most options have default settings for use with EC2.

13.3.1   The Nimrod Architecture

This section describes the architectural details of Nimrod relevant to the EC2 extension. Nimrod utilises a modular architecture that clearly separates the responsibility for various processes to a number of extensible modules. The modules are coordinated via a data model using a relational database management system (RDBMS), which also provides the basis for persistence and failure recovery. A particularly important feature of Nimrod is its use of a remote *agent* that runs on the computational node. The *agent* retrieves work from the *root* server (the server where the other Nimrod modules are running) and will, in a single execution, process as many jobs as available during its allotted time. This contrasts with the usual approach of submitting each job to the middleware separately, and helps mitigate the effects of unpredictable queue wait time on overall execution time. Nimrod, along with Condor [3] (which uses the glide-in mechanism), was one of the pioneering systems to use such a technique. Recent specialised high-throughput systems, such as Falkon [23], follow a similar approach. This approach is also well-matched to existing cloud services, as will be discussed in Section 3.2.

The *agent* is highly portable and can be built for several different architectures and operating systems. Importantly, there is no requirement to install any Nimrod components on the remote computational system prior to running an experiment, as the *agent* is staged in and launched using a variety of supported interfaces. This greatly simplifies system deployment and makes it possible to easily create an ad-hoc high-throughput engine by consolidating multiple computational resources.

Nimrod jobs correspond to executions of a Nimrod *task* for a particular parameter combination. As discussed in Section 2.1, the Nimrod tools use customised computational-task description syntax, similar to a batch script. Depending on the tool being used, all jobs for a particular experiment may be added to the database prior to execution or added dynamically, for example, by some iterative process (e.g. an optimisation/search). While Nimrod is typically used for parametric studies of a statically defined task, it also accommodates assigning a different *task* to every job and thus provides a high-level general-purpose computational middleware service.

Most of the low-level machinery is concerned with interacting with computational resources and services in order to launch *agents* and ensure that those *agents* can contact the *root* – in some cases, this involves launching a *proxy* to bridge between private cluster networks and the *root* machine which is often on the public internet. *Actuators* interact directly with external systems, such as middleware services like the Globus Resource Allocation Manager (GRAM), batch systems, or other meta-schedulers. *Actuators* (1) perform resource information discovery functions (e.g. determining machine architecture), (2) transfer *agents* and their prerequisite files (contact details for modules on the *root* and symmetric cryptography keys for authentication) to resources and (3) subsequently launch or (in)directly queue batch jobs to launch *agents*. *Actuators* can be considered as resource-specific drivers for Nimrod, providing a uniform interface to various types of computational resource.

The *agent schedulers* decide what operations ought to be performed by the *actuator* for a given resource and experiment. They (1) trigger actions by the *actuators* in response to job-to-resource assignments made by *job schedulers,* (2) enforce resource or user-specified limits on *agent* submissions and (3) for some resource types, schedule peripheral tasks such as credential refreshes.

Job schedulers assign work to the available resources using a choice of in-built heuristics, including cost and time minimisation on a per-experiment basis. It is also possible to do one's own job scheduling through a specialised API. The *job scheduler* takes into account dynamic job metadata, collected by the *agents*, and continually refines the schedule throughout execution.

The *database-* and *file-server* provide *agents* with job and control data, and access to the experiment file system on the *root*, respectively. Computational resources can have a number of typical and differing network topologies with regard to connectivity to the internet. A thorough discussion is beyond the scope of this chapter; however, in these cases, Nimrod can launch the *agent* in *proxy* mode on one or more intermediate machines in order to provide network access for the *agents* to connect to the *servers*.

13.3.2   The EC2 Actuator

Figure 13.1 shows the architecture of the EC2 extension. The *actuator* provides the main control flow, an interface to events and data regarding resource configuration, and *agent* commands. Typically, Nimrod *actuators* interface with a library or call

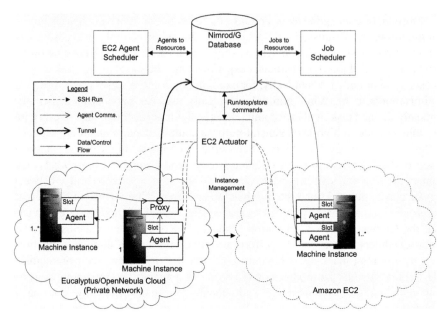

Fig. 13.1 EC2 extension architecture

out to command-line client tools in order to start *agents* on remote resources. A large part of an *actuator's* implementation is devoted to adapting the interface offered by the external middleware or service, to the interface required by the *actuator* model. In Nimrod, this functionality is encapsulated in a *resource* module. The new EC2 *resource* module leverages the Boto (http://code.google.com/p/boto/) library for communication with the EC2 web service. We chose to use Boto because it is implemented in Python, like Nimrod/G, so we did not need to create a command-line wrapper for the AWS Java client tools.

Boto provides client implementation for many of the current AWS query APIs, including EC2, S3, SQS, etc. The EC2 query API has been adopted by a number of other IaaS cloud projects offering software for creating private and hybrid clouds. Notable examples with support in current releases include Eucalyptus and OpenNebula. The EC2 *actuator* can provision Amazon EC2, Eucalyptus and OpenNebula cloud resources for use in Nimrod experiments.

As shown in Fig. 13.1, the EC2 *resource* divides instances into slots based on the number of processor cores per instance and the number of cores required per job. *Agents* are allocated to the slots and then launched via SSH once the instance has been initialised. Owing to limitations of the IPv4 address space, and like compute clusters, a common network configuration for private clouds uses a reserved private IP address range. We postulate that this will become more common as cloud computing is adopted for HTC. External access will be possible via a port-forwarding method from an intermediate device.

In preparation for this, the EC2 extension is capable of launching a *proxy* (with an SSH tunnel back to the *root*) within a cloud, and *agents* will then collect work, etc., via the Nimrod *proxy*.

13.3.3   Additions to the Schedulers

The Nimrod *actuator* acts on commands scheduled to it by the *agent scheduler*, which is responsible for examining pending jobs and scheduling *agents* to consume them. The *agent scheduler* determines initialisation necessary for a computational resource to run Nimrod *agents*, when new *agents* are needed, and when *agents* should be stopped.

Previously, the default *agent scheduler* in Nimrod scheduled *agents* one at a time, in a similar fashion to how they could be launched using external middleware. However, there are now computational middleware standards (e.g. DRMAA [24]) and non-standard interfaces (e.g. to commercial cloud systems such as EC2) in common use that make it possible to request multiple slots or leases at once, and in some cases this can improve provisioning performance. This necessitated changes to the *agent scheduler* to enable it to queue multiple *agents* in a single transaction.

Previously, the *job scheduler* had no notion of accommodating the kind of dedicated resource capacity presented by machine instances in the cloud. In order to ensure that we fully utilise each machine (e.g. avoiding running one uni-processor job on a multi-core machine), it was necessary to alter the *job scheduler* to ensure that it allocated jobs, where possible, in multiples of slots-per-instance.

13.4   A Case Study in High-Throughput Science and Economic Scheduling

In this section, we present a typical Nimrod experiment, along with domain background, as a case study to demonstrate the utility of the Nimrod EC2 extension. We discuss how the Nimrod EC2 extension might be used to improve scientific results and/or meet a deadline. Further, we give economic scheduling and execution data from a scaled version of the original experiment, and provide a cost analysis of the full version.

The research discussed in this case study uses Bayesian statistics for training a predictive model within a *recommender system* for the museum domain (Section 4.1). Importantly, the computational technique being used – a *Markov chain Monte Carlo (MCMC)* approach – is common to other fields where multi-dimensional integration arises (e.g. computational physics, computational biology and computational linguistics). Hence, the discussed example applies to a broad range of computational problems, and demonstrates what can be achieved in other domains with a similar structure.

13.4.1   Introduction and Background

This case study concerns techniques for automatically recommending exhibits to museum visitors, based on non-intrusive observations of their movements in the physical space. In general, *recommender systems* help users find personally interesting items in situations where the amount of available information is excessive [25]. Employing recommender systems in our scenario is challenging, as predictions differ from recommendations (we do not want to recommend exhibits that visitors are going to see anyway). We address this challenge by (1) using a Gaussian *Spatial Process Model (SPM)* to predict a visitor's interests in exhibits [26], (2) calculating a prediction of a visitor's pathway through the museum [27] and (3) combining these models to recommend personally interesting exhibits that may be overlooked if the predicted pathway is followed.

13.4.2   Computational Requirements

SPM has $2n + 3$ model parameters (n is the number of exhibits), which need to be estimated from the observed visit trajectories. To achieve this, we opted for a Bayesian solution. Unfortunately, the integrations required to calculate the parameters' posterior distribution are generally not tractable in closed form. However, the posterior can be approximated numerically using computationally demanding *MCMC* integration methods, such as the *Metropolis-Hastings algorithm* and the *Gibbs sampler*. Following Banerjee et al. [28], we use a *slice Gibbs sampler* [29] to sample from the posterior distribution. This approach is favourable, because it does not require tuning that is tailored to the application (hence, providing an automatic *MCMC* algorithm for fitting Gaussian spatial process models). In our case, we used every twentieth generated *MCMC* sample (to reduce positive autocorrelation between samples) after a burn-in phase of 1,000 iterations, and stopped the sampling procedure after 8,000 iterations. Thus, in total, this procedure provided 350 samples from the posterior.

The statistical quality of the parameter estimates derived from the *MCMC* samples increases with the number of *MCMC* iterations. Figure 13.2 depicts the standard error of the posterior mean estimate of one of *SPM*'s parameters as a function of the number of iterations. Decreasing the standard error by a factor of 10 requires 100 times as many samples. Thus, decreasing the standard error becomes increasingly expensive (the relationship is quadratic). Interestingly, because *MCMC* sampling is linear in time, we see a direct relationship between computation time (measured in *MCMC* iterations) and the statistical quality of the parameter estimates. This relationship between estimation accuracy and computational time is a commonly recurring theme in computational modelling.

Employing an *MCMC* approach for model training is computationally expensive in its own right (in our case, 8,000 *MCMC* iterations were required for acceptable

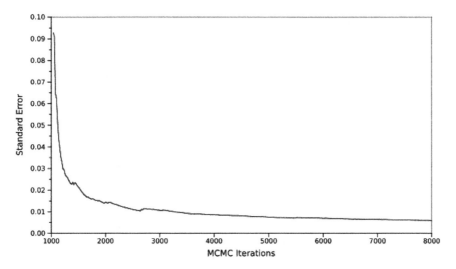

Fig. 13.2   Standard error of one posterior mean estimate over the number of MCMC iterations

accuracy). The computational cost is further increased by using a technique called 'leave-one-out cross validation' to evaluate *SPM*'s predictive performance. That is, for each visitor, we trained *SPM* with a reduced dataset containing the data of 157 of our 158 visit trajectories (following the above-mentioned sampling procedure), and used the withheld visitor pathway for testing. Owing to these factors, evaluating one *SPM* variant with our dataset requires approximately 6 days of compute time on a modern commodity-cluster server such as the East Enterprise Grid (http://www.enterprisegrid.edu.au). This equates to over 22,000 CPU hours. Compounding this is the need to explore a collection of different *SPM* variants, nine over the course of this research, adding up to approximately 200,000 CPU hours for a modest-size research project.

13.4.3   The Experiment

The full-quality (8,000 *MCMC* iterations) experiments were run over a few months using Nimrod/G to distribute thousands of model trainings across university-level computational grid resources that were available on an opportunistic basis. However, relying on opportunistic resources makes it difficult to provide a quality of service (QoS) guarantee on the run-time of the experiment. Hence, if only limited resources are available in the presence of a deadline, one might be forced to reduce the run-time of the jobs, jeopardising the estimation quality. Alternatively, the Nimrod EC2 extension allows the scientist to expand their resource pool for a fee rather than compromising the quality of their research in such a situation.

Table 13.3 Computational resources used for the experiment

Resource	No. of cores	Compute/core	Memory/core	Cost/core
East	120	1.6 GHz Intel Xeon E5310	1 GB	N/A
EC2[a]	152	2.5 EC2 Compute units	0.875 GB	US$0.10
EPC	4	Unknown	0.5 GB	N/A

[a] We used c1.xlarge type instances with AMI-0dda3964, hosted in the US-East EC2 region

To demonstrate the EC2 extension and applicability of Nimrod's existing economic scheduling capabilities, we ran a smaller version of the full sweep experiment – 9 *SPMs* by (158 reduced datasets + 1 complete dataset), totalling 1,431 distinct *tasks*) – by decreasing the number of *MCMC* iterations from 8,000 to 80 (a reduction in the computational requirements by a factor of 100).

A back-of-envelope analysis using the approximate 6-day run-time (for jobs on our East cluster) from the full-quality experiments (scaled down 100 times) reveals that with East alone, this experiment would take at least 17.2 h, though this is below minimum because it also scales input and output file copy time and start-up overhead, which are uniform for the full and scaled experiments.

We enacted a scenario requiring results overnight (a 12-h deadline) with a limited free resource set (listed in Table 13.3). The free resources alone are incapable of meeting the projected throughput requirements. Hence, we added EC2 with a US$100 budget and selected a cost-minimisation strategy from the scheduler (as discussed in Section 2.3). Our free resources included the Eucalyptus Public Cloud (EPC) (http://open.eucalyptus.com/wiki/EucalyptusPublicCloud), so that we could demonstrate Eucalyptus compatibility and the private cloud tunnelling mechanism (the EPC does not allow outgoing connections from machine instances). The EPC is simply a public demo system for testing Eucalyptus, and provides no service guarantees and is not intended for computation. Users can run up to four instances concurrently and a 6-h maximum instance up-time is enforced.

13.4.4   Computational and Economic Results

The number of jobs in execution on each resource over time is shown in Fig. 13.3. All 1,431 jobs were completed successfully within the deadline and budget in 11 h and 6 min, having spent US$68.35 according to the economic scheduler. The scheduler quickly filled the available cores on East and gradually scheduled to EC2, soon adding more jobs to EC2 once East was fully allocated. The delay between the jobs starting on EC2 and East represents the EC2 instance provisioning wait-time. No queue wait-time was experienced on East. Before the halfway point, the scheduler began to estimate that East was capable of finishing the remaining jobs, and because of the cost-minimisation bias, EC2 usage was quickly reduced to nothing despite it having the highest throughput. The EPC, being a low-performance demonstration system, never managed to complete a job before the 6-h instance

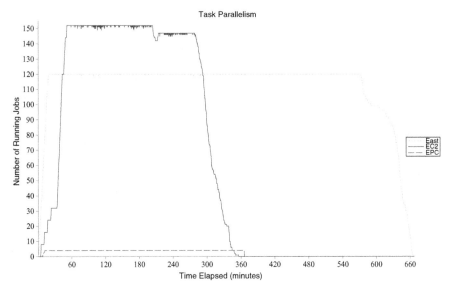

Fig. 13.3 Jobs executing over time

Table 13.4 Completed job statistics

Resource	No. of jobs completed	Tot. job time (h:m:s)	μ / σ Job run time (min)
East	818	1245:37:23	91.36/5.70
EC2	613	683:34:05	66.91/14.23

Note: the EPC is omitted because it did not complete any jobs

limit was reached. The EC2 actuator recovered from this and restarted the proxy on a newly launched instance. However, the jobs were rescheduled to East.

Owing to the economic scheduler not being aware of the time-slice charging of EC2 instances, it underestimated the real cost by approximately US$20. It also does not currently consider data-transfer charges (although transfer statistics are recorded), but here they were negligible. This underestimation may seem considerable. However, it is exacerbated in this case by the high level of instance parallelism and relatively short instance run-time. The schedulers estimate would be much better if, for example, fewer instances were used for longer (the user can enforce this).

Table 13.4 shows run-time statistics of the completed jobs, which provide insight into the performance of EC2. EC2 completed jobs in 74% of the time that East took (25-min better on an average). This is slightly worse than the EC2 compute unit rating suggests (a direct comparison between East and EC2 is possible because East has the same vintage Xeon CPUs as those used in the EC2 rating). Each EC2 core on a c1.xlarge instance should provide roughly 2.5 GHz when compared with East's 1.6 GHz – therefore, we expect EC2 to take approximately 64% of the time of East. Of particular note is the higher run-time standard deviation on EC2. A possible explanation for this is that the physical hardware may have been shared among multiple instances. It is important to note that no fully virtualised infrastructure services, such as EC2, provide QoS guarantees on the performance of hardware sharing.

With this information, we can project the lower bound cost of running the full-quality experiment in a similar situation, again using EC2 as the overflow resource. We scale *MCMC* iterations and hence job run-time by a factor of 100, and similarly, we scale the deadline to 50 days. We assume that the local resource pool has not changed. In 50 days, East can deliver us $50 \times 24 \times 120 = 144,000$ CPU hours, the equivalent of 945 jobs. We need EC2 to complete the remaining 486 jobs, which requires at least 54,197 EC2-core-hours at US\$0.10 an hour, resulting in a potential charge of US\$5,420. Clearly, investing that amount of money into capital expenditure (e.g. to extend the capacity of East) would have made little difference to the overall completion time.

13.4.5 Scientific Results

Using Nimrod/G and associated computer clusters and clouds enabled us to explore a greater variety of *SPM* in a shorter, feasible, time frame without compromising the quality of the results. For instance, we tested the variants of the original model [26], which use different ways of measuring distances between museum exhibits [30]. This led to insights regarding the suitability of the different model variants for certain application scenarios.

In the future, we intend to investigate other ways of incorporating exhibit features into *SPM*. We also plan to extend our model to fit non-Gaussian data.

13.5 Conclusions

This chapter demonstrates the potential for cloud computing in high-throughput science. We showed that Nimrod/G scales to both freely available resources as well as commercial services. This is significant because it allows users to balance deadlines and budgets in ways that were not previously possible.

We discussed the additions to Nimrod/G required for it to use Amazon's EC2 as an execution mechanism, and showed that the Nimrod/G architecture is well suited to computational clouds. As a result, Nimrod/G's cloud actuator allows higher level tools to exploit clouds as a computational resource. Hence, Nimrod/G can be classified as providing a 'Platform as a Service' to job producers/schedulers, and becomes both a cloud client and cloud service in its own right.

The case study showed that computational clouds provide ideal platforms for high-throughput science. Using a mix of grid and cloud resources provided timely results within the budget for the research under discussion.

The economies of scale employed by commercial cloud computing providers make them an attractive platform for HTC. However, questions of national interest and policy issues in spending public research funding with commercial providers remain, especially when they are based overseas. Commercial offerings are motivated by profit, and hence it should be possible to provide a non-profit equivalent more cheaply to better utilise government and university funding, while ensuring the prioritisation of researcher requirements. There is clearly scope for the adoption of similar operational techniques in order to provide HTC resources to the research community.

Commercial computing infrastructure requirements also deviate somewhat from typical HTC requirements[1]. The commercial cloud provider must have sufficient data-centre capacity to meet fluctuating demand, while providing high QoS with regard to reliability and lead time to service. This necessitates reserving capacity at extra expense, passed on to the consumer. On the other hand, HTC workloads are typically not so sensitive. Waiting some time for a processor is of little significance when tens of thousands to millions of processor hours are required. Such considerations may enable higher utilisation and lower capital overhead for dedicated HTC clouds.

Future work will focus on providing accurate cost accounting by implementing a time-slice scheduler and considering data-transfer charges. We also plan to investigate the use of EC2 *Spot Instance* pricing. This could prove ideal for cost minimisation biased scheduling, given the spot price for a particular machine type is typically less than half of the standard cost.

Acknowledgements This work has been supported by the Australian Research Council under the Discovery grant scheme. We thank the Australian Academy of Technological Sciences and Engineering (ATSE) Working Group on Cloud Computing for discussions that were used as input to Section 1. We thank Ian Foster for his helpful discussions about the role of high-throughput science and for his contribution to Section 2.

We acknowledge the work of Benjamin Dobell, Aidan Steele, Ashley Taylor and David Warner, Monash University Faculty of I.T. students who worked on the initial Nimrod EC2 actuator prototype. We also thank Neil Soman for assistance in using the Eucalyptus Public Cloud.

References

1. Abramson D, Giddy J, Kotler L (2000) High performance parametric modeling with Nimrod/G: killer application for the global grid? In the 14th international parallel and distributed processing symposium (IPDPS 2000), pp 520–528
2. Abramson D, Buyya R, Giddy J (Oct 2002) A computational economy for grid computing and its implementation in the Nimrod-G resource broker. Future Gen Comput Syst 18:1061–1074

---

[1]The recently released EC2 *Spot Instance* pricing (http://aws.amazon.com/ec2/spot-instances/) – a supply-demand-driven auctioning of excess EC2 data-centre capacity – is an early example of a scheme to bridge this gap.

3. Litzkow M, Livny M, Mutka M (1988) Condor – a hunter of idle workstations. In the proceedings of the 8th international conference of distributed computing systems. IEEE Press, June 1988, pp 104–111
4. Foster I, Kesselman C (1997) Globus: a metacomputing infrastructure toolkit. Int J Supercomput Appl 11:115–128
5. Erwin DW (2002) UNICORE – a grid computing environment. Concurr Comput Prac Exp 14:1395–1410
6. Laure E, Fisher SM, Frohner A, Grandi C, Kunszt P, Krenek A, Mulmo O, Pacini F, Prelz F, White J, Barroso M, Buncic P, Hemmer F, Di Meglio A, Edlund A (2006) Programming the Grid with gLite. Comput Method Sci Tech 12:33–46
7. Bethwaite B, Abramson D, Buckle A (2008) Grid interoperability: an experiment in bridging grid islands. In the IEEE Fourth International Conference on eScience 2008, pp 590–596
8. Riedel M (2009) Interoperation of world-wide production e-Science infrastructures. Concurr Comput Pract Exp 21:961–990
9. Goscinski W, Abramson D (2008) An infrastructure for the deployment of e-science applications. In: Grandinetti L (ed) High performance computing (HPC) and grids in action. IOS Press, Amsterdam, Netherlands, pp 131–148
10. Schmidberger J, Bethwaite B, Enticott C, Bate M, Androulakis S, Faux N, Reboul C, Phan J, Whisstock J, Goscinski W, Garic S, Abramson D, Buckle A (2009) High-throughput protein structure determination using grid computing. In the IEEE International Symposium on Parallel & Distributed Processing (IPDPS 2009), pp 1–8
11. Sher A, Abramson D, Enticott C, Garic S, Gavaghan D, Noble D, Noble P, Peachey T (2008) Incorporating local Ca2 + dynamics into single cell ventricular models. In: Proceedings of the 8th international conference on computational science, Part I, Springer-Verlag, Krakow, Poland, pp 66–75
12. Baldridge KK, Sudholt W, Greenberg JP, Amoreira C, Potier Y, Altintas I, Birnbaum A, Abramson D, Enticott C, Garic S (2006) Cluster and grid infrastructure for computational chemistry and biochemistry. In: Zomaya AY (ed) Parallel computing for bioinformatics and computational biology, Wiley Interscience, New York, pp 531–550
13. Lynch AH, Abramson D, Görgen K, Beringer J, Uotila P (Oct 2007) Influence of savanna fire on Australian monsoon season precipitation and circulation as simulated using a distributed computing environment, Geophysical Research Letters, 34(20):L20801
14. Abramson D, Lewis A, Peachey T, Fletcher C (2001) An automatic design optimization tool and its application to computational fluid dynamics. In: Proceedings of the 2001 ACM/IEEE conference on supercomputing (CDROM), ACM, Denver, Colorado, pp 25–25
15. Peachey T, Diamond N, Abramson D, Sudholt W, Michailova A, Amirriazi S (Jan 2008) Fractional factorial design for parameter sweep experiments using Nimrod/E. Sci Program 16:217–230
16. Abramson D, Enticott C, Altinas I (2008) Nimrod/K: towards massively parallel dynamic grid workflows. In: Proceedings of the 2008 ACM/IEEE conference on supercomputing, IEEE Press, Austin, Texas, pp 1–11
17. Buyya R, Abramson D, Giddy J, Stockinger H (2002) Economic models for resource management and scheduling in Grid computing. Concurr Comput Prac Exp 14:1507–1542
18. Zhang Y, Mandal A, Koelbel C, Cooper K (2009) Combined fault tolerance and scheduling techniques for workflow applications on computational grids. In: The proceedings of the 2009 9th IEEE/ACM international symposium on cluster computing and the grid – volume 00, IEEE Computer Society, pp 244–251
19. Nurmi D, Brevik J, Wolski R (2008) QBETS: Queue Bounds Estimation from Time Series. Job Scheduling Strategies for Parallel Processing, pp 76–101
20. Buyya R, Giddy J, Abramson D (2000) An evaluation of economy-based resource trading and scheduling on computational power grids for parameter sweep applications. Active middleware services: from the proceedings of the 2nd annual workshop on active middleware services, p 221

21. Nurmi D, Wolski R, Grzegorczyk C, Obertelli G, Soman S, Youseff L, Zagorodnov D (2009) The eucalyptus open-source cloud-computing system. In: The IEEE international symposium on cluster computing and the grid, IEEE Press, Shanghai, China, p 131, 124
22. Sotomayor B, Montero RS, Llorente IM, Foster I (2008) Capacity leasing in cloud systems using the OpenNebula engine. Chicago, IL
23. Raicu I, Zhao Y, Dumitrescu C, Foster I, Wilde M (2007) Falkon: a fast and light-weight tasK executiON framework. In the proceedings of the 2007 ACM/IEEE conference on supercomputing – volume 00, ACM Press, Reno, Nevada, pp 1–12
24. Troger P, Rajic H, Haas A, Domagalski P (2007) Standardization of an API for distributed resource management systems. In the proceedings of the seventh IEEE international symposium on cluster computing and the grid, IEEE Computer Society, pp 619–626
25. Resnick P, Varian HR (1997) Recommender systems. Commun ACM 40:56–58
26. Bohnert F, Schmidt DF, Zukerman I (2009) Spatial processes for recommender systems. In: The 21st international joint conference on artificial intelligence (IJCAI-09), Pasadena, CA, pp 2022–2027
27. Bohnert F, Zukerman I, Berkovsky S, Baldwin T, Sonenberg L (2008) Using interest and transition models to predict visitor locations in museums. AI Commun 21:195–202
28. Banerjee S, Carlin BP, Gelfand AE (2004) Hierarchical modeling and analysis for spatial data. CRC Press, Boca Raton, FL
29. Neal RM (2003) Slice sampling. Annal Stat 31:705–767
30. Bohnert F, Zukerman I, Schmidt DF (2009) Using Gaussian spatial processes to model and predict interests in museum exhibits. In the seventh workshop on intelligent techniques for web personalization and recommender systems (ITWP-09), pp 13–19

Part III
Cloud Breaks

Chapter 14
Cloud Compliance: A Framework for Using Cloud Computing in a Regulated World

Shawn R. Chaput and Katarina Ringwood

Abstract Cloud computing is quickly becoming a significant IT resource, which a typical organization will likely consider at some point. Be it Software-as-a-Service or Infrastructure-as-a-Service, the implications can be significant with respect to compliance with a variety of laws or regulations. The intention of this chapter is to give some insight into the potential compliance pitfalls an organization may experience if ill-prepared, and provide the tools to plan for and navigate around these obstacles before they become insurmountable.

14.1 Using the Cloud

Cloud computing has both advocates and naysayers, each with a variety of reasons for their respective positions. This chapter does not intend to side specifically with either. Rather, the purpose is to demonstrate an organization's minimum requirements with respect to handling the data. It will also be demonstrated that the tasks required are far from trivial and potentially expensive to implement and manage. Thus, whether cloud computing should be considered by an organization is contingent on understanding the costs and obligations.

14.1.1 Overview

First off, using Cloud Providers or Cloud Services (herein referred to as "the cloud"), is neither inherently insecure nor secure. It is highly doubted that a turn-key cloud solution could prove to be the security panacea an organization hopes it

S.R. Chaput (✉)
Privity Systems Inc307, 425 West 8th AvenueVancouver, British ColumbiaV5Y, 3Z5Canada
e-mail: schaput@privityinc.com

N. Antonopoulos and L. Gillam (eds.), *Cloud Computing: Principles,*
Systems and Applications, Computer Communications and Networks,
DOI 10.1007/978-1-84996-241-4_14, © Springer-Verlag London Limited 2010

to be, but neither will it necessarily publicize every piece of Personally Identifiable Information (PII) an organization provides, which is what many fear would happen. The largest challenges with respect to engaging the cloud occur in the preparation of a company for the cloud. This typically includes ensuring strong information security governance and a clear understanding of the organization's legal and regulatory landscape. In fact, outsourcing to the cloud could not be considered successful without previously achieving an organizational security maturity level of four.

Another potential challenge with using the cloud surrounds how significant an influence – if any – an organization can have with respect to modifying the way the cloud operates, imposing and/or strengthening the liability terms of the contracts, requesting and receiving the assurances required from the vendor, and having a firm grasp on the enforcement of the solid legal agreement once it is put in place.

14.1.2 Background

As organizations mature and core competencies are developed, it may seem that onsidering the cloud for specific types of applications, systems, infrastructure, and platforms would be the next logical step. Cloud computing, although potentially more granular and more distributed in nature, is not in fact radically different from traditional outsourcing or off-shoring arrangements: the same amount of diligence and preparation is needed to start such an exercise. Much work on the topic of cloud computing security has already been done by organizations such as the Cloud Security Alliance (http://www.cloudsecurityalliance.org). For more detailed information on the topics discussed here, it is recommended you read the most recent version of their "Security Guidance for Critical Areas of Focus in Cloud Computing". The "audit & compliance" section of version 1 of that document was the foundation for much of this chapter's content, albeit at a higher level. The subsequent releases of the Cloud Security Alliance's Guidance documents will likely go into more detail.

14.1.3 Requirements and Obligations

First, an organization needs to understand the legislative and regulatory landscape in which it resides and operates. If a company processes credit cards, it will likely be subject to the Payment Card Industry's Data Security Standard (PCI DSS).[1] Similarly, if the company handles Personally Identifiable Information (PII), it is

---

[1] https://www.pcisecuritystandards.org/security_standards/pci_dss.shtml

quite likely that it is subject to various privacy legislations, such as the European Union's Data Protection Directive (EU DPD),[2] or Canada's Personal Information Protection Electronic Documents Act (PIPEDA),[3] thus requiring an organization to follow specific guidelines without deviation or compromise regardless of how well they align with internal policies. These are just two examples of how legislation or regulation can shape a company's information security structure and alter or add to the needs with which an organization will approach the cloud provider.

14.1.3.1   Regional Laws

It is nearly impossible to list all of the relevant regional laws, which may shape or otherwise affect the requirements necessary to consider when outsourcing to the cloud. As mentioned previously, privacy is an excellent example of a topic with specific regional laws. When looking at Canada and the United States of America, there are dozens of individual laws that are geographically binding and as a result may take priority over others, even though on the whole they may not be substantially different. To further complicate matters, if an organization operates in more than one jurisdiction, it is likely subject to each respective law. This is an area where the lawyers excel and can help an organization understand which regulations will take precedence over others.

To further add to the confusion, agreements such as the International Safe Harbor Privacy Principles[4] can make an organization subject to laws in areas where it does not even operate. A good example would be the US-EU Safe Harbor agreement[5] meant to provide a streamlined process for companies outside the EU's jurisdiction that will have a chance – by demonstrating compliance with EU Directive 95/42/EC on protection of personal data – to gain the benefits of trade with EU companies requiring reciprocal compliance. This means that not only does an organization need to know its immediate legal responsibilities in respect to the region(s) within which it operates, but it also must stay ahead and aware of the additional types of arrangements to which it is privy and understand the related requirements.

Several Canadian provinces experienced an incredible effect of the Uniting and Strengthening America by Providing Appropriate Tools Required to Intercept and Obstruct Terrorism (USA PATRIOT) Act[6] of the USA, even though the same provinces were not typically subject to foreign laws, not withstanding those of its closest neighboring country. Many government agencies were not permitted to use providers whose systems were physically in the USA, for the fear that their hosted data would

---

[2] http://ec.europa.eu/justice_home/fsj/privacy/docs/lawreport/paper/ispa_en.pdf

[3] http://www.priv.gc.ca/legislation/02_06_01_e.cfm

[4] http://www.trade.gov/td/ecom/shprin.html

[5] http://www.export.gov/safeharbor/eg_main_018236.asp

[6] http://epic.org/privacy/terrorism/hr3162.html

be secretly examined, copied, or seized under the auspices of the Act. Again, not only do organizations need to be aware of the laws that directly affect them, they also need to be aware of the ones to which they do not wish to be privy and make their business decisions accordingly.

14.1.3.2   Industry Regulations

Like the regional laws, industry regulations are wide reaching, complicated, and at times potentially overlapping. Retail and credit card processing are a hot topic of late within the Information Security community, allowing most to become familiar with PCI DSS, American Express' Data Security Operating Policies (DSOP),[7] or Visa's Cardholder Information Security Program (CISP).[8] Similarly, energy producers within North America may need to concern themselves more with North American Energy Reliability Council (NERC)[9] or Federal Energy Regulatory Commission (FERC).[10] Investment Dealers may be subject to the Investment Dealers Association Uniform Securities Legislation (IDA USL).[11] Healthcare has more laws and regulations than most would care to read. The list goes on.

Despite a limited scope of certain laws being mapped to specific types of industries, the awareness in itself is not sufficient to help determine benefits or negative implications on the organization prior to considering using the cloud.

14.2   Cloud Compliance

14.2.1   Information Security Organization

A company's Information Security Organization (ISO) – assuming one is established – has likely already determined which of these laws and regulations are relevant and have documented the requirements thoroughly. The ISO will work towards achieving the information security maturity for the organization, helping on an ongoing basis to establish the best course of action a company needs to take to become or stay compliant. Failing the existence of an ISO, it will likely be incumbent on the company to establish one prior to using the cloud. At a minimum, the ISO can help with the identification of relevant laws and regulations, ensuring

---

[7] https://www209.americanexpress.com/merchant/singlevoice/pdfs/en_GB/American%20 Express%20DSOP%20for%20Merchants%20-%20UK.pdf

[8] http://visa.com/cisp

[9] http://www.nerc.com/

[10] http://www.ferc.gov/

[11] http://www.iiroc.ca/English/Pages/home.aspx

security requirements are met and providing a single point of contact for the various security-related communications likely to occur between the organization and the cloud, while developing new, and integrating existing, strategic company goals.

14.2.2 Data Classification

Assuming that an organization is subject to at least one of their industry-specific regulations or laws, they will be required, at a minimum, to demonstrate some semblance of control over its IT resources, quite likely predicating the existence of an information security program. To meet regulatory obligations, an organization needs to understand the information assets and their related security requirements, which can only be achieved by doing something that most companies try to avoid: proper classification and labeling of their data.

14.2.2.1 Classifying Data and Systems

The exercise of classifying data is incredibly important when looking at allowing others access. An organization needs to be able to provide the security requirements surrounding the data in question at any given point, especially if considering granting another entity the custodianship over said data. This exercise also provides an organization with the ability to pick and choose which data they will provide to outsourcers – and more importantly, which to exclude. By limiting the inclusion of government classified PII or PCI data, for instance, the requirements related to the security of the hosting systems become remarkably more relaxed. Presumably, each of these classifications would have unique and distinct security requirements needed to be passed onto the cloud provider. Reducing those requirements would likely substantially reduce the cost of using the cloud in general, although it may also limit the systems and data the organization possesses from being outsourced. Classification of data and systems will likely lead to a cost-benefit analysis with respect to the use of the cloud as a better understanding of the metadata may reveal shortcomings in the existing security architecture. Knowing what an organization sends to the cloud can help set the expectations on how a provider is required to protect it.

14.2.2.2 Specific Type of Data of Concern

Understanding the requirements of the data is paramount to appropriately securing it. Aside from Personally Identifiable Information, Payment Card Industry data, and the myriad regulations with which an organization would need to be concerned, there are many other types of relevant data to be taken into account.

Government classifies data, in Canada for instance, as Confidential, Secret, Top Secret, or Cosmic Top Secret, and has a variety of requirements, which should be considered relevant to each classification level. Specifically, regardless of the classification level, in order to have access to and store data, an organization would have to have obtained a Facility Security Screening (FSC) clearance with Document Storage from the Canadian and International Industrial Security Directorate (CIISD) of Public Works and Government Services Canada (PWGSC).[12] Depending on the level of access and document sensitivity, the requirements increase – as does the time to validate those requirements. An organization could absolutely not consider hosting data of similar classifications on clouds which do not have these levels of screening from their respective domestic security screening providers.

Data considered "Trade Secrets" within an organization will likely have a bare minimum level of security associated with it. Similarly to data about mergers and acquisitions or financial data, an organization will actively want to protect the trade secret data in a meaningful and defined manner. Although there may not be specific government legislation around it (in the case of publicly traded companies, there most likely are laws governing the integrity of this data at a minimum, such as Sarbanes Oxley in the United States[13]), an organization have no desire to purposely or inadvertently divulge its data, and will likely be willing to take significant steps to protect it.

14.2.2.3   Labeling

Classifying data is only as effective as the exercise of labeling the same data and related systems to reflect their classification. If an organization has undertaken the exercise of classification, it is likely that it has gone through the effort of appropriately labeling it. Of course, by extending an organization to the cloud it becomes incumbent to ensure the appropriate labeling of the relevant systems and data used in the cloud. The challenges of physically labeling virtualized systems persist, and are further compounded by cloud's virtualization of datacenters.

14.2.3   Access Control and Connectivity

Control mechanisms necessary for appropriate user access are another segment of compliance concern with respect to using the cloud. Specifically, it may be necessary to ensure the availability of authentication mechanisms that need to both provide appropriate levels of authorization and accountability as well as integrate

---

[12] http://ssi-iss.tpsgc-pwgsc.gc.ca/index-eng.html

[13] http://frwebgate.access.gpo.gov/cgi-bin/getdoc.cgi?dbname=107_cong_bills&docid=f:h3763enr.tst.pdf

seamlessly with client's environment. This is where out-of-the-box solutions from the cloud provider may not be sufficient for an organization's authentication requirements. Depending on the cloud type – SaaS, PaaS, IaaS – the requirements would vary radically. If using cloud Infrastructure-as-a Service, the capability for remote administration of the related equipment would likely be required; how someone physically and logically connects and authenticates to this environment can have a substantial influence on the cloud provider and client organization's compliance initiatives. For instance, if a computer directly connects to a PCI environment, it runs the potential of being within the scope of the PCI compliance initiative. One way to circumvent this issue would be traversing a demarcation firewall and connecting to a jump point administrative system (such as a terminal server) that uses strong authentication. Mechanisms like this may need to be explored to fully understand the implications of using the cloud and weighing the cost-to-benefit ratio prior to making the decision.

14.2.3.1 Authentication and Authorization

With respect to authentication, how an organization provides access is a subject of great importance. Failing the existence of some sort of universal federated identity or the ubiquity of "Identity 2.0" type technology, offering access to the cloud is not without its substantial obstacles. Many questions immediately arise: Who manages the authentication database? Is the client's organization responsible for providing it and the related links to the cloud or is the cloud managing it entirely? If the latter, how does the client's organization obtain the assurances around appropriate access? Alternatively, if the client is providing the authentication mechanism, how does it leverage the distributed environment of the cloud and the benefits of redundancy without having similar capabilities around its LDAP or other authentication directory? These are all very difficult questions to answer and require sufficient planning and understanding of the risks and technologies.

Authorization suffers similar problems, specifically around ensuring only those with appropriate managerial approval are provided the requisite access. In an outsourced environment, it is difficult – if not impossible – to ensure that all of the access is known and approved. Presumably, the cloud provider may have some access of which the client's organization would not necessarily be aware nor have any significant influence over after the fact.

14.2.3.2 Accounting and Auditing

The issue of authentication is further compounded by the issue of accountability and nonrepudiation. In the case of a cloud provider managing the authentication mechanisms, appropriate logging and monitoring facilities may need to be present depending on the nature of the data in question. In the case of PCI DSS, this is a clear requirement. More so, adequate separation of duties between those who administer the systems and those who monitor the logs should probably exist. Regardless of the specifics, the logging and monitoring will likely be required, presumably in some sort of Security Information and Event Monitoring (SIEM) solution format. This of course begs new questions immediately: is the SIEM part of the cloud provider's standard offering? Should it be? How costly would it be, and how reliable? Would it make more sense to manage the SIEM internally rather than trust it to the cloud? Again, these are questions an organization should be concerned with prior to even looking at engaging the cloud.

14.2.3.3 Encrypting Data in Motion

Given the nature of services cloud offers, as well as the type of requirements most companies have to operate successfully and optimally, a large volume of data will travel between the client and the cloud. How does an organization protect the data in motion? Encryption quickly comes to mind as an immediate solution, especially when it comes to web applications and other Software-as-a-Service offerings, where protocols such as Secure Sockets Layer (SSL) may adequately address the issue. When looking at Platform and Infrastructure-as-a-Service, however, the transit becomes a little more complicated. Should there be a dedicated site-to-site Virtual Private Network (VPN) between the organization and the cloud provider? It is likely that the organization would at a minimum desire some sort of encryption for the authentication traffic and presumably for any administrative activities, but the nature of the data and relevant legislation influencing its usage and storage would otherwise dictate what needs to be protected and how.

14.2.3.4 Encrypting Data at Rest

With respect to specific compliance requirements and the mechanisms needed to be in place to protect various types of information, encrypting data stored in the cloud will also most likely be a requirement. Once the cloud provider has been made aware of it, certain assurances would need to be given with respect to the use of encryption or similar controls that would allow clients to maintain their compliance. One should not, however, underestimate the potential costs of such a solution, nor forget that there would be a need for substantial administrative activities such as key management and key changes.

14.2.4 Risk Assessments

Sufficient research and various assessments should be conducted prior to considering use of clouds. In this context, various frameworks needed to establish the overall impact of the risk of outsourcing to the cloud, as well as the related costs of compliance, would need to be taken into account. During the process of conducting these analyses and assessments, an organization should be able to determine whether utilizing cloud resources is a viable and cost-justified option, while at the same time ensuring that all of the essential regulatory and legislative requirements have been considered. A sample of a few key assessments follows.

14.2.4.1 Threat and Risk Assessments

Without going into detail describing a Threat and Risk Assessment (TRA), an organization must ensure that a TRA with respect to an organization's existing infrastructure is conducted prior to considering switching to the cloud. Through employing a TRA, an organization will at a minimum be able to identify shortcomings of the existing deployment and develop or build a remediation strategy appropriate to the shortcomings, taking into account the likelihood of using the cloud and changes that would be entailed.

There are different options that would allow an organization to exercise due diligence when looking at cloud computing as their new direction. Requesting the cloud provider to supply the results of their own TRA would be one alternative. The client could also conduct its own independent TRA of the cloud. If the data and systems in question are of particular importance and sensitivity, doing a scheduled TRA, or at least one on a regular basis, may be an extremely beneficial tool that would enable the company to ensure compliance to existing laws, and more actively and aggressively monitor the quality of service a provider is giving them. An example of something that is already in place externally would be PCI DSS 1.2, which mandates that a Risk Assessment be conducted at least annually for payment card processing environments.

Frameworks for TRAs tend to be based on Risk Management best practices and are fairly easy to come by. Some of the most common best practices are: AS/NZS 4360:2004 Risk Management[14]; BS 7799–3:2006 Guidelines for Information Security Risk Management,[15] and; ISO/IEC 27005:2008 – Security Techniques – Information Security Risk Management.[16] Adopting any one of these frameworks would ensure easy understanding of the organization's obligations; suggesting the cloud provider use one of these approaches further aligns the cloud with the overall desired course, as well providing a way to confirm TRAs are being conducted and are dependent on the shared and pre-approved best practices methodology.

---

[14] http://www.standards.org.au/

[15] http://www.bsigroup.com/

[16] http://www.iso.ch/

14.2.4.2 Business Impact Assessments

Again, without going into too much detail about defining a Business Impact Assessment (BIA), an organization must identify the business requirements of any one of their systems prior to considering outsourcing it to the cloud. This includes understanding a few key details of the systems in question. For instance, a company should know the Recovery Time Objective (RTO) or the acceptable amount of time to restore the function of the system without gravely affecting the financial stability of the organization of the systems. Another important thing to identify would be the Restore Point Objective (RPO) or the acceptable latency of data to be recovered. Each of these issues can severely impact the cost of outsourcing, so great care and diligence needs to be exercised in the execution. Once completed, the Business Impact Assessment values would need to be communicated to the cloud provider.

14.2.4.3 Privacy Impact Assessments

Where PII is involved, an organization should conduct a Privacy Impact Assessment (PIA) prior to engaging the cloud in order to understand the implications and risk of the engagement. The Canadian Federal Government[17] and Provincial Government of British Columbia (BC)[18] Canada have done an excellent job in providing freely available frameworks and reference materials, all easily found using your favorite search engine.

14.2.5 Due Diligence and Provider Contract Requirements

Once the preliminary requirements have been addressed, and the systems and data with which the cloud is to be seeded have been chosen, it is time to engage the provider and start the rest of the due diligence work. Some of this would be done through capturing those various requirements in contracts and ensuring the organization is aware of the service it is obtaining and all of the impacts that entails. The exercise of diligence can uncover or validate many things. With respect to compliance and security, an organization can verify if the practices in place on the cloud provider's side are satisfactory and align with the client's requirements.

---

[17] http://www.tbs-sct.gc.ca/pubs_pol/ciopubs/pia-pefr/paipg-pefrld-eng.asp

[18] http://www.cio.gov.bc.ca/services/privacy/Public_Sector/pia/default.asp

14.2.5.1 ISO Certification

Practices such as obtaining ISO/IEC 27001:2005[19] certification as a way to demonstrate an understanding and adherence to best security practices may be a valid response; however, the certification is only as useful as the company's defined requirements. Prior to taking the certification as evidence of a solid security foundation, an investigation into the scope and how it pertains to the outsourcing arrangement needs to be conducted. The worst-case scenario would be for a company to pursue a certification that would not be able to address any of the systems and processes to be used as they may be out of scope of that specific certification. On the other hand, even though having a qualification like this may not necessarily address the specific security requirements of the organization, it does demonstrate a certain commitment to ensuring that quality programs are in place in general.

14.2.5.2 SAS 70 Type II

A common type of an externally conducted assessment by North American outsourcing providers is a Statement on Auditing Standards No. 70 (SAS 70)[20] Service Organizations. The "Type II" provides an opinion as to the operating efficiency of the tested controls. Most outsourcers tend to have these assessments conducted periodically (mostly annually) in order to provide or maintain certain assurances to the customers. The associated cost is built into the cost of the outsourcing arrangement. Not entirely unlike the ISO certification, the scope of the assessment is of particular concern for clients; so if a provider is offering such assurances, it is necessary to remember that ensuring the scope is comprehensive and relevant is more important than how often the assessments get done.

14.2.5.3 PCI PA DSS or Service Provider

Relevant for the retail space or any organization processing payment cards, PCI approved Services Providers or Payment Application DSS certified applications may be in scope for the organization. These are fairly easy to research, at least initially, as Visa tends to publish lists of approved vendors for each application on a fairly regular basis.[21] Since an organization cannot outsource to a service provider that has not been pre-approved, nor can it use an application not on the PA-DSS

---

[19] http://www.iso.ch/

[20] http://www.aicpa.org/Professional+Resources/Accounting+and+Auditing/Audit+and+Attest+Standards/Authoritative+Standards+and+Related+Guidance+for+Non-Issuers/auditing_standards.htm

[21] https://www.pcisecuritystandards.org/security_standards/vpa/

confirmed list (at least not without jumping through a whole new collection of hoops), it follows that parts of their compliance, or lack thereof, remains out of their hands. Alternatively, in order to make it, or remain on the pre-approved vendor list, the cloud provider is encouraged to use specific applications to handle client's customer's card numbers data in order to achieve PA DSS certification on an annual basis.

The challenges with respect to requirements like this surround the strategic direction of the cloud provider. If, for instance, the provider is not solely tied to the concept of maintaining a PCI status, problems will ensue for the client. Specific language must be inserted into contracts with respect to ensuring compliance. Further, as a colleague once suggested: plan for the divorce before the wedding. This leads to the concepts of Portability and Interoperability.

14.2.5.4 Portability and Interoperability

Planning for contingency is paramount for outsourcing arrangements and cloud arrangements are no different. It is important to identify who owns the data and ensure that both parties agree. Further, in the event that the arrangement no longer meet the requirements of either party, preparations should take place to allow for smooth transitioning away. This can include simple steps such as ensuring proper termination clauses are inserted into legal agreements, but will likely include more complicated technical considerations. The data being surrendered at contract termination may not be in a universal format, and if returned in a vendor-specific proprietary format might be rendered unreadable. Surely this would not be a desired outcome, and an organization must plan to ensure that a different result is produced by doing their fair share of due diligence while negotiating the terms of their services, rather than after when it may be too late.

14.2.5.5 Right to Audit

If the agreement begins to proverbially "go sideways" or the client organization begins to question the results of an assessment, it may be in the client's best interest to conduct their own assessment of the cloud provider's environment and operating procedures. This action, of course, must be predicated on the existence of a "Right to audit" clause within the contract. Not to be taken lightly, the right to audit clause also indirectly implies that the client will have to be willing to accept relatively large costs from an impartial third party acting as an auditor of the environment. This clause provides the ability to execute the arrangement and hopefully would never need to be used, acting more as a deterrent for the cloud provider to not dismiss their responsibilities to the client throughout the full term of their services.

14.2.5.6   Service Level Agreements

It is also expected that the client organization will be entitled to a bare minimum level of service. It is incumbent on the client to demand relevant, measurable, and specific Service Level Agreements (SLAs) and Service Level Objectives (SLOs) for security-related events, although the client must be aware that there is an inverse relationship with the timeliness of response for most issues and the cost of the service given. This initiative should be linked to the Business Impact Assessment results as well.

14.2.6   Other Considerations

Some of the other considerations to give thought to involve ensuring that the cloud providers have an appropriate governance structure with clearly defined problem-management procedures and escalation paths. Some other key procedures and plans should also be included, such as incident response plans with appropriate roles and responsibilities outlined for both the client and the provider.

14.2.6.1   Disaster Recovery/Business Continuity

An organization needs to be adequately satisfied with the ability of the cloud provider to ensure appropriate availability of the client's corporate assets with which they were entrusted. It may be suggested that the client be privy to reviews of the business continuity plans or disaster recovery plans, or related testing activities. Again, verbiage around this concept should be captured within the contract to ensure suitability and appropriate compensation are considered.

14.2.6.2   Governance Structure

As stated previously, the cloud provider's governance structure should be investigated and arrangements with respect to communication should be formalized. This is required specifically around escalations and problem management, where an official channel needs to be established such that there is always an individual accountable and responsible on both the client and cloud provider sides to ensure adequate completion of the required tasks in a timely and acceptable fashion. There should always be an appropriate escalation point as well, in the event that the responsible individual is unable to complete the necessary tasks as outlined. The governance structure which would outline all of these, amongst many other processes, needs to be formalized and agreed upon prior to contract signing.

14.2.6.3 Incident Response Plan

Many compliance initiatives specifically outline the requirement of incident response teams and their related plans. When dealing both with the cloud and outsourcers in general, this approach needs to be explained, negotiated, documented, and formalized such that there is no room for interpretation when it comes to plan execution. Specifically, the roles and responsibilities for all involved parties ought to be explicitly outlined to ensure that appropriate actions are taken and necessary notifications are made. Breach notification is a particularly troublesome issue with clouds because the laws mandating them tend to be jurisdictional and related to the physical geography of the place of the breach. When developing the responsibilities of the incident response plan, it may be best to consider verbiage that would allow for tying the obligation to determine the actual location of the breach and the related notification requirements for that region to the cloud provider rather than the client.

14.3   Conclusion

As it can be imagined, compliance with the vast array of legislation and regulations when using cloud computing services can be quite complicated and burdensome. However, hopefully the crux of this chapter was not lost and it did not appear as though one should reconsider engaging cloud providers. The intent was rather to ensure client organizations that are already considering outsourcing to the cloud understand which data and systems might be prime (easy) candidates for outsourcing, and which may be prohibitively expensive. The key, as can likely be imagined, is to have firm control over an organization's information assets and a strong understanding of the related legislative and regulatory requirements over that data. Once that concept is understood, and the requirements are gathered, it is achievable to consider the cloud options and obtain and benefit from them at realistic costs.

Bibliography

"Auditing the Cloud", Grid Gurus, http://gridgurus.typepad.com/grid_gurus/2008/10/auditing-the-cl.html, October 20, 2008

Anderson R (2008) Security engineering: a guide to building dependable distributed systems. Wiley, New York

Cloud Computing: Bill of Rights. http://wiki.cloudcomputing.org/wiki/CloudComputing:Bill_of_Rights

Security Guidance for Critical Areas of Focus in Cloud Computing v2.1, Cloud Security Alliance. http://www.cloudsecurityalliance.org/csaguide.pdf, 2009

Hurley W (2009) Beautiful Security. O'Reilly Media

Jaquith A (2007) Security metrics: replacing fear, uncertainty, and doubt. Addison-Wesley Professional

Mather T (March 2, 2009) Cloud computing is on the up, but what are the security issues? Secure Computing Magazine, London

Raywood D (March 9, 2009) Data privacy clarification could lead to greater confidence in cloud computing. Secure Computing Magazine, London

Reese G (2009) Cloud application architectures: building applications and infrastructure in the cloud. O'Reilly Media

Roiter N (March 2009) How to secure cloud computing. Information Security Magazine. http://searchSecurity.techtarget.com/magazineFeature/0,296894,sid14_gci1349670,00.html

Sherwood J (2005) Enterprise security architecture: a business-driven approach. CMP

Wood L (January 30, 2009) Cloud computing and compliance: be careful up there. ITWorld

Chapter 15
Cloud Computing – Data Confidentiality and Interoperability Challenges

Fabrizio Gagliardi and Silvana Muscella

Abstract Interoperability, which brings major benefits for enterprise and science, is key for the pervasive adoption of grids and clouds. The lack of interoperability has impeded broader adoption and the reason, enterprise argues, why the grids have not performed at expected levels. Interoperability between existing grids and clouds is of primary importance for the EU.

This chapter focuses on the guiding principles of interoperability and openness for the development of cloud computing, as they have been for the Internet so far. Therefore, global standardization efforts are emphasized in this chapter and seen as a key priority.

We look at the importance of interoperability and what standardization efforts are taking place surrounding cloud computing, considering how enterprises do not wish to tie their applications to specific providers' remote infrastructure – particularly if there is proprietary technology deployed. Nevertheless, it is still considered early in the market's development for formal standardization of many aspects of cloud computing – except maybe in the area of virtualization technology – but industry leaders recognize the importance of interoperability.

The chapter delivers a snapshot of the impact that cloud computing is making on the European market and the influence of EU regulation in listing the Opportunities for Europe. The concluding remarks and considerations provide a look at the future market drivers and the key challenges of interoperability and data confidentiality.

F. Gagliardi (✉)
External Research, Microsoft Research, EMEA office: 12, Av. des Morgines,
CH-1213, Petit-Lancy (Geneva),
e-mail: Fabrizio.Gagliardi@microsoft.com

N. Antonopoulos and L. Gillam (eds.), *Cloud Computing: Principles,*
Systems and Applications, Computer Communications and Networks,
DOI 10.1007/978-1-84996-241-4_15, © Springer-Verlag London Limited 2010

15.1 Confidentiality of Data and Principal Issues Globally: An Overview

Today, companies considering using a cloud-based service need to obtain a clear understanding of the privacy, security, and legal consequences before signing the SLA with a service provider. Forrester urges in a recent report [1] to develop a checklist of data security and compliance priorities and compare organizational needs to the cloud service provider's policies and procedures.

Other important questions surround confidentiality of data and a variety of related issues including security, privacy, and trust. Who is responsible for the data residing or moving in the cloud, and under which jurisdiction they fall, are common unresolved questions. A key example is the UK National Health Service (NHS) that has a jurisdiction which states that all UK Data must never leave the United Kingdom.

Specific items have to be included in the agreements for companies before signing the contracts, which cover items as to how data are being handled once the service contract is terminated, the kind of data that are returned to the organization, and ensuring the elimination of the data at the host cloud service providers' network. Early adopters have run into a number of hurdles, including not knowing where their data resides, what happens to the data when a decision is made to change the services, and how the service provider guards the customer's privacy. Concern over proprietary data and personal information is a major issue. A cloud provider may not necessarily commit to offering internal auditing on this feature, but understanding through logs and who accesses the data should be available to the company.

Robert Gellman prepared a report for the World Privacy forum indicating that the stored information [2] in the cloud eventually ends up on a physical machine owned by a particular company or person located in a specific country. That stored information may be subject to the laws of the country where the physical machine is located. For example, personal information that ends up maintained by a cloud provider in a EU Member State could be subject permanently to EU privacy laws.

15.1.1 Location of Cloud Data and Applicable Laws

More specifically, Gellman's report goes into greater detail on the explanation of the EU directives, such as the EU's Data Protection Directive [2, 3] that offers an example of the importance of location on legal rights and obligations. Under Article 4 of the Directive, a national data protection law applies when a controller located in the territory of the Member State processes personal information. A cloud provider in an EU Member State could bring personal data obtained from a non-EU-based user under a European data protection law. Once an EU law applies to the personal data, the data remain subject to the law, and the export of that data will thereafter be subject to EU rules limiting transfers to a third country. Thus, if a US company gave its data to a cloud provider based in France, French data protection law would apply and the export of the data back to the United States could be restricted or prohibited. In addition, the subjects of the data would acquire rights of notice, access, correction, etc. under French law. Once an EU Member State's data protection law applies to personal information, there is no clear way to remove the applicability of the law to the data.

The location of a cloud provider's operations may have a significant bearing on the law that applies to a user's data. The actual location may or may not appear in the provider's terms of service. Even if the provider discloses the location of records, the provider may change it, possibly without any notice. The same data may be stored in multiple locations at the same time. A provider who promises to maintain user data in a specific jurisdiction (e.g. the United States) may reduce some of the location risks that a user may face.

15.1.2   Data Concerns Within a European Context

Generally, the question that arises is how national privacy and security standards can be ensured in a global cloud environment. In terms of data privacy and jurisdiction, national standards and regulations have resulted in few providers storing regional hardware, and most choosing, instead, to use European and American infrastructures. Reservations about cloud computing derive from concerns about dependability, vulnerability, and lock-in to providers, as well as security-related issues, when there are no longer true internal systems.

Many users today are choosing to combine internal IT and cloud computing simply due to the fact that by doing this, they are not risking losing control of their sensitive data, especially in the cases where no uniform service level agreements (SLAs) exist. Indeed, loss of data, hardware breakdowns, and a reduction in performance are noted in relation to today's cloud computing offers.

The drawbacks on the current implementations lie primarily on external audits not being currently permitted, limited logs available, the users' trust in the brand such that they have no alternative with regard to data security, and lack of information regarding the actual location or the jurisdiction of data.

Organizations must plan carefully when constructing cloud computing environments to ensure that the flexibility and scalability do not overshadow the necessity for risk-tolerant implementation. As the developments in the EU show, the initial cloud computing implementation must not only be secure, but the whole system must be flexible to accommodate emerging laws and regulations.

The Council of the European Union, in the Adoption of the Council Conclusions on the future of Information Communication Technology (ICT) research, innovation and infrastructures [4], stresses that the digital revolution is still in its early stages and that a research and innovation capacity is essential to be able to shape, master, and assimilate technologies and exploit them to economic, societal, and cultural advantage; in addition, it underlines in this regard the necessity to ensure the availability, appropriate treatment, and conservation of an unprecedented amount of data.

15.1.3 Government Data

Government data are being put online to increase accountability, contribute valuable information about the world, and to enable government, the country, and the world to function more efficiently [5]. All of these purposes are served by putting the information on the Web as Linked Data. Linked data principles provide a basis for realizing the Web of Data by ensuring that data are organized, structured, and independent of any application programs so that it can serve a broad community of people and many applications. The main drivers behind linked data include the value-add of structured content, a mission or mandate to make data linkable, and most importantly, low development barriers. Key enabling technologies span Web 2.0, Mash-ups, Open Source, Cloud Computing, and Software-as-a-Service. Effort toward interoperability can be made where most needed, making the evolution with time smoother and more productive.

15.1.4 Trust

The technology of cloud computing itself is not insecure. However, companies must carefully plan, from the outset, the implications of massively scalable design, storage, and computing. This is especially true if those services are outsourced to cloud providers and not directly under company control. Recently, the Cloud Security Alliance was set up [6] "to promote the use of best practices for providing security assurance within Cloud Computing, and provide education on the uses of Cloud Computing to help secure all other forms of computing." An educational and networking event entitled, SecureCloud 2010, hosted by the European Network and Information Security Agency, the Cloud Security Alliance, and ISACA, which are organizations that help to shape the future of Cloud Computing Security deal with interoperability between cloud providers among other topics, demonstrated the need to immediately address Cloud interoperability in earnest.

In a recent survey carried out by the European Network and Information Security Agency (ENISA) [7], the principal reasons for Small and Medium-sized Enterprises (SMEs) to adopt cloud computing were to avoid capital expenditure in hardware, software, IT support, and information security by outsourcing (70% of SMEs responded in favor of this, and 67% found flexibility, scalability, and IT resources to be key to utilizing cloud). SMEs' main concerns were that 44% were concerned about privacy and the availability of services and 48% were worried over loss of control of their own services. ENISA published a Cloud Computing Report in November 2009 [8] on the benefits, risks, and recommendations for information security, detailing that the cloud's economies of scale and flexibility are both a friend and a foe from a security point of view. The massive concentrations of resources and data present a more attractive target to attackers, but cloud-based defenses can be more robust, scalable, and cost-effective. The paper provided security guidance for potential and existing users of cloud computing.

15.1.5   *Interoperability and Standardization in Cloud Computing*

The development of standards and interoperability between the varying levels of clouds is inevitable. It is also tied directly to the needed adoption by the enterprise. Without clearly defined standards, best practices, and open interoperability, further adoption of the cloud will evolve at a slower pace.

There have been a significant number of publications including those by the UK Government and European Commission itself, which have made the economic case for standards and their utilization in increasing innovation. The central premise of this is that they remove the need for innovative developers and product/service designers to waste time with the lower level functionality that has been developed by others. There can also be the sharing of common solutions between application areas through the utilization of building block technologies that are not subject or area-specific. This will allow increased European competiveness through ensuring that there is a minimization of the lag between early adopters and the main stream. This ensures that organizations of varying sizes are able to contribute to the economy, with their competitiveness not hindered by large scale "vendor lock-in" or proprietary services gaining market dominance.

Dynamic capability is one of the features of cloud that differentiates it from grid by offering resources as and when needed. Virtualization is another key difference. These are among the drivers to adoption. However, there are many challenges to be addressed with grid computing community contributing to cloud needs, above all, for the Open Grid Forum (Open Grid Forum). Interoperability is not the only issue. SLAs are a big challenge, as start-up companies or SMEs, which are currently the major cloud users, want freedom of choice, although Amazon EC2 is the current market leader and the de facto standard cloud service provider. If these companies want to move to another provider, then the problem revolves not only around VM migration, but also other services such as databases that lack compatibility. Other challenges concern how to move existing software packages from internal data centers to external clouds, bearing in mind that the architecture of the majority of this software does not support scale-out, as well as network bandwidth utilization.

It suffices to say that cloud portability, possible via guaranteed standards and interoperability, has to occur in the future, and the major players in this arena have to be involved. The lack of involvement of the major players will lead to standard clouds and nonstandard clouds or companies providing some form of filtering mechanism or converters to allow for portability.

15.1.6   **Open Grid Forum's (*OGF*) Production Grid Interoperability Working Group (*PGI-WG*) Charter**

Open Grid Forum's (OGF's) Grid Interoperation Now Community Group (GIN-CG) and the Production Grid Infrastructure Working Group (PGI-WG) lead the interoperability of global grid infrastructures. The PGI-WG, a spin-off from GIN-CG, brings together members of production grid infrastructures from all over the world to address related challenges, building on the experiences of GIN-CG to create profile documents to be fed into OGF standardization groups. This focus enables work on refined or new OGF specifications. The PGI-WG chiefly focuses on three OGF standards, working closely with the dedicated working groups:

- Job Submission Description Language (JSDL)
- Open Grid Services Architecture-Basic Execution Service (OGSA-BES)
- Grid Laboratory Uniform Environment (GLUE) schema

The efforts of GIN-CG and PGI-WG represent important milestones by enabling other grid infrastructure communities and software providers that intend to implement these specifications to join the standardization activity and contribute their experiences. This work is also a significant step in the grid community's transition to the model proposed by EGI, where e-Infrastructures built from different software will have to operate seamlessly together. Through this work, the ongoing efforts of the Usage Records and Resource Usage Service Working Group will continue and move to include their outputs into the Production Grid Profile being developed.

15.1.7 Achievements in the OGF Open Cloud Computing Interface (OGF-OCCI)

The OGF Open Cloud Computing Interface Working Group (OCCI-WG) is developing a clean, open application programming interface (API) for "Infrastructure as a Service" (IaaS) based Clouds. IaaS is one of the three primary services, alongside Software, and Platform, of the emerging Cloud industry. OCCI-WG is a working group of OGF established in March 2009. The group has active membership of over 160 individuals, and is led by four chairs from industry, academia, service providers, and end users. Several members are from commercial service providers that are committed to implementing the OGF-OCCI specification.

15.1.7.1   What will OCCI Provide?

OCCI is a very slim REST-based API, which can be easily extended as shown in Fig. 15.1. Without the overhead of many similar protocols, the REST approach allows users to easily access their services. Every resource is uniquely addressed using a Uniform Resource Identifier (URI).

Based on a set of operations – create, retrieve, update, and delete – resources can be managed. Currently, three types of resources are considered: storage, network, and compute resources. Those resources can be linked together to form a virtual machine with assigned attributes. For example, it is possible to provision a machine which has 2 GB of RAM, one hard disk, and one network interface.

Fig. 15.1   Example of the REST-based API

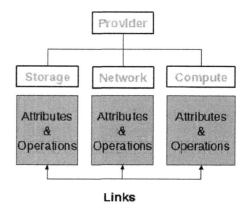

Currently, the OCCI group is finalizing and documenting the initial draft specification. The group is actively collaborating with other groups from the Storage Networking Industry Association (SNIA) for storage, and Distributed Management Task Force (DMTF) for management standards. The work is also featured on the http://www. cloud-standards.org wiki, where Cloud-related standards are coordinated by the major Standards Development Organizations (SDOs).

15.1.7.2   Cloud Data Management Interface (CDMI)

The Storage Networking Industry Association™ has created a technical work group to address the need for a cloud storage standard. The new Cloud Data Management Interface (CDMI) is meant to enable interoperable cloud storage and data management. In CDMI, the underlying storage space exposed by the above-mentioned interfaces is abstracted using the notion of a container. A container is not only a useful abstraction for storage space, but also serves as a grouping of the data stored in it, and a point of control for applying data services in the aggregate.

15.1.7.3   How it Works

The cloud computing infrastructure management, shown earlier supports both OCCI and CDMI interfaces. To achieve interoperability, CDMI provides a type of export that contains information obtained via the OCCI interface. In addition, OCCI provides a type of storage that corresponds to exported CDMI containers. OCCI and CDMI can achieve interoperability initiating storage export configurations from either OCCI or CDMI interfaces as starting points. Although the outcome is the same, there are differences between the procedures using CDMI's interface over the OCCI's as a starting point.

Both OCCI and CDMI are standards working toward interoperable cloud computing and cloud storage. The standards are being co-ordinated through an alliance between the OGF and the SNIA, as well as through a cross-SDO cloud standards collaboration group described subsequently. OCCI will take advantage of the storage that CDMI has provisioned and configured.

Since both interfaces use similar principles and technologies, it is likely that a single client could manage both the computing and storage needs of an application, scaling both to meet the demands placed on them.

15.1.8   SDOs and their Involvement with Clouds

2009 was a significant year for the development of standards efforts in cloud computing. In July 2009, the Object Management Group OMG™ announced a collaboration with leading technology SDOs to coordinate and communicate standards for Cloud computing and storage. Organizations that participate in this round-table style collaboration include the DMTF, OGF, SNIA, Open Cloud Consortium (OCC), and Cloud Security Alliance (CSA). Most SDOs already have many one-to-one liaison relationships, which are effective and productive for handling specific issues. This round-table-style collaboration provides a "bird's eye view" of this broad and complicated technical area, further helping the work already underway between these leading standards bodies. This is the main reason for the establishment of a Cloud Standards Coordination working group. The group has a goal to create a landscape of cloud standards work, including common terminology.

To support this collaboration, a public working group has been established, and anyone with relevant technical skills, interest, and commitment can participate. Participation by enterprise and government IT leaders is encouraged to ensure that their critical standards needs are being addressed. The work is an outgrowth of the already existing Standards Development Organization Collaboration on Networked Resources Management (SCRM) working group that has coordinated management standards in general [9]. The organizations involved have created a wiki to describe each organization's standards and efforts in this space.

15.1.9   An Example of Cloud Computing Interoperability
at Microsoft

Interoperability at Microsoft is important, and in recent years the interoperability team has been working actively to make Windows the best platform to run PHP applications [10]. The PHP Toolkit for ADO.NET Data Services, ADO.NET Data Services, is shipped as a part of .NET 3.5 SP1 and provides a RESTful interface in data services and an efficient way to surface your data to the web. The data are then easily consumable, served up in JSON or XML (POX). The PHP Toolkit for ADO.NET Data Services is an Open Source project that provides a set of utilities and libraries for PHP developers to easily take advantage of these ADO.NET Data Services. This toolkit was recently highlighted at the Gov 2.0 Summit in Washington DC to explore how technology can enable transparency, collaboration, and efficiency in government.

The Zend Framework [11] has invited the open-source community and software vendors to participate in the formation of a Simple Cloud API. IBM, Microsoft, Rackspace, Nirvanix, and GoGrid have already joined the project as contributors. In the coming months, they will work together to define APIs for these cloud application services, enabling a new generation of native cloud applications written in PHP.

The Simple Cloud API is an open-source project that makes it easier for developers to use cloud application services by abstracting insignificant API differences. One of the design goals of the project is to encourage innovation. To this end, the Simple Cloud API can be used for common operations, while users can easily drop down to vendor libraries to access value-add features. The Simple Cloud API is an example of Microsoft's continued investment in the openness and interoperability of its platform. Currently, Microsoft Azure also supports the full Java stack including open-source tools such as the Apache web server. An example of the Azure Services Platform is given in the subsequent paragraph (Fig. 15.2).

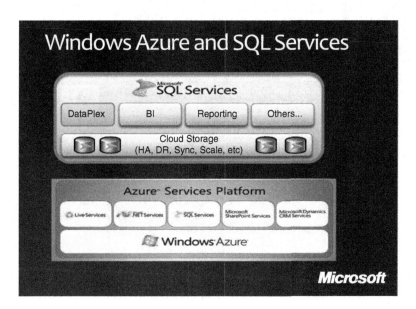

Fig. 15.2 Windows Azure and SQL services

15.1.10   A Microsoft Cloud Interoperability Scenario

At the Gov 2.0 summit, Microsoft presented a cloud interoperability scenario that takes advantage of the recently announced Toolkit for PHP with ADO.NET Data Services to view public government data with Windows Azure and PHP [12]. This scenario allows a Windows Azure application that exposes data in a standard way (XML/Atom), and shows how you can simply "consume" this data from a PHP web application. This scenario takes advantage of the Open Government Data Initiative (OGDI) [13] and Microsoft's Open Government effort, built on the foundation of transparency, choice, and interoperability. Using open standards and API, developers and government agencies can retrieve the data programmatically for use in new and innovative online applications or mashups. Publicly available government data sets have been loaded into Windows Azure Storage, and the OGDI team built a data service that exposes the data through REST web services, returning data by default in the Atom Publishing Protocol format (Fig. 15.3).

15.1.11   Opportunities for Public Authorities

More governments are making a commitment to cloud computing in order to address rising IT costs and making efficient use of labor, as well as for environmental

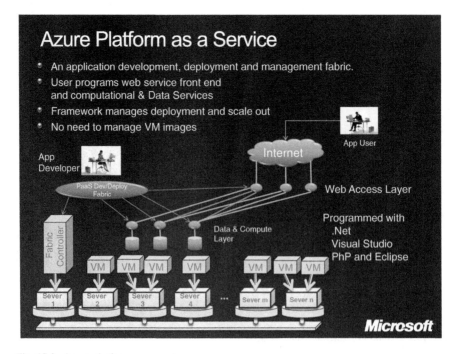

Fig. 15.3 Azure platform as a service

responsibility and openness to innovation. Cloud computing offers a number of benefits to government and public authorities, such as simplifying acquisition, budgeting, policy planning, and architecture along with the technological benefits, such as increased storage, automation, flexibility, mobility, and a shift in IT focus. As economies continue to struggle, governments need to take a deeper look at their expenses and make smarter, cost-effective decisions. In both London and Washington, the definition (as well as possibly the development of a government cloud, nicknamed G-Cloud) is constantly discussed. Therefore, open-source software is certainly losing momentum and political appeal, while cloud computing is gaining press coverage and executive interest according to a recent Gartner report [14].

The US Government has been one of the leaders in outlining concrete plans to implement cloud-like technologies in areas such as desktop management (i.e. remote help desk) and secure provisioning, portals and collaboration, content and records management, workflow management, business intelligence, a Software-as-a-Service, as well as a data center that calls for government-to-government, government-to-contractor, and contractor-to-contractor modes of service delivery.

A few barriers exist in that government's sensitive and secret data must continue to be maintained in government-owned, government-operated facilities. In May 2009, the EU launched a broad consultation on whether it should consider revising the 1995 data protection directive. Cloud computing and new business models are challenging government systems. Currently, around 90% of organizations in the EU do not engage in transfers of data outside the region, but cloud computing is very likely to change that. There are in fact a few examples of governments starting to take advantage of the emerging technology.

15.1.12 Future Market Drivers and Challenges

As the current landscape of cloud computing has been described, it is important to understand where it is going in the future. Ultimately, the market will drive the overall adoption, but it is equally important to outline what it will take to prove it as a fully viable solution.

Just a short time ago, there was an issue with a lack of referenceable successes, with few large players offering clouds. Amazon were leading the field, (with EC2, S3, SimpleDB, CloudFront, and SQS), but with every passing month, larger IT players have been unveiling their new cloud solutions, such as IBM BlueCloud, Microsoft Azure, etc.

It is important, however, to define what are the catalysts for cloud computing in terms of the provider, the user, the technology itself, and available business models. The catalyst for business is to leverage clouds to get to market with new business models as well as the generation of Web 2.0 startups, to receive a better reliability through service-level contracts, availability of open standards to reduce lock-in, and concrete solutions to data-security issues. Finally, the technology itself needs to be able to scale to support massive enterprise applications, provide seamless support for third party applications, and easily substitute in-house management and monitoring tools.

The current opportunities are for the next generation of cloud computing virtualization providers (e.g. 3Tera, Xen), computing giants with massive data centers (e.g. Amazon), bridging providers and integrated Platform as a Service (PaaS) (e.g. Google, Elastra), and for SaaS systems providers for databases, app servers, and business intelligence (e.g. salesforce.com).

Overall, hyper-competitive markets are pushing the business to demand ever faster time to market, reduced entry/exit barriers, while reducing IT costs, allowing SMEs to have world-class enterprise application functionality at affordable price points, and startups to build their infrastructure on clouds to gain cost advantages. Existing companies are starting to consider migrating just to remain at par.

15.1.13   Priorities Moving Forward

While many cloud providers' solutions for extending applications between physically distributed resources are still at the concept stage, the market should expect significant developments over the coming months by hosting services to the providers, which bridge the gap between dedicated application hosting and cloud-based infrastructure services.

These two approaches have plenty in common, perhaps, the most important being that the larger Grid infrastructures and Clouds run on shared infrastructure accessed via the network, often remotely.

It is this common attribute that results in shared problems that both the Grid and Cloud communities need to address, including, but not limited to, the portability of services and data between grids or clouds, the secure access to and operation of those services, the secure movement and storage of data, the need for location awareness to cater for disparate regulatory requirements, unified management for both internal and external platforms, etc.

15.2   Conclusions

Standardization and interoperability are invaluable characteristics to a successful application of distributed computing, either the already mature grid e-Infrastructure efforts or the momentum around its cloud-focused counterparts in the industry. As grids made the transition from academic and research exclusivity to potential industry adoption, the role of standardization took precedence. The same must be done for clouds, but being mindful that its arrival has taken quite a different path. Contrary to the evolution of grid, cloud computing has seen its growth through business interest as the practical Infrastructure as a Service (IaaS) model. The challenge now is to see how this can be best adapted toward further strengthening of e-Infrastructure and its e-Science communities.

One of the Ten Cloud Computing Predictions for 2009, by Michael Sheehan [15], was the obvious conclusion that Cloud adoption will be significant in 2009. Moreover, Sheehan also insisted that the government will play a much larger role too. The French government's mission is to bring the Cloud to their government infrastructure. With the 2008 US Election, Barack Obama proved how critical an online presence was to furthering the concept of change in many EU27 governments. Cloud computing certainly implies risks as discussed in this chapter, but creates economies of scale that can benefit large as well as small government organizations.

One of the major concerns in today's society is still data security. Cloud providers will give you a list of legal terminology about what will happen to the data in the cloud and who it is invisible to, and the customer may request to lock down sets of machines by building a firewall. Moreover, if the customer requires tighter controls beyond the service offered by default due to regulatory issues, then this becomes open to further discussion and no doubt ambiguous interpretation. If the customer has publicly available data, then this is a non-issue, but is still an area of further analysis. A recent Avanade study found that on a margin of five to one, consumers placed a higher priority of security of their data in the cloud over potential economic benefits and efficiencies [16]. These are not new issues; nevertheless, some further challenges for the future in the scope of cloud computing cover the analysis of internal data protection, communication, foundational security between the provider and the customer, and virtualization security.

At a Cloudscape event organized in Brussels in January 2009 to explore the cloud computing landscape and its impact on enterprise Information Technology in collaboration with an EC-funded project OGF-Europe [17], some thought-provoking conclusions were drawn to the extent that a follow-up was organized in February 2010 to address the points further. A clear need for grid/cloud standardized operation guidelines emerged from interactive discussions exploring enterprise feedback on standards requirements.

Areas of further efforts among the e-Science and industry communities lie in pursuing the clarification of grid/cloud taxation aspects while operating grids/clouds, introducing guidelines for handling/guaranteeing privacy in clouds and grids (liability issues), and in general providing guidelines for work across legislative domains.

Finally, while Enterprise and Government are pioneering fields, it is expected that industrial adoption will proceed apace as organizations seeking to gain energy efficiency and offload expensive data center infrastructure to be replaced by on-demand access to cloud resources. We anticipate that this field will be cost-sensitive, and in spite of much fear about security, 80% or more of the organizations' IT implementation could be via cloud computing resources in the future.

References

1. Section 1 How secure is your cloud? A close look at cloud computing security issues. This is the first document in the "Secure Cloud Computing" series by Chenxi Wang, Ph.D. with Jonathan Penn, Allison Herald
2. Privacy in the clouds: risks to privacy and confidentiality from cloud computing. Prepared by Robert Gellman for the World Privacy Forum, Date February 23, 2009 World Privacy forum. http://www.worldprivacyforum.org/cloudprivacy.html
3. Directive 95/46/EC of the European Parliament and of the Council of 24 October 1995 on the protection of individuals with regard to the processing of personal data and on the free movement of such data. http://ec.europa.eu/justice_home/fsj/privacy/docs/95-46-ce/dir1995-46_part1_en.pdf and http://ec.europa.eu/justice_home/fsj/privacy/docs/95-46-ce/dir1995-46_part2_en.pdf
4. Adoption of Council Conclusions of the future of ICT research, innovation and infrastructures – 16128/09 of the 25th November 2009, Brussels, BE
5. http://www.w3.org/DesignIssues/GovData.html Putting Government Data Online by Tim-Berners Lee
6. http://www.cloudsecurityalliance.org/
7. Privacy, Security and Identity in the Cloud Giles Hogben European Network & Information Security Agency ENISA. http://www.enisa.europa.eu/
8. Cloud Computing Report Benefits, risks and recommendations for information security http://www.enisa.europa.eu/act/rm/files/deliverables/cloud-computing-risk-assessment/
9. http://cloud-standards.org. Every SDO has representatives that maintain the wiki updated
10. Dave Bost, Developer Evangelist at Microsoft focusing on the Visual Studio tools and the .NET application platform
11. ZEND Framework – http://framework.zend.com/about/overview
12. Jean-Christophe Cimetiere – Sr. Technical Evangelist, Microsoft. http://blogs.msdn.com/interoperability/archive/2009/09/10/viewing-public-government-data-with-windows-azure-and-php-a-cloud-interoperability-scenario-using-rest.aspx?CommentPosted=true#commentm essage
13. http://www.microsoft.com/presspass/press/2009/may09/05-07OpenGovDataInitiativePR.mspx
14. Is Cloud Computing Killing Open Source in Government? Gartner September 2nd, 2009
15. Ten Cloud Computing Predictions for 2009, Written by Michael Sheehan on Dec 2nd, 2008. Filed under: cloud computing, features, general, GoGrid, Hosting, Industry, Partners, ServePath. Read more: http://blog.gogrid.com/2008/12/02/ten-cloud-computing-predictions-for-2009/#ixzz0TOFX54F5
16. http://www.avanade.com/us/_uploaded/pdf/pressrelease/uscloudsurveyreleasefinal053414.pdf. Avanade is an IT consultancy joint venture between Microsoft and Accenture
17. CLOUDSCAPE – A Workshop to explore the cloud computing landscape and its impact on enterprise IT, January 2009 Multiple perspectives on cloud & Grid computing learn more at www.ogfeurope.eu

Chapter 16
Security Issues to Cloud Computing

Cyril Onwubiko

Abstract With the growing adoption of cloud computing as a viable business proposition to reduce both infrastructure and operational costs, an essential requirement is to provide guidance on how to manage information security risks in the cloud. In this chapter, security risks to cloud computing are discussed, including privacy, trust, control, data ownership, data location, audits and reviews, business continuity and disaster recovery, legal, regulatory and compliance, security policy and emerging security threats and attacks. Finally, a cloud computing framework and information asset classification model are proposed to assist cloud users when choosing cloud delivery services and deployment models on the basis of cost, security and capability requirements.

16.1 Introduction

As organisations seek new ways of driving businesses forward, increasing demands are now placed on computer networks to provide competitive edge and create new opportunities at reduced cost. This has accelerated business and technological initiatives that promise to provide services at comparably low infrastructure and operating costs. The rapid growth of cloud computing is a good example.

This new model of service (cloud computing) offers tremendous reduction in operating cost; unfortunately, it has also introduced a set of new and unfamiliar risks. Most networks today are borderless, spanning across different network estates, security domains and enterprise, whose security policies, security protection mechanisms and business continuity plans are different, varying and diverse. Consequently, new security requirements are needed, new forms of protection strategies become essential and existing practices may require reviewing.

C. Onwubiko (✉)
Security & Information Assurance, Research Series Limited, 1 Meadway,
Woodford Green, IG8 7RF, Essex, UK
e-mail: cyril.onwubiko@research-series.com

N. Antonopoulos and L. Gillam (eds.), *Cloud Computing: Principles,*
Systems and Applications, Computer Communications and Networks,
DOI 10.1007/978-1-84996-241-4_16, © Springer-Verlag London Limited 2010

To address the inherent risks in cloud computing, fundamental security issues that exist in traditional networks must be evaluated in relation to cloud computing. Risks to cloud computing delivery models, such as software as a service (SaaS), hardware as a service (HaaS), platform as a service (PaaS) and infrastructure as a service (IaaS) must be identified and discussed in detail. Interdependent risks and cumulative risk arising from private, public, virtual private, localised and federated clouds must be outlined and discussed. Issues of information ownership, trust, confidentiality, integrity, privacy and anonymity must be addressed. It is pertinent to note that understanding risks that exist in the cloud is fundamental to understanding how best to treat risks inherent in cloud computing.

16.2   Cloud Computing ('The Cloud')

Cloud computing is an emerging technological development that leverages the Internet to provide unparalleled distributed computing service based on service-oriented architecture (SOA) and virtualisation. Cloud computing appears to be ubiquitous, dynamically scalable and on-demand, which can be purchased on a 'pay-as-you-go' basis without under or over provisioning or prior subscription. According to NIST, 'cloud computing is a model for enabling convenient, on-demand network access to a shared pool of configurable computing resources (e.g., networks, servers, storage, applications, and services) that can be rapidly provisioned and released with minimal management effort or service provider interaction [1,2]'. This implies that cloud computing offers on-demand self-service, a highly scalable shared pool of network resource that offers broad network access to users. These services are dynamic and affordable with minimal consumer configurable interfaces.

There are five main attributes of cloud computing:

- On-demand self-service
- Ubiquitous network access
- Location independence and homogeneity
- Elastically scalable
- Measured service

First, the cloud offers on-demand self-service; this means that the cloud can be used as and when required without prior subscription. It does not require pre-booking or 'phased-delivery' for the consumer; hence, there is no need for under or over subscription in the cloud.

Second, the cloud offers almost infinite network access to vast infrastructure and computing resources, such as storage facility, memory, processor, hosting and myriad applications. Third, the cloud uses a shared pool of resources, platforms and infrastructure residing on the Internet, which is located at various parts of the world, making the cloud location-independent. The services offered in the cloud are homogenous. The same service is provided exactly in the same way to all users.

This is because of its multi-tenancy delivery model. Fourth, cloud computing capabilities, such as storage, computing power, processing and hosting are elastic; resources are pooled together to provide vast amount of computing power. Finally, cloud computing services are measured; each service purchased or utilised by a consumer is measured and billed accordingly.

With the economic downturn in 2009, cloud computing has become a viable business and technological proposition, because of the significant reduction in both infrastructure and operational costs that it offers when compared with the traditional IT services. The cloud offers huge economies of scale and enhances outsourcing and consumerisation. It is understandable that cloud computing is attractive to users who range from government agencies, financial institutions, individual and corporate users to cybercriminals. This opportunity to cohabit and share a pool of resources with all consumers including cybercriminals brings to bear a significant element of risk. Therefore, a cloud computing environment requires an implicit level of trust as well as explicit level of vigilance and risk management to ensure success [3].

Figure 16.1 is a cloud computing deployment and delivery model. It comprises five cloud delivery models, namely, public or external cloud, community cloud, agency cloud, private and hybrid clouds. The models consist of three service methods, namely, cloud software computing (SaaS), cloud platform computing (PaaS) and cloud infrastructure computing (IaaS).

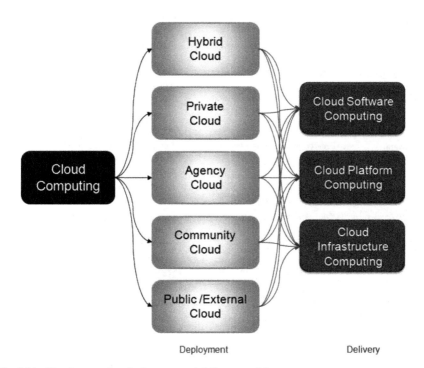

Fig. 16.1 Cloud computing deployment and delivery model

A public or external cloud is a general-purpose cloud computing environment managed by a cloud provider. The cloud provider could be external provider, such as Amazon EC2, Google Apps, Salesforce, Rackspace, etc. that leases third-party cloud resource to the consumer. However, a cloud could be public even when third-party cloud resources are not used; the most important aspect of a public cloud is its content. A community cloud is a cloud specifically consumed by a particular set of community, such as financial institutions cloud, health services cloud, etc. An agency cloud is a form of community cloud solely for the military, agency, or defence institutions, such as the Defense Information Systems Agency (DISA) cloud [4] and the NBC Federal Computing Cloud [5]. Agency clouds are not for public consumption. They are regulated and operated by the agencies themselves. A private (localised) cloud is an enterprise-owned cloud exclusively accessed for its operation or activity. It is not shared or co-owned with another enterprise, such as the Microsoft Azure on-premise platform cloud [5]. A hybrid cloud comprises two or more clouds, such as a private cloud joining another vendor's provisioned public cloud. For current cloud offerings, see Fig. 16.2 [4].

Cloud Market Types	Types of Offerings	Examples
Software-as-a-Service	• Rich Internet application web sites • Application as Web Sites • Collaboration and email • Office Productivity • Client apps that connect to services in the cloud	• Flikr • Myspace.com • Cisco WebEx office • Gmail • IBM Bluehouse
App-components-as-a-Service	• APIs for specific service access for integration • Web-based software service than can combine to create new services, as in a mashup	• Amazon Flexible Payments Service and DevPay • Salesforce.com's AppExchange • Yahoo! Maps API • Google Calendar API • zembly
Software-platform-as-a-Service	• Development-platform-as-a-service • Database • Message Queue • App Servicer • Blob or object data stores	• Google App Engine and BigTable • Microsoft SQL Server Data Services • Engine Yard • Salesforce.com's Force.com
Virtual Infrastructure-as-a-Service	• Virtual servers • Logical disks • VLAN networks • Systems Management	• Akamai • Amazon EC2 • CohesiveFT • Mosso (from Rackspace) • Joyent Accelerators • Nirvanix Storage Delivery Network
Physical Infrastructure	• Managed Hosting • Collocation • Internet Service Provider • Unmanaged hosting	• GoDaddy.com • Rackspace • Savvis

Fig. 16.2 Current cloud market offering [4]

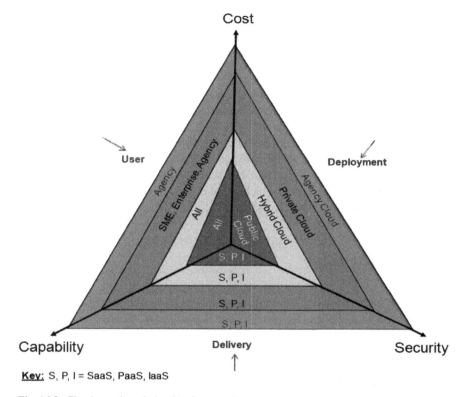

Key: S, P, I = SaaS, PaaS, IaaS

Fig. 16.3 Cloud security relationship framework

The risks inherent in cloud computing are similar irrespective of the cloud model in use; however, there are unique security and information assurance requirements for each cloud deployment model. For example, security requirements for private clouds are different from that of a public cloud. Private clouds are perceived to be more secure than public clouds. Similarly, privacy concerns vary from private to public clouds.

To provide a realistic risk management to cloud computing, each cloud deployment model must be evaluated in its own right. In this respect, a cloud security relationship framework is proposed to provide this assessment (see Fig. 16.3). A cloud security relationship model is a theoretical framework to evaluate cloud deployment and delivery models based on security, cost and capability requirements.

16.3   Understanding Risks to Cloud Computing

A major concern with cloud computing is that the cloud provider offers the resources in the cloud, that is, the software, platform and infrastructure to the user (cloud consumer). In addition, user data/information also reside with the cloud provider. The risk with this type of service is that user information could be abused, stolen, unlawfully distributed, compromised or harmed. There is no guarantee that user's information/data could not be sold to its competitor. Unfortunately, this particular risk applies to all the three types of cloud delivery models, namely, SaaS, PaaS and IaaS.

Other risks to cloud computing also exist, and range from privacy, data protection, ownership, location and lack of reliable audit standard to data security procedure of most pioneer cloud providers, such as Google, Amazon, etc. According to Rick Gordon of Civitas Group, a concern with regard to cloud providers, especially Google Apps includes the lack of reliable security audit standard, data lock-in and Google's opacity regarding its internal data security procedures [7].

In this section, risks to cloud computing are discussed with the view to outlining technical, administrative and ethical controls to provide guidance to cloud users.

16.3.1 Privacy Issues

Privacy even with traditional information security systems and networks is difficult to satisfy, and is a challenging issue to cloud computing. Cloud computing has significant implications for the privacy of personal information as well as maintaining the confidentiality of business and government information [6]. Concerns over privacy with current cloud computing offerings are apparent and real. For example, in a letter from Pam Dixon, executive director of the World Privacy Forum to the Los Angeles Mayor, Antonio Villaragosa, it was stated that, 'our concern is that the transfer of so many City records to a cloud computing provider may threaten the privacy rights of City residents, undermine the security of other sensitive information, violate both state and federal laws, and potentially damage vital City legal and other interests [7]'. This concern is valid and true, especially with public clouds where sensitive individual and corporate information is put in the hands of third-party cloud providers, whose cloud infrastructure may not be regulated, and could traverse through geographical borders that impact both legal and regulatory requirements of the information being transported or stored.

Further, information in the cloud is perceived to have weaker privacy governance over that held in a personal physical computer system [6]. Hence, cloud users must be aware of the terms of contract they sign with a provider, and should be informed of the provider's privacy and security guidelines and practices.

We recommend that privacy and security requirements of the different forms of cloud models are investigated and assessed, because not all cloud models raise the same privacy and confidentiality issues. As shown in Fig. 16.3, each cloud model offers unique security requirements, privacy capabilities and varying cost implications. For example, private or agency clouds are most suitable for protectively marked materials or classified information, but are more expensive to operate, while public clouds are suitable for personal non-confidential information such as sharing photos or pictures with friends.

Again, it is important that cloud consumers (individual or corporate) assess the information requirements and understand the underlying regulatory and compliance requirements of their assets before migrating such assets to the cloud. Otherwise, they risk violating or undermining privacy, regulatory and compliance requirements of such assets.

Finally, users must apply due diligence on each cloud provider they intend to use, and must ensure that the necessary privacy laws are included in the service contract issued by the cloud provider.

16.3.2   Data Ownership and Content Disclosure Issues

Another issue to consider before migrating to the cloud includes ownership of information or data residing on the provider's cloud. The moment a user puts data to the cloud, not only could the privacy of the data be lost, but also the ownership 'authority' over the data and right of disclosure could well be lost (by alienating ownership to the cloud provider). Although the lawful ownership and right of disclosure remains with the originating data owner, this could change quite quickly. Some providers retain the right of disclosure as data custodians, while others do not. This practice is gradually changing depending on the terms of the contract, which the provider issues to its customers.

There is a concern when the cloud provider becomes both the data owner and the data custodian. Even with traditional IT services, it is best practice to have separation of duties, where a different individual is the data owner, while another individual or group is the data custodian. This shifting paradigm with the cloud means that the cloud provider is both the data owner and data custodian for all data stored or transmitted from their cloud, including data from 'delinquent organisations', such as cybercriminals and organised crime groups. This practice violates the principle of separation of duties and job rotation; a fundamental principle of information security best practices.

We recommend that cloud users protectively mark their information and explicitly specify the ownership of information in the service contract. The service contract must be signed and indorsed by the cloud provider in form of a declaration. Protective marking is an administrative control used to classify information assets based on the degree of sensitivity afforded to that asset. For example, information can be protectively marked as 'TOP SECRET', 'SECRET', CONFIDENTIAL, etc.

16.3.3   Data Confidentiality

When a user puts information to a public cloud, what control does that user have over the data, its confidentiality, integrity or availability? When we consider small to medium-sized organisations or individual users, one could easily discuss the risks associated with cloud computing services. What happens to the government, the enterprise in relation to the cloud? Can the cloud be used for government-protected marked information? For example, 'SECRET' document for defence agencies, such as for the CIA, MI5 or the MOD. I certainly do not think so, especially at this current stage of the cloud. These agencies have their own clouds, such as the MOD cloud, the DISA cloud, etc.; however, what is put in these clouds are still of great concern. It is pertinent to note that cloud computing is not ideal for all use cases. For example, protectively marked information asset up to the level of 'SECRET' or 'TOP SECRET' is not suitable for cloud computing (see Fig. 16.4). Similarly, 'STRICTEST IN CONFIDENCE' and 'IN CONFIDENCE' data may not be suitable for the cloud.

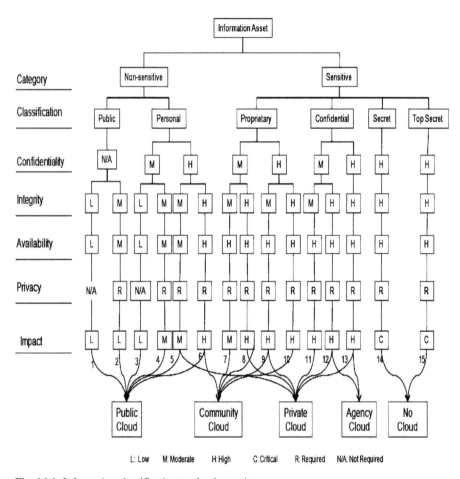

Fig. 16.4 Information classification to cloud mapping

We recommend a risk-management approach when evaluating information assets to be migrated to the cloud, giving conscious attention to the security and information assurance requirements of those assets.

16.3.4 Data Location

Where does the data that an end-user has created on an MCSP's system reside? Location of end-user data is of great importance. For example, the EU Directive on Data Protection (Safe Harbour [8,9]) stipulates countries where EU private and personal data can and cannot reside or traverse.

The EU Directive on Data Protection of 1998 [9] is a comprehensive data protection legislation that orders its member states to establish a legal framework to protect the fundamental rights to privacy with respect to processing personal data that has *extraterritorial effect*. It prohibits the transfer of personal data or health records data to non-EU nations that do not meet the European '*adequacy*' standard for privacy protection. The US and the EU share the goal of enhancing privacy protection for their citizens [9]. Clearly, achieving regulatory and legislative compliance in the cloud requires concerted effort from both the user and the provider, where the user knows the information requirements and is able to communicate that clearly to the provider, and in return, the provider is transparent and thus willing to address the regulatory and legislative mandates required with regard to the assets.

With the infrastructure as a service, the cloud provider can dynamically use localised infrastructures that exist outside the EU or US territories. This may contravene or abuse fundamental privacy and legislative mandates, especially if the end-user is not aware of where the information is held or transported to/from. This applies specifically to EU and US cloud consumers, SMEs, government and enterprise who may wish to use the cloud for delivering service. Other countries have other legislations that should be considered when using the cloud. Certain types of assets may easily be abused with cloud computing, for instance, personal medical data (health record data) are subjected to strict compliance act, such as the health information privacy and portability act (HIPPA). A significant concern is that personal medical data can be easily circumvented with the SaaS or IaaS models of the cloud. This highlights some of the inherent risks that exist with cloud computing [10].

That being said, there are cloud providers that operate territorial cloud service. For example, there are UK cloud providers that lease zoned UK only localised resources. In addition, there are US and Canadian cloud providers that offer localised provincial cloud services.

Cloud users whose information assets require location-specific data storage or transit requirements must confirm these with cloud providers that offer location-based cloud service, and must ensure that they are included in the service contract offered by the cloud provider.

16.3.5 Control Issues

It is not until recently that many cloud security interest groups, such as the Cloud Security Alliance [11], the Cloud Computing Interoperability Group [12] and the Multi-Agency Cloud Computing Forum [4] began to seek ways of delivering efficient and effective controls in the cloud to ensure that information in the cloud are secure and protected.

Currently, clouds are hugely uncontrolled, especially the public ones. Recommendations like the use of legal, regulatory, compliance and certification practices have been suggested in order to adequately control cloud services and practices [3,11,12]. Unfortunately, maintaining compliance with regulatory and legislative requirements in the cloud can be much more difficult to demonstrate. The attributes of cloud computing as being location-independent, with unclear borders and boundaries, providing shared pool of resources on a multi-tenancy architecture further make achieving demonstrable regulatory security compliance untenable.

The legal landscape, regulatory compliance and certification are constantly changing, and organisation must understand and evaluate current legal, regulatory compliance needs of their information before moving them to the cloud.

16.3.6 Regulatory and Legislative Compliance

Regulatory compliance and certification are security initiatives with significant impact on information security practices [8]. Standards regulate how information security management is being implemented, managed and conducted. For example, ISO 27001–2005 is a security standard that recommends best practices for information security management. Organisations seeking accreditation go through a regulatory compliance process. Compliant organisations are perceived to possess essential drivers to earn trust, and hence, attract business relations with other organisations. This proposition applies to cloud computing. In fact, obtaining certification to a particular standard is not going to be the only driver, and the coverage of each security accreditation or certification is anticipated to contribute towards establishing trust. Furthermore, compliance to regulatory authorities will certainly earn some 'Brownie points' for corporate organisations. For example, corporate organisations that are regulated by the financial services authority (FSA) must seek advice before using public clouds for their operations or risk of facing huge fines, and could possibly lose their practicing license. There should be guidance on what corporate financial institutions can put out in the cloud and what may not be permissible. As the cloud phenomenon unfolds and inherent risks understood, adequate guidelines must follow.

The legal landscape of traditional IT is continuously changing. A significant concern is that some of these legislations are territorial, even within a country, with separate pieces of jurisdiction. For example, the California Security Breach Information Act (SB-1386) legislation mandates Californian organisations that maintain personal information about individuals to inform those individuals if the security of their information is compromised [13]. This piece of legislation stipulates the disclosure of security breaches only in California. The application of SB-1386 and other legislations in the cloud are unclear.

16.3.7 Forensic Evidence Issues

Information security forensic evidence and e-discovery possess a challenge too. In the cloud, what information constitutes legally acceptable forensic evidence? How is such information received in relation to the different cloud deployment models? If evidence is gathered from a public cloud, how authentic is that information perceived to be compared with when similar information is obtained from a private cloud? Similarly, with pre-trial discovery and e-discovery, as the cloud provider is the data custodian, while the user is the lawful owner of the data, who should provide pre-trial evidence in a court of law, and who is responsible with respect to discovery and other litigation subjects? With copies of most information at different clouds, which information/data constitutes an authentic copy of the information that is admissible in a court of law?

It is pertinent to note that the different cloud deployment models offer varying levels of security, privacy and acceptability; therefore, it is imperative that cloud users must evaluate the security, legal, regulatory and legislative requirements of their valued assets before choosing a particular cloud model, and a cloud vendor or provider.

16.3.8 Auditing Issues

Auditing for security management aims to evaluate policies, practices, operations and technical controls of an organisation in order to assess compliance, detection, protection and security forensics [14]. The need for regular security audits is essential, and should not focus only on the reactive audits done when an incident has occurred, but also on proactive security audits done in order to assess whether security controls, security processes, procedures and operations are adequate and practical in protecting critical assets of the organisation. Two factors make demonstrating security audit in the cloud a critical issue:

First, cloud providers must demonstrate their security audit procedure to their customers. Second, the level of audit coverage being conducted must be acceptable, bearing in mind the myriad of diverse and varied information assets that the cloud providers are data custodians for.

Auditing security requirements in a cloud environment can be difficult and significantly challenging [15]. One approach to addressing auditing issues in the cloud is transparency from the cloud provider in managing information security. That is, the cloud provider must make its customers aware of its audit processes and the different levels of audit coverage. In this way trust and good relationship between the provider and its customers can be achieved.

16.3.9 Business Continuity and Disaster Recovery Issues

Cloud computing is dynamic and offers ubiquitous network access to vast amount of significant resources, and these resources are meant to be available swiftly and on-demand to legitimate users. Unfortunately, there have been cases when the availability of data in the cloud has become a major concern. For example, Amazon's Elastic Compute Cloud (EC2) service in North America was temporarily unavailable at significant times due to 'lightning storm that caused damage to a single power distribution unit (PDU) in a single availability zone [16]'. This highlights the importance of disaster recovery and business continuity plans in the cloud. The availability of resources in the cloud is of least importance to users according to most surveys. This is because the cloud offers ubiquitous and on-demand network access. Unfortunately, information in the cloud could still be unavailable when needed due to natural disasters, vulnerability exploits and deliberate attacks.

There are three reasons why cloud users must be concerned with the availability of their valued assets in the cloud. First, most cloud providers rent computing and data-centre infrastructures from other cloud providers. This means that when one cloud infrastructure is affected (unavailable), most probably, other providers will suffer similar losses, hindering the availability of resources to a wilder audience much more possible than with the traditional IT networks.

Second, the possibility that a cloud provider can file for bankruptcy, where the provider goes out of business with consequential financial liability to offset makes the availability of cloud resources a serious issue to consider. Finally, cross-vulnerability in the cloud due to the multi-tenancy implementation of cloud infrastructures and services makes the availability of resources in the cloud an important issue to consider.

In these respects, we recommend that users engage with their cloud providers to understand their disaster recovery processes and procedures, and where possible, make inputs as to how best this can be achieved. For instance, users may be provided backup copies of data on a monthly basis as part of the agreement. This practice can be extremely helpful, for example, in the case of bankruptcy of a cloud provider, or when natural disaster threatens the existence of a data centre. Further, users must be aware of their provider's business continuity plans, for instance, whether the provider has hot-standby sites and whether resilience is built as an abstraction to all layers of its services.

16.3.10 Trust Issues

Trust in both the traditional IT services and cloud computing must be earned. Trust is a major issue with cloud computing irrespective of the cloud model being deployed. Nevertheless, the cloud like traditional IT services can be secured, protected and dependable. It is believed that the cloud offers security advantages.

For example, intruders do not have access to the source code and providers often work hard to provide clean, unbreakable barriers between the customers [17]. However, this requires conscientious effort from both cloud providers and users; in addition, cloud providers must be transparent about their security policies, audit practices, data backup procedures and certification/accreditation. Once users are comfortable with a particular provider's practices, together with the service level agreement (SLA) agreed upon, they are more willing to do business.

Nevertheless, cloud users must be open-minded and must not whole-heartedly trust a provider just because of the written-down service offerings, without carrying out appropriate due diligence on the provider and where certain policies are not explicit, they should ensure that missing policies are included in the service contract. By understanding the different trust boundaries, each cloud computing model assists users when making decision as to which cloud model they can adopt or deploy. For example, with infrastructure cloud computing, a great trust relationship is created because user data backup is possible and applicable, where copies of a user's data are backed up. Similarly, there is a possibility for the user to create and configure additional and customised access controls to protect its data. This level of trust is not possible with software cloud computing, for instance.

16.3.11   Security Policy Issues

Whose security policy governs the cloud, the user or the MCSP? Obviously, the cloud provider's security policy is what stipulates acceptance uses, specifies service level agreements and governs the cloud environment. What if the security policy of the MCSP is not acceptable to a cloud user, because the policy may be missing some policies that the users consider essential towards achieving the security and information assurance requirements for their assets? To ensure that information assets in the cloud are adequately maintained, we recommend that cloud users must:

* Carry out due diligence on the provider
* Appropriately classify the information assets to determine their security, regulatory and compliance requirements
* Consider the viability of each cloud model in relation to their information assets requirements
* Consider return on investment (RoI) of the cloud in relation to the security of the asset

16.3.12   Emerging Threats to Cloud Computing

New and unfamiliar threats to cloud computing are emerging. Examples include cross-virtual machine (VM) exploits, inter-processor exploits and cross-application vulnerability exploits. Although most of these widely publicised attacks to cloud computing are theoretical [18], it is possible that within the next couple of years, these attacks may be realised. Therefore, precautionary measures must be put in place; mitigation plans and risk treatment plans must exist to address emerging vulnerability exploits and current attacks to cloud computing.

Above all, to appropriately profile cloud computing risks, each cloud service and deployment model must be evaluated against its security requirements (see Fig. 16.4).

16.4   Cloud Security Relationship Framework

Managing security in the cloud is different from managing security in traditional IT systems or networks. The difference is significant from the level of trust of machine data to management of information in the cloud. Cloud computing is a new and emerging technology, and hence, inherent and cumulative risks to cloud computing are new, evolving and unfamiliar. Like any new technology, new and unfamiliar risks exist. Therefore, conscientious effort must be dedicated towards understanding risks that exist, in addition to finding appropriate ways of addressing such risks.

The current stage of the cloud is very immature. A lot of the offerings are geared towards adopters with little to no risk and a lot to gain from low-cost, pay-as-you-go resources [19]. Thus, current cloud computing deployments are not suitable for all use cases. However, like other utility services, such as electricity, cloud computing can be secured. To make the cloud secure, security must be built into every aspect of the cloud starting from its foundation stage.

To understand risks associated with cloud computing, risks that exist with traditional IT must be properly evaluated (as discussed in Section 3), while new and emerging risks to the cloud are investigated on a per cloud service and deployment model basis. To assist with this assessment, a framework is proposed (see Fig. 16.3). A cloud security relationship framework is a framework for assessing cloud computing offerings (cloud service model, cloud deployment model and use cases) on the basis of cost, security and capability. The cloud computing framework comprises three components, *deployment*, *delivery* and *user*. These components are evaluated against three metrics, *cost*, *security* and *capability*.

Cost relates to the amount that users pay to use a particular cloud computing service operating on a specific delivery model in a given deployment. A *cloud delivery model* is a cloud computing service, for instance, SaaS, PaaS and IaaS, where each delivery model provides a set of specific functionalities. A *cloud deployment model* is a cloud computing type that offers a set of unique attributes and coverage, such as private, public, hybrid, community, localised, virtual private and external clouds. There is a considerable number of cloud computing models currently being used and developed. These terminologies are used loosely in many publications today; however, early taxonomies are provided in [20,21].

Security relates to the protection afforded to cloud computing services, such as confidentiality, integrity and availability. It is difficult to quantify security offerings in the cloud. Thus, instead of using formal (mathematical) metrics as those discussed by Pfleeger [22], we have used metrics (low, medium and high) that are in current use and applicable to many use cases. In this study, low security is when one security requirement (confidentiality, integrity and availability) can be achieved; medium security is when two of the requirements are achievable, while high is when all the three requirements can be achieved.

Capability relates to the variety of offerings available with each cloud computing deployment. There is a direct relationship between cost and security of the cloud deployment models, such as public, community, agency, hybrid and private. This implies that private clouds provide 'pre-requisite' security requirements when compared with hybrid or public clouds. Similarly, the cost implication for the same type of service grows from public to private clouds, while the capability (service-offering capabilities) is directly related to the cloud service type deployed. For example, infrastructure cloud computing (IaaS) offers more capabilities than PaaS or SaaS.

It is pertinent to note that not all cloud computing deployment models (public, private, agency, community and hybrid) raise the same security concerns, or offer the same confidentiality, integrity, availability or privacy of data or information. Certain cloud deployments are most appropriate to certain organisations. For example, government, financial or health institutions are more inclined to hybrid or private clouds than public clouds. Similarly, users transmitting or storing classified information, such as confidential information, should use hybrid or private clouds (see Fig. 16.4), while agencies, such as MOD, CIA or DISA, must use agency or privately operated clouds.

The cloud security framework (see Fig. 16.3) must be used in conjunction with the information assets classification model (see Fig. 16.4) when deciding which information assets need to be mitigated to the cloud.

We have shown that based on security and privacy requirements of information assets (confidentiality, integrity, privacy and impact), some assets are not suitable for the cloud. For example, 'SECRET' and 'TOP SECRET' information assets (information assets #14 and #15) are not suitable for the cloud (see Fig. 16.4).

Similarly, information assets #12 and #13 require minimum agency cloud, but can also use private clouds. Information asset #13, for instance, is classified as 'confidential' and needs high confidentiality, high integrity, high availability and privacy requirements. However, if this asset is to be compromised, then the impact to the organisation will be critical. Therefore, based on the information requirements and impact level of this information asset, agency cloud, at the minimum, is required to host, store and transport this asset.

Information assets #1–#6 can be hosted in a public cloud, and information assets #6–#10 require a community cloud of some sort. For example, a financial community cloud, if the information assets are owned by a financial institution, or a health community cloud, if owned by a medical or health institution.

Note that while information asset #5, for example, may require at the minimum a public cloud, this information asset may well be hosted in a private cloud too. The zoning of information assets to clouds is done based on the minimum security and privacy requirements of that information asset (see Fig. 16.4).

16.4.1 Security Requirements in the Clouds

A private (localised) cloud is a solely owned cloud, operated and used by an enterprise. It may be regulated and governed like other clouds, and most importantly, it is for 'restricted' users only. Private clouds are more secure than public clouds, and therefore, private clouds are most suitable for transmitting classified information, such as confidential and/or proprietary information. Information assets with lesser security requirements, such as personal information may still use a private cloud (see Fig. 16.4). It is pertinent to note that the use of a private cloud offers no guarantee as to the security or privacy of the information assets that it stores or transports. For example, the use of Microsoft Azure on-premise cloud platform does not provide any guarantee to the security and compliance of information that is stored or transported using this cloud. We recommend that organisations seeking to use the cloud for classified information or regulated transactions should use a private cloud, but must do so bearing in mind that the necessary security requirements of that information asset are constantly assessed and reviewed. Furthermore, private clouds come with a prize; for instance, the cost to rent, deploy or operate a private cloud is comparably and considerably higher than a public cloud.

A public cloud is an open cloud maintained by a cloud vendor for the general use of everyone including cybercriminals. A public cloud is most probably the most currently used cloud, such as Salesforce, Amazon EC2 and Amazon web services (see Fig. 16.2, [4]). A public cloud is relatively safe and offers a wide range of capability at reduced cost.

Agency clouds, like private clouds, are perceived to be secure and reliable because they are privately owned by the military or defence agencies. Hence, rigorous and complex security requirements are thought to be applied. Defence agency cloud may require separate legal, regulatory and security compliance measures different from those of public clouds. For example, the DISA cloud is subject to government legislation, while UK government clouds would be subject to CESG information assurance compliance and protective handling.

A community cloud is governed by the regulatory controls of that community,for example, health and financial institutions clouds. Integrated (hybrid) clouds combine a set of requirements from two or more co-joining clouds. These requirements are bound to vary depending on the specific requirements of the co-joining clouds. It is an illusion to think that hybrid clouds provide 'high' security. Each cloud must be assessed in its own right to determine its privacy, security and regulatory policies and practices.

16.5 Conclusion

Cloud computing is an emerging technology that offers unparalleled distributed computing resources at affordable infrastructure and operating costs. The cloud requires conscientious and diligent attention from both users and providers due to the inherent risks associated with its operating paradigm, such as ubiquitous network access, multi-tenancy service delivery, location independence, homogeneity and openness.

In this chapter, cloud computing has been explained. Three of the widely used cloud services, namely, software computing, platform computing and infrastructure computing, and five of the deployment models, namely, private (localised), public, community, agency and hybrid clouds have been discussed.

Cloud computing, like existing utility services such as electricity, water and telephone, can be secure, safe and reliable; however, this can be achieved when security issues that exist with traditional IT services are evaluated in relation to cloud computing. Unfortunately, cloud computing offers varying levels of security and privacy based on the cloud model being deployed.

The proposed cloud security framework to assess cloud offerings provides a systematic assessment of cloud computing services based on cost, capability and security. It has been shown that the three cloud service models offered unique security requirements. Similarly, the capability of the deployment models (public, community, agency, private and hybrid) has been found to be unique and varied.

As organisations use the framework and information classification model proposed in this chapter to evaluate cloud services and information requirement respectively, we recommend that they do so by knowing that not all information assets should be migrated to the cloud.

About the Author

Dr. Cyril Onwubiko is a CLAS Consultant at Cable and Wireless, where he is responsible for providing information assurance to information assets of varying business impact levels (ILs) in accordance with the HMG security policy framework. Cyril is also currently the chair of the Security and Information Assurance Committee, E-Security Group at Research Series.

Prior to C&W, Cyril was an Information Security Consultant at British Telecom (BT), providing strategic information security undertakings. Earlier, Cyril worked at COLT Telecommunications Group for 8 years, participating in several projects, while helping COLT develop their IP VPN service – IP Corporate, a Pan-European IP VPN service for managed customers. Cyril also assisted COLT to roll out their enterprise-MPLS VPN core and was a focal engineer supporting SWIFT. He is experienced in VPN Security, Security Information and Event Management (SIEM), Data Fusion, IDS and Computer Network Security, and knowledgeable in Information Assurance, HMG Security Policy Framework (SPF) and Risk Assessment and Management.

Cyril holds a Ph.D. in Computer Network Security from Kingston University, London, UK, a Masters of Science degree (M.Sc.) in Internet Engineering from the University of East London, London, UK and a Bachelors of Science and Technology degree (B.Sc.), first class honours, in Computer Science and Mathematics from Federal University of Technology, Owerri. He is the author of two books, 'Security Framework for Attack Detection in Computer Networks' and 'Concepts in Numerical Methods'.

References

1. Mell P, Grance T (2009) Draft NIST working definition of cloud computing. http://csrc.nist. gov/groups/SNS/cloud-computing/index.html. Accessed 16 Sept 2009
2. Mell P, Grance T (2009, August 12) Effectively and securely using the cloud computing paradigm, NIST
3. Kaufman LM (2009 July/August) Data security in the world of cloud computing. IEEE Sec Priv 7(4):61–64
4. Greenfield T (2009) Cloud computing in a military context – Beyond the Hype, Defense Information Systems Agency (DISA), DISA Office of the CTO. http://www.govinfosecurity. com/regulations.php?reg_id = 1432. Accessed 20 Sept 2009
5. NBC Federal Cloud Playbook (2009) National business center, Department of the Interior, Washington DC. http://cloud.nbc.gov/PDF/NBC%20Cloud%20White%20Paper%20 Final%20(Web%20Res).pdf. Accessed 23 Sept 2009
6. Microsoft Azure Services, http://www.microsoft.com/azure/services.mspx. Accessed 23 Sept 2009
7. Gellman R (2009) Privacy in the clouds: risks to privacy and confidentiality from cloud computing. http://www.worldprivacyforum.org/pdf/WPF_Cloud_Privacy_Report.pdf. Accessed 17 Sept 2009
8. Claburn T (2009) Google Apps contract in LA hits security Headwind, http://www.informationweek.com/news/showArticle.jhtml?articleID=218501443. InformationWeek. Accessed 20 July 2009
9. Onwubiko C, Lenaghan A (2009, March) Challenges and complexities of managing information security. Int J Elect Sec Digit Forensic IJESDF 3(2). ISSN (Online): 1751-9128 – ISSN (Print): 1751-911X
10. Safe Harbour (1998) European commission's directive on data privacy and protection legislation, http://www.export.gov/safeharbor/SafeHarborInfo.htm. Accessed 17 Sept 2009
11. Onwubiko C (2008) Security framework for attack detection in computer networks. VDM Verlag, Germany
12. Cloud Security Alliance (2009), http://www.cloudsecurityalliance.org/. Accessed 19 Sept 2009
13. Cloud Computing Interoperability Forum (2009), http://www.cloudforum.org/. Accessed 17 Sept 2009
14. SB-1386, The California Security Breach Information Act (2002) SB1386 amending civil codes 1798.29, 1798.82 and 1798.84. http://en.wikipedia.org/wiki/SB_1386. Accessed 20 Sept 2009
15. Onwubiko C (2009), A security audit framework for security management in the enterprise. Commun Inform Sci 45:9–17, Springer. ISSN 1865-0929 (Print) 1865-0937 (Online)
16. Chaput SR (2009) Compliance and audit, security guidance for critical areas of focus in cloud computing, Cloud Security Alliance
17. Cohen R (2009) Lightning knocks out amazon's compute cloud. Cloud Comput J. http:// cloudcomputing.sys-con.com/node/998582. Accessed 11 June 2009
18. Viega J (August 2009) Cloud computing and the common man. IEEE Comput 42(8):106–108
19. Ristenpart T, Tromer E, Shacham H, Savage S (2009) Hay, you, get off of my cloud: exploring information leakage in third-party compute clouds. ACM Computer Communications Security Conference CCS'09, November 2009
20. Cheesbrough P (2008, Dec) Into the cloud, lessons from the early adopters of cloud computing. Information Age
21. Youseff L et al. (2009) Toward a unified ontology of cloud computing. http://www.cs.ucsb. edu/~lyouseff/CCOntology/CloudOntology.pdf Accessed 15 Sept 2009
22. OpenCrowd (2009) The OpenCrowd cloud taxonomy. http://www.opencrowd.com/views/ cloud.php. Accessed 26 Sept 2009
23. Pfleeger SL (May/June 2009) Useful cybersecurity metrics. IEE IT Pro J 11(3):38–45

Chapter 17
Securing the Cloud

James P. Durbano, Derek Rustvold, George Saylor, and John Studarus

Abstract Despite the excitement surrounding the cloud, a relatively small percentage of organizations have actually begun incorporating cloud computing into their technology portfolios. Of the many obstacles to adopting the cloud model of delivery and consumption of computing resources, the number one concern, from users to CIOs/CTOs, is security. The lack of strong security controls can resonate through the cloud, opening all of the applications and services that are running across the cloud to exploitation. In this chapter, we examine cloud security, focusing our discussion on gaps within the existing ISO 27002 security controls when applied to cloud computing. These gaps are used to build a list of potential security concerns that may not be addressed by traditional (non-cloud) data center policy and procedures. Using the results of this gap analysis, a set of recommendations on how to incorporate security into the cloud is provided. Additionally, case studies of both public- and private-cloud provider security mechanisms are presented.

Abbreviations

AWS	Amazon Web Services
CIO	Chief Information Officer
CTO	Chief Technical Officer
EC2	Elastic Compute Cloud (Amazon EC2)
FIMSA	Federal Information Security Management Act
GLBA	Gramm–Leach–Bliley Act
HIPAA	Health Information Portability and Accountability Act
ISO	International Organization for Standardization
IT	Information Technology
NIST	National Institute of Standards and Technology
RAM	Random Access Memory

J.P. Durbano (⊠)
Northrop Grumman 1840 Century Park East Los Angeles, CA 90067-2199, USA
e-mail: james.durbano@ngc.com

N. Antonopoulos and L. Gillam (eds.), *Cloud Computing: Principles, Systems and Applications*, Computer Communications and Networks, DOI 10.1007/978-1-84996-241-4_17, © Springer-Verlag London Limited 2010

SLA   Service Level Agreement
SOX   Sarbanes–Oxley

17.1 Introduction

Cloud computing represents an exciting evolution of application and infrastructure solutions, prompting Information Technology (IT) departments around the world to investigate what the cloud can do for their organizations. Despite the excitement surrounding the cloud, a relatively small percentage of organizations have actually begun leveraging cloud computing, citing concerns such as vendor lock-in, lack of acceptable service-level agreements (SLAs), and limited governance procedures. Of the many obstacles to adopting the cloud model of delivery and consumption of computing resources, the number one concern, from commercial users to developers to CIOs/ CTOs, is security [1]. These concerns are motivated by a variety of factors including:

1. Handing over control of hardware resources to a third party
2. The fact that other companies (including competitors) may also utilize the same cloud platform
3. Meeting the requirements of existing regulations

The lack of strong security controls can resonate throughout the cloud, opening all of the applications and services to exploitation. Put simply, a single vulnerability can contaminate the entire cloud. Providing a cloud environment with strong, demonstrable security controls is desired by all cloud users. In fact, certain user communities, such as those subject to regulatory compliance, must maintain strong security controls in order to consider the cloud a viable platform. For example, government customers must satisfy FISMA [2], healthcare providers are bound by HIPAA [3], publicly traded companies follow SOX [4], and financial institutions are subject to GLBA [5].

To secure the cloud, we begin by applying traditional data center security techniques. However, the very nature of cloud computing (i.e., multitenant, geographically distributed, virtualized, etc.) introduces new security challenges. A structured approach to identifying these security issues includes an analysis of the new technologies introduced by cloud computing and a gap analysis against current standards, such as the ISO 27002 security controls.

In this chapter, we examine cloud security. It is impossible to present a complete overview of cloud security issues and possible resolutions in the context of a single chapter, and the reader is referred to the excellent work being performed by organizations such as the Cloud Security Alliance [6]. For this reason, we focus our discussion on gaps within the existing ISO 27002 security controls when applied to cloud computing. These gaps are used to build a list of potential security concerns that may not be addressed by traditional (noncloud) datacenter policy and procedures. Using the results of this gap analysis, a set of recommendations on how to incorporate security into the cloud is provided.

17.1.1   What Is Security?

Before we can discuss how to secure the cloud, we must first define what is meant by "security." What does it mean to have a "secure" cloud? What aspects must be addressed by any cloud security solution?

For the purposes of this chapter, we state that a "secure" cloud is one that addresses the following information security principles: confidentiality, integrity, availability, identity, authentication, authorization, and auditing. Representative questions from potential cloud adopters include:

- *Confidentiality*: Can anyone else see my data when it is in the cloud?
- *Integrity*: Can anyone else modify my data when it is in the cloud?
- *Availability*: Will my data/applications always be up and running? What if the cloud provider goes out of business?
- *Authentication*: When people access my data and applications, how does the cloud ensure that they are who they claim to be?
- *Authorization*: How does the cloud ensure that people can only access the data and applications that they are allowed to access?
- *Auditing*: How can I verify that all of these items are consistently addressed?

Now that we have sufficiently scoped our definition of security, we examine the existing security controls to identify gaps in coverage associated with cloud computing.

17.2   ISO 27002 Gap Analyses

ISO 27002 (formerly ISO 17799) "establishes guidelines and general principles for initiating, implementing, maintaining, and improving information security management in an organization" [7]. Although the standard offers a high-level description for providing information security, it does not include detailed information on how the security controls should be implemented.

By comparing the ISO 27002 security controls against the technologies and use cases of cloud computing, a number of security gaps were identified and are discussed below. Because cloud computing extensively leverages virtualization technologies, much of the discussion is focused on virtualization gaps.

This information is intended to provide a high-level overview of some of the challenges associated with securing the cloud. There are additional gaps against the ISO standard that are not discussed and many other issues to consider. The interested reader is referred to [6] for more details.

Because ISO 27002 is organized around "families" of related controls, our discussion follows this organization. In this section, we address the following ISO 27002 families:

- Asset Management
- Communications and Operations Management

- Information Systems Acquisition, Development, and Maintenance
- Information Security Incident Management
- Compliance

17.2.1   Asset Management

The goal of Asset Management controls is to protect organizational assets. Within this family, gaps were identified in the following: Asset Tracking.

Traditionally, physical access is required to insert new servers into the network. In a cloud data center, virtual environments can be provisioned without the need for physical access to the network. Thus, it may be possible to have rogue virtual servers on the network. Controls must be introduced to track these new virtual assets across the network to make sure appropriate security measures are in place.

Also, it is important to develop a consistent naming scheme for servers on the network in order to maintain accurate logs and to track events. Naming schemes for data center hosts are typically location- and application-centric. However, these schemes are not always applicable to virtual servers, which migrate from server to server and even across physical sites. Similarly, servers may be shared by multiple applications, making application-based naming ineffective.

Finally, in a virtualized data center, there will be virtual devices that may come and go as instances are modified. Instances are simply cloud resources, and could represent virtual machines, software-as-a-service modules, storage units, etc. Examples of virtual devices include network interfaces, consoles, serial ports, USB ports, floppy, CD ROMs, and storage systems. These virtual devices could be used to gain unauthorized access to the system or to copy data on/off the instances.

17.2.2   Communications and Operations Management

The goal of Communications and Operations Management controls is to maintain the availability and integrity of information and equipment. Within this family, gaps were identified in the following controls: Change Management, Capacity Management, System Utility Access Control, Patch Management, System Audits, Media Destruction and System Reuse, Data Encryption, Logging and Monitoring, and Backups.

Change Management: Existing data center change control processes are simplified by the fact that many times individual hosts are assigned exclusively to an application. In a cloud environment, one physical server typically runs many virtual machines and is responsible for a number of business tasks. Thus, a change to a single host may impact multiple applications within the data center.

Capacity Management: There are three primary issues associated with capacity management in the cloud. First, the cloud environment must be effectively sized. One of the benefits of using a cloud environment is the ability to rapidly provision new instances. As such, there must be mechanisms in place to determine the number of instances the existing infrastructure can handle without impacting business tasks.

Second, all applications running within the same physical segment of the cloud are, in effect, competing with each other for the same CPU, memory, storage, and networking resources. Because of this, it may be possible for a single application to cause a denial-of-service attack within the cloud by demanding a large amount of resources (thereby negatively impacting other applications).

Finally, an application 'X' running in a cloud may be able to gather information about the state of other applications due to the number of resources available to application 'X'. For example, if application 'X' notices that available CPU, disk, or network resources have been reduced, it may be able to deduce that the other applications on the cloud are running at a higher level than normal. This information might be useful to a malicious individual trying to gather information about the state of the cloud.

System Utility Access Control: Cloud computing will result in new utilities and management consoles that must be used in a secure manner. These are unlike traditional system administration tools, since they effectively provide administrator capabilities (e.g., create, destroy, and move) to "standard" users. These tools must support controls to prevent misuse.

Patch Management: There are two primary concerns associated with applying patches in a cloud environment: patching the underlying "cloud" infrastructure and patching individual instances. New controls will need to be put into place to patch the underlying host operating system (hypervisor) without impacting the virtualized servers running on that host. Instances may need to be migrated to an alternative host, especially if rebooting is required. Also, individual instances may be offline when patches are applied and thus will need to be patched immediately when brought online. Instances will need to be scanned when brought online to make sure they are not missing any patches.

System Audits: Traditionally, physical systems are audited when first built and put into production. In a cloud environment, virtual instances of operating systems may be built and put into production with little or no oversight. Procedures will need to be modified to include audits at the creation of the system and every time a virtual system comes back online after having been modified.

Media Destruction and System Reuse: New controls will be needed to guarantee that, upon destruction, the instance is indeed removed completely from the cloud environment. This includes all of the file systems, memory paging files, and metadata. For the most critical data, such as classified government information, the persistent storage may need to be physically removed and destroyed.

Data Encryption: A malicious user copying off a dormant image of an instance can view not only the file system associated with the image but also the volatile memory image that is stored to disk. Passwords and other confidential data, normally encrypted on disk but not in memory, may end up stored on disk in an unencrypted format. New controls are required to encrypt an instance while it is stored on disk and as it is being migrated between servers.

Logging and Monitoring: With the introduction of the cloud, a new operating system, the hypervisor, must be monitored. Additionally, individual logs from physical servers and virtualized instances will need to be gathered, processed, and aggregated into a centralized location. The distributed nature of the data processing across the cloud will require sophisticated log processing to correlate information across multiple logs from many sources in different log formats.

Backups: The backup of a single physical resource may contain information from a number of instances. Policies and procedures must ensure that no data leaks can occur between instances.

17.2.3 Information Systems Acquisition, Development, and Maintenance

The goal of Systems Acquisition, Development, and Maintenance controls is to prevent information loss and errors, as well as unauthorized modification or access. Within this family, gaps were identified in the following controls: Message Integrity and Technical Standards.

Message Integrity: The introduction of new tools, user interfaces, and APIs to support and interact with the cloud will introduce new control messages across the network. Such messages will be used to create, launch, and deprovision cloud resources, as well as to implement and verify various security controls. As such, these messages are obvious targets for attack and must be protected to ensure that they cannot be altered, duplicated, or deleted.

Technical Standards: Cloud computing is beginning to leverage new technologies that require changes in how software is developed, tested, deployed, and managed. Existing controls, policies, and procedures will need to be modified to handle these new types of software to prevent poorly written and untested software from being introduced into production. Additionally, new standards are required for hypervisor operating systems.

17.2.4 Information Security Incident Management

The goal of Information Security Incident Management controls is to ensure that, when security incidents occur, a consistent process is followed to remedy the situation. Within this family, gaps were identified in the following controls: Reporting Security Events and Collection of Evidence.

Reporting Security Events: With the introduction of the hypervisor, there are new security events that must be logged, reported, and possibly investigated (such as moving an instance across physical resources). Existing procedures will need to be expanded to handle these new security events.

Collection of Evidence: With virtual servers, the controls and procedures in which evidence is gathered must be modified. This could vary from taking the physical servers offline (and migrating off any nonimpacted instances) to simply hibernating and cloning the affected instances. Performing digital forensics on virtual machines has important implications that have yet to be fully explored. When a virtual machine is powered off, its disk image remains available to the host operating system. This exposes the instance to potential tampering in a manner that does not exist with physical machines. Defining acceptable methods for collecting evidence in a virtualized environment will be essential to performing incident response and forensics.

17.2.5 Compliance

The goal of Compliance controls is to ensure that systems comply with all relevant laws, regulations, and any other constraints imposed on the system. Within this family, gaps were identified in the following controls: Technical Compliance and Audit Tools

Technical Compliance: Compliance issues are paramount when operating within a highly regulated environment. Just as with traditional data centers, auditors will demand that cloud environments remain compliant. The physical location of data will be of particular importance in the cloud, especially in the context of data privacy, business continuity planning, incident response, and forensics.

Audit Tools: Audits must identify rogue instances on the network and other suspicious activity or control failings. New tools are required to verify that all instances are in compliance. These compliance checks must be run automatically against instances immediately after provisioning, after maintenance, and again when decommissioned.

17.3 Security Recommendations

In the previous section, we identified a number of security gaps against the ISO 27002 standard that are unique to virtualized systems and cloud computing. In this section, we provide a list of 20 recommendations (summarized in Table 17.1) that attempt to address many of these gaps. Although some of these recommendations are not unique to cloud environments, they become more critical to address when working in a cloud. This is by no means an exhaustive list of steps necessary to protect a cloud environment. Instead, it is meant to provide the reader with some of the many actions that must be taken to ensure a reliable, secure cloud.

1. Provide globally unique names to every instance in the cloud that allow key instance attributes to be identified. From the name, one should be able to identify the application as well as the owner. All instances created across the cloud should be assigned a name provided by the cloud. This is a globally unique

Table 17.1 Summary of cloud computing security recommendations

Recommendations
1. Provide globally unique names to every instance in the cloud that easily allows key instance attributes to be identified
2. Record resource locations, both physical and virtual, throughout an instance's entire lifecycle to enable traceability
3. Do not implicitly trust the cloud or any instances in the cloud; every interaction in the cloud demands authorization and authentication
4. Encrypt instances and data when stored to disk and while migrating between servers
5. Restrict dynamic utilization of resources to predetermined levels to prevent an "internal" denial-of-service attack
6. Virtually "shred" retired instances and data when no longer needed
7. Assign priorities (i.e., SLAs) to every instance in the cloud to ensure appropriate availability and resource utilization
8. Utilize a single management, logging, and monitoring system capable of supporting the entire cloud
9. Restrict console access (physical and virtual) to users with a defined business need
10. Create new instances according to defined, tested, and approved specifications
11. Execute applications across multiple physical servers to improve reliability
12. Provide centralized authentication and authorization services
13. Provide a centralized key management system to allow the cloud to communicate sensitive information
14. Digitally sign control messages within the cloud in order to prevent tampering and unauthorized use
15. Restrict data ingress/egress points in the cloud to mitigate the introduction of malicious software and removal of private data
16. Record the current state and lineage records (from creation to destruction) of physical and virtual resources
17. Isolate suspicious instances and replace with alternate instances
18. Scan the cloud for unauthorized instances in order to identify, isolate, and remove them
19. Audit resource utilization records to detect suspicious activity
20. Audit instances at "life" events, such as creation, migration, hibernation, and startup, to ensure compliance

    identifier that is used to cross-reference information about the instance. Instance names are kept for the life of the cloud to preserve records and logging integrity. If instance names are to be viewed by unprivileged personal or processes, then the instance name itself should not reveal any useful information about the application or the data being stored within the instance. A user-defined name (i.e., "alias") may be permitted for convenience, but the globally unique name will be the standard identifier used within the cloud.

2. Record resource locations, both physical and virtual, throughout an instance's entire lifecycle to enable traceability. Records of physical resources and data that were used or generated by an instance should be maintained from creation to destruction. This is important for successful incident response and digital forensics. See Recommendation 16 for additional details.

3. Do not implicitly trust the cloud or any instances in the cloud; every interaction in the cloud demands authorization and authentication. Neither the cloud nor

any instances should trust each other. When an instance stores any data within the cloud, it should encrypt the data. Similarly, the cloud should not trust any particular instance. This includes limiting the amount of cloud resources that are usable by any particular instance (i.e., to prevent a denial-of-service attack). See Recommendations 4 and 5 for additional details.

4. Encrypt instances and data when stored to disk and while migrating between servers. All instances should be encrypted by the cloud provider when being stored to disk or in transit from one physical server to another across the network. This is to prevent unauthorized access to the information stored within the instance. Additionally, individual instances should take their own precautions and encrypt sensitive information, including virtual memory (RAM), that may persist on disk (e.g., through paging files or if the instance is hibernated to disk).

5. Restrict dynamic utilization of resources to predetermined levels to prevent an "internal" denial-of-service attack. Automatic growth should be capped at a predetermined level. A cloud administrator can manually override this limit after a review. Without this limit, it may be possible for one business application to consume vast amounts of resources on the cloud and effectively cause a denial-of-service for all other applications.

6. Virtually "shred" retired instances and data when no longer needed. When there is no longer a business use for an instance or data, it should be removed from the cloud and disposed of properly. The image on the file system should be virtually shredded (i.e., overwritten with random data).

7. Assign priorities (i.e., SLAs) to every instance in the cloud to ensure appropriate availability and resource utilization. When a new instance comes online within the cloud, it should be allocated a business criticality. This rating is used to determine the order in which resources are allocated across applications within a cloud. Those applications with a higher business criticality will have first rights to cloud resources.

8. Utilize a single management, logging, and monitoring system capable of supporting the entire cloud. The cloud should have a singular management interface to control and check the status of the various aspects of the cloud. The implementation of this management interface could be centralized or distributed, allowing for multiple consoles that provide the same information. However, any one console should be able to display information about the entire cloud. Logs and events across all instances should be consolidated and presented in an aggregated manner.

9. Restrict console access (physical and virtual) to users with a defined business need. Access to device consoles (physical or virtual) within the cloud should be restricted to users with a defined business need. The ability to start and stop an instance on the network should be restricted to the owner of the instance and authorized delegates.

10. Create new instances according to defined, tested, and approved specifications. New instances should be built, ideally through an automated process, to predefined, tested, and approved technical specifications (such as templates). Arbitrary instances should not be allowed onto the cloud without going through an approved process that includes defining a technical specification.

11. Execute applications across multiple physical servers to improve reliability. Distributing a business task in an intelligent manner across a number of physical servers improves the reliability of the task, since it is no longer reliant on any one server.

12. Provide centralized authentication and authorization services. Authentication, the verification of the identity of a process or individual, should be handled by a centralized service within the cloud. By centralizing the authentication of users and processes, it is easier to detect suspicious activity, such as failed logins. This also reduces the number of copies of sensitive data, such as usernames and passwords, across the cloud.

13. Provide a centralized key management system to allow the cloud to communicate sensitive information. Centralized key management provides a mechanism for the cloud to securely communicate sensitive information. Segregation of this key management from the cloud provider, and by roles within the same provider, is a worthwhile consideration because of the separation of access and enhanced level of data privacy that can be provided. At a minimum, each administrative user on the cloud would be assigned a public/private key pair that could be used to facilitate secure communications. This key management infrastructure should be used for distributing initial super user credentials and for managing instances.

14. Digitally sign control messages within the cloud in order to prevent tampering and unauthorized use. The key infrastructure described above should be used to encrypt all messages, such as the control messages to create, destroy, or otherwise modify instances on the cloud. If needed, these control messages would be encrypted in addition to being signed. Time stamping of all control messages should be required to prevent replay attacks.

15. Restrict data ingress/egress points in the cloud to mitigate the introduction of malicious software and removal of private data. Interfaces where data can be copied to and from the cloud should be restricted to administrator use and monitored. This includes network and storage media interfaces. Physical access to media (e.g., tapes, disk drives, USB interfaces) should be restricted to prevent unauthorized data access. Cloud storage clients should use approved network interfaces to upload, download, and access cloud data. Network data ingress and egress should be monitored for malicious software and unauthorized data transfers.

16. Record the current state and lineage records (from creation to destruction) of physical and virtual resources. As instances are brought online and destroyed, it is important to keep a list of all approved instances. This list will be used to audit the cloud, ensuring that there are no rogue instances running. These records should include the physical location of each instance, state (e.g., running, suspended, isolated, destroyed), and owner. Historical records of instances should be maintained after an instance is removed from service.

17. Isolate suspicious instances and replace with alternate instances. If suspicious activity is noticed, the offending instance should be frozen and replaced with an alternate instance. The suspect instance would then be isolated from the rest of

the cloud for analysis. It may also be necessary to isolate the physical server used by the suspicious instance. In this case, all instances currently running on the same hardware must also be isolated for inspection and transitioned to new physical resources.

18. Scan the cloud for unauthorized instances in order to identify, isolate, and remove them. The introduction of rogue instances is a significant concern, and the cloud should be scanned frequently to ensure only legitimate instances exist. Any instance that is not on the list of authorized instances should be removed from the cloud and isolated. It may also be necessary to isolate the physical server used by the suspicious instance. In this case, all instances currently running on the same hardware would have be isolated for inspection and transitioned to new physical resources.

19. Audit resource utilization records to detect suspicious activity. Resource utilization is an important tool to identify suspicious activity on the cloud. An audit of the total resource usage, including memory, disk, CPU, and network activity, across all instances on the cloud, can be used to locate suspicious instances. This data should also be compared against historical records to identify potential anomalies.

20. Audit instances of "life" events, such as creation, migration, hibernation, and startup, to ensure compliance. After an instance is brought to life on the cloud, it may go through various life events, such as hibernation, a move across physical hardware platforms, or an increase/decrease in available resources. At each life event, the instance should be assessed for compliance with the cloud's security requirements. If the instance is no longer in compliance, it should be isolated.

17.4   Case Studies

Many of the 20 recommendations proposed above are actively being applied by both public and private cloud providers. In this section, we describe some of the security features offered by two particular providers, Amazon.com and a Fortune 100 company, in order to show alignment with our recommendations.

17.4.1   *Private Cloud: Fortune 100 Company*

The first case study is for a private cloud built for a Fortune 100 company. Although a private cloud, the need for security and privacy is not removed; proprietary information is still hosted in the cloud and must be protected. Table 17.2 identifies 7 of our 20 security recommendations that this company has incorporated into their security model.

Table 17.2 Fortune 100 customer private cloud security features alignment with cloud security recommendations

No.	Recommendation	Private cloud implementation
3	Do not implicitly trust the cloud or any instances in the cloud; every interaction in the cloud demands authorization and authentication	A hardware appliance is used to provide multiple security contexts and restrict communication between tenants.
9	Restrict console access (physical and virtual) to users with a defined business need	Separate controls are provided to users to enable management (e.g., VM creation/deletion/sizing) that do not involve console access.
10	Create new instances according to defined, tested, and approved specifications	Templates are provided to users in order to instantiate preconfigured VMs.
11	Execute applications across multiple physical servers to improve reliability	Users are free to launch VMs across dozens of servers to support their high availability needs
12	Provide centralized authentication and authorization services	A centralized Active Directory service provides these services.
15	Restrict data ingress/egress points in the cloud to mitigate the introduction of malicious software and removal of private data	All network traffic (i.e., user-entered data) flows through the same firewall; only administrators can bypass this mechanism and access is tightly controlled.
19	Audit resource utilization records to detect suspicious activity	Every VM is monitored for resource "spikes" (e.g., memory, processor, network); triggers are configured to notify administrators.

17.4.2 Public Cloud: Amazon.com

The next case study is Amazon Web Services (AWS) Elastic Compute Cloud (EC2). Amazon acknowledges that maintaining security and privacy in a cloud environment is more complex than when managing a single datacenter. Table 17.3 identifies 6 of our 20 security recommendations that Amazon has incorporated into their security model. Detailed security information for Amazon is beyond the scope of this chapter, and the interested reader is referred to [8].

17.5 Summary and Conclusion

Of the many obstacles to adopting the cloud model of delivery and consumption of computing resources, security ranks at the top of the list [1]. The lack of strong security controls can resonate through the cloud, opening all of the applications and services that are running across the cloud to exploitation.

Table 17.3 AWS security features alignment with cloud security recommendations

No.	Recommendation	Amazon implementation
3	Do not implicitly trust the cloud or any instances in the cloud; every interaction in the cloud demands authorization and authentication	Every AWS interaction requires a "signed" API call (see also recommendation no. 14).
6	Virtually "shred" retired instances and data when no longer needed	When customer storage is no longer used, every block of data is automatically wiped. AWS also uses a proprietary disk virtualization layer to ensure customer data remains private when virtual disk blocks are returned to resource pool.
8	Utilize a single management, logging, and monitoring system capable of supporting the entire cloud	AWS utilizes bastion hosts for cloud management.
9	Restrict console access (physical and virtual) to users with a defined business need	Administrative access, both physical and virtual, is strictly controlled according to legitimate business requirements. Those access privileges are immediately revoked when an employee no longer has a need for access. Each administrator is assigned unique cryptographically strong SSH keys. Access to bastion hosts is logged and audited on a regular basis.
12	Provide centralized authentication and authorization services	AWS utilizes bastion hosts for cloud management.
14	Digitally sign control messages within the cloud in order to prevent tampering and unauthorized use	Customers are issued a unique key. This key, or an authorized X.509 certificate, must be used to sign all Amazon EC2 API calls. Signing API calls ensures that control messages within the cloud are authorized and prevents tampering. API calls in transit are encrypted with SSL.

First and foremost, the cloud is a data center and therefore traditional data center protections should be applied. It is not necessary to "start over" with security in the cloud. Many of the existing protections can and should be applied to the cloud. However, there are a number of gaps in existing coverage because of the unique aspects of cloud computing. In this chapter, we identified a number of these gaps (as compared against the existing ISO 27002 security controls). From these gaps, we provided 20 recommendations to help alleviate security concerns.

This chapter was intended to serve as an introduction to some of the many issues surrounding security in the cloud. There are additional gaps against the ISO standard that were not discussed and many other security issues to consider. Fortunately, groups such as the Cloud Security Alliance are actively investigating these issues. Also, this chapter focused on the ISO controls, but similar analyses could be performed against other controls (e.g., NIST 800-53) and regulatory documents (e.g., SOX, GLBA) unique to communities of interest.

There is certainly a tremendous amount of work remaining to "secure" the cloud. However, it is important to note that every new computing paradigm has brought with it unique security challenges. The Internet is an excellent example of this; certainly, allowing remote users and computers to access internal resources has proved incredibly challenging to protect. However, the Internet has changed how we do business, communicate, and live our lives. Therefore, the goal of security is to mitigate risk to an acceptable level. Business is centered on risk management and cloud computing will be treated as any other business decision. If the community can develop controls to address the issues outlined in this chapter, then businesses will move to the cloud for the benefits that it offers.

References

1. IDC Enterprise Panel (2009) http://cloudcomputing.sys-con.com/node/1048317. Accessed Aug 2009
2. Federal Information Security Management Act (2009) http://csrc.nist.gov/groups/SMA/fisma/index.html. Accessed Aug 2009
3. Health Insurance Portability and Accountability Act of 1996 (2009) http://www.hhs.gov/ocr/privacy/index.html. Accessed Aug 2009
4. Sarbanes–Oxley Act of 2002 (2009) http://en.wikipedia.org/wiki/Sarbanes-Oxley_Act. Accessed Aug 2009
5. Gramm–Leach–Bliley Act (2009) http://www.ftc.gov/privacy/privacyinitiatives/glbact.html. Accessed Aug 2009
6. Cloud Security Alliance (2009) http://www.cloudsecurityalliance.org. Accessed Aug 2009
7. ISO/IEC 17799:2005 Information Technology Security Techniques (2009) http://www.iso.org/iso/support/faqs/faqs_widely_used_standards/widely_used_standards_other/information_security.htm. Accessed Aug 2009
8. Amazon Web Services Security, Overview of Security Processes (2009) http://s3.amazonaws.com/aws_blog/AWS_Security_Whitepaper_2008_09.pdf. Accessed Dec 2009

Part IV
Cloud Feedback

Chapter 18
Technologies for Enforcement and Distribution of Policy in Cloud Architectures

K.W. Scott Morrison

Abstract Service-Oriented Architecture (SOA) has demonstrated the value of defining a decoupled policy layer for applications. This design pattern promotes a declarative-style approach to policy enforcement and offers a basis for reuse of rule sets. When an intermediary applies policy to a communication stream, it has utility beyond the simple application of authentication and authorization. In this role, policy is the language to articulate all actionable functions on a protocol stream, including (but not limited to) general cryptography, message transform, content validation, routing, orchestration, service level agreement enforcement, counters, audit, event management, and monitoring. Policy thus becomes the underpinning for the security and management of applications and data. This chapter is about the application of decoupled policy enforcement technology to cloud computing. It explores the use of the SOA Policy Enforcement Point (PEP) as a policy gateway in the cloud and shows this to be an effective security model for cloud services.

18.1 Introduction

Security of applications and data remains the primary concern among early adopters of cloud technology [3, 11, 24, 28]. This is not surprising, as the cloud community has struggled with articulating a comprehensive and cohesive security model. Early efforts from organizations such as the Cloud Security Alliance show promise [4], but cloud has fundamental challenges around trust that technology alone will not overcome. In this chapter, we demonstrate that a design pattern and associated technology that matured in the Service-Oriented Architecture (SOA) space, the intermediary SOA Policy Enforcement Point (PEP), can form the basis of an effective security model for applications and data residing in clouds.

K.W.S. Morrison (✉)
Layer 7 Technologies, 1200 G Street, NW, Suite 800, Washington, DC 20005, USA
e-mail: smorrison@layer7tech.com

N. Antonopoulos and L. Gillam (eds.), *Cloud Computing: Principles,
Systems and Applications*, Computer Communications and Networks,
DOI 10.1007/978-1-84996-241-4_18, © Springer-Verlag London Limited 2010

SOA builds on earlier formalized approaches to distributed application development and integration, and indeed contributes to other emerging methodologies [29]. Arguably, it is the most successful paradigm for large-scale application development among heterogeneous systems. Cloud applications are borrowing heavily from SOA methodologies and philosophical stance [12], so clearly successful technological solutions developed under SOA are worthy of consideration for migration to cloud architectures [14]. Indeed, many of the security challenges solved by SOA architects now appear in cloud deployment [20].

The enforcement of policy governing access to services – which at its simplest covers only authentication, authorization, and audit – can be complex to implement because of the diversity in application platforms and architecture. Thus, the best practice for policy enforcement is to decouple this from services. This strategy has a number of favorable outcomes. It allows for the consistent management and enforcement of policy across a broad spectrum of services; it offers the opportunity for reuse; it simplifies necessary integration with identity infrastructure; and finally it transcends limitations imposed by the existing languages and libraries. As a side effect, this approach allows modeling of policy as an aspect of an application or service module. This promotes a declarative approach to rule sets, offering responsive change and no direct coupling to compiled and linked application builds.

The purpose of this chapter is to propose the deployment of SOA PEPs into cloud environments as a means of providing a flexible and robust security and monitoring layer for cloud-based applications and data. It will specifically explore how differences between cloud environments and on-premise IT (the traditional deployment locale for SOA) affect the SOA PEP. Where appropriate, it will suggest ways to overcome issues caused by characteristic differences in the cloud environment.

This chapter will restrict its view to SOA PEPs used in intersystem communication, under application-layer protocols such as SOAP and the related WS-* embellishments. This is not to diminish the role of Web browser to server communications in cloud scenarios (indeed, at present this constitutes the bulk of the transaction volume in cloud computing). However, Web-oriented policy enforcement is largely a solved problem and the existing implementations transfer to cloud-based deployments with little challenge, as evidenced by the growing adoption among SaaS providers of security models based on SSL and SAML, OpenID, or OAuth. This chapter will instead acknowledge the increasing importance of application-to-application XML-based traffic in enterprise-centric cloud computing and focus on the specialized issues faced in governing these transactions both within cloud providers and across the public Internet.

18.2 Decoupling Policy from Applications

The capabilities and constraints of an architectural model drive the scope of the policy used to manage system entities residing in it. The Web, for example, benefited greatly from a highly constrained architectural model [9]. All resources can be addressed through the URI [2]; this identifier is relatively unambiguous, visible, and inexpensive to parse within the HTTP. HTTP offers few options for identity claims and SSL provides a decoupled security layer protecting transmission. The high degree of constraint and rigor that defines the Web allows policy to consist of little more than confidentiality and integrity, authentication, authorization, and some audit – all elements that promote a clear separation between Web application and policy enforcement.

Web architecture is the basis of Web services. However, in contrast to its foundation, Web services are less constrained, vastly more complex, and suffer from an approach to standardization that is highly distributed. The basic processing and security models offer a breadth of scope that leaves considerable underspecification [17]. This has made implementation in application servers complex and prone to issues with interoperability.

In the SOA community, one approach to these challenges has been to separate security and monitoring functions into a PEP decoupled from the application services themselves. Policy, which is a concrete language for asserting the requirements that constitute the run time governance of services, is the logical place to accommodate the more diverse needs of Web services and to articulate a strict message-processing model for enforcement points. Policy enforcement thus takes on a much more significant role in facilitating service-oriented communications than for the conventional Web.

The canonical model for decoupled policy enforcement promotes a separation of concerns between the system entity responsible for enforcement, the Policy Enforcement Point (PEP), and the system entity responsible for decision-making, the Policy Decision Point (PDP), recognizing that the latter is often a centralized resource shared among many lightweight enforcement instances [30]. This has been well described in the context of Web applications [16], but the model is of similar value when applied to Web services transactions.

18.2.1   Overlap of Concerns Between the PEP and PDP

The essential tension in this model is between the desire to have centralized, authoritative decision-making and the practical need for distributed enforcement. The PDP requires visibility of key elements of a transaction to render decisions effectively; the PEP has full visibility, but it cannot practically relay this entire context to the PDP. Identity-centric PDPs should be in proximity to directories and serve as unambiguous authority for decision-making. To meet performance, security, and reliability demands, PEPs should reside with applications. The communication between PEPs and PDPs must reflect an optimization of data necessary to render an effective decision without significantly degrading transactional throughput. This has ramifications for cloud deployment.

In the conventional Web, the policy model segments cleanly because of the limited scope of policy in the architecture. Web PEPs are responsible for enforcing privacy and integrity expectations of policy locally; to escalate an access control decision, the PEP simply bundles identity claims, intended actions, and target URI and relays this to a PDP.

Web services transactions, in contrast, blur the distinction between these system entities because a lot of the decision-making demands additional message context that is not practical for a PEP to relay to a central PDP. Thus, SOA PEPs retain considerable internal decision-making responsibility. This independence is a crucial factor when deploying into cloud-based environments, where communication with a centralized PDP (which may reside on-premises instead of within the cloud) could be impractical for reasons of security or latency. Distribution of authority comes at a cost of increased policy management and provisioning.

18.2.2   Patterns for Binding PEPs to Services

There are two common deployment patterns for PEPs: as agents, which integrate directly into the application container and as intermediaries, which are independent of the application container and often reside on a separate physical or virtual host. There are tradeoffs associated with each approach that have particular ramifications in the context of cloud deployment. The important consideration here is how to secure the point of interface between the PEP and the relying party service (which in general resides inside an application server container). This defines the trust model between these entities.

18.2.3   Agents

The agent-based model of PEP deployment uses a plug-in that integrates directly into the execution model of the application container. The point of interface is an application server API.

There are a number of reasons that make this strategy attractive. The tight binding between the PEP and the application server execution context means that validated identity claims can be propagated directly into the application, using technologies such as JAAS in Java application servers or thread impersonation in systems supporting a high degree of integration between OS and application server (such as Microsoft environments). Collapsing this into a single execution context trivially provides security and establishes trust across *the last mile* – the hop between the PEP and the application. Agents distribute security processing along with applications, thereby benefiting from scalability strategies associated with the application and avoiding potential security bottlenecks.

However, there are issues with this approach. The tight, code-level binding between PEP and application server has its own challenges. With the exception of the Java servlet filter API, there are no standardized and widely adopted interfaces to application server execution context. This implication is that organizations with a large number of heterogeneous systems (including simple version and patch differences between like-servers) find agent-based PEPs difficult to deploy broadly and consistently.

In practice, this leads to a lowest-common-denominator approach to functionality in agents. For simple Web application agents, requiring little more from policy than authentication, authorization, and audit, this is sufficient; however, it has limited agent applicability for Web services PEPs, as these require advanced policy processing capabilities. Furthermore, introducing third-party code into application servers injects manageability risks. This has fostered a pejorative association with agents in the commercial marketplace, leading some vendors to explicitly promote their "agent-less" architecture.

The colocation of a PEP and an application server may be concealing other potential risks. Binding the PEP to a generalized application server install makes this critical security layer subject to the integrity of the underlying OS. Hardening modern operating systems is a complex and highly specialized task, and the best practices may be compromised to accommodate server needs or simply from a lack of appreciation of their importance. If an attacker successfully compromises the OS, the entire security model collapses, rendering the PEP superfluous.

Agents have been widely successful in conventional Web servers, both on-premise, in SaaS applications, and in generalized cloud deployment of Web applications. In these cases, HTTP servers tend to be monocultures, de-emphasizing diversity issues with the agent interface. The limited demands of Web policy also allow Web agents to be lightweight and simpler to package with server installations.

18.2.4   Intermediaries

The intermediary model delegates PEP processing to an independent unit that can simultaneously serve one or more downstream relying parties. It operates as a policy-driven reverse-proxy to these applications. The point of interface here consists of basic network (e.g. TCP) and application layer (e.g. HTTP) protocols. These of course benefit from standardization and widespread support – this maturity makes deployment essentially universal.

The conventional on-premise SOA deployment of PEP intermediaries consists of hardened, performance-optimized appliances that are physically separate from application servers. This model invests PEPs with a high degree of trust; they serve as an independent policy layer that fully gates all communications to and from less policy capable internal services. PEPs are tuned for high-performance processing of common traffic profiles, particularly XML-based transactions where significant benefit is realized by leveraging purpose-built acceleration chips for essential operations such as schema validation, transform, and query. Intermediary PEPs are rarely a performance bottleneck because of the vertical scalability benefits of such optimizations and the horizontal scalability potential that comes from placing additional units in parallel.

The intermediary model has the benefit of a network hop to clearly define layering between policy and service. However, in the cloud, the underlying networks are inherently untrustworthy; this adds considerable complication to the security model between the PEP and relying party, demanding that it becomes more explicitly protected than with agents. The following table describes this:

Issue	Details	Solution
Trust model	Relying party must trust PEP.	Trust of PEP security tokens (username/password, X.509 certs, Kerberos, etc.)
Subject declaration	PEP must propagate *validated* principal identity.	Use of authoritative vouching mechanism, such as SAML tokens, or various proprietary approaches (IBM's LTPA or TAI, custom headers, etc.)
Privacy and integrity	Securing the communications between PEP and its relying party.	SSL/TLS or message-based security models such as WS-Security
Relying party server resiliency	Make relying party inaccessible except through PEP.	Internal and external firewall rules to reject connections other than to/ from PEP. Highly restrictive local access control

The commercial sector markets intermediaries for Web servers as Web application firewalls. Despite their advantages, this product category sees less deployment than agents-based solutions, primarily because of the ease with which agents can handle the more limited policy requirements of the Web.

Intermediaries, in contrast, are the dominant solution for SOA Web services. Here, the lack of definition and constraints on the architecture demand much greater functionality from policy and thus greater sophistication from PEPs than the limited operating environment of an agent can uniformly support. Web services is fundamentally an approach to integration – an insight that implies a potential diversity of service provider hosts that make agent integration impractical.

18.3   PEP Deployment Patterns in the Cloud

The term *cloud computing* suffers greatly from industry hype, ambiguity, and overload of meaning. NIST offers a reasonably comprehensive definition that characterizes cloud in terms of essential characteristics, service, and deployment models [18]. NIST acknowledges that community debate is continually refining our understanding of the term, and they have updated their paper in response to evolving perception.

There is wide acceptance of the three cloud service models NIST describes. These can be characterized not just in terms of functionality offered to customers, but also by where the boundary of control lies in the stack between customer-managed and provider-managed elements (where the stack defines layers including host and network infrastructure, operating systems, applications, data, etc.). The opportunities for deployment of SOA PEPs into the cloud are largely a function of where these control boundaries lie. Cloud-based PEPs are virtual appliances that consist of a policy execution engine operating under a security-hardened and performance-optimized operating system. Thus, deployment of virtual PEPs in the cloud requires a customer-accessible hypervisor execution environment.

18.3.1   Software-as-a-Service Deployment

Software-as-a-Service (SaaS) offers no real opportunities for SOA PEP deployment. SaaS implementations are thin-client Web applications operated entirely by the provider, but open to minor configuration by the customer, such as Salesforce.com or Google GMail. Policy enforcement for Web applications, by virtue of its limited scope (the security model simply consists of basic authentication, sometimes SAML SSO and federation, and SSL/TLS transport protection), is generally integral to the host application servers and is therefore under complete control of the provider.

SOA PEPs, however, do have a role to play in securing access of on-premise services by SaaS applications. This is a conventional, edge-of-network PEP deployment in the on-premise DMZ, implemented using either hardware or virtualized SOA PEPs.

18.3.2   Platform-as-a-Service Deployment

Like SaaS, Platform-as-a-Service (PaaS) offers no current opportunity for deployment of virtual PEP appliances. Although PaaS relaxes the boundaries of control to offer customers access to an application deployment environment, the container-based execution model – such as Google's AppEngine – is generally too restricted to support the diverse connectivity and operating requirements of a mature SOA PEP code base.

18.3.3   Infrastructure-as-a-Service Deployment

Infrastructure-as-a-Service (IaaS), in contrast to SaaS and PaaS, offers the greatest degrees of freedom of control to the customer, and thereby an opportunity for virtualized PEP deployment. IaaS offerings such as Amazon's Elastic Compute Cloud (EC2) shift the boundaries of customer control to an abstracted hypervisor, which can host a virtualized PEP and virtualized, subordinate SOA services under PEP management. By providing finely grained, policy-based control over all communications to or from a cloud-resident service, the PEP allows a cloud customer to reassert control over IaaS-resident applications. This higher level of visibility and control serves to offset the loss of lower-level, physical controls necessarily surrendered to the cloud provider. This deployment model is the focus of this chapter (Fig. 18.1).

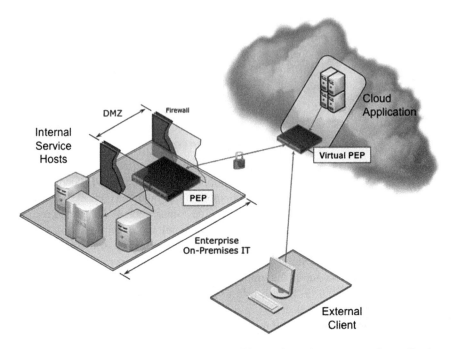

Fig. 18.1 Virtual PEPs deployed in the cloud provide security and management for applications in the cloud. When paired with on-premise PEPs, they can create a secure tunnel between application in the internal network and cloud instances

18.3.4 Alternative Approaches to IaaS Policy Enforcement

There is a number of existing approaches to securing services in IaaS clouds. Both simple Web security and VPNs offer the advantage of simplicity, generality and familiarity. However, both suffer from significant limitations in their scope that make virtual PEPs, which consolidate a broader range of capabilities under policy control, a much more attractive choice.

18.3.5 Basic Web Application Security

Simple security models – consisting of basic credentials in HTTP, interface to conventional LDAP directories for authentication and authorization, and SSL for confidentiality and integrity – are widely supported in application servers hosting rich Web services. But application servers do not uniformly or consistently support more sophisticated message-based security models, SLAs, threat detection, orchestration, content-based routing, load distribution, etc. – all valuable functions in SOA messaging environments with diverse service consumers and producers.

SOA PEPs, in contrast, consolidate and parameterize all of these capabilities under a policy that is bound to each individual service.

18.3.6 VPN-Based Solutions

In mid-2009, Amazon introduced its Virtual Private Cloud (VPC) offering as a solution to securely integrate EC2 with on-premise enterprise networks. VPC consists of a standards-based VPN server and an undisclosed mechanism for isolating EC2 instances to a specific customer domain. Other vendors, such as CohesiveFT, have promoted VPN solutions for securing communications to the cloud.

VPN-based solutions have the advantage of providing generalized confidentiality and integrity for all tunneled protocols. This has the distinct advantage of supporting virtually all communication protocols and therefore access to applications that are not service-oriented. But VPNs suffer from a lack of constraint with respect to service entitlements. VPNs secure networks, not applications. In environments with a significant trust imbalance – such as between on-premise IT and a cloud provider – VPNs can potentially offer an open vector for attack if a system hacker compromises a cloud-resident application or operating environment.

SOA PEPs put channel (or message) encryption subordinate to the entire execution context of policy, which can incorporate authentication, authorization, threat detection, optimized content validation, SLA enforcement, load distribution, and audit. Because policy is ultimately bound to individual services, this severely limits the attack surface available to compromised applications.

18.4 Challenges to Deploying PEPs in the Cloud

The NIST definition illustrates that cloud computing is characterized by five essential characteristics, including resource pooling and rapid elasticity. PEPs deployed into IaaS clouds face unique challenges around performance, security, and management because of the underlying architecture that supports these characteristics. The following sections examine these challenges.

18.4.1 Performance Challenges in the Cloud

The commoditization of processing cost in the cloud is attractive, but there are special considerations that go into making effective use of this. For PEPs deployed in IaaS facilities, these include fault tolerance, scalability, clustering, generalized acceleration, and content encoding.

18.4.2   Strategies for Fault Tolerance

SOA PEPs achieve fault tolerance through system redundancy; however, traditional methods for providing independent, high-availability failover may not function in the cloud. Failover techniques that make use of gratuitous ARP – such as Linux-HA – will certainly be restricted because of the risk of IP hijacking by an instance.

A better approach is to load balance incoming HTTP traffic across two or more PEPs using conventional HTTP application delivery controllers. This basic infrastructure is commonly available in cloud installations because it is the basic scaling strategy for conventional Web applications, which at present constitute the majority of cloud provider's business. Load balancer failover makes more economic use of deployed resources than a running instance in standby as failover occurs with no interruption of service. This also provides the basis for a practical scalability model.

18.4.3   Strategies for Scalability

Elasticity is a basic characteristic of cloud computing, which offers an opportunity to better manage PEPs operating under traffic load that is unpredictable and in a continual state of flux. As load increases, new PEP instances can launch on-demand; as it decreases, underutilized instances can terminate (to use Amazon nomenclature). This offers a distinct advantage over on-premise SOA PEP deployments with fixed capacity.

As with fault tolerance, for HTTP-based transports, the existing HTTP load balancers can distribute traffic across the breadth of the running instances. Vendors such as Citrix have pioneered a model under which the HTTP load distribution system controls application instance launch. This should focus on PEP instances, which in turn control the launch of applications under their policy control, thus creating a cascade pattern of elasticity.

Elasticity, however, does introduce new challenges with provisioning of PEP instances on launch, and the potential for loss of critical state information on termination. Clustering is a strategy that addresses some of these issues.

18.4.4   Clustering

Clustering can overcome some provisioning and operational challenges when deploying multiple PEPs simultaneously. In addition to providing a means for sharing configuration and policy information between nodes, clustering offers a fast channel for synchronization of time-critical information such as shared counters or coordination against replay attacks exploiting the WS-Security model.

However, traditional application clustering technologies may not be deployable in cloud environments. Clustering assumes a locality of deployment to reduce latency, and potentially to allow propagation of broadcast or multicast protocols for synchronization. In on-premise computing, it is common to group PEPs on a single rack and integrate these through a switch allowing physical control over such a distribution. Cloud environments offer no such deployment specification. PEP instances may be geographically isolated, resulting in isolation by router boundaries or at a minimum multiple switch hops that will not propagate this traffic. Amazon, for example, abstracts their operating environment into coarse divisions they call *availability zones*. These roughly map to distinct data centers within an operating region; however, Amazon does not publically provide deeper architectural details of how these are organized.

PEPs thus need to operate independently and synchronize exclusively off shared persistent storage. Amazon was the first public cloud provider to create a range of persistence mechanisms as services, including Simple Storage Service (S3), SimpleDB, Elastic Block Storage (EBS), and Relational Database Service (RDS). As a continuum, they illustrate the spectrum of tradeoffs between scalability, reliability, availability, trustworthiness, and traditional versus cloud-centric architectural models. Issues to consider for PEPs are unpredictable latencies that may affect time-sensitive operations such as replay detection or policy synchronization. For example, the use of shared underlying infrastructure, such is the case with EBS, may provide highly nondeterministic performance. Similarly, the underlying data propagation realities that account for Amazon's eventual consistency strategy may prove difficult to reconcile with the PEP need for high-performance access to a persistent store.

18.4.5 Acceleration Strategies

Optimization is always an exercise in balancing tradeoffs. In SOA PEPs, the computationally expensive operations are XML processing and basic cryptographic calculations. Appliance-based SOA PEPs use custom hardware to accelerate these that is not applicable in virtualized environments. An important design tradeoff is therefore to sacrifice low-level optimization for the overall gains realized through elastic scalability in cloud environments.

18.4.5.1 Accelerating Message Processing

Specialized hardware can accelerate low-level XML processing, including XSLT, XML Schema validation, and XPath query into documents [13, 26]. Similarly, regular expression parsing benefits from application in specialized hardware.

However, a new generation of software-based, highly optimized libraries is emerging. These include pure software approaches (Excentric Works), and optimization that utilizes the existing architecture in commodity chips [5].

18.4.5.2 Acceleration of Cryptographic Operations

Cryptographic operations, such as RSA key operations, also see benefits from hardware acceleration. This hardware may integrate higher-level protocol optimization (such as SSL acceleration), FIPS-compliant cryptographic algorithms, and Hardware Security Module (HSM) protection of keys (nCipher, Sun, Safenet). HSM modules in particular find wide application in military and intelligence markets.

FIPS-compliant software cryptographic libraries are widely available (RSA, Certicom), and drawing on the benefits of elastic deployment can offset cryptographic optimizations.

Protection of key material is an open problem for clouds. In private clouds, it is conceivable to interface with a physical HSM shared between virtual images. In public clouds, a software-based secure key store is the only alternative. This has inherent risk as virtual images may leave behind residual disk images on termination, potentially exposing key stores to scavenging and brute force decryption.

18.4.6 Transport Content Coding

Message content compression can be economically advantageous between on-premises computing facilities and cloud providers. HTTP includes content coding [8], but only on the response message; this is insufficient for bidirectional SOAP messaging (or highly parameterized REST requests). A similar nonstandard model, also leveraging algorithms like zlib, gzip, and compress (or dictionary substitutions of common SOAP idioms), could extend to requests. However, the challenge is that PEPs at either end must synchronize compression parameters out of band, or utilize proprietary negotiation protocols.

18.4.7 Security Challenges in the Cloud

The great challenge with PEPs deployed in the cloud – and indeed, in all distributed computing – is the secure propagation of identity context between tiers. Privacy and integrity may act in support of this fundamental issue.

18.4.8 The PEP Air Gap

The virtual PEP deployed in the cloud acts as a policy air gap between the external Internet and internal applications. It deliberately breaks transport semantics into ingress and egress segments, kept separate and mediated through policy. This affects all transport layers, including TCP, SSL, and message transport such as HTTP or message-oriented middleware (MOM). With the latter in particular, the policy air gap may break QoS characteristics (such as transactional context, guaranteed one time delivery, end-to-end delivery reliability, etc.) unless explicitly propagated using protocols like XA.

Propagation, however, may not be entirely desirable in cloud environments. The policy-mediated air gap is an important design pattern because it establishes a clear, customer-managed demarcation between the inside of the cloud and the outside Internet. Both sides have a distinct set of security challenges and demand different approaches to threat mitigation and establishment of trust.

The air gap pattern also serves as a reminder to application designers to build for resiliency. Cloud providers are highly visible and accessible, making these natural targets for system cracking attempts. Recent attacks against public cloud-resident applications such as Bitbucket (Nohr 2009) underscore the need to recognize that all cloud services may be subject to continuous assault and should be hardened in the manner of traditional DMZ-based applications – notwithstanding the protective capacity of the PEP. This is not a typical design imperative for on-premise SOA applications.

18.4.9   Binding PEPs and Applications

As with any multi-tenant facility, the internal cloud network must be considered a hostile environment. All communications to or from application instances must pass through the PEP security and management layer. There are two strategies to bind PEP and managed application in the cloud: intermediary isolation and the protected application stack.

18.4.9.1   Intermediary Isolation

In the intermediary isolation model, a single PEP can simultaneously protect one or more virtualized cloud application instances. The PEP runs in its own virtual instance; this is self-contained, hardened against attack, and optimized for high throughput.

The challenge here is providing last mile security and isolation of the application. Protect the hop between the PEP and each application instance with SSL with mutual certificate authentication. Application servers universally support SSL and it is appropriate for such point-to-point transmissions in a single hop, synchronous environment. Use of WS-Security message-oriented security models is not recommended as this does not add any value for such a localized transmission and suffers from increased processing overhead, complexity, and uneven support. An exception to this is some WS-Security token profiles, as these solve trust problems in a standardized framework. If there is a need to propagate a statement describing attributes, entitlements, or an act of authentication on the PEP, utilize the SAML sender-vouches model [19]. Application server support for SAML is growing, but for many it remains an unfortunate gap. External firewall rules (called security groups in Amazon's Cloud Front) should block access to the internal application. Internal firewalls on the application instance should block all connections, except those originating from the PEP addresses protecting it and from explicit administrative hosts.

The administrative overhead of this bidirectional binding can be considerable if the number of PEP or application instances routinely changes in response to transaction volume. Policies in the PEP must register application hosts to route requests to, using internally addressable IP addresses. Each time an administrator deploys a new application instance, policy will need to change across all PEPs. Launch of a new PEP forces a change to the internal firewall rules and the trusted SSL client list on each application instance to allow connections. At present, this has no satisfactory solution. Use of technology such as Rightscale's framework for on-demand application configuration may address some of these issues.

18.4.9.2   The Protected Application Stack

In the protected application stack (or colocation) model, PEPs and applications are coresident in a single virtualized image. The application thus inherits hardening of the base operating system applied for the PEP. Internal firewall rules allow only the PEP ingress or egress communications; the application therefore cannot initiate or accept external communications except by proxy through the PEP.

This model differs subtly from the agent model. It does not integrate PEP and application into a single process space through an API. Instead, the point of interface between these remains the network layer using local host connections. It also inverts the application hierarchy: the application is now subordinate to the secure container of the PEP. The OS is hardened with the perspective and expertise of a PEP architect, rather than that of an application server.

VM colocation trivially solves last mile issues because it confines this hop within the security context of the hardened operating system. As a side effect, the binding between PEP and application is static, thus greatly simplifying elastic deployment.

There are disadvantages to this approach. The initial configuration is more complex because of the potential for conflict between installation and operational expectations of the PEP code base and the application. There is also some risk of compromise to the underlying OS hardening to accommodate application resource requirements. This runs counter to the design intentions of an appliance-based security PEP.

18.4.10   Authentication and Authorization

The fundamental challenges around authentication and authorization in cloud deployments concern the strength of security tokens and the accessibility of identity information for the purpose of validation or attribute retrieval. These challenges conspire to suggest a particular approach to access control in the cloud. This approach promotes a shift away from identity-centric authorization, toward authorization based on evaluation of a broad range of transaction characteristics.

Cloud-based PEPs are unlikely to have access to corporate directories or conventional IAM systems to validate security tokens (the latter being tightly bound to directories). Few organizations make these internal systems directly accessible outside their firewall. Even with a VPN bridging on-premise and the cloud, the latency incurred for access makes their use highly impractical.

Directories and IAM systems are certainly deployable in the cloud (though subject to many of the same issues explored here). PEP themselves may have internal directories that are valuable for development and test, but may not be practical for production deployment. However, the real risk with any cloud-resident directory is that it creates a new identity silo that is independent of existing on-premise identity stores. This is clearly undesirable.

Cloud-based PEPs must function independently. They must validate tokens against trust models locally; this collapses much of the traditional functionality of a PDP into PEP basic services, expressed through local policy. This influences both the token types that are practical to use in the cloud and the approach to service authorization.

Weak security tokens – such as user name and password pairs – have no place in the cloud. Public cloud providers are highly visible and accessible targets for system crackers. Brute force attacks against basic access control are trivial to implement and a positive result can often compromise an entire application and its data. Anecdotally, in our own recent deployments of applications on Amazon, we have observed random attack rates exceeding 8,000 attempts in the initial 72 hours of operation. These are largely naive password guessing attacks that may fail to gain access, but succeed in locking out legitimate access. Amazon recognizes this threat and mandates a public key-based, mutual authentication approach to govern access to the root shell of virtual instances. This overrides the traditional basic authentication mechanisms on Unix images.

Every policy governing access to cloud services should adopt a similar approach. It is reasonable to assume that any service residing in the cloud – not just the root shell – will be subject to continuous password guessing attacks. Policies therefore must not assert requirements for basic security token types. WS-Security Username Token Profile [22] and HTTP basic authentication, even using highly randomizing password rules, introduce unacceptable risk. Preferred are multifactor authentication schemes using physical devices that cycle through one time passwords (there are a number of manufacturers of these devices, and Amazon now supports a similar offering). No standardized bindings exist to Web services, so these may require proprietary bindings to HTTP or customized WS-S security tokens to function.

Certificate-based authentication mechanisms – including approaches that leverage PKI such as SAML – are a stronger approach. This provides a strong authentication model that offers a higher level of assurance to parties in a transaction. In addition, certificate extensibility offers authoritative statements from trusted third parties about attributes associated with a key holder. This can help to decouple authorization from pure identity – which may be impractical to administer at remote cloud sites – and move toward access decisions based on evaluation of a broad number of characteristics – such as organizational unit, membership, rank, etc. In combination with other transactional characteristics communicated by the sender, this can become the basis of formalized authorization models such as Role-based Access Control (RBAC) (RBAC 2009), and Attribute-based Access Control (ABAC) [15].

SSL/TLS offers optional client-side certificate authentication (in addition to server authentication and channel confidentiality and integrity) [6, 10]. WS-Security x509 Certificate Token Profile [23] articulates a means to sign message contents, binding this to a certificate. Commercial PEPs may include integral CA capabilities for creating and managing certificates.

Certificates associated with identities are typically long lived (usually on the order of years); nevertheless, it remains important to evaluate their current validity. On-premise SOA deployments could often overlook certificate revocation because of in-place security mechanisms and procedures. Cloud-based PEPs, however, by virtue of their global accessibility, must be rigorous in applying revocation checks. This implies regular CRL updates or use of the OCSP protocol. Both are practical in the cloud, but both can place a very high processing cost on clients. CRLs generated by the U.S. Department of Defense have grown so large and unwieldy that simple distribution and evaluation has become largely impractical [7, 27], necessitating a move to OCSP despite its added latency.

Certificates are also not practical containers for authoritative statements about ephemeral attributes or entitlements. SAML tokens, in contrast, support these. SAML has the benefit of offering short lifetime of the assertion (solving revocation issues by forcing an aggressive timeout), a binding to subject evidence (such as key pairs), and providing a means to make statements about acts of authentication, authorization, and arbitrary name/value attributes. Profiles exist describing the use of SAML in HTTP and for Web services.

SAML provides a means to make explicit declarations about authorization. This allows central, on-premise administration of entitlements, issued by a local Security Token Service (STS), relayed with a message to a cloud-based PEP, and evaluated under the trust model in effect. This has the advantage of centralized administration for both on-premise and cloud entitlements.

Despite this, it is a more common practice in cloud architectures to impose a separation of concerns between authentication and authorization. In this model, initial validation of identity claims is made in the enterprise, and thus, close to authoritative directories. Authorization, in contrast, is moved close to services to be enforced on cloud-based PEPs.

There are various approaches for articulating entitlements for suitable for remote, cloud-based evaluation. Native PEP policy can express authorization rules; this approach has the advantage of direct association with services. XACML [21] is a more standardized, albeit complex, alternative. In general, XACML is administered and evaluated in a centralized, cloud-based PDP, accessible to all PEPs using the XACML *Request* element embedded into SOAP messages. It is also possible to locally encapsulate XACML within PEP policy context.

Most SOA PEPs also provide the ability to accept Kerberos security tokens in message or transport [23]. In practice, Kerberos has less practicality to the cloud because of the high administration cost of local key management and integration into ticket services.

Finally, while much of this last section concerned validation of sender identity, server-based authentication is also critically important to the client, particularly for clients sending a message to applications hosted in public cloud-provider. SSL and the WS-Security message security model both address this as side effects of the privacy and integrity policy.

18.4.11   Clock Synchronization

Clock synchronization is very important when using short-lived security tokens like SAML or Kerberos tickets. Even minor time deviations between token issuers and PEPs can cause approval problems. Virtual instances inherit their clock from the host, and unpredictable clock skew was a common issue with early virtualization technologies. Virtual cloud PEPs should synchronize clocks regularly with an authoritative time source shared by all participants in a transaction.

18.4.12   Management Challenges in the Cloud

A number of open issues exist around management of PEPs deployed into IaaS facilities. These center around secure persistence, provisioning, and visibility issues in high latency environments (such as those that exist between on-premise operational consoles and cloud providers).

18.4.13   Audit, Logging, and Metrics

Auditing, logging, and accumulation of metrics are important operations in any application infrastructure. In the cloud, these face challenges associated with persistence and collection.

Audits record events of significance; they are distinguished from logs, which document day-to-day operational information. Elements of policy often generate audits explicitly to record important runtime transaction events, such as detection of an attack signature, or even recording of entire message content. Audits also record noteworthy events in the operational lifecycle of the PEP – an update to policy is a typical example. The high value of audit data demands persistence and integrity. Logs, in contrast, have immediate relevancy for diagnostic purposes, but less long-term value for forensics. As a result, logs commonly rotate automatically over old entries to keep the collection size within reasonable bounds.

Persistence of logs and audits in cloud providers is problematic. Audits (and optionally logs) must stream to long-term resilient storage instead of local disks that will be lost on instance termination. Syslog is one accepted mechanism to do this. Audits, however, should also be cryptographically secure to prevent disclosure of sensitive message contents (such as security credentials), and to guard against alteration. This can be computationally expensive to apply at run time.

Audit volumes can be very large. Data transfer costs between cloud providers on-premise faculties can be very high [1], making streaming or export of audit and log data to existing tools impractical.

Metrics collection may also produce very large data volumes. It is often necessary to record historical transaction rates for purposes of future load planning, so most SOA PEPs maintain sliding counters describing each service under their management. Depending on the time granularity of the bin, these data structures can become extremely large. Regular transfer to on-premise storage can incur considerable cost. Leveraging inexpensive local cloud storage can offset this, as evaluation of this data generally involves a rollup inside a reporting engine that can reside in the cloud.

Other existing SOA PEP alerting mechanisms may also be infeasible in the cloud. Policy-driven alerts that use SNMP to communicate with on-premise management infrastructure may be impractical because of security risks and latency. SMTP-based altering, common in on-premise SOA, may not be feasible to implement in the cloud. Cloud providers do not want their platforms to become a launching pad for spam traffic, so may block outgoing SMTP traffic. Furthermore, there are anecdotal reports of organizations blacklisting mail from Amazon AWS IP ranges because of the threat of spam [25].

A final issue is event correlation between infrastructure elements during forensic investigation. In traditional on-premise SOA, logs from routers, load balancers, and conventional firewalls provide extremely valuable data to operators investigating issues, such as an attack or transaction failure. These data are not available to customers in the cloud.

18.4.14 Repositories

One of the challenges of virtualized cloud environments is the ephemeral nature of the operating environment. Centralized policy and configuration repositories provide an important service in cloud environments to manage this. They function as the system of record – that is, the central authoritative source for policy and configuration that can be pushed to PEP enforcement points. Repositories must leverage long-term, scalable storage in cloud environments to mitigate potential loss of data on instance termination.

Commercial SOA registry/repository offerings, such as those from SoftwareAG, HP, and IBM, take on management of all the metadata associated with services. These incorporate workflow around asset creation and authorization, environment migration, and deployment of policy and service into production. At present, these are not cloud-centric. Turnkey cloud management and security solutions, such as RightScale and Symplified, implicitly have some of these capabilities in their offerings, but these are not general cloud registry/repositories. The generalized cloud policy registry/repository will become an important infrastructure component for cloud-based PEPs, but at present, there are no commercially successful implementations of this.

18.4.15 Provisioning and Distribution

Policy naturally assimilates dependencies on local information that may change as the policy moves between environments. Consider a migration from development, to QA, and finally into production environments: the IP addresses change, as do dependencies on external systems such as PDPs, representations of identity, etc.

Elastic computing exacerbates the dependency problem. Policy content may change in response to variation in traffic volume. Some of these changes are deterministic and thus solvable using simple mappings applied to policy documents. At present, there is no comprehensive and standardized solution to this challenge.

18.4.16 Policy Synchronization and Views

Synchronization of policy between PEPs in the on-premise DMZ and PEPs deployed in the cloud is an open issue. The existing protocols address some simple aspects of security. SSL/TLS, for example, incorporates a negotiation mechanism that converges on a cipher suite common to both parties. A similar approach is required for other aspects of policy.

WS-Security Policy (Nadalin et al. 2007) provides a means for a service provider to declare a means to secure a transaction using either SSL or WS-S message-based security. Its scope includes confidentiality, integrity, and security tokens.

This approach provided the much-needed declarative policy around security, but much work remains. There is a need for a standardized approach to negotiate a reciprocal policy contract (like SSL does), as well as declaration of traditionally out-of-band parameters of policy such as transport compression. In the absence of this, synchronization of policy remains largely a manual operation.

The determination of appropriate policy views for a client, based on factors such as identity and entitlements, is an open area of research. All policies contain elements not intended for client consumption, such as authorization rules or internal routing. Accurate and secure resolution of suitable externally facing views of policy is an unresolved problem in need of further investigation.

18.5   Conclusion

Too often, technological trends focus on what is new and fail to learn the lessons of the past. In the cloud community today, there is a misperception that SOA largely failed and that cloud will be the approach that successfully drives down IT costs and increases agility in the enterprise. In truth, cloud advocates can – and should – learn from the lessons of SOA. There is much to gain from recognizing cloud computing as an evolutionary step and a logical deployment model for services developed under the principles and guidance of SOA.

The adherents of SOA are careful to promote the discipline not as technology, but as an architectural approach. Technology may not be a perfect realization of the philosophical goals of SOA; however, it is a pragmatic lens through which one can explore the more practical aspects of the discipline, especially when applied to an emerging sector like cloud computing. This chapter was about such a technology.

This chapter proposed the use of SOA PEPs, a security technology with proven value in on-premise SOA, as a means to secure and manage application services residing in the cloud. We found that a number of new challenges arise from the changes in control and operating environment that is inherent to cloud computing. The approach shows promise, though there remain open areas for research, particularly around cloud-based policy repositories and provisioning of PEP instances. Nevertheless, a run time, cloud governance architecture, based on the existing virtualized PEP infrastructure, is a practical and pragmatic approach.

Acknowledgments This author acknowledges the many valuable discussions with Jay Thorne, Director of Development, Tactical Team at Layer 7 technologies.

References

1. Armburst M et al (2009) Above the clouds: a Berkeley view of cloud computing. Electrical Engineering and Computer Sciences University of California at Berkeley. Technical Report No. UCB/EECS-2009-28. 10 Feb 2009
2. Berners-Lee T, Fielding R, Masinter L (2005) RFC 3986 Uniform Resource Identifier (URI): Generic Syntax. IETF
3. Brodie S (2008) Barriers to cloud computing adoption. http://blog.skytap.com/2008/06/barriers-to-cloud-computing-adoption/. Accessed 20 June 2010
4. Brunette G et al (2009) Security guidance for critical areas of focus in cloud computing V2.1. Cloud Security Alliance
5. Cameron R, Herdy K, Ehsan A (2009) Parallel bit stream technology as a foundation for XML parsing performance. In: Proceedings of the international symposium on processing XML efficiently: overcoming limits on space, time, or bandwidth. Balisage Series on Markup Technologies, vol. 4 (2009), Montreal, Canada
6. Dierks T, Allen C (1999) The TLS Protocol version 1.0. RFC 2446
7. Fickes M (2005) Validating DOD. Government Security Magazine. http://govtsecurity.com/mag/validating_dod/. Accessed 20 June 2010
8. Fielding R, Getty J, Mogul J, Frystyk H, Masinter L, Leach P, Berners-Lee T (1999) Hypertext transfer protocol – HTTP/1.1, IETF

9. Fielding RT (2000) Architectural styles and the design of network-based software architectures. Ph.D. thesis, University of California, Irvine
10. Frier A, Karlton P, Kocher P (1996) The SSL 3.0 Protocol, Netscape Communications Corp.
11. Hollis C (2009) Barriers to private cloud adoption. http://chucksblog.emc.com/chucks_blog/2009/06/barriers-to-private-cloud-adoption.html/.Accessed 20 June 2010
12. Langley K (2008) Cloud computing: get your head in the clouds. http://www.productionscale.com/home/2008/4/24/cloud-computing-get-your-head-in-the-clouds.html/. Accessed 20 June 2010
13. Leventhal M, Lemoine M (2009). The XML chip at 6 years. In: Proceedings of the international symposium on processing XML efficiently: overcoming limits on space, time, or bandwidth. Balisage Series on Markup Technologies, vol. 4 (2009), Montreal, Canada
14. Linthicum D (2009) Cloud computing and SOA convergence in your enterprise: a step-by-step guide. Addison–Wesley, Reading, MA
15. Lingyu W et al (2007) A logic-based framework for attribute based access control. In: Proceedings of the 2004 ACM workshop on formal methods in security engineering, Washington DC, USA
16. Maler E et al (2003) Assertions and protocols for the OASIS security assertion markup language (SAML) V1.1. OASIS Standard, September 2003
17. McIntosh M et al (2009) Basic Security Profile V1.1 Web Service Interoperability Organization
18. Mell P et al (2009) NIST Definition of Cloud Computing. NIST Computer Security Division. http://csrc.nist.gov/groups/SNS/cloud-computing/. Accessed 20 June 2010
19. Monzillo R et al (2006) Web services security: SAML token profile 1.1. OASIS Standard Specification
20. Morrison KS (2009) Steer safely into the clouds: why you must have cloud governance before you move your apps. Layer 7 Technologies
21. Moses T (2005) eXtensible access control markup language (XACML) version 2.0. OASIS Standard
22. Nadalin A et al (2006) Web services security: username token profile 1.1. OASIS Standard Specification
23. Nadalin A et al (2006) Web services security: Kerberos token profile 1.1. OASIS Standard Specification
24. Ness G (2009) The 3 major technology barriers to cloud computing. http://seekingalpha.com/instablog/275505-gregory-ness/3681-the-3-major-technology-barriers-to-cloud-computing/. Accessed 20 June 2010
25. Reese G (2009) Cloud tips: sending email from an EC2 instance. http://broadcast.oreilly.com/2009/01/sending-email-from-ec2.html/. Accessed 20 June 2010
26. Salz R, Achilles H, Maze D (2009) Hardware and software trade-offs in the IBM DataPower XML XG4 processor card. In: Proceedings of the international symposium on processing XML efficiently: overcoming limits on space, time, or bandwidth. Balisage Series on Markup Technologies, vol. 4 (2009), Montreal, Canada
27. Van Cleave D (2003) MITRE helps the air force implement PKI. The Mitre Digest May 2003
28. ZDnet Interviews (2009) Experts highlight barriers to cloud adoption. http://news.zdnet.co.uk/internet/0,1000000097,39661584,00.htm/. Accessed 20 June 2010
29. Service-Oriented Architecture (2009) http://en.wikipedia.org/wiki/Service-oriented_architecture Role-based Access Control. http://en.wikipedia.org/wiki/Role-based_access_control. Accessed 20 June 2010
30. Yavatkar R et al (2000) A framework for policy-based admission control RFC2753 Internet engineering task force

Chapter 19
The PRISM On-demand Digital Media Cloud

Terry Harmer, Ron Perrott, and Rhys Lewis

Abstract Over the last 5 years, the digital media sector has undergone a radical change in its business model. An industry once focused on broadcasting to a fixed published schedule must now support an on-demand usage model across a wide range of fixed and network devices using a variety of content formats. This media revolution has brought significant changes to user viewing patterns and demanded significant changes in the broadcaster's business model. In turn, this has resulted in significant changes to the content creation workflow and radical changes in the infrastructure that is used to support digital media creation, distribution, delivery and archive. For the last 7 years, the Belfast e-Science Centre (BeSC) has worked with the British Broadcasting Corporation (BBC) to research emerging network-centric technology and their applications within the broadcasting sector. This work pioneered the use of grid technology within the broadcasting sector and evolved, over the last 4 years (the PeRvasive Infrastructure of Services for Media (PRISM) project), into piloting a cloud-based media infrastructure that supports traditional and network-centric access to BBC content. The PRISM media cloud has services and test users across the United Kingdom and brings together owned and on-demand resources to support its user content access services. The service cloud is deployed on demand using owned and on-demand resources, and operates as a dynamic market selecting services based on need and usage criteria. In this chapter, we describe the PRISM cloud and the market ideas that underpin its operation.

T. Harmer (✉)
Belfast e-Science Centre, the Queen's, University of Belfast, Belfast, UK.
e-mail: t.harmer@besc.ac.uk

N. Antonopoulos and L. Gillam (eds.), *Cloud Computing: Principles,*
Systems and Applications, Computer Communications and Networks,
DOI 10.1007/978-1-84996-241-4_19, © Springer-Verlag London Limited 2010

19.1   Introduction and Background

Digital media has become a pervasive part of people's lives. Once video was transmitted to the home and viewed on a television. The focus for the broadcaster was on creating programmes to be broadcast according to a well-defined broadcasting schedule; creating an attractive schedule was an important part of the broadcaster's business model to ensure success. There were generally few television stations and each targeted a broad audience with peak adult viewing and targeted programmes for children. There has been a rapid expansion in the number of television channels, such as CBeebies children's channel or the Science Fiction channel, which target increasingly narrower audiences.

In addition, it is now the norm for video to be available on-demand from a range of *content providers* such as established television broadcasters, offering for example new catch-up services such as the British Broadcasting Corporation's (BBC's) *iPlayer* [6], or newer content providers such as YouTube [14]. This on-demand content is available at home using set-top boxes from cable or satellite providers, and via broadband network connections directly to network enabled in-home devices. It is commonplace that media is downloaded on-demand to a networked device at home or on the move when required; or it might be downloaded to a device and stored for future use. New companies and a new economy have been established that sell and deliver content directly to a user for use on their networked device using the network as the sales and delivery platform, such as Apple's iTunes Store or Amazon's Download service.

This media revolution has led to significant changes in the way the industry operates and the resulting workflows. A traditional broadcaster, such as the BBC, must now support a range of user access mechanisms, or *platforms*, in their day-to-day operation. Their traditionally small number of (schedule-driven) *linear* broadcasting channels has increased rapidly, from two channels 5 years ago to seven channels today, and they sit alongside cable, satellite, online news services and content on-demand services, and support conventional and high-resolution material. Each of these platforms requires content and metadata management, and they often have different content control access rights. For example, online content from the BBC's iPlayer is available for 7 days after transmission and only within the UK. A broadcasting infrastructure must manage these platforms efficiently and cost-effectively in the cost-sensitive media domain.

What makes digital media an interesting domain to work in is that it is a *golden example* that combines large-scale data requirements, millisecond-based quality of service (QoS) requirements and high security needs because (to the broadcaster) digital content is its lifeblood. Thus, for example, digital media combines data needs that are currently larger (and rising faster) than that projected for the Large Hadron Collider [1] and must support many millions of users all with high degree of reliability. For any new technology, the digital media domain is a demanding one.

The Belfast e-Science Centre has been working with the BBC for 7 years, researching the use of emerging technology within the broadcasting domain. Initially, BeSC and the BBC pioneered the use of grid technology [2] within the broadcasting chain for traditional terrestrial broadcasting in the Gridcast project [3]. More recently, we have been working with a wider range of partners[1] to demonstrate the use of network-centric applications and cloud infrastructures to create dynamic, highly scalable infrastructures to support the multi-platform digital media infrastructure

In this chapter, we discuss the evolution of our early cloud work within the Gridcast project into the dynamic service cloud that is used to support on-demand content access within the PeRvasive Infrastructure of Services for Media (PRISM) project. The PRISM infrastructure has been in field deployment for over 2 years to support a test consumer group. It provides content access via a set-top box to streamed or downloaded content from the BBC, or streamed content directly to networked enabled devices, such as mobile phones, computers and games consoles. The PRISM infrastructure uses auto-deployment and auto-scaling and has no human operators managing the service infrastructure – infrastructure is auto-provisioned when required and failed services are re-deployed automatically when failure is detected. This automation acts as a market of resources that are capable of hosting services and services that need compute resources.

19.2   A Media Service Cloud for Traditional Broadcasting

Traditional terrestrial broadcasting is a complex operation – traditional broadcasters, like the BBC, are usually collections of affiliate or regional broadcasters that operate sometimes to the same broadcasting schedule and sometimes modified versions of a core broadcasting schedule. The infrastructure is most often built to assume the distribution of live content from a controller location. In the simplified example of Fig. 19.1, as discussed later, three of the BBC's regional networks (BBC Northern Ireland or BBCNI, BBC Scotland and BBC Wales) are fed from a large-scale store of content centralised in London.

Content for the common core, or *network*, schedule is distributed at its scheduled broadcast time (as-if-live) to the affiliates for distribution to the supported platforms. Broadcast automation manages content delivery to the broadcast platforms that are supported. If content is not being broadcast at the scheduled network time, then it is recorded at the affiliate for time-shifting and that content is managed locally. The core network infrastructure is designed to support live and high-quality video transmission – which will always be an important part of the broadcasting infrastructure requirements.

19.2.1   Gridcast the PRISM Cloud 0.1[2]

The traditional broadcasting infrastructure model, outlined above, gives a robust and reliable infrastructure – however it does reduce the flexibility of the business

---

[1] Partners in the later work included Qinetiq plc and BT plc.
[2] *The diagrams here depict the services as clouds are from the initial technical discussions with the BBC in the summer of 2003.*

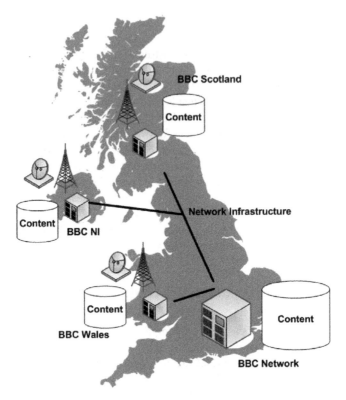

Fig. 19.1 BBC nations and regions infrastructure

as it makes customisation and consumer market targeting more difficult for the affiliates. In the Gridcast project, we created a cloud infrastructure to support the traditional broadcasting activities that were deployed and in test use in autumn 2003 – it was written using the Globus Toolkit Version 3, developed initially in GT3 Alpha1 and it tracked GT3 development to an architecture release to coincide with that Globus toolkit release (Fig. 19.2).

The Gridcast infrastructure consisted (from today's perspective) of a collection of service clouds that provided the outward presence of the affiliate broadcaster and the associate core network control. The services permitted remote technical service sharing and the coordination of content output – one of the early motivations was in line with the grid ideas of permitting resource sharing and optimisation of infrastructure usage.

The support of schedule-based broadcasting is implemented by content being shared from the central repositories or the broadcasters themselves to the point of use. Thus, for example, the scheduling services for BBCNI would request a copy of the content to support its scheduled output – live output, such as for news programmes, is shared using a live network feed. This architecture thus defined a typical IT focused content sharing network with collections of repositories sharing content.

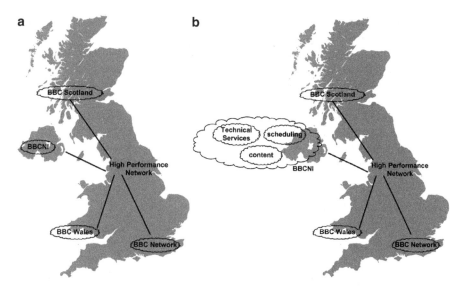

Fig. 19.2 (a) Broadcaster Cloud. (b) Broadcaster Services

However, sharing is not just a simple matter of copying content. Content sharing must be performed securely and the Gridcast infrastructure had a role-based security model that used role-annotated X509 digital certificates [5] to denote the rights of a requesting user – and thus all requests for content where made using secure service exchange that validated these user credentials. Each individual content item within the infrastructure could have an associated security policy that defined who could copy the material and indeed where it could be stored and for how long. In practice, the rights to content were defined by a few large-scale content policies based on the genre of the content; for example, a policy that defined news content or one for drama. A content policy could require that content was shared in a rights-protected fashion and thus demand a key to unlock it for viewing.

In addition to security considerations, content sharing across the Gridcast infrastructure was managed to support scheduled broadcasting – storage within the regional broadcast locations is limited and the content is not required for extended periods by the individual affiliates. The Gridcast content movement was organised by a transport broker that was driven by the broadcast schedule and the quality of service required by that schedule, as depicted in Fig. 19.3.

The Transport Broker is charged with organising content movement within the broadcast organisation to ensure that each affiliate has the content required when it is required and in the correct broadcasting format – if a required format did not exist when requested, then it would be created in time for the required sharing of that content. Within the infrastructure, we integrated a collection of transport types that varied from open source, such as GridFTP [7], proprietary content delivery networks to live switched feed. The selection by the transport broker was made using a market-driven approach – each transport offers its QoS for a transaction and defines an associated cost of delivering that QoS and the broker chooses based on the required QoS and the cost defined by the requester.

This content-sharing approach brings significant business benefits to the broadcaster and its affiliate broadcaster enabling them to construct reactive schedules tailored to the needs of the target audience. Further, sharing can be from copies of content held across the broadcaster community and not just the central content repositories, enabling load sharing of content requests across the broadcasting infrastructure. The Transport Broker API evolved within the Gridcast infrastructure towards the end of the project (2004) to manage the various content stores within the broadcast infrastructure as a collection of content storage clouds, as depicted in Fig. 19.4a.

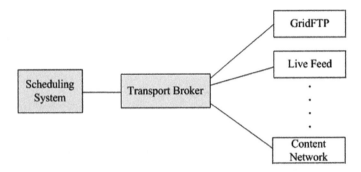

Fig. 19.3 A content broker for content sharing

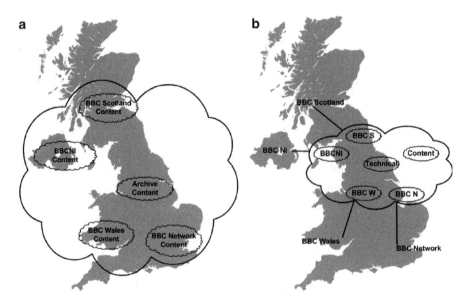

Fig. 19.4 (**a**) A content cloud. (**b**) The Gridcast service cloud.

The transport broker's role is then to provide a simple and implementation-independent view of available content – effectively the broker gives the view that it had access to all content and in any format that was required, and its underlying services moved content to support this view and external technical services enable content processing when required, Fig. 19.4b. This cloud implementation enabled automatic load balancing of content transfers and also the pre-emptive format conversion and placement of content to satisfy predicted content requests.

This (as we view it now) cloud approach also extended to the organisations and the technical services within the broadcasters – effectively creating a location-independent collection of broadcaster clouds. A broadcaster cloud managed the output for a particular broadcaster and cooperated with its affiliates. This approach enabled the broadcasting cloud's role to be changed dynamically. Thus, all broadcasters could act independently, or act to the same schedule or to change the role as to which broadcaster was managing the core schedule – bringing resilience to the broadcast infrastructure. A more detailed discussion of the architecture, the supporting broadcasting services and a broadcasting service management infrastructure can be found in [3, 9].

19.3 An On-demand Digital Media Cloud

Gridcast was focused on issues internal to a broadcaster – the sharing of content and technical services that enabled the broadcaster to fulfil its business role. This is still a significant issue to a broadcast and indeed any technical organisation. However, as discussed earlier, a mainstream broadcaster must manage this traditional broadcasting role along with managing access via satellite, digital terrestrial broadcasting and increasingly on-demand content access – each of which places different requirements on the broadcast infrastructure.

In addition, the broadcasting economy has changed significantly over the last 3 years. The broadcaster would have once expected in-house resources to manage the content workflow from commissioning through to delivery to the consumer; today, the broadcaster must interact with an increasingly diverse collection of service providers, each delivering one component of the final product (e.g. post-production, subtitle, playout, etc.) Each of these service providers must be integrated within the content workflow and be part of the broadcast content management infrastructure. In essence, there is a content economy, as depicted in Fig. 19.5, where content is traded and shared across broadcasters and service providers.

It is commonplace for broadcasters to cooperate in sharing technical resources and content. Basic technical services might be contracted to third-party specialist media companies, delivery of content to platforms might be managed by a broadcast company, such as Red Bee in the UK who provide playout services for a number of broadcasters, and web content managed by a web streaming specialist. This diverse economy places significant emphasis on managing relationships between economy members.

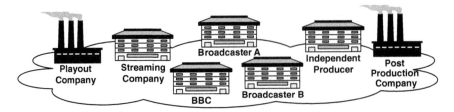

Fig. 19.5 A media economy

In Fig. 19.6, the high-level service architecture for the PRISM infrastructure is depicted. At the core of the architecture is a cloud store that manages all content within the infrastructure – this cloud store is a development of the one used within the Gridcast infrastructure and is a managed, loosely coupled collection of individual cloud stores that provide a single view of all available content. The user has a collection of devices on which content may be accessed. These devices use commercial gateway providers to provide content for a user – so a satellite box is necessary for access content from satellite transmissions, a broadband network box provides access to the Internet, etc. The role of the infrastructure is to enable managed access to the content that is available to the user enabling multi-platform content access.

Within a broadcaster, broadcast control staff interact with the content cloud to manage the availability of content – for example, broadcasting schedulers managing content release or legal specialists reviewing and commenting on content prior to its release. The content cloud is supported by local in-house and third-party service providers that enable content to be prepared and refined for release – for example, providing content conversion or specialist quality control services.

To the broadcaster, a platform is managed by a content provider that has an established (and often contractual) relationship with that broadcaster to provide content to users – this relationship will define when content will be made available, for how long it is available and in what form it is provided by the broadcaster and by the provider to the user. The exchange of content may also require the exchange of supporting metadata to enable the content to be indexed and classified by the provider – for example to enable its designation to be suitable for particular age groups or to enable user searches for locating particular content.

The traditional ways to manage this type of business relationship would require human control of the transfer or (more recently) using automated content management workflows as part of content development lifecycle management. In the PRISM infrastructure, the focus is on automation and fine-grained control of behaviour and the approach is to control behaviour using content policies that focus on individual content management and expected behaviour given operations and events on that content. A content policy is a Security Access Mark-up Language (SAML) [10] document that specifies who exercises control over content, the operations that can be performed and by which type of user, and any consequent action that should be performed if an operation succeeds or fails. Each user and service within the infrastructure is identified by a security credential that identifies

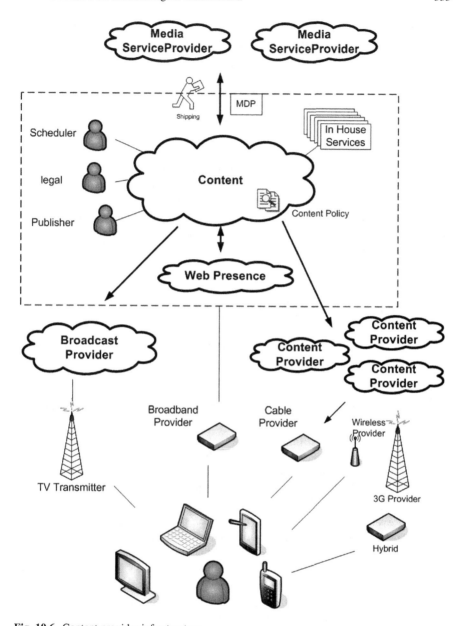

Fig. 19.6 Content provider infrastructure

them and their role within the infrastructure – for example, specifying an individual as a scheduler for particular content. Individual content can have a specific content policy and extend, restrict or relax generic content policies for the group or genre of content it belongs to. Thus, a global broadcast policy might be defined, which is refined by an affiliate broadcaster; this in turn is refined by its genre and specialised by the individual content. Content policies can be changed dynamically and can include actions that should be performed when a policy itself is changed – enabling a highly dynamic environment to be created.

Thus, the relationship between a broadcaster and a content provider is an action within a content policy – for example, when content is made available, an action with a content policy might define that it is automatically shared with particular content providers, or simply define that it is available to share. The means of sharing, the format and the timing of sharing are also defined by policies within the cloud store. This policy-driven approach also manages content sharing and processing by external service partners. For example, when content is to be transcoded, a content policy may define that it is done by a third-party company and define how the transfer to the service company is to be performed. This might mean that a physical copy of the content is created and dispatch by courier requested, or more generally within the infrastructure that the Media Dispatch Protocol [12] is used to auto-negotiate and initiate the transfer of content directly to the chosen content service provider.

19.4   PRISM Cloud Implementation

An implementation of a broadcasting infrastructure presents a significant challenge in that it includes activities that are scheduled and predictable, and activities that are demand-driven and unpredictable. In delivering content to users, a minimum QoS is expected; otherwise, users will not use the content services. And, yet, the predictable and scheduled activities required by a broadcaster within the infrastructures must be maintained.

In addition, a broadcast infrastructure includes fixed assets, potentially mobile assets and an increasing need to scale the infrastructure dynamically to meet user demand. Thus, large-scale content stores will be in fixed and defined locations within broadcast locations – for example, the BBC may implement a single, centralised large-scale content store with smaller stores available within affiliate broadcasters or even at the premises of its production partners. This situation is further complicated by specialist service equipment being clustered around these content stores to support content processing – where the locality to the content reduces the need to move large-scale content across congested networks. A solution must live with this reality and permit these fixed assets to be supplemented to support predicted and unpredicted spikes in demand – for example, the rush of users requesting content for a new programme shortly after it is released.

19.4.1   Cloud Resources

The PRISM infrastructure is defined as a collection of resource clouds that can be used to support services within the media infrastructure. The cloud is composed of fixed

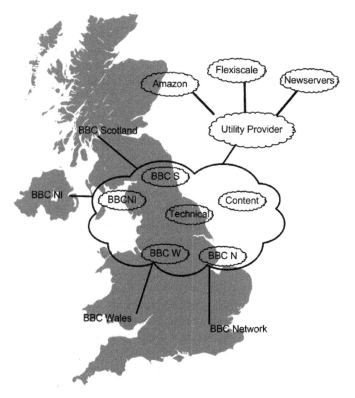

Fig. 19.7 A resource cloud

service assets that provide defined functionality and utility assets that can be used to support these fixed assets – these utility assets can be services, compute resources and storage resources, and be owned or bought on demand, as depicted in Fig. 19.7.

This model enables the media cloud to scale as demand increases and to occupy a low resource footprint when demand is low – thus, for example, at night when most of the affiliate broadcasters are operating the same broadcasting schedule and user on-demand usage is low, the individual affiliate services can be shut down and their resources are released, with all affiliate services operated by a single broadcasting service and online infrastructure reduced. (The PRISM auto-deployment system will power-off owned resources or will release utility resources to reduce the infrastructure cost as needed.)

The API to these various clouds is uniform and defined using the libcloud library [4], which provides a standard and simple model for resource end-to-end management. The library uses a *find* (to locate a suitable resource) operation, *reserve* (to hold a resource) operation, *instantiate* (to make a resource available) operation and *discard* (to release a resource) operation model. The *find* operation takes a collection of *restrictions* that define resource properties – these enable selection based on resource characteristics through to location and cost.

This multi-provider cloud approach has shown to offer a flexible and highly resilient infrastructure. For example, if the broadcaster has no in-house infrastructure available, then the infrastructure is allocated entirely on utility resources – the only weak link is the physical connection to the broadcast platforms. As demand increases, the availability of utility resources enables the services to scale to meet this demand.

19.4.2   Cloud Service Deployment and Management

The PRISM service cloud is managed by the Debut auto-deployment and management infrastructure (an overview of Debut is given in [9]) that provides service, virtual machine and application deployment, monitoring and scaling. Debut operates as a cloud broker in selecting resources for services/storage/applications, as a deployment layer and as a monitor and SLA layer for deployed resources. Each deployment block (in Debut terms), which is one or more applications/services/stores, defines its deployment requirements – following the libcloud model these are defined as restrictions that specify basic items such as version of software, trusted software providers and host operating system, infrastructure requirements such as network bandwidth and firewall requirements, and locality requirements such as particular location. The restriction framework is a generic one and can easily be extended by a user to specify particular needs in a deployment. The restrictions are used to select the resources that are suitable for a deployment from the clouds that are being managed.

The Debut deployment layer performs software deployment driven again by restrictions that specify the kind of environment, such as bare metal or virtual container type, on a selected resource and either notify a user of the allocated location or link this location into other applications that use the deployed software, and thus enable a large-scale infrastructure to be composed as a series of deployments. The management layer also performs automatic service scaling and enables SLA requirements such as response time or load factors on applications or services that will trigger automatic scaling of an application/service/store.

19.5   The PRISM Deployment

The PRISM infrastructure is currently supporting a non-public content access trial with users able to access content from a range of locations and devices as illustrated in Fig. 19.8.

At its core, the PRISM infrastructure has a cloud that implements the traditional broadcasting infrastructure, as outlined earlier, that provides digital media content in terms of audio from radio broadcasts and video from TV broadcasts. This infrastructure also provides access to live streaming broadcasts for all of the supported BBC channels.

A content cloud implements a large-scale media store with associated processing capabilities and metadata indexing and search capabilities. The content store for

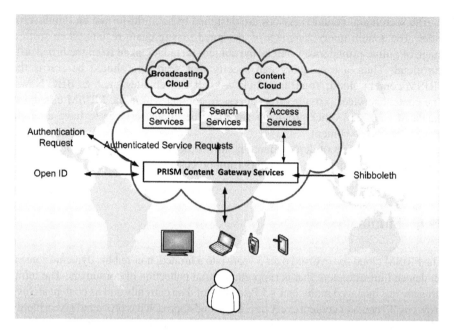

Fig. 19.8 The deployed PRISM cloud

supporting a traditional broadcast channel has been extended to publish content automatically along with its metadata to the on-demand content cloud. This publication is controlled by automatically applied content policies outlined earlier.

Content is accessed through content access services that provide authenticated and multiple protocol content use. The content services support direct access to media by devices using an open collection of metadata search and content transport services. In addition, the content access services support a web interface with thumbnail-based browsing and searching based on TV Anytime metadata [12]. For example, it is possible to search for a programme based on artist, title, description, language, subtitling, audio description and approximately 1,000 fields that describe the nature and lifecycle of the media content. In the current user trial, the infrastructure is actively accessed by different devices types including a prototype set-top box developed for the BBC; computers using a range of web browsers; mobile phones or computer games consoles.

The infrastructure requires user authentication when using the content services. The services use a range of access protocols such as Open ID [8], Shibboleth [11] and X509 certificates. For most users in the trial, Open ID has been the authentication mechanism of choice as it enables their current online accounts, at Google, Hotmail, Facebook, etc., to provide user authenticated access services. Once authenticated, the access services assign a user a profile that controls their access to content. Thus, the service provides role-based views of content that control all aspects of use from ability to search and the content that can be searched, to the type of delivery mechanism that can be used, such being able to download and whether the media is rights protected when downloaded.

The search and content services are designed to be multi-format and multi-provider. The search query language is designed to aggregate results taken from a range of online providers as well as the content metadata taken from the broadcasting cloud. Thus, a user query can specify that searching should be across the PRISM content cloud, YouTube, Flickr as well as web sites, such as BBC News. The content services provide direct access to content within the PRISM cloud and mediated access to other providers enabling the client services to have a single point of access to content.

Over the 1.5 years of deployment, the infrastructure has managed more than 1.5 PetaBytes of content along with supporting processing and metadata.

19.6   Summary

The PRISM cloud has evolved over 3 years into a limited, non-public, dynamic content on-demand infrastructure that is supporting a trial collection of consumers. The infrastructure has managed more than 1.5 PetaBytes of data currently and its content archive grows by 30 hours of content every day. The cloud approach has proven to give a highly reliable and scalable infrastructure, which can cope with equipments and network loss – for example, the infrastructure has coped with losing one of its large-scale content stores by automatically deploying backup resources to on-demand providers.

19.7   Content Note

The PRISM project is an R&D project and as such it is not a statement of BBC technology direction or internal infrastructure requirements – it is an experimental infrastructure that is evaluating approaches and technologies and how they might be used within a broadcasting infrastructure.

Acknowledgements The authors acknowledge the support of the UK Technology Strategy Board under grant TP/3/PIT/6/l/15656, the EPSRC under Platform Award EP/F066139/1 and our co-researchers in QinetiQ plc and BT plc.

Many people have worked on this project and the authors wish to highlight the role of Christina Cunningham, Stephen Craig, Chris Chambers, David Butler, Tanya Beech, Gerry Robinson and the development teams at Belfast e-Science, BBC Research and Innovation, QinetiQ ISTAR, and BT (Ireland).

References

1. http://lhc.web.cern.ch/lhc/
2. Foster I, Kesselman C (1999) The grid: blueprint for a new computing infrastructure. Morgan Kaufmann, San Francisco, CA. ISBN 1-55860-475-8

3. Harmer TJ (2007) Gridcast – a next generation broadcast infrastructure? Clust Comput 10:277–285. ISSN: 1386-7857
4. Harmer TJ et al (2009) Provider-independent use of the cloud. In: 15th international Euro-Par conference, Delft, The Netherlands, August 25–28, 2009, pp 454–465. ISBN: 978-3-642-03868-6
5. Housley R, Ford W, Polk W, Solo D (1999) Internet X.509 public key infrastructure certificate and CRL profile. IETF-Network Working Group, The Internet Society, RFC 2459
6. http://www.bbc.co.uk/iplayer
7. Kettimuthu R et al (2007) GridCopy: moving data fast on the grid. In: Proceedings of the fourth high performance grid computing (IPDPS 2007), Longbeach, CA
8. http://openid.net
9. Perrott R, Harmer TJ, Lewis R (2008) e-Science infrastructure for digital media broadcasting. IEEE Comput 41(11):67–72
10. http://saml.xml.org
11. http://shibboleth.internet2.edu
12. SMPTE (2007) Media Dispatch Protocol, SMPTE Standard 2032-1-2007. http://www.smpte.org/. Accessed 20 June 2010
13. http://www.youtube.com

Chapter 20
Cloud Economics: Principles, Costs, and Benefits

Asoke K. Talukder, Lawrence Zimmerman, and Prahalad H.A

Abstract Cloud computing is an important next step in the trend toward inexpensive and universal access to information and sophisticated computing resources that help close the digital divide between the computer haves and have-nots. In cloud computing, the end-users can access fully functional software and services online at little or no cost using inexpensive computers or mobile communication devices that connect them via the Internet. Innovative service providers no longer need to own and maintain development or production infrastructures and can automatically scale their production operations to meet growing demand much more easily and economically than possible with internal data centers, traditional hosting, or managed services arrangements. The cloud's inherent ability to dynamically scale up or scale down the infrastructure commitment as demand changes on a pay-as-you-go basis has a positive impact on the service provider's overhead costs, energy costs, and in reducing its carbon footprint.

Cloud economics as presented in this chapter refers to the economic forces, business drivers, and structural issues affecting the broad costs and benefits of adopting the cloud technologies or the creation of private or public utility clouds. Here, cloud economics also deal with the economy inside the cloud, which includes monetization, charging, billing, and taxation of products and services inside the cloud.

20.1 Cloud Computing Reference Model

The cloud can be divided into three major verticals, namely, the *cloud user*, the *cloud vendor*, and the *original cloud provider* (OCP) as shown in Fig. 20.1. The cloud vendor is an organization that has a local tax registration and offers the cloud services to the *cloud user* with guaranteed *quality of experience* (QoE) and *quality of service* (QoS)

A.K. Talukder (✉)
Geschickten Solutions, Bangalore, India
e-mail: asoke.talukder@gmail.com

N. Antonopoulos and L. Gillam (eds.), *Cloud Computing: Principles,*
Systems and Applications, Computer Communications and Networks,
DOI 10.1007/978-1-84996-241-4_20, © Springer-Verlag London Limited 2010

within the framework of a *service level agreement* (SLA). A cloud vendor can be a compute, storage and application brokerage and clearing house that provides prenegotiated access to the cloud services such as *infrastructure as a service* (IaaS) provider, *platform as a service* (PaaS) provider, and *software as a service* (SaaS) provider [1]. The IaaS service provider offers the physical computing hardware that includes the processing power through a set of *central processing units* (CPUs) in a cluster. IaaS will also provide the online memory (Random Access Memory – RAM) and the disk storage. The PaaS provider is responsible for supplying and managing all the middleware platforms necessary to enable the software to run over the cloud. Finally, the SaaS provider will offer the software applications that will be used by the end-user.

The cloud vendor offers the QoE and the QoS that the end-user requires; the cloud vendor will provide the data security and meet the regulatory and legal requirements as required by the user or the regulators. The cloud vendor ensures that SaaS, PaaS, and IaaS are available to the end-user as services that are elastic and can scale up or scale down on demand. The cloud vendor also guarantees that the cloud service is fault-tolerant and is available on a continuous basis with proper security that includes *confidentiality, integrity, availability, authentication, authorization, accounting, and anonymity* (CI5A) [2]. The cloud vendor will charge the end-user for the consumed cloud resources based on the QoE.

At one time, energy companies used to manufacture power transmit it from generating stations to the distribution center, and finally deliver it to a household for a fee. The same was also true with telecommunications vendors who used to own the entire infrastructure starting from customer premises equipment to the transmission line. However, today many telecom and energy resellers are virtual operators who do not own any infrastructure. They use energy and telecom infrastructures from different providers to offer better QoS, cheaper tariffs, or value-added services.

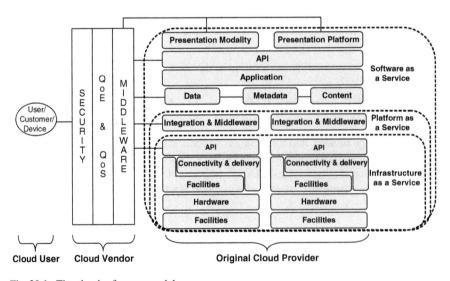

Fig. 20.1 The cloud reference model

This helped competition and improvement in service quality with new job creation and economic opportunities. Similarly, in the cloud, the cloud vendor is a virtual organization that offers the last-mile services to the end-user. It may not even own any cloud infrastructure – it will source cloud resources from various original cloud providers such as SaaS, PaaS, or IaaS from different parts of the world to offer the cloud services that meet certain SLA. The original cloud provider such as an IaaS, PaaS, or SaaS can also become a cloud vendor by offering guaranteed services quality and meeting local tax requirements.

In many cases, the *small and medium enterprises* (SMEs) or a household will interact only with the cloud vendor at the last-mile and may not even know the original cloud providers. The service model for the cloud vendor will mainly be driven by the end-to-end services they provide based on QoS, SLA, and QoE. These services may be the entire computing environment starting from software application to data storage and management or even simple resources such as four processors for 1 hour. The service can be private or public and accessible through any network whether wire-line or wireless. The pricing of the resources by the original cloud provider will be driven by some fixed price derived from raw computing power and the storage (memory and disk), whereas the pricing of the cloud service to the end-user will depend on the SLA and QoE the user perceives.

Currently, many large cloud providers are actively recruiting vendors and resellers of their services. Like any value-added reseller sales channel, the providers are looking to leverage the vendor's sales efforts, client relationship management expertise, and value-added services such as cloud application development or customization, legacy system integration, etc., to increase the provider's revenues and to maximize the utilization of their facilities. Cloud vendors will create new economic opportunities that promise to increase innovation and entrepreneurship in the delivery of the cloud services that will directly impact the QoS and QoE of the end-users.

20.2 Cloud Economics

Cloud economics as presented in this section refer to the economic forces, business drivers, and structural issues affecting the costs and benefits of adopting the cloud technologies.

20.2.1 Economic Context

As this chapter is being written, every enterprise in the world is facing a global economic recession that has profoundly affected all developed countries as well as those developing countries that develop products sold in those markets. Uncertain times also bring opportunities, but taking advantage of strategic opportunities typically must now be done quickly without additional capital funds or corporate resources.

In addition, for information technology (IT) managers, energy cost management is not a small issue[1]. The challenge today is to increase computing power utilisation with lower energy consumption. In addition, the maintenance of legacy enterprise data centers absorbs the majority of IT budgets and IT managers are looking for ways to create increased capacity and flexibility within their current computing facility and hardware footprint, thereby lowering costs and increasing their return on assets (ROA). There has been increasing attention paid to alternatives that provide the pay-as-you-go options, unlimited scalability, quick deployment, and the minimal maintenance requirements. Cloud computing is a paradigm that promises to meet all these requirements.

20.2.2 Economic Benefits

Occasionally used to refer to the economics of cloud computing, the term "Cloudonomics" was coined by Joe Weinman in a seminal article entitled "The 10 Laws of Cloudonomics" [4]. While far from being a comprehensive or exhaustive list of economic factors, his "10 Laws" serve as a useful starting point in our discussion. He examined the strategic advantages provided by public utility cloud services over private clouds and traditional data centers. He posits that public utility clouds are fundamentally different from traditional data center environments and private clouds. For individual enterprises, cloud services provide benefits that broadly fall into the categories of lowering overall costs for equivalent services (you pay only for what you use), increased strategic flexibility to meet market opportunities without having to forecast and maintain on-site capacity, and access to the advantages of the cloud provider's massive capacity: instant scalability, parallel processing capability, which reduces task processing time and response latency, system redundancy, which improves reliability, and better capability to repel botnet attacks. Further, public cloud vendors can achieve unparalleled efficiencies when compared with data centers and private clouds because they are able to scale their capacity to address the aggregated demand of many enterprises, each having different peak demand periods. This allows for much higher server utilization rates, lower unit costs, and easier capacity planning netting a much higher return on assets than is possible for individual enterprises. Finally, because the location of the public cloud vendor's facilities are not tied to the parochial interests of the individual clients, they are able to locate, scale, and manage their operations to take optimum advantage of reduced energy costs, skilled labor pools, bandwidth, or inexpensive real estate.

These are not the only benefits that have been identified. Matzke [5] suggests that the levels of required skills or specialized expertise along with the required

---

[1] IBM cites a study [3] that reports that US data center managers are anticipating a 35% increase in energy expenses over the next 4 years.

economies of scale drive the optimum choice for resourcing IT initiatives. For him, the availability of scalable skills combined with other economies of scale are among the compelling benefits of cloud computing[2]. This is especially true for enterprises that are located in labor markets that have very few or only very expensive IT staff resources available with the requisite skills.

20.2.3 Economic Costs

The costs associated with cloud computing facing early adopters include the potential costs of service disruptions; data security concerns; potential regulatory compliance issues arising out of sensitive data being transferred, processed or stored beyond defined borders; limitations in the variety and capabilities of the development and deployment platforms currently available; difficulties in moving proprietary data and software from one cloud services provider to another; integration of the cloud services with legacy systems; cost and availability of programming skills needed to modify legacy application to function in the cloud environment; legacy software CPU-based licensing costs increasing when moved to a cloud platform, etc.

20.2.4 Company Size, Economic Costs, and Benefits of Cloud Computing

The economic costs or benefits of implementing cloud services vary depending on the size of the enterprise and its existing IT resources/overheads including legacy data center infrastructure, computer hardware, legacy software, maturity of internal processes, IT staffing, and technical skill base. These factors determine the strategic costs and benefits that accrue to individuals and corporations depending on their relative size.

In the past, large corporations have had an advantage over small corporations in their access to capital and their ability to leverage their existing human, software, and hardware resources to support new marketing and strategic initiatives. However, since the advent of cloud computing, the barriers to entry for a particular market or market segment for a startup company have been dramatically reduced and cloud computing may have tipped the balance of strategic advantage away from the large

---

[2] Those with low requirements for economy of scale and skills can be addressed with on-site resources. Initiatives with low scalability requirements but higher skill requirements can be handled through traditional outsourcing arrangements. Projects with high scalability requirements but low skill scalability requirements can be addressed through collocation or traditional hosting arrangements. Finally, projects that require both economies of scale as well as scalable skills are best addressed by cloud computing all other things being equal [4].

established corporations towards much smaller or startup companies. A small, dedicated, and talented team of individuals can now pool their individual talents to address a perceived market need without an immediate need for venture capital funds to provide the necessary IT infrastructure. There are a number of cloud providers who provide software development environments that include the requisite software development tools, code repositories, test environments, and access to a highly scalable production environment on pay-as-you-go basis.

Also contributing to this trend is the open-source movement. While licensing issues, support, and feature considerations may dissuade larger enterprises from using open-source software in the development and deployment of their proprietary products, the availability of open-source software in nearly every software category has been a boon to SMEs, the self-employed, and startups.

As these small companies grow into midsize and large companies, they face changing cost equations that modify the relative costs and benefits of cloud computing. For instance, at certain data traffic volumes, the marginal costs of operating with a cloud provider's infrastructure may become more expensive than providing the necessary IT infrastructure in-house. At that point, there may be advantages of a mixed-use strategy in which some of the applications and services are brought in-house and others continue to be hosted in the cloud. The following tables will identify the differences that SMEs and large enterprises face in both the benefits and costs of cloud services (Tables 20.1 and 20.2).

20.2.5 The Economics of Green Clouds

The development of green data centers and green clouds is shaped by two important factors. The first is a global awareness of the devastating potential of climate change due to human activity primarily through carbon emissions. The second is the rising costs of energy. These two factors have focused IT infrastructure planning and decision-making on energy cost reduction, dynamic resource allocation strategies, and have moved green issues from the category of nice-to-do to strategically important for all midsize and large corporations. In 2008, IBM did more than 30 energy assessments around the world and found that 60–70% of the energy used in the data centers was used for indirect purposes such as cooling and lighting the facilities with only 30–40% of the energy being used directly by the computing hardware [3].

Public cloud providers locate their data centers where bandwidth, cheap energy, abundant water for cooling, and proximity to markets are optimal. Google [6] and other cloud providers have focused on creative approaches to efficient resource usage including not only electricity usage but also water recycling and equipment recycling upon disposal. Through purchasing servers and other equipment designed to minimize energy usage, these cloud providers minimize the non-computing energy overhead and maximize their utilization rates through the dynamic allocation of

Table 20.1 Economic benefits of cloud adoption

Economic benefits	Small and medium enterprises (SMEs)	Large enterprises
Strategic flexibility	Critical in getting quickly to market. Cloud services allow startups to rapidly develop and deploy their products as long as they can use the open source or proprietary development platforms of the cloud providers. As the cloud market offerings mature, there will be many more platform options available.	Cloud services can provide large enterprises the same strategic benefits as startups for new initiatives as long as legacy software integration and data issues are not significant. With appropriate software development talent, operating units can rapidly develop and market test new innovations without putting additional strain on IT budgets, staff, or hardware. Longstanding internal IT management policies and standards may have to be re-examined and modified to allow this to happen.
Cost reduction	Pay-as-you-go pricing may be critical if operating capital or venture capital funding is not available. With cloud services, growth can more easily be funded through operating revenues and there may be tax advantages to converting what would have been longer-term depreciation expenses to fully loaded current expenses.	Cloud services provide the same cost benefits for isolated and exploratory initiatives. Instant availability and low setup costs for new development and deployment environments allow operating units to explore new initiatives quickly at low cost without increasing internal IT hardware or staff overheads. For high data traffic volumes, it may become more economical to bring the operations in-house. Because maintaining legacy hardware and software absorb the majority of IT costs, large corporations may see significant costs savings by selectively moving noncritical applications and processes to external clouds.
Software availability	Software as a Service (SaaS) and Platform as a Service (PaaS) provide necessary software and infrastructure at low entry cost. Limited online version functionality may be more than offset by dramatic cost savings.	Existing volume licensing of legacy desktop and process-integrated enterprise software may make the status quo more attractive if end-user retraining, process modifications, and other change costs are high. Legacy desktop software may have more features and functionality than is currently available in SaaS versions. But the legacy software licensing costs may dramatically increase if it is hosted in a private cloud environment.

(continued)

Table 20.1 (continued)

Economic benefits	Small and medium enterprises (SMEs)	Large enterprises
Scalability	One of the most dramatic benefits for SMEs and startups. If successful, applications designed to autoscale can scale endlessly in a cloud environment to meet the growing demand.	Large enterprises with significant hardware, legacy software, and staff resources can benefit from cloud scalability by identifying CPU-intensive processes such as image processing, PDF conversion, and video encoding that would benefit from the massively scalable parallel processing available in clouds. While this may require modifying legacy applications, the speed benefits and reduced local hardware requirements may far outweigh the software modification costs.
Skills and staffing	While the proper design of cloud applications requires high-level software development skills, their maintenance and support is vastly simplified in the cloud environment. Cloud providers handle all maintenance and support issues for both hardware and platform software at costs that are either bundled into the usage fees or available in various configurations as premium services. This allows significant cost savings through reduced staff overheads.	Because the majority of enterprise IT costs goes to support legacy applications and hardware, the greatest staffing benefits will be seen in new cloud initiatives that do not add to the staffing burden. Longer term, as the enterprise begins to analyze cloud technology potential for its legacy operations, retraining of existing staff or bringing in new staff with cloud technology skills will be necessary to take advantage of the new paradigm. Thus, some investment will have to be made before large-scale or long-term benefits will be seen. The staffing investment may be significant if the enterprise is attempting to create a private cloud to handle dynamic resource allocation and scalability across its operating units. In this case, it may face significant staff investment as well as the required hardware, software, and network investment to implement and maintain their private cloud.
Energy efficiency	Because SMEs can dramatically reduce or eliminate local servers, cloud computing provides direct utility cost savings as well as environmental benefits.	Even very large enterprise IT data centers cannot achieve the energy efficiencies found in the massive facilities of public cloud providers even with aggressive high-density server and virtualization strategies. In periods of economic downturns, green initiatives typically cannot compete for scarce capital funds. By employing a mixed strategy that off-loads applications and processing to external clouds when feasible, IT managers are able to minimize their energy costs and carbon footprint.

(continued)

Table 20.1 (continued)

Economic benefits	Small and medium enterprises (SMEs)	Large enterprises
System redundancy and data backup	This is a large benefit for SMEs, the majority of which are poorly prepared for hardware failures and disaster recovery [3]. Cloud storage can reduce downside risks at low cost.	Because cloud technologies distribute both data storage and data processing across potentially large number of servers, the likelihood of data loss due to hardware failure is much lower than in most large private data centers. The cloud data storage can provide a cost effective supplemental back-up strategy.

computing resources. This combination of lower energy overhead amortized over a much higher server utilization rate allows cloud suppliers to provide computing services far more efficiently with a much smaller energy and carbon footprint.

Because of the scale of operations of large cloud providers, they are able to achieve efficiency rates and server utilization rates that are unachievable in even large corporate data center operations. Thus, cloud computing holds the promise of not only providing attractive cost savings at the enterprise level but also may contribute to the larger societal objectives of energy efficiency and environmental protection and sustainable development.

20.3 Quality of Experience in the Cloud

To retain and recruit customers in the cloud, the experience of the customer has to be managed in a very sensitive fashion. In the cloud, experience will be measured in terms of experience in a *virtual environment* (VE) [8] where challenges will relate to user-agents and devices, the virtualized environments used, the presence attributes, and the tasks to be performed. *Experience assurance* (AE) in the cloud will deal with a community of vendors, providers, and partners; where the cloud vendor will empower the customer – the customer will be able to choose and measure the perceived value of a service. In addition, the cloud vendor must be proactive – communicating a problem before the customer discovers it; also, a remediation must be in place before customer asks for it. Experience happens through *moment of truth* (MoT), when people meet people; therefore, the cloud vendor must be in constant touch with the customer and also must improve based on the feedback from the customer.

To ensure security and service quality in the cloud, a cloud vendor has to go beyond its own domain of control. This becomes even more complex when the cloud vendor is a virtual organization and does not own service infrastructures. For example, to provide a secure and fault-tolerant service, the cloud vendor must ensure that all the original cloud providers in the value-chain agree on some level of security

Table 20.2 Economic costs of cloud adoption

Economic costs	Small and medium enterprises (SMEs)	Large enterprises
Data security	SMEs are better able to use third-party services such as payment processing to handle secure transactions.	Data is an enterprise's most important IT and operating asset. Current uncertainty regarding the security of the data assets stored in public clouds is one of the most significant barriers in cloud adoption. Large enterprises may not want their data stored in countries where intellectual property piracy is prevalent. Some companies may not want their data stored on equipment used by their competitors.
Data confidentiality	SMEs face the same data confidentiality issues as large enterprises.	One of the advantages of cloud computing and storage for confidentiality is that the data transfer and storage algorithms encrypt the data into units that are difficult to reconstruct without the specialized algorithms/keys if the data are intercepted in transfer or the cloud security is compromised.
Data regulations	SMEs face the same regulatory data location issues as large enterprises.	Depending on the company's industry, there may be significant regulatory issues regarding data location. Data that identifies the individual in certain health and financial contexts are subject to US regulations. Similarly, the EU has laws that restrict the transfer of certain data outside of its borders.
Data integrity	The data integrity and reliability of cloud suppliers may be higher than that provided by the existing internal systems.	Cloud technologies are relatively new and storage and data transfer algorithms slice the data into small units, which are stored and transferred dynamically within the storage region. Estimating and factoring the risks of potential data corruption of mission critical data at this early stage of cloud implementation may be difficult leading to nonadoption, especially if the existing internal systems, processes, and protocols are working.
Data transfer costs	For new initiatives that do not require the transfer of legacy data to the clouds, transfer costs are minimal. Getting locked into a particular cloud service provider is currently a market concern due to the lack of open standards among the providers.	Moving the existing data sets to clouds requires data integrity check to ensure that all of the data has been transferred fully and that it has not been corrupted. For very large data sets, this may represent significant staff costs. Cloud vendors typically charge data transfer costs. If the data set is large and there is significant data churn due to transaction processing, it may be more cost-effective to look at more traditional hosting options.

(continued)

Table 20.2 (continued)

Economic costs	Small and medium enterprises (SMEs)	Large enterprises
Integration costs and legacy application reengineering	In startups and small companies, potentially little or no integration is required between cloud applications and legacy applications.	Potentially significant costs to have new cloud applications interact with legacy applications or to modify legacy applications to offload processing to cloud-based components. Conversely, there may be advantages to reengineering legacy applications and hosting them in a public cloud when integrating Web 2.0 functionality with legacy applications.
Software licensing	Cloud services (SaaS, PaaS) provide significant software licensing cost savings for startups and small companies.	Migrating large enterprises to cloud based SaaS may not be cost-effective relative to the existing enterprise licensing agreements. Depending on the licensing agreements for third-party software, especially if licensing fees are based on the number of CPUs using the software, hosting legacy applications in a cloud environment may involve significantly increased licensing costs or noncompliance with the agreements if the software is installed on a machine image used for autoscaling as the user demand increases.
Cloud availability – "rolling brownouts"	Unavailability of the cloud services or slow performance due to heavy traffic is a serious concern when choosing a cloud vendor.	Same as with SMEs. Currently, even large vendors have experienced slow performance or suspended service due to overwhelming utilization.

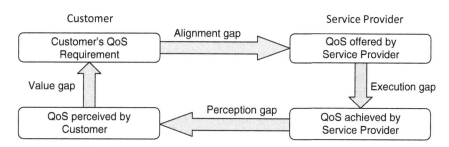

Fig. 20.2 Viewpoints of quality of service

policy and QoS guarantee. The cloud vendor can learn from telecom industry and implement the ITU Recommendation G1000 [9] where QoS is expressed on a service-by-service basis. For QoS to be truly useful across the industry, it must be meaningful from four viewpoints, which are illustrated in Fig. 20.2. These viewpoints are:

- Customer's QoS requirements
- Service provider's offerings of QoS (or planned/targeted QoS)
- QoS achieved or delivered
- Customers' survey ratings of QoS (perceived QoS)

To address these viewpoints in a timely manner, the cloud vendor can consider the *grade of service* (GoS) used in telecom traffic engineering [10]. The GoS deals with resource instead of services – it deals with number of controls to provide a measure of adequacy of a group of resources under specified conditions. The key point to conform to GoS standards is to apportion individual values to each network element in a fashion that the target end-to-end QoS is obtained.

The challenge here is that the GoS and QoS have different interpretations. While the QoS views the situation from the customer's point of view, the GoS takes the provider's point of view. To resolve the ambiguity, it is necessary to introduce *service level agreement* (SLA) in this context. An SLA is a contract between a customer and the cloud vendor to define QoE. The purpose of SLA will be to ensure that QoE is understood in the same manner by the customer and the cloud vendor. Also, it can be implemented in the cloud using definitions and rules [11]. Furthermore, the SLA defines what is to happen in case the terms of the contract are violated [12].

The security challenges in the cloud will be higher and more complex compared with what the world has seen earlier. The major difference is that a user does not have full control of the infrastructure and the people who manage the data and the cloud infrastructure. Many security attacks that were not possible in a private network will be possible in the cloud owing to its large attack surface. Therefore, in addition to standard security offered by the cloud providers, there will be separate end-to-end security services provided by the cloud vendor.

To realize QoS, QoE, and security, we propose the *cloud service quality manager* (CSQM) architecture as shown in Fig. 20.3. There are six entities in this architecture.

1. Access requestor (AR)
2. Policy decision point (PDP)
3. Policy repository (PR)
4. Policy enforcement point (PEP)
5. Cloud decision point (CDP)
6. Service Quality Manager (SQM)

The *access requestor* (AR) is an endpoint device or user-agent seeking access to some service or resource from the service provider. The *policy decision point* (PDP) is a system where a policy decision related to security requirement or QoS requirement is made. Typically, the policies fall into two main categories: general policies that are applicable to all the users; specific policies that are applicable to an individual user, a particular service, or a group of users or services defined in an SLA. The SLA is designed to meet certain *key performance indicators* (KPIs) based on certain *key quality indicators* (KQIs). Policies are stored in *policy repository* (PR). The PR will coordinate with other databases such as inventory for services, resources, and GoS. The policy server will host the PR and evaluate the policy

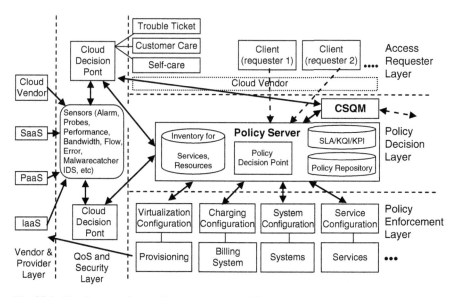

Fig. 20.3 The cloud service quality management architecture

conformance through the PDP. The *policy enforcement point* (PEP) is responsible for enforcing a policy. Because policy may not directly be understood by all equipments or applications, it is necessary to translate these policies into service-specific configuration rules and enforce through activation and control systems. The *cloud decision point* (CDP) captures, interprets, and decides about the events received from the cloud vendor and original cloud providers like SaaS, PaaS, and IaaS. These events are alarms, performance, and security data collected in proactive and reactive fashion. A CDP works like a sensor that processes various events and sends them to the PDP for review and policy enforcement. All these policy servers and CDPs will be managed by the *cloud service quality manager* (CSQM).

20.4   Monetization Models in the Cloud

In the cloud, there are four different models of monetization:

1. Each and every service is priced and charged to the consumer. IaaS and PaaS will fall in this category – IaaSs and PaaSs will monetize the services they offer. All single tenancy resources will fall into this category – in single-tenancy a resource can be used by only one user at any given point in time – here demand-supply-driven pricing will prevail. Some SaaS services will also fall in this category – this model for SaaS will evolve from the earlier model of *application service provider* (ASP). This model is quite successful in the wireless networks where network operators are in control of the network and therefore all the services that are offered through these networks are monetized. Monetization of

SaaS will be transaction-based. Even a multitenancy object will be converted into single-tenancy object through *digital rights management* (DRM).

2. The second model of monetization will be offering part of the service free and part of the service as chargeable. Here, the free part of the service will mainly be match-making platforms, such as job sites portals, dating sites, search engines, or the virtual travel agents. Here, the monetization will be through the match or completion of a transaction. In this model, the service provider will offer the *content* free and determine the *intent* of the user for using this content. Once the intent is known, the provider will propose a match and commit a business transaction.

3. The third model is where a service is free. The user is free to use or modify the service or content. This will follow the principle of *Bhikshu economy*. Bhikshus are Buddhist monks who offer service for free – in return, community supports their livelihood ("366: A Bhikshu who, though he receives little, does not despise what he has received") [7]. If one finds a value in it, one makes a contribution. Unlike a capitalistic economy, pricing is not dependent on demand and supply – one can pay any amount that is worth the experience. Another interesting concept of *Shramadana* from Buddhist philosophy will prevail in the cloud, wherein public pays back by joining the community and offering their intellect, time, and labor instead of cash. Wikis and GNU software are examples of this practice.

4. The fourth model is free service that might have some restriction for monetization. Many governments are following the principle that all outcomes of research projects funded by governments will be open-domain where not only the results but also the data will be available in the open domain for not-for-profit usage. Healthcare-related projects in the USA and other parts of the world fall in this category.

Data logistics will play a significant role in the cloud monetization. Data logistics will include functions like

- Data acquisition
- Data cleaning
- Data transformation
- Data transportation
- Data storage (offline)

Data acquisition or cleaning of data will be a complex process where it might be a service provided by the SaaS provider or the cloud vendor. Though not likely, data acquisition and cleaning service might be offered by the IaaS or the PaaS through a partner. Data acquisition will deal with a first-time user where the data need to be transformed into the electronic form. Data might exist in paper form or some other nonelectronic form, which need to be converted into electronic form understandable and accessible by the software application. In data cleaning service, the data will be examined and validated to ensure that the data that has been captured is indeed correct and free from redundancy or missing components. Data transformation will be a service where the data of the end-user is transformed into a format that is understandable by the software application. Transportation of data will mainly be the role of the cloud vendor where the data is transported from the end-user's premise to the computing infrastructure in the cloud.

20.5   Charging in the Cloud

The charging for the resources and invoicing the end-user will be the responsibility of the cloud vendor. For the cloud usage, the cost to the end-user will be the combination of communication cost and the charges the user will pay to the cloud vendor. Communication will be provided by an *internet and communication service provider* (ICSP). The ICSP charges will mainly be based on the traditional spatial and temporal properties of the single-tenancy resource usage like bandwidth, and duration of usage. Cloud computing has the following three characteristics.

1. Infinite virtual computing resources available on demand, thereby eliminating the need for cloud computing users to plan far ahead for provisioning.
2. The elimination of an upfront commitment by cloud users, thereby allowing companies to start small and increase hardware resources only when there is an increase in their needs.
3. The ability to pay for use of computing resources on a short-term basis as needed (e.g., processors by the hour and storage by the day) and release them as needed, thereby rewarding conservation by letting machines and storage go when they are no longer in use.

Capital expenses (capex) versus *operational expense* (opex) is one of the advantages of using cloud computing. There have been many discussions comparing the cost of a 24 × 7 use of a cloud infrastructure from a cloud vendor like Amazon EC2 instance against the cost of hosting a server within the data center. Usually, providers take the average price of a 1U server, divide it by 36 (the number of months in the typical expected service life of a piece of equipment), and compare the savings. If operational costs like energy, cooling, manpower, etc. are included, the cloud looks very attractive from an operational costs' point of view.

20.5.1   Existing Models of Charging

The existing models of charging can be divided into charges by the IaaS, PaaS, and the SaaS. In case of a SaaS business with varying demand over time and revenue proportional to user hours in an IaaS, Armbrust et al. [13] have proposed the tradeoff charging model through the following equation:

$$UserHours_{cloud} \times (revenue - Cost_{cloud}) \geq UserHours_{datacenter} \times (revenue - \frac{Cost_{datacenter}}{Utilization})$$

They also proposed the revenue equation for adverts-supported model in which the number of adverts served is roughly proportional to the total visit time spent by end-users on the service.

20.5.1.1 On-Demand IaaS Instances

On-Demand Instances from an IaaS allows a customer to pay for compute capacity by the hour with no long-term commitments. This frees the customer from the costs and complexities of planning, purchasing, and maintaining hardware and transforms what are commonly large fixed costs into much smaller variable costs. For example, at Amazon for an Extra Large Instance with 15 GB of memory, 8 EC2 Compute Units (four virtual cores with two EC2 Compute Units each), 1,690 GB of instance storage, 64-bit platform will cost $0.80 per hour. However, there are hidden costs in many of these charging models; one such hidden cost worth mentioning here is the data access. Some cloud vendors offer storage at a very attractive price but charge on transactions that accesses the disk.

20.5.1.2 Reserved IaaS Instances

Reserved Instances by an IaaS gives the customer an option to make a low, one-time payment for each instance the customer wants to reserve and in turn receives a significant discount on the hourly usage charge for that instance. After the one-time payment for an instance, that instance is reserved for the customer, and the customer has no further obligation.

Simple statistics reveal that *reserved instances* though give a cloud customer the option to make a low, one-time payment for each instance, they are not suitable for a short-term usage. Hence, we envisage a new charging model of *Value Instance*. Here, the one-time payment for each instance to be reserved is calculated taking into consideration a percentage of the on-premise hardware cost.

20.5.1.3 PaaS Charging

Just getting the computing resource from the IaaS provider may not be sufficient; the charges for the PaaS need to be provisioned. PaaS cloud vendors enable an application where they charge their platforms on rental basis. These rentals are based on the number of servers or number of instances of PaaS the customer will need to use. If the application is not cloud ready, there could be additional charges for cloud enablement. There are different charging models for the PaaS user. These are sometimes charged per-resource like a piece of middleware, which might be in a range of $100–500 a year. Some of the PaaS providers charge on a per user basis, a model similar to Google App Engine.

20.5.1.4 Cloud Vendor Pricing Model

Because QoS and SLA play a significant role in the cloud, the cloud vendor will have a back-to-back QoS and SLA with both the ICSP and the cloud providers that will need to provide QoE- and SLA-based charging as well. If there is an SLA violation, a credit to the user will have to be initiated.

20.5.1.5 Interprovider Charging

There will be many cases where the revenue collected by the cloud vendor needs to be shared with partners and other providers who are part of the value-chain. This demands an inter-provider charging agreement that will rate and calculate the charges payable to or receivable from the partner provider like the SaaS, PaaS, or the IaaS. This will be driven by the following considerations:

1. Bill & keep – this is a special type of billing agreements between the providers where the provider keeps [14] all the money they collect from the subscriber. Nobody shares any revenue with any other provider.
2. Usage of resource is measured, rated, and billed at the *point of interconnection* (POI). Rates will be determined by service combined with spatial, temporal, and instance attributes.

20.6 Taxation in the Cloud

It is easy to formulate a taxation policy for tangible movable or immovable assets; it is also possible to formulate a taxation policy when these assets cross the border of a state. Tax is levied at the point of consumption of the service; therefore, conventional taxation principles will not be able to support the complex needs of taxation in a virtual cloud environment. Cloud computing is predicated on a concept of borderless global services. Governments, for one reason or another, do not like this idea – at a basic level, governments need borders.

The taxation in the cloud will be the responsibility of the cloud vendor who will have a local tax registration and be governed by the local tax regulations. Taxation in the cloud can be managed with similar taxation model as mobile network operators or *mobile virtual network operator* (MVNO). A mobile subscriber can consume the service of the home service provider while at the home network; the subscriber can use the service of a foreign network being present at the home network. The subscriber can also be roaming in a foreign country with different taxation policies and consume services of the foreign network or the home network. Similarly, in the cloud, the end-user could be in one country and the cloud vendor could be in another country offering services from providers that originate in other countries.

Over a period of time, we believe that there will be clearing houses that will manage the interstate and intercountry taxations of the consumables. This might lead to a situation where there are dangers of double taxation. If tax is based on the location of the registered office of a cloud computing company, then there is always an option to the virtual offices to be located in a lower tax or tax-free export zone.

References

1. Security Guidance for Critical Areas of Focus in Cloud Computing (2009, April) Prepared by the Cloud security alliance
2. Talukder AK, Chaitnya M (2008) Architecting secure software systems. CRC Press, Boca Raton, FL
3. Lee S, Cooper LF (2009, August) IT managers discover the high cost of ignoring data center efficiency problems. BizTechReports.Com. Cited in an IBM WebEx presentation entitled: dynamic infrastructure in action: reducing costs while increasing value. http://researchlibrary. theserverside.net/detail/RES/1254491035_498.html
4. Weisman J (2008) GigaOM network: the 10 laws of Cloudonomics. BusinessWeek Online. http://www.businessweek.com/technology/content/sep2008/tc2008095_942690.htm. Originally posted 6 September 2008
5. Matzke P (2008, November) Cloud computing: from vision to reality. http://download.sczm.t-systems.de/t-ystems.de/en/StaticPage/55/02/30/550230_10_Presentation_Cloud-Computing-ps.pdf. Original presentation given 25 November 2008
6. Google (2009). Efficient computing: data center efficiency measurements. http://www.google. com/corporate/green/datacenters/measuring.html. Accessed September 2009
7. The Bhikshu (Mendicant) from The Dhammapada, A Collection of Verses. http://www. sacred-texts.com/bud/sbe10/sbe1027.htm
8. Gaggioli A, Bassi M, Delle Fave A (2003) Quality of experience in virtual environments. In: Riva G, Davide F, IJsselsteijn WA (eds) Being there: concepts, effects and measurement of user presence in synthetic environments. Los Press, Amsterdam, p 121
9. ITU-T Recommendation G.1000, Communications quality of service: A framework and definitions
10. ITU-T E.600, Terms and definitions of Traffic Engineering, 1993
11. RFC3644, Policy Quality of Service (QoS) Information Model
12. Oodan A et al (2002) Telecommunications quality of service management: from legacy to emerging services. Institution of Electrical Engineers
13. Armbrust M et al (2009, Feb 10) Above the clouds: a Berkeley view of cloud computing. UC Berkeley Reliable Adaptive Distributed Systems Laboratory. http://radlab.cs.berkeley.edu/
14. Berger U (2004) Bill-and-Keep vs. cost-based access pricing revisited. http://ideas.repec. org/p/wpa/wuwpio/0408002.html

Chapter 21
Towards Application-Specific Service Level Agreements: Experiments in Clouds and Grids

Bin Li, Lee Gillam, and John O'Loughlin

Abstract Service Level Agreements (SLAs) become increasingly important in clouds, grids and utilities. SLAs that provide bilaterally beneficial terms are likely to attract more consumers and clarify expectations of both consumers and providers. This chapter extends our existing work in SLAs through evaluating application-specific costs within a commercial cloud, a private Eucalyptus cloud and a grid-based system. We assess the total runtime, as well as the wait time due to scheduling or the booting time of a virtual instance. With relatively short processes, this start-up overhead becomes insignificant. In undertaking these experiments, we have provided some justification for a recent hypothesis relating to a preference for job completion time over raw compute performance [4].

21.1 Introduction

Cloud computing [14, 17], and its recent forefathers of grid systems [1, 2, 3, 6] and utility computing [5, 14], have led to a number of organisations reappraising their IT infrastructures. Organisations with existing IT infrastructures are increasingly questioning the ownership model of computing, with cost management [7] being a key concern. Clouds, grids and utilities have also become the basis for, or a core part of, other businesses, and are typified by the strong emergence of Software as a Service (SaaS). The move towards SaaS, essentially Internet-based software applications, is reported by producers and consumers alike to be both strategically and financially beneficial. Removing the need for physically locating, powering and cooling, certain kinds of core and bespoke infrastructure – with regular maintenance schedules and

B. Li (✉)
Department of Computing, Faculty of Engineering and Physical Sciences, University of Surrey, Guildford, Surrey, United Kingdom, GU2 7XH
e-mail: B.Li@surrey.ac.uk

N. Antonopoulos and L. Gillam (eds.), *Cloud Computing: Principles,*
Systems and Applications, Computer Communications and Networks,
DOI 10.1007/978-1-84996-241-4_21, © Springer-Verlag London Limited 2010

concomitant staffing – presents a different cost model for IT. Though email is typically given as a prime example of a widely used SaaS, software such as Google Apps, SalesForce, Zoho, g.ho.st and MobileMe can support a variety of uses. Such software may be offered for free up to certain limits, beyond which differential costs will be applied to specific levels of support or quantities of storage; models for such costs will vary by provider, requiring the consumer to ascertain the best value for money offering. Popular SaaS offerings with relatively fixed characteristics, such as email, readily scale to the number of users and user demands, implying that utilisation can be maximised and the resulting cost-efficiencies can be passed on to consumers.

While SaaS may offer solutions for generic software needs, specific computational activities that rely on mechanisms of distributed computing for complex calculations, Web Services for remote access, P2P networks for file sharing and distribution, and so on, present different challenges. Cloud computing has grown to encompass wider infrastructural issues for businesses, offering organisations and individuals the opportunity to use different forms of commoditised computer systems, with various associated costs for processor hours and storage in managed facilities. Such facilities can be used by organisations internally, or as part of the external-facing business activity, or as part of an overall customer offering in which the offering may encompass the costs of processor hours and storage. Although accessing such systems has long been technically possible, the costs have typically been rather less transparent and efficiently maximising use of the infrastructure has been of less economic importance. Traditionally, peak requirements tended to dictate the size of a system; now it is possible to run 1,000 servers for a short period without having to own them, and the costs of doing so should not far exceed that of using a server for 1,000 hours. The IT infrastructure can grow and shrink as needed, with costs directly proportionate. Businesses are exploring solutions within this space that might help with cutting costs; however, the range of choices is substantial.

Cloud systems may not be to everybody's tastes for a variety of reasons: lack of bandwidth makes such systems either difficult or impossible to use; organisations may prefer the existence of tangible assets; legislative/regulatory issues may be too great; and concern may exist over vendor dependency or so-called *lock-in*. Alongside such issues, we would also include the importance of having well-specified bilateral Service Level Agreements (SLAs) that provide generally understandable clauses for assurances of availability, reliability and liability. In previous work [10–13], we have explored the construction of SLAs such that a price comparison service – as exists for other products. Commercial Cloud systems enable us to capture price–performance information relating to specific applications with relatively well-known demands on systems, and to be able to determine how such a comparison service may be formulated. Such a comparison service will necessarily depend on both the performance requirements of the user and the current availability of the system, as well as the price willing to be paid by the consumer. A variety of factors are involved in determining the best value: a supercomputer may be able to undertake specific kinds of analysis at a much faster rate than a commercial cloud system [15] once the required work has been appropriately initiated.

On the other hand, if the system is unable to perform such a task for an extended period, or there is a larger overhead due to scheduling [4], running more slowly on available systems may be specifically advantageous depending on the value of the results and time at which they are provided. These factors of price, performance, time to completion (availability), likelihood of completion (probability of failure) and penalty (liability) are key to being able to produce such a comparison service, and necessary alongside the description of the required service itself in order to populate the SLA.

In this chapter, we build on previous work in SLAs through experiments with a public cloud, a private cloud and a grid system to determine the relative costing as would be required for such a price comparison service. We use a Value-at-Risk (VaR) Monte Carlo Simulation on a public cloud (Amazon EC2) to obtain costing information, and contrast the performance with a private cloud (Eucalyptus install at the University of Surrey) and grid system (Condor install at the University of Surrey) to determine an exchange rate. While a recent study compared performance characteristics of EC2 and Eucalyptus, addressing storage, CPU, network transfer and network latency [1], start-up time for these systems appears not to have been accounted for, yet can be a major overhead for large numbers of short processes. Applications such as VaR emphasise the importance of overall time to completion, and a Monte Carlo approach is readily parallelised but may favour particular levels of parallelism depending on the number of simulations. In relating price and performance, at minimum we may ascertain when it is appropriate to scale across private and public clouds, and potentially which direction is favoured.

21.2 Background

Commercial grid and utility computing was largely driven by big technology vendors such as IBM, Sun, HP, Oracle and Microsoft. Products and services such as IBM's Computing On-Demand, Sun's network.com, Oracle 10g and Microsoft's High-Performance Computing (HPC) cluster solution were variously labelled as grid and utility, and variously priced and packaged. Sun's network.com had a relatively clear pricing – US$1 per CPU hour. However, limited uptake meant that the service was eventually closed down. The US$1 price point was used in 2003 to equate computing resources [6]. An updated consideration of this price point suggests that substantially improved performance is now available, but the costs are most likely to vary according to the application when elements of the cost are treated separately: 'most applications do not make equal use of computation, storage, and network bandwidth; some are CPU-bound, others network-bound, and so on [14]. Specific application requirements need to be reckoned with when determining how best to configure the cloud system. Prices for Amazon AWS are typically used to exemplify this: here, CPU, memory and storage often move together (Table 21.1), while network transfers and persistent storage necessitate further calculations.

Table 21.1 Prices for Amazon AWS showing different classes of priced instances with different (virtualised) hardware specifications (prices as on January 2010)

Type	Small	Large	Extra large	Medium (high-CPU)	Extra large (high-CPU)
Memory (GB)	1.7	7.5	15	1.7	7
Compute units[a]	1	4	8	5	20
Virtual cores per unit	1	2	4	2	8
Storage (GB)	160	850	1,690	350	1,690
Platform (X-bit)	32	64	64	32	64
Price (on-demand instances, EU, US$ per hour)	0.095	0.38	0.76	0.19	0.76

[a] One EC2 computer unit provides equivalent to 1.0~1.2 GHz Intel Opteron or Xeon processor

If we have good understanding of the requirements of an application such that we are able to find matching resources at the right price, then we may begin to search through the options on offer. Here, the consumer is attempting to achieve the best approximate fit. However, the best value may have come if a wider variety of configurations were available or could be specifiable. The consumer would outline their needs, and a range of providers would make offers to the consumer in order to secure their business. Consumers may get better pricing depending on a variety of factors, and the service for comparability would offer opportunities for markets in computational equivalents of financial instruments – where these may be contracts of different values based on the SLAs – and even derivatives of such instruments. These SLAs may need to reference a portfolio of computational resources, introducing some notion of risk into the SLA itself (see, for example, [9]). This would further suggest that organisations may offer variable SLAs in which price accounts for risk – cheaper resources imply more risk and less liability in the event of failure. Here, we have been inspired by the notions of tranches and subordination in financial CDO models such that higher-value SLAs are those that shall be satisfied first [10–12]. We believe that such a framework might assist providers or brokers to optimise system utilisation and offer the best value for money with dynamically configured systems. As such, cloud markets may emerge based on such considerations and others made previously in relation to grid economics [8]. However, much of the work of understanding applications in order to derive the required service description terms and guarantee terms for the SLAs is still needed, and initial comparability across resources, as described in the remainder of this chapter, is a vital step towards this.

21.3 Experiment

21.3.1 Target Application: Value at Risk

Value at Risk (VaR) typically computes a value from a distribution of returns (profit or loss against the previous day) of financial instruments. The value obtained from this analysis is the largest *expected* loss at a specific confidence level for a given time horizon. In previous work, we have implemented three approaches for VaR using Java – Historical Simulation (HS), Variance–Covariance (VC) and Monte Carlo Simulations (MCS) – focussed on linear option-free financial portfolios [11, 12]. These VaR methods can be characterised to promote reusability in implementation, and results of HS and VC can be used to validate the expected loss produced by the MCS. For VaR in general, job completion is potentially the most vital factor: the faster the result, the more useful it may be and the lower the likelihood that the 'history' has now changed with new data that renders the analysis meaningless.

For our experiments, we capture the total completion time of MCS VaR for 95% confidence with 20 assets, with an evenly distributed notional (investment), and using 1 year of historic market data with 640,000 simulations. This application requires a relatively short run time, so the time taken before the application starts is significant.

21.3.2   Target Systems

Our target systems comprise a Condor pool, Amazon EC2 and a private cloud based on Eucalyptus. We do not attempt to equate the configurations of these systems, since the relative performance figures are of interest. Furthermore, we control data transfer by having input data local to the analysis. The MCS is run using up to 32 nodes on all three systems, and also on 64 for EC2 and Condor. Furthermore, we have produced a Directed Acyclic Graph of the MCS for Condor's DAGman; however, for a better comparison we run jobs independently (non-DAG).

21.3.2.1   Condor

Software for distributed computing is based on a scheduler, typically used in grids, developed by the University of Wisconsin in Madison. Our Condor pool comprises 128 cores provided by 32 IBM HS21 Woodcrest Blades (two Intel dual core processors, 2.66 GHz, 1,333 MHz FSB with 4 GB RAM per blade), with Red Hat Enterprise Linux 4 and Condor version 6.6.6.

21.3.2.2   Amazon EC2

Our choice of public cloud is offering on-demand servers. We built an Ubuntu 9.04 (jaunty) 32-bit image containing the MCS application with all necessary input files. The 32-bit image works in EC2 as m1.small and c1.medium instance types. The application executes immediately once the image has been started, captures results and timing information using web requests to a publicly available web server and self-terminates following successful completion.

Table 21.2 Platform hardware specification comparison

	EC2 (m1.small)	Eucalyptus (m1.small)	Condor
OS Architecture	32-Bit	32-Bit	32-Bit
Compute unit	One virtual core	One	One physical CPU
Compute unit type	Intel 1.0–1.2 GHz 2007 Opteron or 2007 Xeon processor	Intel 1.0 GHz 2007 Xeon	Intel 2.66G dual core processor
Number of compute unit	One	One	Two
Ram (GB)	1.7	256M	4

21.3.2.3 Eucalyptus

Eucalyptus [8] is open-source software for building cloud systems on top of conventional compute clusters, with a similar API and protocols to EC2. Our private cloud is built using Ubuntu Linux server 9.04 (kernel 1.6.28-27) with Eucalyptus version 1.61 and consists of two servers, each with two Quad Core Intel Xeon E5540s at 2.53 GHz and 32 GB RAM. Currently, only the m1.small instance type is available, offering a maximum of 40 instances of 1.0 GHz per compute unit and 256 MB RAM. We are able to reuse the 32-bit image built for EC2 within this system.

The specification for nodes within the three systems is shown in Table 21.2.

21.3.3 Results

Values obtained for MCS VaR from all three systems are within tolerance of the VC VaR, and the standard error is within the necessary 1% tolerance up to 32 nodes but outside this tolerance at 64 nodes, consistent with expectations based on prior work.

We separate the start-up time from the application run-time and investigate the averages: for Condor, this gives us an average scheduling overhead; for EC2 and Eucalyptus, this provides the average image boot time. Results from this separation are shown below (Figs. 21.1–21.3).

We obtain an average boot time for 32 virtual machines of 106 s in EC2 and 234 s in Eucalyptus, both of which are lower than a speculated 5 min [4]. For EC2, similar boot times are obtained for all our chosen configurations, and we have found that such times are consistently achievable for morning and afternoon runs over a 7-day period. However, times for both Condor and Eucalyptus are progressively increasing with increasing demands. Condor requires 76 s for 32 processes, which appears to be favourable performance over EC2, but EC2 is offering better times at 64.

Once the application is 'booted', Eucalyptus appears to offer best run performance: for 32 instances, Eucalyptus takes 4.1 s, EC2 (m1.small) 7.9 s and Condor 19 s (Fig. 21.4). We have also found that EC2 (c1.medium) can outperform these at 3.7 s. Coordinating the analysis in Condor using DAGman magnifies the start-up time to around 500 s, and making it particularly unfavourable.

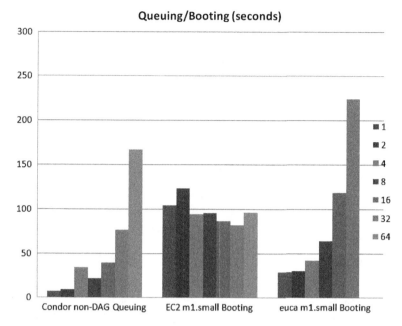

Fig. 21.1 Performance comparison (queuing/boot time)

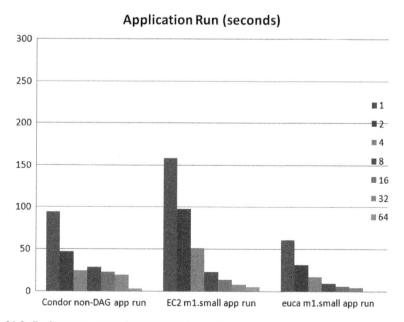

Fig. 21.2 Performance comparison (application run)

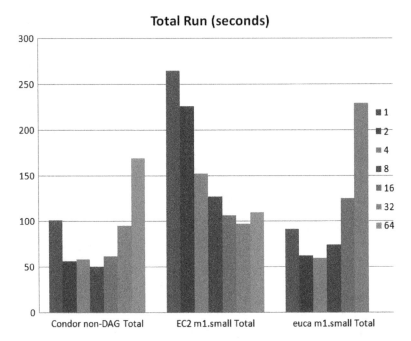

Fig. 21.3 Performance comparison (total run)

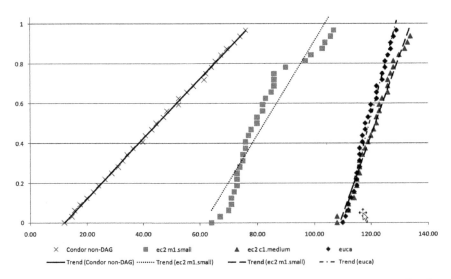

Fig. 21.4 Probability of completion. To show the general trend, we excluded one outlying data point in ec2 c1.medium, which is considerably to the right of other data in that set

The total run time in Eucalyptus produces a similar 'smile' curve (Fig. 21.3) to Condor. In both systems, performance is improving up to a given number, then drops away as more instances are demanded. EC2's total run time appears to show a slight increase at 64, but well within the previous range.

21.3.4 Job Completion

We consider the probability of completion of the analysis in Condor, Eucalyptus (m1.small) and EC2 (both m1.small and c1.medium) for 32 processors (Fig. 21.4). Condor manages to start all parallel tasks first, followed by EC2 (m1.small), Eucalyptus and EC2 (c1.medium). Note, however, the regression slope gradients: Condor shows the greatest variance for start-up time ($\sigma = 19.53$), followed by EC2 m1.small (11.81), EC2 c1.medium (7.11) and Eucalyptus (5.41).

The probability of completion of VaR on AWS is 100% after the average AMI booting time of 97 s, provided all have been provisioned. This may not always be the case.

We show the speed up for each platform in Fig. 21.5 by considering the gain achieved in using double the number of instances each time. Here, the point at which performance appears to begin to degrade becomes apparent (Eucalyptus, 4; Condor, 8).

21.3.5 Cost

We estimated the cost of running VaR MCS on EC2 by reference to the Amazon pricing scheme in July 2009 (Table 21.3), which appeared similar to Sun's network.

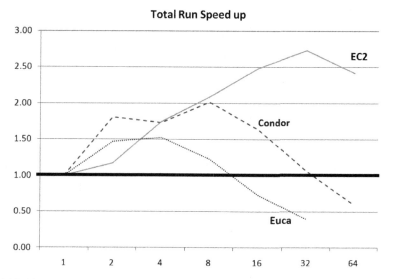

Fig. 21.5 Total run speed-up, showing gain achieved in doubling the number of instances, and performance degradation

Table 21.3 Cost of VaR MCS (Dec 2009)

	AWS m1.small moderate I/O hourly charges (US$)	One off MCS (640,000 simulations) charges with 434M Ubuntu AMI m1.small (US$)
EC2 VM per Instance instance-hour (or partial hour)	0.11	0.11
EC2 I/O in	0.10	0.01
EC2 I/O out	0.17	0.01
S3 I/O out (monthly cost)	0.17	0.01
S3 others	0.30	0.30
VAT (%)	15	15
Total cost (incl. VAT)	0.98	0.51

com charges of $1 per CPU-hour integrating costs that are individually priced here. The actual cost of an MCS VaR in EC2 (m1.small), for 640,000 simulations is about $0.51, and the running costs of 640,000*1 instance is similar to that of 10,000*64 instances. Use of higher performance units, 64-bit machines and Windows-based machines will result in variant performance and costs, not least since a Windows machine initially costs more than a Linux machine [17]. With Sun's network.com running 64-bit systems, some of Amazon's costs may be higher than those for a system that was closed down.

VaR MCS with 640,000 simulations, in EC2, costs US$0.51, but takes only 90 s. The same application running in Condor and Eucalyptus takes 95 and 228 s, respectively. The EC2 cost equivalent would be: Condor – $0.54; Eucalyptus $1.29. This emphasises the importance of careful choice of provider. However, a system that takes longer should price more competitively, and equivalent performance would be: Condor – US$0.48; Eucalyptus – $0.20. Price differences would reflect system performance with different applications and different configurations of those applications. Significant data capture will be required to address the scope of these differences.

21.4 Conclusions and Future Work

In this chapter, we have used a Value at Risk (VaR) Monte Carlo Simulation (MCS) to compare run information from a public cloud (Amazon EC2), a private cloud (Eucalyptus) and a grid system (Condor). We considered the impact of the scheduling and booting overhead on an application with a relatively short run time, and used this information to relate system costs. We have previously reported on introducing risk into Service Level Agreements [10–12], and how price information helps to create guarantee terms of SLAs and contributes to required future work on resource availability prediction. The experiments presented here help us to consider further how to build SLAs such that a price comparison service for computing resources could be feasible. Such price information may be applicable to classes of applications that have similar characteristics in order to estimate costs without prior knowledge of performance. However, obtaining reliable information will necessitate numerous runs across multiple systems, likely involving parameter sweeps. These efforts will be combined with autonomic use of SLAs, and are geared towards demonstrating the provision of a computational price comparison service.

With reference to [4], it is entirely feasible that a public cloud (EC2) may be faster than a supercomputer for a certain set of applications with known requirements and performance, and given certain availability constraints and scheduling overheads. The experiments presented here also show the potential for using current commercial clouds over grid-type infrastructures.

During our experiments, we encountered several occasions where one or two instances simply failed to start properly, even given almost 9 (chargeable) hours. Such occurrences merely emphasise the need for, and potential value of, application-specific SLAs.

References

1. Baun C, Kunze M (2009) Building a private cloud with eucalyptus. In: Proceeding of the 5th IEEE International Conference on e-Science Workshops, Oxford, UK
2. Buyya R, Giddy J, Abramson D (2001) A case for economy grid architecture for service-oriented grid computing. In: 10th IEEE international heterogeneous computing workshop, San Francisco, CA
3. Chetty M, Buyya R (2002) Weaving electrical and computational grids: how analogous are they? Comput Sci Eng 4:61–72. http://buyya.com/papers/gridanalogy.pdf
4. Foster, I (2009) What's faster – a supercomputer or EC2? http://ianfoster.typepad.com/blog/2009/08/whats-fastera-supercomputer-or-ec2.html
5. Germano G, Engel M (2006) City@home: Monte Carlo derivative pricing distributed on networked computers, Grid technology for financial modelling and simulation, 2006
6. Gray J (2003) Distributed computing economics, Microsoft research technical report: MSRTR-2003-24 (also presented in Microsoft VC Summit 2004, Silicon Valey, April 2004)
7. Greenberg A, Hamilton J, Maltz DA, Patel P (2009) The cost of Cloud: research problems in data centre networks. ACM SIGCOMM Comput Commun Rev 39(1). http://ccr.sigcomm.org/drupal/files/p68-v39n1o-greenberg.pdf. Accessed January 2009
8. Kenyon C, Cheliotis G (2003) Grid resource commercialization: economic engineering and delivery scenarios. In: Nabrzyski J, Schopf J, Weglarz J (eds) Grid resource management: state of the art and research issues. Kluwer, Dordrecht, The Netherlands
9. Kerstin V, Karim D, Iain G, James P (2007) AssessGrid, economic issues underlying risk awareness in grids. LNCS, Springer, Berlin/Heidelberg
10. Li B, Gillam L (2009) Towards job-specific service level agreements in the cloud. In: Proceeding of the 5th IEEE international conference on e-Science workshops. Oxford, UK
11. Li B, Gillam L (2009) Grid service level agreements using financial risk analysis techniques. In: Antonopoulos N, Exarchakos G, Li M, Liotta A (Eds) Handbook of research on P2P and grid systems for service-oriented computing: models, methodologies and applications. IGI Global, USA
12. Li B, Gillam L (2009) Risk informed computer economics. In: IEEE international symposium on cluster computing and the grid (CCGrid 2009, ServP2P). Shanghai, China
13. Li B, Gillam L (2008) Grids for financial risk analysis and financial risk analysis for grids. In: Proceedings of UK e-Science programmes, all hands meeting 2008 (AHM 2008), Edinburg

14. UC Berkeley Reliable Adaptive Distributed Systems Laboratory (2009) Above the clouds: a Berkeley view of cloud computing, white paper. http://radlab.cs.berkeley.edu/
15. Walker E (2008) Benchmarking Amazon EC2 for high-performance scientific computing. http://www.usenix.org/publications/login/2008-10/openpdfs/walker.pdf
16. Eucalyptus Cloud: http://www.eucalyptus.com/
17. Amazon, EC2, S3 Pricing (2009), Amazon EC2 Developer Guide (2006). http://aws.amazon.com

Index